The Regional Multinationals
MNEs and "Global" Strategic Management

Although many firms label themselves "global," very few can back this up with truly global sales and operations. In *The Regional Multinationals* Alan Rugman examines first-hand data from multinationals and finds that most multinationals are strongly regional, with international operations in their home regions of North America, or Asia. Only a tiny proportion of the world's top 500 companies actually sell the same product and deliver the same services around the world. Rugman exposes the facts behind the popular myths of doing business globally, explores a variety of regional models, and offers an authoritative agenda for future business strategy. *The Regional Multinationals* is the essential resource for all academics and students in International Business, Organization, and Strategic Management, as well as those with an interest in finding out how multinationals really work in practice and how future strategy must respond.

Alan M. Rugman is L. Leslie Waters Chair of International Business at the Kelley School of Business, Indiana University, where he is also Professor of International Business and Professor of Business Economics and Public Policy. His numerous publications include *International Business* (2000, 2003), *The End of Globalization* (2000), and *The Oxford Handbook of International Business* (2001).

The Regional Multinationals
MNEs and "Global" Strategic Management

Alan M. Rugman

Indiana University

CAMBRIDGE
UNIVERSITY PRESS

PUBLISHED BY THE PRESS SYNDICATE OF THE UNIVERSITY OF CAMBRIDGE
The Pitt Building, Trumpington Street, Cambridge, United Kingdom

CAMBRIDGE UNIVERSITY PRESS
The Edinburgh Building, Cambridge, CB2 2RU, UK
40 West 20th Street, New York, NY 10011–4211, USA
477 Williamstown Road, Port Melbourne, VIC 3207, Australia
Ruiz de Alarcón 13, 28014 Madrid, Spain
Dock House, The Waterfront, Cape Town 8001, South Africa

http://www.cambridge.org

First published 2005

Printed in the United Kingdom at the University Press, Cambridge

Typefaces Swift 9.5/12.5 pt. and Formata   *System* LaTeX 2ε   [TB]

A catalogue record for this book is available from the British Library

Library of Congress cataloguing in publication data
Rugman, Alan M.
The regional multinationals / Alan M. Rugman.
   p.   cm.
Includes bibliographical references and index.
ISBN 0 521 84265 4 (hardback) – ISBN 0 521 60361 7 (paperback)
1. International business enterprises.   I. Title.
HD2755.5.R83567   2004   338.8′8 – dc22   2004052681

ISBN 0 521 84265 4 hardback
ISBN 0 521 60361 7 paperback

Contents

Figures

Tables

Acknowledgments

In preparing this book, four people in particular have provided tremendous help. First, Cecilia Brain of Toronto has been an excellent research assistant, working with me to prepare the data on the 500 firms from annual reports and websites. She has also helped in preparation of material for the fifty cases discussed in the book. Second, Professor Alain Verbeke has helped me develop new analytical insights into the regional and global theories of multinationals, as can be seen in this important co-authored work in chapters 3, 4, 10, and 12. Third, Mildred Harris has worked very diligently in preparing the drafts of chapters, tables, and all of the final manuscript for publication. Fourth, in the preparation of the manuscript for the book and in previous drafts of the chapters, excellent proof-reading was undertaken by Helen Rugman.

I am pleased to acknowledge help and support from the Kelley School of Business, Indiana University, Bloomington, Indiana, and its Center for International Business Education and Research. In particular, they supported the research assistance of Ms Cecilia Brain in 2003/04. I also received support and an encouraging research environment at Templeton College, University of Oxford, for parts of summers 2002 and 2003 when I was working on research for this book. I have received helpful comments from colleagues and doctoral students at these institutions and at various conferences and seminars where previous versions of this work have been presented over the 2001–04 period. In particular, helpful comments on various chapters have been provided by Karl Moore, Steven Kobrin, Rob Grosse, Peter Buckley, Arie Lewin, Don Lessard, Jing Li, Nessara Sukpanich, Stéphane Girod, Saliya Jayaratne, and several anonymous reviewers of the book proposal. In addition, Peter Snow provided editorial advice on the book proposal. I am appreciative of their help and insight and I alone am responsible for any errors in this book.

Finally, thanks to Katy Plowright, Alice Ra, Chris Harrison, and others at Cambridge University Press for their enthusiasm for this book.

I am also pleased to acknowledge several journals who have published previous versions of some of these chapters:

Chapter 4, a revised and shorter version, was co-authored with Professor Alain Verbeke and was published in *Journal of International*

Business Studies 35(1): 3–18 in January 2004. An earlier version of chapter 4 was presented at the Duke University JIBS and CIBER Conference on "Emerging frontiers in international business research", 6–9 March 2003. We are pleased to acknowledge the help of Arie Lewin in stimulating this article. Helpful comments on earlier drafts have been provided by Vern Bachor, Paul Beamish, Peter Buckley, Yves Doz, John Dunning, Michael Enright, Stéphane Girod, Robert Grosse, Mike Kotabe, Mitchell Koza, Klaus Meyer, John Mezias, Karl Moore, Mona Sellers, and Lorn Sheehan. We also acknowledge the excellent research assistance of Cecilia Brain.

A previous version of chapter 5, co-authored with Stéphane Girod, appeared in *European Management Journal* (February 2003). Thanks to Cecilia Brain for comments and assistance with the data.

An edited version of the appendix to chapter 3 appeared as a book review in the Academy of Management *Executive* 16:3 (August 2002): 157–59.

An abbreviated version of chapter 7, co-authored with Cecilia Brain, appeared in *Management International Review*, vol. 44 (2004), as did part of the second half of chapter 12, co-authored with Alain Verbeke.

1

Introduction

Contents

KEY THEMES OF THIS BOOK

The world's largest 500 companies are often called multinational enterprises (MNEs), i.e. they produce and/or distribute products and/or services across national borders. These MNEs have repeatedly been identified as the drivers of globalization. Yet, very few are "global" firms, with a "global" strategy, defined as the ability to sell the same products and/or services around the world. Instead, nearly all the top 500 firms are regionally based in their home region of the "triad" of North America, the EU, or Asia. It follows that a firm can be internationally active across its home-region market but not be global.

A large firm can have what appears to be an international "global" strategy within its home region. This occurs if the firm's successful strategy includes selling the same products and/or services in the same manner within its home region of the triad, allowing the firm to gain all the potential economies of scale and scope and/or differentiation advantages within its home region market. The data presented in this book show that there appear to be no additional scale, scope, or differentiation advantages to be gained by going global.

If firms have exhausted their growth in their home region of the triad and still go into other regions, they then face a liability of foreignness and other additional risks by this global expansion. In other words, the advantages of standardization can be achieved within the home region of the triad, especially if the home-region government pursues policies of an internal market such as social, cultural, and political harmonization (as in the EU) or economic integration (as in NAFTA and Asia).

A related point is that inter-block business is likely to be restricted by government-imposed barriers to entry. The EU and the United States are now fighting trade wars and are responsive to domestic business lobbies seeking shelter in the form of subsidies and/or protection, as in the case of the steel and agricultural sectors. There will remain cultural and political differences between members of the triad, but there will be fewer of these within each triad block. Increasingly, there will be European firms, North American firms, and Asian firms. They will continue to have 70% or more of their sales in their home region of the triad. There are only a handful of purely "global" MNEs in the world's largest firms. Globalization will remain a mirage in that regionalism will continue to dominate international business strategy.

In *The End of Globalization* (Random House, 2000) I developed evidence for this regional triad theme mainly at aggregate level for the core triad of the United States, EU, and Japan. The intra-regional trade and FDI across the "broad" triad of North America (NAFTA), Europe, and Asia (including Oceania) were also examined and twenty cases of the regional strategies of multinationals were analyzed. In this book, new database at the firm level for the world's 500 largest companies and calculate their sales across the regions of the broad triad. This is discussed in detail in chapter 2. The new database is a unique contribution which then permits new analysis of the strategies of these 500 companies, arranged by industry sector, size, and region. Chapter 5 examines the 49 largest retail firms in the world; chapter 6 the world's largest financial institutions; chapter 7 the pharmaceutical firms; and chapter 8 the automobile companies. Chapter 9 looks at strategies of twenty-two other large firms. Theoretical discussion of the regional nature of international business strategy is developed in chapters 3, 4, 10 and 12, with the public policy implications of regional multinationals discussed in chapter 11.

In summary my research suggests that both globalization and the use of global strategy is a myth. Far from taking place in a single global market, most business activity by large firms takes place within regional blocks. Government regulations and cultural differences segment the world into the broad triad regions of North America, the EU, and Asia-Pacific. Rival multinational enterprises from the triad compete for regional market share and so enhance economic efficiency. As a result, top managers now need to design triad-based regional strategies, not global ones. Global markets are not becoming homogenized, nor is there a trend towards globalization. Rather there is a trend, over the last quarter century, towards regionalization and increased intra-regional economic activity. Only in a few sectors, such as consumer electronics is a global strategy of economic integration viable. For most other manufacturing, (such as automobiles, chemicals, energy, etc.) and for all services, (such as retail, banking, etc.) regional strategies are required. The implications of this for corporate strategy and public policy are discussed in chapters 10, 11, and 12.

THE EMPIRICAL CONTRIBUTION OF THE BOOK

In this book, the top 500 firms are examined, both across sectors and in a set of individual case studies arranged by triad regions. Data are presented on the percentage intra-regional sales for all of the 500 firms for which data can be obtained. No data are available for 120 firms. Virtually all of these are extremely domestic (home country) in their sales, e.g. the US Post Office (ranked at 29) and the Central Japan Railway (ranked at 460). Of the remaining 380, the vast majority (320) are home-region based, having less than 50% of their sales in the other two parts of the triad. For another fifteen there are insufficient data. Twenty five are "bi-regional", with at least 20% of their sales in two parts of the triad, and less than 50% in their home triad. Eleven are host-region based with more than 50% of their sales in a foreign region. Only nine of the 500 are truly "global", with at least 20% of their sales in all three parts of the triad, but less than 50% in one region of the triad. This is a picture of regionalization, not globalization. As such, the 500 largest MNEs in the triad need a regional solution to strategy.

A powerful indicator of triad/regional economic activity is the concentration of the world's largest firms in the core triad of the United States, EU and Japan. In 2001, of the world's largest 500 firms, 428 were in these core triad regions, see table 1.1. In 1996, it was 443; in 1991 it was 410, and back in 1981 it was 445. Over the last twenty years the trend has shown a decrease in the proportion of US firms, from 242 in 1981 to as few as 157 in 1991, but up to 162 in 1996, and 197 in 2001. The EU number is very consistent, being 141 for the old EEC members in 1981 but up to 155 for the enlarged EU in 1996, and down to 143 again by 2001.

Those 500 firms dominate international business. They account for over 90% of the world's stock of FDI and nearly 50% of the world trade. These firms are the "unit of analysis" for research in international business. They are the key vehicles for both FDI and trade. Furthermore, research presented in this book reveals that the majority of their sales, on average, are intra-regional, and for

Table 1.1. The world's largest 500 multinational enterprises

Country	1981	1991	1996	2001
United States	242	157	162	197
European Union	141	134	155	143
Japan	62	119	126	88
Canada		9	6	16
South Korea		13	13	12
China			3	11
Switzerland		10	14	11
Australia		9	5	6
Brazil		1	5	4
Others	55	48	11	12
Total	500	500	500	500
Triad total	445	410	443	428

Source: Fortune, 'The Fortune Global 500," July 22, 2002.

Table 1.2. Classification of the world's largest 500 firms	
Type of firm	No. of firms
home-region oriented	320
bi-regional	25
host-region oriented	11
global	9
insufficient data	15
no data	120
Total	500

the great majority of them this intra-regional trade is concentrated in their home region of the triad. Very few of these 500 large firms actually have any significant presence in all three regions of the triad. (In fact only a handful, such as IBM, Coca Cola, and LVMH qualify as "global" firms.) A somewhat larger subset of the 500 have a strong presence in at least one other part of the triad in addition to their home region. These four types of firms are:

(i) firms in their home region of the triad: these are labeled home-based MNEs, or home-region oriented firms;

(ii) firms in two regions of the triad: these are labeled "bi-regional" firms;

(iii) firms in a foreign region of the triad; these are "host-region oriented firms";

(iv) firms in all three regions of the triad: these are labeled "global" firms.

It should be noted that firms in all groups may be "international", but not necessarily global. Only group (iv) firms are actually "global", but group (ii) bi-regional firms may be regarded as partly global. Clearly, group (i) and group (iii) firms are not global by any definition.

THE REGIONAL SALES DATA IN THE BOOK

In this study of the 500 largest firms in the world, shown in table 1.2, the intra-regional sales of these firms across the three regions of the triad can be calculated for 380 firms, based on information in the annual reports and web pages. The 380 firms in table 1.1 can then be classified according to those that are global, bi-regional, and domestic. There are no data for 120 firms (most of which are entirely domestic) and insufficient data for another fifteen firms. The main results are:

(a) home-region oriented: of the top 500 firms, 320 have at least 50% of their sales in their own region of the triad;

(b) bi-regional: only 25 of the 500 firms are bi-regional, with over 20% of their sales in at least two parts of the triad plus less than 50% of sales in their home region;

(c) host-region oriented: 11 host-region oriented firms with over 50% of sales in a triad region other than their own;

(d) global: only nine of the top 500 MNEs are global, defined as having sales of 20% or more in each of the three regions of the triad, but less than 50% in any one region.

Of these classifications, the intra-regional average sales for each group is:

- 80.3% for the 320 home region oriented firms;
- 42.0% for the 25 bi-regional MNEs;
- 30.9% for the 11 host-region ranked firms;
- 38.3% for the nine global MNEs;

The average intra-regional sales for all 380 firms with available data is 71.9%.

The book's tables (especially in chapter 2) include notes on individual companies and their different reporting systems. Of the 380 companies with data on regional sales, 200 are service companies and 180 are manufacturing companies. There are sixteen broad industry categories, with nine manufacturing categories and seven service categories. All of these points are discussed in detail in chapter 2. These data indicate that the top 500 MNEs operate on a home-region basis for 320 of 380 cases of MNEs for which data are available. This is very strong evidence of regional/triad activity. There are few "global" MNEs – indeed so few as to render the concept of "globalization" meaningless. "Global" strategy is a special case, not the general case.

These data confirm in a robust manner the analysis of Rugman (2000) on the myth of global strategy and the nature of triad-based business activity rather than globalization. These data also confirm the study of the 49 retail MNEs in the 500, in Rugman and Girod (2003). In that study, only one retail MNE was found to be global, namely LVMH. This result is evident across all industry sectors except for electronics, which includes seven of the nine global firms in the set.

THE REGIONAL AND GLOBAL CASE STUDIES IN THE BOOK

In this book I analyze up to sixty firms in detail, as can be seen in chapters 4 through 9. This study of individual firms, whose operations are often described as global, shows that most are mainly dependent on their home region of the triad for their revenue stream. Some of the well-known companies discussed in this book are:

McDonald's
Nike
Wal-Mart
Carrefour
Volkswagen
Toyota
Honda

In fact, Wal-Mart derives over 94% of its revenue from its home-region of North America. Over 80% of Carrefour's revenues are in its home region of Europe. McDonald's and Nike are bi-regional in Europe and North America. Toyota is bi-regional in Japan and North America. Finally, Honda is a host-region oriented company with over 50% of its sales in the North American market. Not one of these, traditionally thought of as global companies, is, in fact, global.

Of the 500 companies studied, nine are global companies with over 20% of their sales deriving from each of triad regions. Of these, the five most relevant cases are included in this book.

1. IBM
2. Canon
3. Coca-Cola
4. Flextronics
5. LVMH

Seven of the nine global companies in the top 500 are in the computers, office, and electronics industry. IBM, Canon, and Flextronics illustrate the nature of this highly mobile manufacturing industry. IBM is the largest and one of the most global companies in the world. Of the other global companies, Coca-Cola is the only global food manufacturer, while LVMH is a manufacturer and luxury retailer and the only service provider with a global scope.

SUMMARY OF THIS BOOK

It is widely accepted that multinationals drive globalization. The top 500 multinationals dominate international business, accounting for over 90% of the world's FDI and nearly half its trade. But globalization, as commonly understood, is a myth. Far from taking place in a single global market, business activity by most large multinationals takes place within any one of the world's three great regional blocks – North America, Europe, and Asia-Pacific.

Of the world's largest 500 multinationals in 2001, 428 were in the USA, the EU, and Japan. Only a handful – nine – were by my definition truly global. These took at least a fifth of their sales from each of the three regions but less than half from any one region. Most – 320 out of 380 – were stay-at-home multinationals, deriving on average four-fifths of their sales from their home regions. There were 25 "bi-regional" multinationals, deriving less than half of their sales from their home region but over a fifth from one other region. Eleven "host-country" oriented multinationals derived over half their sales from a region other than their own.

There is no discernible trend towards either global branding or standardization. Only a few multinational brands, with Coca-Cola leading the way, are global. Even McDonald's is bi-regional, not global. In terms of the value chain, a few multinationals outsource offshore. Nike has 99% of its production outside of the United States, almost all of it in Southeast Asia. Yet its brand name drives sales on a regional basis: most of its sales are in North America and Europe.

International manufacturing is dominated by large multinationals in location-bound clusters. The best example is the automobile industry. The data on foreign sales of the world's largest automobile multinationals shows that the majority of these sales were made in their home regions. GM at 81% and Ford at 61% have most of their sales in North America. In contrast BMW and VW have most of their sales in Europe. Assembly and production of vehicles, however, is generally carried out regionally in each market served.

The service sectors are even more regional. In retail, only one of the largest forty-nine retail firms was global – LVMH. In banking, all the companies had the vast majority of their assets in their home regions. Citigroup had 80% of its assets in North America. Insurance is even more local. Even knowledge-intensive services industries are largely local. For example, professional service firms are located locally with partners largely immobile and their networks, at best, regionally based.

Most R&D is undertaken by the world's largest 500 multinationals in their back yards. Patents, for instance, are registered in local regions. Active multinationals first attempt to register at the US Patent Office. To overcome regulatory barriers to marketing and distribution pharmaceutical R&D then spreads through separate national patents. Similarly, health care is not global but delivered locally, subject to local regulations. Global markets, therefore, are not becoming homogenized. Only in a few sectors, such as consumer electronics, is a global strategy of economic integration viable.

It is possible that the "back end" production of the value chain is more globalized than the "front end" of sales. However, even there we find a picture of regionally based production clusters and networks similar to the automobile sector. Only in electronics is production likely to be globalized, as transportation costs are low relative to assembly. Otherwise, production in chemicals, resources, and services is likely to be highly localized. In retailing, a few multinationals, such as Nike and Wal-Mart, outsource a significant part of their products from other regions; but, again, most production is localized in order to address national preferences.

All of this has major implications for business. Managers need to design regional strategies, not global ones. Only in a few sectors does a global strategy make sense. For most other sectors, strategies of national responsiveness are required.

However, there is nothing to stop a multinational pursuing a "global" strategy within its home region. By this, a multinational will sell the same product or service in the same way across all the countries of its home region, allowing it to gain economies of scale. Only when a multinational exhausts the possibilities for growth in its home region, does it need to venture into other regions.

In other words, all the advantages of global homogeneity can be achieved regionally, especially if the governments of that region pursue internal market policies such as social, cultural, and political harmonization (as in the EU) or economic integration (as in NAFTA and in Asia).

2

Regional multinationals: the data

Contents

The world's 500 largest firms derive most of their revenue from their home-region markets. For instance, most European firms derive over 50% of their revenues from their marketing operations in European countries. The same can be said for companies in the North American and Asia-Pacific regions. Indeed, in 2001, the average intra-regional revenue for the 380 firms for which data was available was 71.9%. These 380 companies account for 76% of the world's 500 largest firms and 79.2% of their revenues. The following methodology describes how the data were gathered and categorized.

METHODOLOGY

Data on the "Regional Nature of Global Multinational Activity" (the RNGMA database) used in this book were collected from official documents of the world's 500 largest companies according to *Fortune*, "The *Fortune* Global 500" (2002). Wherever possible the annual report and, in the case of United States companies and those with large operations in the United States, SEC filings were used to obtain data on regional sales. Companies failing to publish this information were contacted directly. For companies that did not disclose the information, relevant information (number of stores, net income, etc.) was used to estimate regional revenue. Of the largest 500 firms, intra-regional sales data were obtained for 380 companies.

Throughout this chapter, companies are classified as home-region oriented; bi-regional; host-region oriented; or global. Home-region oriented companies derive at least 50% of their revenues from their home region. Bi-regional companies derive at least 20% of their revenues from two regions (including their own) but less than 50% in any one region. For host-region oriented companies, a foreign region must account for at least 50% of sales. A global company derives at least 20% of its sales from each of the three main regions of North America, Europe, and Asia-Pacific, but less than 50% in any one region.

Each company defines regional segmentation based on its organizational structure and not by a universal definition of region. The database includes notes on individual companies and their different reporting systems.

To calculate intra-regional sales in Europe, data on Europe as a whole were given preference. For companies that only reported data for the EU, this number was used to estimate Europe as a whole. Wherever there is a superscript "m", Europe refers to Europe, the Middle East, and Africa (the EMEA region). For a small number of companies, only information on the UK is available. These companies are recognized by a "u" superscript.

For the purpose of this study, Asia-Pacific refers to Asia and Oceania. It does not include Pacific countries in the Americas. Many companies only report sales in the Japanese market. These companies are recognized by a superscript "j". A small number of companies report their Asian figures include Africa. These companies can be recognized by a superscript "f".

The database defines North America as the members of the North American Free Trade Agreement: Canada, Mexico, and the United States. When a company does not report sales in NAFTA, the next best alternative is used. For companies that only report sales in the US the superscript "z" has been used. If the company defines North America as Canada and the United States we use the superscript "a". In the case of the Royal Bank of Canada, which only reports revenues in Canada, the superscript "c" has been used. If there is no entry for North America, but instead there is an entry for the Americas, this number is used to estimate the region and is denoted by the superscript "l".

Some companies segment revenues according to origin of the sales transaction while others segment sales according to location of customer. In some cases, both types of data are reported. Wherever possible, location of customer is used because exports are important to a company. For companies for which this information was not reported, sales at origin were used to estimate geographic sales. Comparisons across companies should take into consideration these limitations.

Europe's GDP is relatively at par with North America's. In Asia, however, GDP is much lower. If we weighted the regional sales, according to GDP, percentages in Asia-Pacific would become more significant. It is therefore important to note that this study only relates to the relative importance of the three regions to the companies in regards to revenue and not to the relative influence of companies within each region.

Intra-regional sales were reported as >90% for companies that reported foreign sales as less than 10%. For calculation purposes, this number was estimated at its lowest point of 90%.

Of the 380 companies, 200 are service companies and 180 are manufacturing companies. The database simplifies The *Fortune* Global 500 industry classifications codes into sixteen broad categories. Of these, nine are manufacturing categories and seven are service categories as discussed later.

THE INTRA-REGIONAL NATURE OF THE WORLD'S LARGEST FIRMS

The 500 largest companies in the world accounted for over $14 trillion of total sales (revenues) in fiscal year 2001. The average revenue for a firm in the top 500 was $28 billion, ranging from Wal-Mart at $220 billion to Takenaka at $10 billion. The average sales of a firm in the set of 380 is $29.2 billion. Although a company's level of intra-regional sales varies from as little as 9% to as high as 100%, an estimated 84.2% of the 380 companies have over 50% of their sales in their home region. For the entire set, intra-regional sales average 71.9%. This is displayed in table 2.1.

Only 6.6% of the 380 companies are bi-regional, having less than 50% of their sales in their home market and having at least 20% of their sales in two regions (including their own region). Lafarge, the French cement company is one example of a bi-regional firm. It derives 40% of its revenue from its home-region market of Europe, but it also has a significant presence in the North American market from which it derives an additional 32% of its revenues. An additional 2.9% of companies are host-region oriented. This can be considered another type of bi-regional firm and is defined as having over 50% of their sales in a host region. The

Table 2.1. Classification of the top 500 firms				
type of MNE	no. of MNEs	% of 500	% of 380	% intra-regional sales
global	9	1.8	2.4	38.3
bi-regional	25	5.0	6.6	42.0
host-region oriented	11	2.2	2.9	30.9
home-region oriented (1)	320	64.0	84.2	80.3
insufficient data	15	3.0	3.9	40.9
no data	120	24.0		na
Total	500	100.0	100.0	

Notes: (1) Intra-regional sales were reported as >90% for companies that reported foreign sales as less than 10%. For calculation purposes, this number was estimated at its lowest point of 90%.
Data are for 2001.
Numbers might not add up due to rounding.

Figure 2.1. Regional multinationals, by degree of intra-regional sales
Note: mid-points have been used to graph the data. Data are for 2001

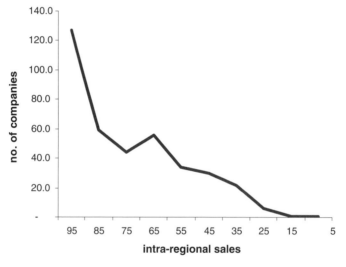

Australian company News Corp., with 9% of its sales in its home region and 75% in the US market, is one such a firm. Only 2.4% of companies fit the definition of global, that is, companies that have at least 20% of their revenues in the three different regions of North America, Europe, and Asia-Pacific, but less than 50% in any one region. Royal Phillips Electronics is an example of a global firm. These companies tend to put significantly more emphasis on global strategy than other firms. There are insufficient data to categorize the remaining 3.9% firms.

Figure 2.1 confirms the home-region bias in the activities of the top 500 firms for the 380 firms for which data can be classified by percentiles. Of these, 58 are purely domestic (15.3% of the total). The majority of these firms are service companies, such as merchandizers, banks and other financial services, telecommunications, and utilities. Another 69 have over 90% or more of their sales at home (18.2%), and a total of

230 have over 70% or more of their sales in their home region of the triad. Those with over 50% or more intra-regional sales add up to the 320 identified above as home-region based. This reflects an extraordinary degree of regionalization, rather than globalization. These data confirm, in a robust manner, the analysis of Rugman (2000) on the myth of global strategy and the nature of triad-based business activity rather than globalization. These data also confirm the study of the 49 retail firms in the 500, Rugman and Girod (2003). In that study, only one retail firm, LVMH, was found to be global, see chapter 5.

Global firms

Among the world's largest MNEs, nine stand out as being the most global in terms of generating their revenue across the three largest regions of North America, Europe, and Asia-Pacific. These are listed in table 2.2. Headquarters for these companies are evenly distributed across these three dominant regions. All global companies are in the manufacturing sector except for LVMH/Dior, which is well known as a luxury goods retailer. (In the data for 2001, LVMH is ranked 459 and is listed as a separate firm from Dior, listed at 446; as these two firms have subsequently merged, they are treated as one firm in this book.)

Bi-regional firms

Bi-regional companies are listed in table 2.3. These companies have a significant presence – more than 20% – in two major regions, including their own, but less than 50% of their sales in their own home region. The largest such company is British Petroleum (BP) with 174.2 billion in sales. BP derives 36.3% of its revenues from the European market and 48.1% from the US market. Together these two markets account for 84.4% of the company's revenue. Bi-regional expansion seems to be most common for European firms, which account for sixteen of the twenty-five bi-regional firms in the RNGMA Index. Of these sixteen firms, only one, L. M. Ericsson, has Asia as its other major host region. The other fifteen are European/North American firms. These companies are lured to North America to benefit from the profit opportunities of the faster growing US market.

Some of the companies listed in table 2.3 might actually fall under the home-region oriented category, but a lack of home-region data prevents such conclusion. For instance, both Toyota Motors and Nissan Motors have nearly 50% of their sales in Japan. If the rest of Asia and Oceania accounted for even a small fraction of total revenues, these companies would have been listed under home-region oriented despite a significant presence in the North American market. The same can be argued about

Table 2.2. Global firms

	500 rank	company	region	revenues in bn US$	F/T sales	% intra regional	North America % of total sales	Europe % total sales	Asia-Pacific % of total sales
1	19	Intl. Business Machines	North America	85.9	64.8	43.5	43.5[l]	28.0[m]	20.0
2	37	Sony	Asia-Pacific	60.6	67.2	32.8	29.8[z]	20.2	32.8[j]
3	143	Royal Philips Electronics	Europe	29.0	na	43.0	28.7[a]	43.0	21.5
4	147	Nokia	Europe	27.9	98.5	49.0	25.0[l]	49.0	26.0
5	162	Intel	North America	26.5	64.6	35.4	35.4[z]	24.5	40.2
6	190	Canon	Asia-Pacific	23.9	71.5	28.5	33.8[l]	20.8	28.5[j]
7	239	Coca-Cola	North America	20.1	na	38.4	38.4	22.4[m]	24.9
8	388	Flextronics International	Asia-Pacific	13.1	na	22.4	46.3[z]	30.9	22.4
9	459	LVMH	Europe	11.0	83.4	36.0	26.0[z]	36.0	32.0
		weighted average*		33.1		38.3			
		Total		298.0					

Data are for 2001.
Numbers might not add up due to rounding.
Notes: [a] Canada and the US; [z] United States; [l] Americas; [m] Europe, Middle East and Africa; [j] Japan.
* Weighted average is calculated by using the size of firms according to revenues.

Table 2.3. Bi-regional firms

	500 rank	company	region	revenues in bn US$	F/T sales	% intra regional	North America % of total sales	Europe % of total sales	Asia-Pacific % of total sales
1	4	BP	Europe	174.2	80.4	36.3	48.1^z	36.3	na
2	10	Toyota Motor	Asia-Pacific	120.8	50.8	49.2	36.6	7.7	49.2^j
3	58	Nissan Motor	Asia-Pacific	49.6	50.3	49.7	34.6	11.0	49.7^j
4	68	Unilever	Europe	46.1	na	38.7	26.6	38.7	15.4
5	138	Motorola	North America	30.0	56.0	44.0	44.0^z	14.0	26.0
6	140	GlaxoSmithKline	Europe	29.5	50.8	28.6	49.2^z	28.6	na
7	153	EADS	Europe	27.6	na	44.9	33.7	44.9	10.2
8	158	Bayer	Europe	27.1	na	40.3	32.7	40.3	16.1
9	210	L. M. Ericsson	Europe	22.4	97.0	46.0	13.2	46.0	25.9
10	228	Alstom	Europe	20.7	88.0	45.1	28.0	45.1	16.1
11	230	Aventis (q)	Europe	20.5	87.2	32.1	38.8^q	32.1	6.4^j
12	262	Diageo	Europe	18.6	na	31.8	49.9	31.8	7.7
13	268	Sun Microsystems	North America	18.3	52.6	47.4	47.4^z	30.2^m	17.2
14	285	Bridgestone	Asia-Pacific	17.6	61.2	38.8	43.0^l	10.1	38.8^j
15	288	Roche Group	Europe	17.3	98.2	36.8	38.6	36.8	11.7
16	316	3M (q)	North America	16.1	53.1	46.9	46.9^z	24.6	18.9
17	317	Skanska	Europe	15.9	83.0	40.0	41.0	40.0	na
18	340	McDonald's (q)	North America	14.9	62.4	40.4	40.4^q	31.9	14.8
19	342	Michelin	Europe	14.6	na	47.0	40.0	47.0	na
20	386	Eastman Kodak	North America	13.2	na	48.5	48.5^z	24.7^m	17.2
21	386	Electrolux	Europe	13.1	na	47.0	39.0	47.0	9.0
22	390	BAE Systems	Europe	13.0	82.7	38.1	32.3^q	38.1	2.7
23	408	Alcan	North America	12.6	95.4	41.1	41.1^q	39.6	13.9
24	415	L'Oréal	Europe	12.3	na	48.5	32.4	48.5	na
25	416	Lafarge	Europe	12.3	na	40.0	32.0	40.0	8.0
		weighted average*		31.1	42.0				
		Total		778.3					

Numbers might not add up due to rounding.
Data are for 2001.
Notes: ^{a} Canada and the US; ^{z} United States; ^{l} Americas; ^{u} United Kingdom; ^{m} Europe, Middle East and Africa; ^{j} Japan.
^{q} 3M: Data for Europe include the Middle East; Aventis: Estimated using sales for core business; McDonald's: Data for Asia include the Middle East and Africa.
* Weighted average is calculated by using the size of firms according to revenues.

Eastman Kodak, whose 48.5% intra-regional sales do not include data on Canada or Mexico.

Host-region oriented

The eleven host-region oriented MNEs are reported in table 2.4. Another type of bi-regional, these companies have over 50% of their sales in a

Table 2.4. Host-region based MNEs

	500 rank	company	region	revenues in bn US$	F/T sales	% intra regional	North America % of total sales	Europe % of total sales	Asia-Pacific % of total sales
1	7	DaimlerChrysler	Europe	136.9	na	29.9	60.1	29.9	na
2	20	ING Group	Europe	83.0	77.3	35.1	51.4	35.1	3.4
3	38	Royal Ahold	Europe	59.6	85.0	32.8	59.2	32.8	0.6
4	41	Honda Motor	Asia-Pacific	58.9	73.1	26.9	53.9	8.1	26.9^j
5	136	Santander Central Hispano Group	Europe	30.4	66.1	44.3	55.7^l	44.3	na
6	245	Delhaize 'Le Lion'	Europe	19.6	84.0	22.0	75.9	22.0	1.0
7	301	Astra Zeneca	Europe	16.5	na	32.0	52.8^z	32.0	5.2^j
8	364	News Corp.	Asia-Pacific	13.8	na	9.0	75.0^z	16.0^u	9.0
9	476	Sodexho Alliance	Europe	10.6	na	42.0	50.0	42.0	na
10	482	Manpower	North America	10.5	80.9	19.1	19.1^z	68.6	na
11	487	Wolseley	Europe	10.4	79.1	28.7	66.3	28.7	na
		weighted average*		40.9		30.9			
		Total		450.1					

Numbers might not add up due to rounding.
Data are for 2001.
Notes: ^{z} United States; ^{l} Americas; ^{u} United Kingdom; ^{j} Japan.
* Weighted average is calculated by using the size of firms according to revenues.

region other than their own. Host-region oriented MNEs include Daim-lerChrysler as one of eight European-based firms with more than half of their sales in North America. There is also one Asian business, Honda, and the Australian-based News Corp. that also have most of their sales in North America. Only one US MNE, Manpower, has more sales in Europe than in its home market. Most of these MNEs are attracted by the US economy and their strategies are market-access ones.

The expansion strategies of host-region MNEs have often been implemented through merger and acquisition, as when German Mercedes Benz purchased Chrysler, one of the big three US automakers. The Spanish bank, Santander Central Hispano Group, has 55.7% of its sales in the Americas, which it achieved by purchasing banks that were being auctioned as a result of government privatization efforts across Latin America. The most host-region oriented company listed in table 2.4 is Australian News Corp., owner of Fox, The New York Post, TV Guide, among others (in the United States) and of *The Times*, *The Sunday Times*, and *The Sun*, among others (in the UK).

Home-region oriented

Of the 320 home-region oriented MNEs, the largest twenty-five are listed in table 2.5. None of these firms can be considered a global firm. They

	500 rank	company	region	revenues in bn US$	F/T sales	% intra regional	North America % of total sales	Europe % of total sales	Asia-Pacific % of total sales

Table 2.5. The top 25 home-region based companies

	500 rank	company	region	revenues in bn US$	F/T sales	% intra regional	North America % of total sales	Europe % of total sales	Asia-Pacific % of total sales
1	1	Wal-Mart Stores (q)	North America	219.8	16.3	94.1	94.1	4.8	0.4
2	3	General Motors	North America	177.3	25.5	81.1	81.1	14.6	na
3	5	Ford Motor	North America	162.4	33.3	66.7	66.7^z	21.9	na
4	9	General Electric	North America	125.9	40.9	59.1	59.1^z	19.0	9.1
5	12	Mitsubishi	Asia-Pacific	105.8	13.2	86.8	5.4^z	1.7^u	86.8^j
6	13	Mitsui	Asia-Pacific	101.2	34.0	78.9	7.4	11.1	78.9
7	15	Total Fina Elf	Europe	94.3	na	55.6	8.4	55.6	na
8	17	Itochu	Asia-Pacific	91.2	19.1	91.2	5.5	1.7	91.2
9	18	Allianz	Europe	85.9	69.4	78.0	17.6^l	78.0	4.4^f
10	21	Volkswagen	Europe	79.3	72.3	68.2	20.1	68.2	5.3
11	22	Siemens	Europe	77.4	78.0	52.0	30.0^l	52.0	13.0
12	23	Sumitomo	Asia-Pacific	77.1	12.7	87.3	4.8^z	na	87.3^j
13	24	Philip Morris	North America	72.9	42.1	57.9	57.9^z	25.8	na
14	25	Marubeni (q)	Asia-Pacific	71.8	28.2	74.5	11.6^z	na	74.5
15	26	Verizon Communications	North America	67.2	3.8	96.2	96.2^z	na	na
16	27	Deutsche Bank	Europe	66.8	69.0	63.1	29.3	63.1	6.5
17	28	E.ON	Europe	66.5	43.4	80.1	9.4^z	80.1	na
18	29	US Postal Service (q)	North America	65.8	3.0	97.0	97.0^z	na	na
19	30	AXA (q)	Europe	65.6	77.3	51.2	24.1^z	51.2	19.9
20	31	Credit Suisse	Europe	64.2	73.3	60.9	34.9^l	60.9	4.1^f
21	32	Hitachi	Asia-Pacific	63.9	31.0	80.0	11.0	7.0	80.0
22	34	American International Group	North America	62.4	na	59.0	59.0^a	na	na
23	35	Carrefour	Europe	62.2	50.8	81.3	na	81.3	6.6
24	36	American Electric Power	North America	61.3	12.3	87.7	87.7^z	11.8^u	na
25	39	Duke Energy	North America	59.5	13.1	96.5	96.5	na	na

Data are for 2001.
Notes: ^{a} Canada and the US; ^{z} United States; ^{l} Americas; ^{u} United Kingdom; ^{j} Japan; ^{f} Africa. ^{q} Wal-Mart: Estimated using number of stores; Marubeni: Asia includes only Japan and Singapore; US Postal Service: US data reflect an Annual Report statement that says less than 3% of total revenues originate outside the United States; AXA: Europe represents France, the UK, Germany and Belgium.

pursue essentially a domestic intra-regional strategy. The average intra-regional (home) sales of these 320 firms is 80% – a long way from being global.

The largest home-region oriented firm, Wal-Mart, is also the largest company in the world with revenues of $219.8 billion. The company's international presence is relatively low. Only 16.3% of its sales are outside of its home market of the United States. Of these, 10.4% of its sales are

Table 2.6. The "near miss" global companies

500 rank	company	region	revenues in bn US$	F/T sales	% intra regional	North America % of total sales	Europe % of total sales	Asia-Pacific % of total sales
2	Exxon Mobile	North America	191.6	69.6	37.5	37.5^a	8.9^u	10.4^j
8	Royal Dutch/Shell Group	Europe	135.2	na	46.1	15.6^z	46.1	na
55	Nestlé	Europe	50.2	na	31.6	31.4	31.6	na
117	Compaq Computer	North America	33.6	62.0	38.0	38.0^z	36.0^m	na
230	Aventis (q)	Europe	20.5	87.2	32.1	38.8^a	32.1	6.4^j
316	3M (q)	North America	16.1	53.1	46.9	46.9^z	24.6	18.9
340	McDonald's (q)	North America	14.9	63.7	40.4	40.4^a	31.9	14.8
341	Anglo American	Europe	14.8	86.7	46.1	18.9	46.1	17.8
383	Eastman Kodak	North America	13.2	na	48.5	48.5^z	24.7^m	17.2

Data are for 2001.
Notes: ^{a} Canada and the US; ^{z} United States; ^{u} United Kingdom; ^{m} Europe, Middle East and Africa; ^{j} Japan. ^{q} 3M: Data for Europe include the Middle East; Aventis: Estimated using sales for core business; McDonald's: Data for Asia include the Middle East and Africa.

derived from operations in other North American Free Trade Agreement (NAFTA) members, Canada and Mexico. Together, the European and Asia-Pacific markets account for only 5.2% of the company's revenues. The remaining 0.4% of revenues is derived from operations outside the largest regional economic blocks.

A large portion of the companies listed in table 2.5 are very home-region oriented, with over 90% of intra-regional sales. Yet, other companies listed in this table have a more significant presence in countries outside their own region. For instance, French TotalFinaElf has 44.4% of its sales outside of its home-region market. Another example is Siemens, which derives 52% of its sales intra-regionally but has a significant presence in the Americas, which accounts for 30% of its sales.

Some special cases

"Near miss" global

Insufficient information makes categorization difficult for a number of companies. Table 2.6 highlights special cases of companies that could have been categorized as global had sufficient information been available, and other companies that barely miss the requirements of a global company.

Coca-Cola and McDonald's

The two MNEs always regarded as "global", indeed as the agents of globalization, are Coca-Cola and McDonald's. Yet only Coca-Cola is truly a global

MNE. Ranking at 129 in the 500 list, it has over 20% of its sales across all three parts of the triad: 38.4% in North America; 22.4% in Europe, the Middle East and Africa; and 24.9% in Asia. Of Coca-Cola's sales in Asia, 74% are in Japan, but the company is attempting to increase its market in China. In contrast, McDonald's, ranked at 340, is a bi-regional MNE. It has 36.6% of its sales in North America, 37.1% in Europe; but only 13.8% in Asia.

Nike

Nike is another interesting case. It sources 99% of its product offshore, in China (38%), and South East Asia (61%). Yet Nike is a business with the majority of its sales in the Americas (58.2%); indeed it has 52.1% of sales in its home market of the United States. Nike also competes in Europe with 29% of its sales there, but not much in Asia with only 12.9% of sales there. Nike is not one of the largest 500 firms, with sales of under $10 m, and it is not a global business except in terms of part of its supply chain, as discussed further in chapter 3.

Colgate Palmolive

Very few of the 380 firms in this book have any significant sales outside of the "broad" triad regions of the EU, North America, and the Asia-Pacific. Few have, for example, any significant strategic presence in Latin America, Africa, or the subcontinent of India and Pakistan.

One exception is *Colgate Palmolive*, a US firm which is too small to be in the top 500, with revenues of only $9.3 billion in 2001. Colgate has two major business segments. One is Pet Nutrition, with sales of $1.2b, of which $0.7 is in the home country US market. Its other business unit is much larger, at $8.1b – this is the oral, personal, household surface and fabric care segment. For this, its geographic sales are:

North America	2.4 b and 29.3%
Latin America	2.2 b and 27.2%
Europe	2.0b and 24.5%
Asia Pacific	1.5 b and 19.0%

While Colgate has 56.5% of its sales in the Americas, it is one of the few large firms to have such a large presence in Latin America, at 27.2%. Colgate is a "near miss" global firm, as just an additional one percent of its sales in Asia/Africa would put it into the global category of 20% of sales in each major triad region. If a substantial amount of Colgate's Pet Nutrition business is in Japan, then its overall geographic sales may be classified as global, but the published data do not allow us to so classify the firm.

Table 2.7. The regional nature of global MNEs, by industry and type					
industry category	global	bi-regional	host-region oriented	home-region oriented	insufficient information
manufacturing	9	24	3	131	13
1 aerospace and defense	0	2	0	8	1
2 chemicals and pharmaceuticals	0	4	1	11	2
3 computer, office and electronics	7	4	0	22	3
4 construction, building materials and glass	0	2	0	9	0
5 energy, petroleum and refining	0	1	0	27	3
6 food, drug and tobacco	1	2	0	9	2
7 motor vehicle and parts	0	4	2	23	0
8 natural resource manufacturing	0	1	0	15	1
9 other manufacturing	1	4	0	7	1
Services	1	1	8	189	1
1 banks	0	0	1	39	0
2 entertainment, printing and publishing	0	0	1	8	0
3 merchandizers	1	0	2	60	0
4 other financial services	0	0	1	26	0
5 telecommunications and utilities	0	0	0	27	0
6 transportation services	0	0	0	13	0
7 other services	0	1	3	16	1
Total	10	25	11	320	14

Data are for 2001.

INTRA-REGIONAL SALES BY INDUSTRY CATEGORIZATION

In the RNGMA database companies have been classified into 16 categories. Nine are manufacturing categories, and seven are service categories as listed in table 2.7.

Expansion of marketing operations into foreign regions is more common in the manufacturing sector than in the service sector. Nearly all, 95% of the 200 service firms studied in the RNGMA database, are home-region oriented compared to 73% for the 180 countries in the manufacturing sector. In contrast, only one of the ten global companies listed in the RNGMA database is from the service sector. Table 2.7 illustrates the different levels of globalization among RNGMA industries.

The manufacturing industry accounts for most bi-regional companies. Only one service company, McDonald's, is bi-regional. Surprisingly, the largest number of host-region oriented companies comes from the service industries. Eight out of eleven host-region companies are in the service industry and include banks, retailers, and insurance companies, among others.

"Location-bound" sectors show the highest percentage of intra-regional sales across industries. Location-bound industries face barriers to international expansion in the form of government regulations, dependence on geographic location, transportation costs, and cultural barriers. For example, most countries heavily regulate their banking industries. Some countries, such as France and Japan, regulate the size and location of large retailers. Another example comes from the mobile phone network providers. In this industry, companies must bid for the licenses to operate in each market and adapt to the different types of platforms that are permitted in each national/regional jurisdiction. Many large utilities are government owned and depend on national infrastructure and natural resources. Finally, cultural barriers in the form of cultural attitudes, ethics, and language

Table 2.8. Average sales in the service and manufacturing sectors

industry category	weighted average intra-regional sales
manufacturing	
1 natural resource manufacturing	77.6
2 construction, building materials and glass	73.5
3 aerospace and defense	66.3
4 energy, petroleum and refining	66.0
5 motor vehicle and parts	60.6
6 other manufacturing	57.8
7 chemicals and pharmaceuticals	56.5
8 computer, office and electronics	56.2
9 food, drug and tobacco	55.0
Services	
1 merchandizers	87.9
2 telecommunications and utilities	87.6
3 transportation services	83.7
4 banks	78.3
5 other services	75.8
6 entertainment, printing and publishing	73.1
7 other financial services	71.9

Data are for 2001.

make exporting cultural products across borders very difficult. This is most important in the entertainment, printing, and publishing sector, where most international expansion occurs through the acquisition of already established and locally managed companies.

All service sectors are location bound, with over 71% of revenues deriving from home-region markets. In the manufacturing sector, the relatively more "location-bound" sectors, show intra-regional sales of 66% or higher. In sectors in which value added-in production is made at the customer end, intra-regional sales are lower. Such sectors include food, drugs, and tobacco; computers and electronics; and chemicals and pharmaceuticals. Table 2.8 lists the average intra-regional sales for RNGMA industries.

The manufacturing sector

Despite being relatively more global than the service sector, there remain barriers to trade in the manufacturing sector. This is true even within regional markets. For instance, in North America, the United States imposed tariffs on Canadian softwood lumber that crippled the industry. In Asia, Japanese electronic companies have threatened to lobby their government to keep less expensive foreign electronics parts, especially from South Korea, from entering their home market.

Aerospace and defense

Of the largest eleven companies in the aerospace and defense industries nine are from North America (all are US with the exception of Canadian Bombardier) and two are European. For the ten for which there is enough information, the eight North American based companies are home-region oriented. The two European based companies are bi-regional, with over 30% of their sales originating in their host-region market of North America.

Chemical and pharmaceutical

The chemical and pharmaceutical industries are heavily regulated by national and regional governments in the form of price controls and approval processes. In addition, a firm's liability varies across jurisdictions and must be considered when generating a market strategy. For those firms who have entered the crop-science business, cultural perceptions of genetically modified crops and national/regional regulations will also impact decision making at a national/regional level.

The vast majority of European companies in this sector are bi-regional. AstraZeneca is a host-region based company formed by the merger of Sweden's Astra and UK's Zeneca in 1998. All North American companies are home-region based. This trend of European companies entering the North American market while North American companies rely heavily on their home market is because the United States is the largest world market for pharmaceuticals. It is important to note that the effect is due to pricing, not quantity.

Computer, office, and electronics

With average intra-regional sales of 56.2%, the computer, office, and electronics industry is one of the most global. Seven of the ten global firms in the RNGMA database are from this industry. A strong reliance on the global supply chain and standardized computer parts explains the industry's relative higher international scope. No company in this industry derives less than 10% of its revenues from foreign regions.

The three triad regions are heavily represented in this industry. Among global companies, two are North American, two are European, and three are from Asia-Pacific.

Electronics manufacturing service providers

The emergence of "electronics-manufacturing service providers" (EMS), has led corporate rivals such as Sony and Philips, or Ericsson, Alcatel, and Motorola, to use the same factories to manufacture their competing products. Indeed, companies unknown to the public, such as Flextronics, Solectron, Sanmina-SCI, Celestica, and Jabil, among others, produce such well-known products as IBM PCs, the Microsoft Xbox video console, Web TV set-top boxes for Philips and Sony, and portable phones for Ericsson, Alcatel, and Motorola. In 2002, EMS industry revenues were estimated at $134 billion. The two largest EMS companies, Flextronics and Solectron, account for 9.7% and 9.2% of this market respectively.

That the electronics industry is pioneering contract manufacturing is no accident. The industry's products are easily transported by air, allowing parts to travel the world over before the finished product is completed. This allows an EMS to identify the specific advantages of each region and to develop a worldwide production network that coordinates pro-curement, inventory management, vendor management, packaging, and services that minimizes both time-to-market and production costs.

Today's electronic manufacturers have come a long way from the cheap labor-based contractors that used to dominate the industry. Robotic automation is now a significant part of the production process and is mostly handled by specialists. It is their manufacturing expertise that makes for lower costs, but EMSs provide many more advantages to OEMs. They decrease the risk of manufacturing because OEMs no longer need to make large investments on a new factory to introduce a new product that might or might not be successful. EMSs can also purchase inputs at lower prices because they are not only making cell phones for Alcatel, but also for Motorola and Ericsson, strengthening their purchasing power.

Contract manufacturing accounts for less than one-fourth of electronic manufacturing; however, EMS companies might dominate the industry in the future. This process will redefine the role of OEMs in the electron-ics industry to that of design and marketing while increasing its global nature in all parts of the production cycle.

Construction, building materials, and glass

The second most location-bound manufacturing industry is construction, building materials, and glass. All companies for which data is available are based in Europe and Asia-Pacific. The two bi-regional companies are European with large operations in the United States.

Energy, petroleum, and refining

All but four of the companies in the energy, petroleum, and refining industry have intra-regional sales of over 50%. The four companies that depend more heavily on markets in foreign regions are British Petroleum (BP), Exxon Mobile, Royal Dutch/Shell Group, and ChevronTexaco. BP is clearly bi-regional in Europe and North America. There is not enough information to assess the remaining three companies.

Food, drug, and tobacco

The manufacturing industry with the second lowest intra-regional sales is food, drug, and tobacco. The only global company in this industry is Coca-Cola. Two European companies, Unilever and Diageo, operate bi-regionally in Europe and North America.

Nestlé, for which no sufficient data are available, is either a bi-regional or a global company. Unlike many other RNGMA companies, Nestlé derives a large percentage of its revenue from non-triad markets.

Motor vehicles and parts

The automotive sector presents a combination of bi-regional, host-region, and home-region oriented companies. Two bi-regional companies are Asian car makers, Toyota and Nissan, which operate in the North American and Asian markets. The other two bi-regional companies are tire makers, Bridgestone of Japan and Michelin of France. Both of these companies depend heavily on the North American market for their international revenues.

The North American market is also the dominant foreign region for the two host-region oriented companies, DaimlerChrysler and Honda Motor. Their expansion into this market is markedly different, however. DaimlerChrysler was formed by the merger of German Daimler Benz and North America's third largest carmaker, Chrysler. In contrast, Honda's entry into the US market was fueled by fears of protectionism in the American market in the 1980s.

Natural resource manufacturing

Natural resource manufacturing refers to producers of forest and paper products, metals, mining, and crude oil production. This is the most "location bound" of all RNGMA manufacturing industries with 77.6% intra-regional sales. Canadian Alcan is the only bi-regional company in this industry.

Other manufacturing

Other manufacturing industries include household and personal products; industrial and farm equipment; scientific, photo and control equipment; and miscellaneous manufacturers. Many well-known companies, such as 3M, Kodak, L'Oréal, and Fuji, are listed as other manufacturing.

The service industries

Government regulations and large differences in the markets have made it more difficult for service companies to expand outside of their home region, or even their home country. For instance, even despite attempts at integrating the Canadian, US, and Mexican economies under the NAFTA, many barriers remain in place in the service sector. Canadian chartered banks, for instance, are heavily regulated and must maintain a certain level of local ownership. Some utilities are highly dependent on local infrastructure and act as natural monopolies. Corporate, labor, environmental laws, and other government regulations differ significantly across nations and regions.

Banking

Thirty-nine of the forty banks for which there is information derive 50% or more of their revenues from their home-region markets. Some banks are very international but remain home-region oriented. For instance, 73.3% of Crédit Suisse sales are derived from outside of Switzerland, but less than 40% derive from outside of Europe. Five of the thirty-nine home-region oriented banks derive 100% of their sales from their home region: Bank One, Wachovia Corp., Washington Mutual, US Bancorp of North America, and Nordea of Europe.

The only host-region oriented bank is Santander Central Hispano Group. In 2001, 66.1% of its sales were derived from foreign countries. Of this, 55.7% originated in the Americas, mainly Latin America, where the company undertook a series of acquisitions in the late 1990s.

Entertainment, printing, and publishing

Most entertainment, printing, and publishing companies are home-region oriented. Only Australia's News Corp, which owns media companies in the United States and the UK, is host-region oriented. Cultural barriers in the form of different attitudes, ethics, and language make exporting cultural products across borders very difficult. This is most important in the entertainment, printing, and publishing sector, where most international expansion occurs through the acquisition of already established and locally managed companies.

Merchandizing

Merchandizing is the most location bound of all industries reported in the RNGMA database. Nearly 88% of all sales by merchandizers are intra-regional. Only one company, France's LVMH, is global. The company is a manufacturer and retailer of luxury goods that appeal to the wealthy in all regions.

Royal Ahold and Delhaize "Le Lion" of Europe are both host-region oriented companies with North America as their main host-region market. Royal Ahold derives 59.2% of its revenue from North America. Delhaize "Le Lion" of Belgium derives nearly 76% of its sales from North America.

Although traditionally thought of as global companies, France's Carrefour and American Wal-Mart are home-region based companies with over 80% of their sales derived intra-regionally.

Other financial services

Other financial services include: diversified financials, such as General Electric; insurance, such as Allianz; and securities, such as Morgan Stanley. Government regulations, similar to those imposed on the banking industry, make this a very location-bound industry with 71.9% intra-regional sales. Of the twenty-seven companies in this sector, only one, ING, is not home-region oriented. ING derives over 50% of its revenue from its host-region market of North America. Only 35% of its sales are in Europe.

Telecommunications and utilities

All of the twenty-seven companies in telecommunications and utilities industries are location bound. There are a number of reasons for this, including (1) dependence on local natural resources (particularly in the case of gas and electric utilities); (2) a history of government ownership and control; (3) high level of government regulation (e.g. licensing for telephone operations), and (4) many of these firms have traditionally been called natural monopolies. For instance, telephone companies require physical equipment that is costly and inefficient to duplicate for each company. Those controlling the equipment have a natural monopoly that is often regulated and may be open to competitors through regulation.

Transportation

The transportation industries in the RNGMA database are very location bound, with over 50% of their sales in their home-region markets. Except for Air France and British Airways, all other transportation companies in the RNGMA list derive over 70% of their sales in their home regions.

Other service industries

Other service industries include computer and data services; diversified outsourcing services; food services; healthcare providers; oil and gas equipment services; and other services not included elsewhere. Sixteen of the twenty firms listed, for which there is sufficient information, are home-region oriented. McDonald's is the only bi-regional company. Three companies are host-region oriented.

INTRA-REGIONAL SALES BY REGION

Across the three economically dominant world regions of North America, Europe, and Asia, the results are similar in that most companies sell their products intra-regionally. Nonetheless, North American firms have the highest percentage of home-region based firms while European firms have the lowest percentage of home-region firms and the highest percentage of bi-regional and host-region oriented firms.

The average intra-regional sales of North American firms is 77.2%, higher than that of the Asia-Pacific region, with 74.3%, and the European region, with 62.8% (see table 2.9).

Table 2.9.   Average sales by triad region

region	total no. of firms for which some information is available	weighted average intra-regional sales*
North America	185	77.2
Europe	119	62.8
Asia-Pacific	75	74.3
other	1	88.0
Total	380	72.2

Data are for 2001.
*weighted average is calculated using number of firms in each region.

Table 2.10.   The regional MNEs, classified by triad

region	global	bi-regional	host-region oriented	home-region oriented	insufficient information
North America	3	6	1	167	8
Europe	4	16	8	86	5
Asia-Pacific	3	3	2	66	1
other	0	0	0	1	0
Total	10	25	11	320	14

Data are for 2001.

Europe has the highest number of global, bi-regional, and host-region oriented firms. For the European bi-regional and host-regional oriented firms, the most important foreign market is North America.

North America accounts for the highest number of firms in the RNGMA database, but the region is more inward oriented. In fact, 167 of the 185 North American firms listed in the RNGMA database are home-region oriented.

Asia-Pacific companies are also more home-region oriented than their European counterparts, but less than for North American companies. For Asian companies, North America is also the most important foreign region, see table 2.10.

North America

The United States accounts for nearly 90% of North American firms in the RNGMA database. Compared to Canada, American firms are more intra-regional. The only Mexican firm in the RNGMA database is petroleum producer Pemex. The company is highly intra-regional at 91.7%.

The largest twenty-five firms in the RNGMA database are US based. These include such well-known firms as Wal-Mart, Exxon Mobile, General Motors, and Ford.

Of all 189 North American companies, three are US-based global companies: IBM, Intel, and Coca-Cola. IBM and Intel are both in the computer, office, and electronics industry, the second most global of all RNGMA industries. Coca-Cola is in the most global industry, food and beverages.

In all industries except computers, office, and electronics and in other manufacturing, North American manufacturing firms are consistently more intra-regional when compared with world averages. All North American services show higher levels of intra-regional sales when compared to world averages.

Europe

Of Europe's 119 companies, eighty-five are headquartered in three countries: Britain, France, and Germany (this number includes Unilever and Royal/Dutch Shell which operate in Britain and the Netherlands).

The countries with the highest intra-regional sales are Luxembourg and Denmark, but the RNGMA database has few firms from these countries, making overall conclusion difficult to assess.

Belgium and the Netherlands have very low intra-regional sales, but the low number of companies from these countries allows biases from individual companies. For instance, the intra-regional number for Belgium is heavily influenced by Delhaize "Le Lion," a host-region oriented firm. Spain shows a similar situation; the low level of intra-regional sales in Spain reflects the propensity of the two Spanish firms in the RNGMA database to invest heavily in Latin America.

The two largest European companies in the RNGMA database, British BP and DaimlerChrysler, have higher percentage intra-regional sales in North America than in their own home region. Of the largest twenty-five European firms, five are more reliant on the North American market than their own home market. These companies derive a very small percentage of their sales from the Asia-Pacific region.

Despite the relatively more extra-regional nature of European firms, eighteen of the largest twenty-five firms derive over 50% of their sales from their home region.

Three of Europe's four global companies are manufacturing companies. Two of these are electronics companies Royal Phillips Electronics and Nokia. Dior, the other manufacturing company, was purchased in 2001 by LVMH, the only service company in Europe's global list.

All European bi-regional companies are in the manufacturing sector and depend heavily on the North American market. L. M. Ericsson is the only European bi-regional firm that depends more on the Asian market than on the North American market.

Europe has the highest number of host-region oriented companies in the RNGMA Index. Two manufacturing companies, AstraZeneca and

DaimlerChrysler, are host-region oriented, with North America as their dominant market. Six service companies in the banking, merchandizing, other financial services, and other services industries are host-region oriented, with the North American market being the dominant market.

The vast majority of European firms (72%) are home-region oriented. Across all industries, European firms consistently show lower intra-regional sales than the world average. Food, drug, and tobacco show the lowest intra-regional sales (36.4%) followed by chemicals and pharmaceuticals (37.6%).

Asia-Pacific

Japan is the country with the highest number of companies in the RNGMA database, accounting for 88%. The country is also the most developed economy in the region. Excluding Taiwan, whose only firm derives all its revenue nationally, Japanese firms tend to be more intra-regional than firms in neighboring Asian countries.

A number of Asian companies depend heavily on the US market. Seven of the twenty-five largest Asian firms derive 20% or more of their sales from North America. This includes Toyota, Sony, Honda, Nissan, Ito-Yokado, Mitsubishi Tokyo Financial Group, Mitsubishi Electric, and Canon. On the other hand, Europe is not as important a market for Japanese firms. Only Sony has over 20% of its sales in Europe.

All Asian global companies (Sony, Canon, and Flextronics) are in the computers, office, and electronics industry. The region's bi-regional companies are all in the motor vehicles and parts industry (Toyota, Nissan, and Bridgestone). Honda is the only host-region oriented company manufacturing sector. News Corp. of Australia is the only host-region company in the Asian market. For all firms with less than 50% of their sales in their home region, North America is the most important host region.

As is the case with North American and European firms, the majority of firms headquartered in the Asia-Pacific region (88%) are home-region oriented.

Eleven of the fifteen Asia-Pacific industries (Asia-Pacific has no companies in aerospace and defense) in the RNGMA database display higher intra-regional sales when compared to the world average. In the manufacturing industries, these industries include: chemical and pharmaceuticals; computer, office, and electronics; construction, building materials, and glass; energy, petroleum, and refining; food, drug, and tobacco; and other manufacturing. In the service industry these include: other financial services, telecommunications and utilities, transportation services, and other services.

Motor vehicles and parts; natural resource manufacturing; banks; entertainment; printing and publishing; and merchandisers all have

Table 2.11. The intra-regional sales of 60 firms in 2002

rank 2001	rank 2002	company	region	F/T sales	% intra regional	North America % of total	Europe % of total	Asia-Pacific % of total	C
3	2	General Motors	North America	25.7	82.3	82.3	14.1	na	D
5	6	Ford	North America	33.3	66.7	66.7^z	21.7	na	D
7	7	DaimlerChrylser	Europe	84.5	31.1	58.7	31.1	na	S
9	9	General Electric	North America	40.2	59.8	59.8^z	18.5	9.1	D
10	8	Toyota	Asia-Pacific	55.0	45.0	38.8	8.8	45.0^j	B
11	13	Citigroup	North America	65.0	70.0	70.0	na	na	D
15	14	TotalFinaElf	Europe	79.8	54.8	11.7	54.8	na	D
18	12	Allianz	Europe	70.9	75.0	20.2^l	75.0	4.8^f	D
21	20	Volkswagen	Europe	72.5	69.3	19.9	69.3	5.9	D
27	47	Deutsche Bank	Europe	67.0	66.9	24.2	66.9	7.2^f	D
31	48	Credit Suisse	Europe	67.4	64.5	28.0^l	64.5	4.0^f	D
41	28	Honda	Asia-Pacific	74.6	25.4	56.3	7.7	25.4^j	S
47	64	Bank of America	North America	6.7	93.5	93.5^a	3.4^m	2.4	D
50	44	Assicurazioni Generali	Europe	65.3	94.2	1.4^a	94.2	na	D
55	38	Nestlé	Europe	na	32.2	21.7^a	32.2	12.3	I
62	50	Merck	North America	16.0	84.0	84.0	na	na	D
84	93	NEC	Asia-Pacific	17.1	82.9	5.0	na	82.9^j	D
121	101	Johnson and Johnson	North America	38.1	61.9	61.9^z	21.0	11.5^f	D
127	106	Pfizer	North America	35.9	64.1	64.1	na	29.8^j	D
134	120	United Parcel Service	North America	16.0	84.0	84.0^z	na	na	D
138	156	Motorola	North America	55.0	45.0	45.0^z	14.0	28.0	B
139	130	BT	Europe	26.6	87.0	8.3^l	87.0	4.7	D
140	119	GlaxoSmithKline	Europe	95.7	28.6	50.9^z	28.6	na	S
141	126	Mitsubishi Electric	Asia-Pacific	26.3	83.1	8.9	6.0	83.1	D
142	123	BASF	Europe	78.4	58.9	24.2	58.9	15.7^f	D
147	136	Nokia	Europe	98.8	54.0	22.0	54.0	24.0	D
152	145	Dow Chemical	North America	59.2	40.8	40.8^z	33.4	na	I
155	133	Saint-Gobain	Europe	68.8	74.3	22.4	74.3	na	D
158	143	Bayer	Europe	na	41.3	30.6	41.3	16.6	B
172	172	DuPont de Nemours (E.I.)	North America	52.4	53.4	53.4	26.3^m	7.3	D
207	207	Alcatel	Europe	na	62.9	19.8^z	62.9	7.4	D
213	247	Cisco	North America	na	59.0	59.0	24.8	15.5	D
218	252	Bristol-Myers Squibb	North America	37.6	62.4	62.4	22.2^m	na	D
230	238	Aventis	Europe	91.2	36.4	44.8^a	36.4	6.4	B
239	234	Coca Cola Company	North America	na	40.2	33.1^a	26.9	25.8	G
257	214	Novartis	Europe	98.0	47.0	47.0	33.0	17.0^f	B
259	251	Credit Lyonnais	Europe	28.0	80.0	11.0^l	80.0	6.0	D

(*cont.*)

Rank 2001	Rank 2002	Company	Region	F/T Sales	% intra regional	North America % of total	Europe % of total	Asia-Pacific % of total	C
261	412	Solectron	North America	61.2	50.7	50.7	16.6	32.7	D
288	245	Roche Group	Europe	98.2	37.1	38.0	37.1	13.6	B
291	221	Norsk Hydro	Europe	90.7	76.7	11.1[a]	76.7	5.9	D
301	253	AstraZeneca	Europe	na	31.9	55.6	31.9	5.5[j]	S
309	263	Abbott Laboratories	North America	37.8	65.1	65.1[a]	na	na	D
340	321	McDonald's	North America	64.8	39.3	39.3[a]	33.3	15.4	B
350	317	Mitsubishi Chemical	Asia-Pacific	16.0	85.5	na	na	85.5	D
354	340	Wyeth	North America	36.7	63.3	63.3	5.1[u]	na	D
364	326	News Corp.	Asia-Pacific	na	7.2	80.3[z]	12.5[u]	7.2	S
383	394	Eastman Kodak*	North America	53.2	46.8	46.8[z]	26.2[m]	17.5	B
388	378	Flextronics	Asia-Pacific	na	24.4	30.1[l]	45.5	24.4	G
407	383	Akzo Nobel	Europe	94.0	52.0	27.0[a]	52.0	11.0	D
409	313	Compass Group	Europe	70.3	65.0	35.0	65.0	–	D
415	373	L'Oréal	Europe	na	49.9	30.3	49.9	na	B
423	419	Stora Enso	Europe	98.5	76.4	11.6[a]	76.4	na	D
436	na	Henkel	Europe	78.9	71.1	13.8[a]	71.1	7.5	D
441	456	Eli Lilly	North America	41.0	59.0	59.0	19.5[w]	na	D
452	466	Corus Group	Europe	71.0	80.0	12.0	80.0	6.3	D
465	323	Sun Life Financial Services	North America	72.0	80.0	80.0[a]	8.0[u]	3.0	D
474	433	Cosmo Oil	Asia-Pacific	<10	>90	na	na	>90[j]	D
na	na	Starbucks*	North America	16.2	91.3	91.3[a]	na	na	D
na	na	Nike	North America	47.9	58.2	58.2	29.0[m]	12.9	D
na	na	Kao	Asia-Pacific	na	86.0	na	na	86.0	D

Notes: [a] Canada and the US; [z] United States; [l] Americas; [u] United Kingdom; [w] Western Europe; [m] Europe, Middle East and Africa; [j] Japan; [f] Africa.

lower than average intra-regional sales. News Corp. of Australia, a host-region oriented company, highly influences downwards the intra-regional sales percentage for the entertainment, printing, and publishing industry.

UPDATED DATA

Table 2.11 shows data on the intra-regional sales of sixty of these top 500 firms in 2002. The findings are very similar to the data presented in this book for the year 2001. Indeed, only two of these sixty firms were re-categorized. A slight increase in the percentage of sales that originated in the United States shifted GlaxoSmithKline from a bi-regional firm to a host-region oriented firm. Nokia, which was a global company in 2001, slightly increased its sales in its home-region market and is now reclassified as a home-region oriented firm. Additional information allowed us to now classify Solectron and Citigroup as domestic firms (previously they could not be classified at all). It is extremely time con-suming to calculate the intra-regional sales of these top 500 firms, but this check with updated 2002 data across 15% of the 380 firms, which report geographic segment data for sales, confirms the robust nature of our data and classifications for 2001.

In addition in table 2.11 data are reported for 2002 sales for three interesting firms not in the top 500; all are home-region based. Starbucks has 91.3% of its sales in North America; Nike had 58.2%; and Kao has 86% in Asia. As we go down the list of firms it is even more likely that firms will become home region or domestic, and we are even less likely to find global firms.

In the remainder of this book these issues will now be discussed in more detail in the following two chapters which present analysis of the regional nature of multinational firms. This is followed by four chapters looking at key sectors, and then detailed analysis of some forty to fifty individual firms.

3 Two regional strategy frameworks

Contents

The theme of this book is that, today, much economic activity (both in manufacturing and services) is location bound, taking place in clusters in the principal regions of the broad "triad" of the EU, North America, and Asia. The geography of location has been summed up in the phrase "sticky places" and these rigidities influence the strategic management decisions of firms, including multinational enterprises (MNEs). In practice, the choice of entry mode and choice of location are complementary strategic management decisions of profound importance to MNEs.

The key theoretical driver behind this book is the insight from MNE scholars, such as Dunning (2001), Enright (2000), and Rugman and Verbeke (2001), that in most regional clusters of value-added activities in the triad the MNEs are embedded as leading participants. The most extreme articulation of this viewpoint is that of Rugman and D'Cruz (2000) who argue that MNEs act as "flagship firms" to lead, direct, co-ordinate, and manage strategically the value-added activities of partner firms in a business network, including key suppliers, key customers, and the non-business infrastructure. While Dunning (2001) refers to flagships as leaders only of vertical clusters (as in autos), Rugman and D'Cruz (2000) also include horizontal clusters (as in textiles, financial services, etc.).

In this chapter, the strategies of the top 500 firms are examined across the regions of the triad. Given the data presented in the last chapter it is clear that the vast majority of the 500 largest MNEs need to develop a regional solution to strategy, rather than rely on continued discussion of global strategy. Authors who argue for a simplistic global strategy only, ignoring the realities of regionalization include: Vijay Govindarajan and Anil K. Gupta (2001); J. P. Jeannet (2000); and George Yip (2002). My problem with these books is illustrated in the Appendix to this chapter, which is a detailed review of Govindarajan and Gupta (2001).

In the first half of the chapter a basic firm and country framework of corporate strategy is revised and then extended to take triad regions into account as well as the local and country levels. In the second half of the paper an extension of the well-known integration/responsiveness matrix is developed and extended to permit analysis of regional and global strategies. Both frameworks are applied at actual firms. These frameworks are then used over chapters 5–9 as more detailed cases are developed. Further theoretical extensions appear in chapter 4, and these are applied at business unit level and to upstream production in chapter 10.

BASIC ANALYSIS OF REGIONALIZATION

The basic model of the international business field distinguishes between country-effects and firm-level effects. In earlier work a matrix of country-specific advantages (CSAs) and firm-specific advantages (FSAs) was developed, Rugman (1981), Rugman and Verbeke (1992). Much of the analysis in this book can be synthesized within a simple framework of CSAs and FSAs which are the two basic building blocks for international business strategy.

First, there is a set of firm-specific factors that determine the competitive advantage of an organization; we call these firm-specific advantages (FSAs). An FSA is defined as a unique capability proprietary to the organization. It may be built upon product or process technology, marketing, or distributional skills. The FSAs possessed by a firm are based ultimately on its internalization of an asset, such as production, knowledge, managerial, or marketing capabilities over which the firm has proprietary control. FSAs are thus related to the firm's ability to coordinate the use of the advantage in production, marketing, brands, or the customization of services.

Second, there are country factors. These, of course, are highly relevant to firms involved in international trade and investment. They can lead to country-specific advantages (CSAs) which affect a firm's strategy. For example, the CSAs can include political, cultural, economic, and financial

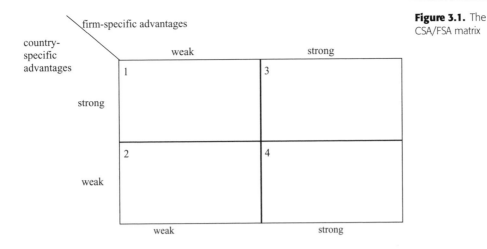

Figure 3.1. The CSA/FSA matrix

factors which are parameters exogenous to the firm. The CSAs can be based on home-country natural resource endowments (minerals, energy, forests) or on the labor force and cultural factors. If CSAs draw on natural factor endowments of a nation then they include the key variables in its aggregate production function. For example, CSAs can consist of the quantity, quality, and cost of factor endowments such as natural resources, labor, and land. But CSAs also include demand conditions, the political, cultural, and regulatory systems, and infrastructure. In Porter (1990) terminology, the CSAs form the basis of the global platform from which the multinational firm derives a home-base "diamond" advantage in global competition. Tariff and non-tariff barriers to trade and other government regulation also influence CSAs. Building on these CSAs, the firm's leading managers make decisions about the efficient global configuration and coordination between segments of its value chain (operations, marketing, R&D, and logistics). The skill in making such decisions represents a strong managerial, indeed organizational, firm-specific advantage (FSA), which can be dynamic in a Penrose sense, Rugman and Verbeke (2002).

THE CSA/FSA MATRIX

Managers of most MNEs use strategies that build upon the interactions of CSAs and FSAs. They do this so that their firm or business units can be positioned in a unique strategic space. To help formulate the strategic options of the MNE, it is useful to identify the relative strengths and weaknesses of the CSAs and FSAs they possess. Figure 3.1, the CSA/FSA matrix, provides a useful framework for discussion of these issues. It should be emphasized that the "strength" or "weakness" of FSAs and

CSAs is a relative notion. It depends upon the relevant market, the CSAs and the FSAs of potential competitors.

Cell 1 firms are generally resource based and/or mature firms producing a commodity-type product. They have production-based FSAs due to location and low costs, which are then the main sources of the firm's competitive advantage. Thus these firms are following low-cost price competition strategies. Some firms can be positioned in cell 1 when they benefit from government policies such as discriminatory subsidies, taxes and/or tariffs, a type of "shelter" CSA. Firms in cell 4 are firms with strong FSAs in marketing and customization. These firms may, for example, have strong brand-name products, and they can follow a differentiation strategy. In cell 4 the FSAs dominate, and the home-country CSAs are not essential. Cell 2 firms represent inefficient, floundering firms with no strong CSAs or FSAs; these firms are preparing to exit or to restructure. Cell 2 can also represent domestically based small and medium-sized enterprises (SMEs) with little foreign exposure. In cell 3 both FSAs and CSAs are strong, e.g. where resource-based CSAs are complemented with strong FSAs in production and/or marketing.

In terms of business strategy, cells 3 and 2 are unambiguous in their implications. A cell 3 firm can benefit from strategies of both low cost and differentiation. Such a firm is constantly evaluating its production mix. By adopting new product lines, developing dynamic organizational capabilities, and maintaining an effective strategy, the firm can maintain its overall position in cell 3. In cell 2 there is no alternative but to restructure or to eventually leave the market.

Cells 4 and 1 are credible positions for different types of firms. For instance, a cell 4 firm that has strong FSAs in marketing (brands or customization) can operate internationally without reliance on the CSAs of the home or host nations. For such a firm, cell 4 does not signal a CSA weakness; the CSA is not relevant. In contrast, cell 1 can have resource-based multinationals with product lines determined more by CSAs than by FSAs. By improving potential FSAs in marketing or product innovation and increasing value added through vertical integration, the cell 1 firm can move to cell 3, where it is no longer just a producer of staple products, but it has added new FSAs in marketing or innovation.

It is useful to note the following two points. First, if the firm has a conglomerate structure it would be more useful to situate each division or product line individually, recognizing that different units of the diversified firm would use different generic strategies. Second, changes in the trading environment, such as the EU 1992 single market measures, or the EU 1999 single currency, or the Canada–US Free Trade Agreement and NAFTA, could affect the relative CSAs of the firms. To the extent that CSAs are improved, the firms will tend to move to cell 3, and to the extent that the CSAs are hampered, the firm or some of its product lines

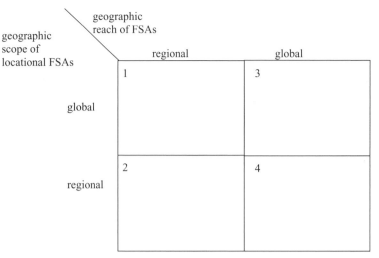

Figure 3.2. The regional and global dimensions of FSAs

may move to exit, as in cell 2. In other words, regulatory changes directly affect the CSAs whereas the FSAs are indirectly affected.

THE REGIONAL MATRIX

This two-by-two FSA/CSA matrix can now be modified into a new matrix, as shown in figure 3.2. On the horizontal axis is shown the regional or global reach of the FSAs of a firm. On the vertical axis is shown the regional or global scope of the locational advantages of a firm. The regional matrix can now be used for analysis of firm strategy in connection with the geographic reach of FSAs and the geographic scope of locational FSAs. It differs from the CSA/FSA matrix as now both axes represent aspects of corporate strategy. On the horizontal axes the firm's FSAs are exploited either regionally or globally. On the vertical axis the firm's geographic scope (either regional or global) determines the locus of competitive advantage for the firm. In turn, this depends upon the nature and impact on the firm of relevant CSAs, but the CSAs themselves are parameters to which managers react.

The regional matrix will allow us to position the 380 firms in this book for which data on intra-regional sales can be obtained. The vertical axis becomes operational for managers as, for each firm there are data available reflecting its geographic scope. Of course, as seen in chapter 2, for 320 of the 380 firms with data, there is an average of 80% of their sales in their home region – all of these firms will be on the lower (regional) half of the vertical axis. Only nine of the 380 firms are unambiguously "global" in their geographic scope. The bi-regional firms are also constrained in their geographic scope to the regional half of the vertical axis. We now turn to analysis of these three types of firms, using this new regional matrix.

On both axes of the regional matrix, a distinction is made between regional and global dimensions. For example, on the vertical axis, at the regional level, the relevant indirect CSA affecting a firm's geographic scope can be a national government regulation or an EU or NAFTA regulation; at the global level it is a WTO, IMF, or UN type of instrument. As discussed earlier, other locational effects of CSAs on a firm can also be modeled to include culture, infrastructure, and resource-endowment factors at local/regional, or world levels. On the horizontal axis the geographical reach of an FSA can be based, for example, on a national patent or a regional EU "eco" labels green capability, Rugman and Verbeke (1998b). For a global reach to the FSAs it is necessary for the FSA to become a global standard or a global brand, and/or have global benefits of integration, with economies of scale and scope. This matrix does not handle "national responsiveness" directly, and a second matrix to handle location-bound FSAs is introduced later in this chapter to do so.

In this regional matrix, only cell 3 is purely global. A firm can be both global in the reach of its FSAs and in the scope of its locational advantages; the latter based on the CSAs relevant to the firm. In contrast, cell 2 is purely regional. By regional is meant home region. A firm can be purely regional when the reach of its FSAs is limited to its home country and/or home region, while the geographic scope of its locational advantage is also limited to its home region.

In contrast, in cell 4, bi-regional firms appear. These have a global reach to their FSAs, but their geographic scope of location is not fully global but is limited to two regions. The bi-regionals have more than 20% of their sales in two regions of the triad and less than 50% in any one region. They are more "global" than the home-region firms in their reach of FSAs, and individual cases will need to be analyzed to find the specific reasons for their positioning in the regional matrix.

Finally, cell 1 is a case not observed often, where there is only a regional reach of FSAs, despite a potentially global scope for locational advantages. Firms remain in cell 2 when the regional reach of their FSAs acts as a constraint on the development of their geographic scope.

This leads to the following key analytical classifications:

Cell 3: Global firms – these have a global reach of their FSAs and a global scope for locational advantages; they are in all three regions of the triad;

Cell 4: Bi-regional firms – these have a global reach for their FSAs, but they are not global in their geographic scope, as they only have a significant presence in two regions of the triad;

Cell 2: Home-region firms – they have FSAs with a reach only in their home region, and they also have a home-region locational scope;

Cell 1: Firms with home-region FSAs but a global scope in location – there are very few of these in practice, although many firms think that they are global in scope; data show, however, that they are actually home-region based, in cell 2. We call cell 1, the "myth" of global scope.

In cell 1 firms cannot develop the complementary FSAs with a global reach that are required to exploit the global scope of their locational advantages. While the environment of international business is becoming more global, it is very difficult for firms to transfer their successful regional FSAs into global FSAs. Often it requires developing new FSAs in "national responsiveness", discussed later in this chapter, and in chapter 10. Thus many of the potential cell 1 firms remain in cell 2, where their regional reach of FSAs is matched by a locational advantage in one specific region – usually their home region. The literature on globalization and global strategy has tended to ignore the complexities involved in this cell of the myth of global scope, and it has usually been assumed that global scope is all a firm needs to become global. But firms also need a global reach of their FSAs, and this can only be achieved by a new alignment of strategy and structure, since a global reach of FSAs needs a different type of firm than one with a local or regional reach of FSAs. These complexities of global and regional strategy and structure will be explored further in the second half of this chapter, and in chapters 4 and 10.

Next we apply the framework of figure 3.2 to analyze some specific firms in each of the major cells. This will help us to classify the differences between regional and global strategies of the world's largest firms.

Cell 3: Here a firm follows a pure global strategy, such as Levitt's standardization of production with economies of scale, or a global brand, but there are few such examples. One is the luxury products of *LVMH*, whose global FSAs in branding and distribution is only possible as a result of its relatively homogeneous customer base of wealthy individuals around the world. For other global firms, strategy is more complex. For example, *Coca-Cola*, though global in terms of sales, needs to adapt its products to local tastes. This type of firm has a strong global FSA in terms of its brand name, but it is also "nationally responsive" in its product lines, distribution, and even the recipe of its best-known product, to local tastes. The strategy of national responsiveness cannot be fully analyzed in figure 3.2, so we will develop another framework later in this chapter to look into this issue.

Cell 2: Here local companies are affected by local, home-country regulations – a good example in the list of the world's 500 largest companies is the *US Post Office*. Others are retail firms like *Kroger*. *Carrefour* is a cell 2 firm with regional FSAs. It is subject to regional regulations affecting its location. Carrefour expanded from its French-based FSAs across Europe as a result of the expansion of the EU (a regional level locational factor). It is discussed in more detail below (in the retail section).

Cell 4: Here a bi-regional company, such as *Toyota Motors* (which has 36.6% of its sales in NAFTA) has a regional scope for its location but a global reach in its FSAs. Toyota has developed global brands in quality and style, but it has to operate bi-regionally. It can assemble cars across the Canada–US border, as there is regional free trade in NAFTA, see Rugman (1990). In addition, Toyota has a strong home base, with 49.2% of its sales in Asia; it is bi-regional, as are many other firms in cell 4. Some European pharmaceutical firms are also bi-regional, with large sales in North America. An example is *GlaxoSmithKline*. While most pharmaceutical firms think that they have global FSAs in their patented drugs, in practice local regulations prevent the development of a standardized distributional system. Even within the EU there are country differences in the healthcare systems which can prevent a regional solution. These local regulatory pressures keep pharmaceutical firms in cell 4.

News Corp. is a company in cell 4 that has regionally-based locational factors, but it has global reach to its FSA. The Australian firm, News Corp., operates on a North American and European basis; it is a host-region oriented company with over 75% of its sales in North America, 16% in Europe, and only 9% in the home region of Asia. It benefits from a global reach in entertainment FSAs based on satellite TV technology. Yet it has only regional scope for its locational advantages as its brand names of Fox in North America and Sky in Europe and Asia are segmented by telecommunications regulations.

Nike is an example of a home-region company in cell 4 with a global reach of FSAs. It has 58% of its sales in North America and 29% in Europe, but with only 13% of sales in all of Asia, making it bi-regional rather than global. This firm outsources 99% of its production to South East Asia, but its brand is now subject to lobbying by NGOs on a global basis. In terms of employment, of the 22,000 Nike employees, over half are located in the United States (54.7%). If we include other countries in the Americas, this number rises to 60.2%. Europe, the Middle East, and Africa account for another 24.9%. Asia and the Pacific account for about 14.9% (or 3,000 employees), but this region is also home to about 660,000 employees of independent contract companies that supply Nike products. These independent contractors are not owned by Nike, but are part of its supply network. Nike is only indirectly responsible for the working conditions of the employees working for these independent firms. Yet, due to the adverse perceived impact to its brand image of "sweatshop" conditions in these factories, Nike is now assuming some responsibility for the labor conditions in the factories of its independent suppliers.

The Nike case indicates the importance of understanding the precise firm-specific advantages (or capabilities) of an MNE. Nike is not successful because it outsources in Asia. Instead, it beats other competitors because of its business model, in which its brand name is the dominant FSA. This brand name signifies high quality, stylish, "cool" shoes. All its competitors

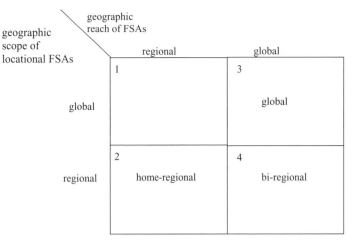

Figure 3.3. Firms in the regional and global matrix

also outsource significant portions of production in Southeast Asia. This access to cheap labor is a country factor condition, not an FSA. In a similar vein, *Wal-Mart* (discussed next) beats other firms due to its unique business model, not by outsourcing to China. The Nike and Wal-Mart cases illustrate the crucial importance of the sales data used in this book. These are the best data available on the strategic positioning and success of MNEs.

MATRIX STRATEGIES OF LARGE MNEs

In this section the positioning of an additional set of the world's largest MNEs is considered. In general, as shown in figure 3.3, most of the firms can be generically classified as global in cell 3; home-region based in cell 2; and bi-regional in cell 4.

Retail firms

Wal-Mart – Currently the world's largest MNE is Wal-Mart. This is a cell 2 firm; its FSAs are home-region based, even local to the United States. They are built on the large, wealthy US suburban consumer demand, cheap land for extensive parking lots for customers to encourage bulk shopping, and a US based supply of competent IT workers who have helped design key supplier relationships with other US firms such as Procter and Gamble. This places the geographic scope of its locational advantages as local.

Its expansion into the other member countries of the NAFTA also highlights the regional scope of its locational advantages. While Canada shares some of the characteristics of the US market, Mexico shows a different business landscape. The suburban population is relatively poor and so is a large part of the city dwellers; but there is a rising low-to-middle-class that seeks affordable prices. Land costs, however, remain low across the country.

Wal-Mart's regional FSAs are well known: its brand equity with a business model yielding enormous buying power, and a strong supplier network with key suppliers tied in with an advanced IT infrastructure. All these regional FSAs allow it to offer "everyday low prices". Its return on equity was 20.1% in 2001, well above the industry average of 13.5%. These regional FSAs have now been taken to the two other members of NAFTA as Wal-Mart has 500 stores in Mexico and 174 in Canada, with 94% of its sales in NAFTA. While in 2000 it purchased the Asda group of the UK, and it also has a 34% interest in Seiyu Ltd. of Japan, clearly the reach of Wal-Mart's FSAs is regional, not global. Some analysts, like Govindarajan and Gupta (2001) argue that Wal-Mart is in cell 3 or cell 1; yet the sales data deny a global scope of locational advantages to Wal-Mart.

Wal-Mart is not a cell 1 or cell 4 firm, as its FSAs remain US based, and these have been reinforced by its expansion within NAFTA to Mexico and Canada, rather than changed to a global basis. To be in cell 4 Wal-Mart would need to have FSAs that are transferable to other regions of the triad. Yet with over 80% of its sales in the United States, and 94% in NAFTA the scope of its operations remains regionally grounded. Other large US retailers, like Kroger, are also in cell 2, and these strong local rivals also have locally-based regional FSAs.

Carrefour can be positioned in cell 2 of the matrix. As a French based company it has mainly grown throughout Europe as the EC deepened into the EU. Indeed, 90% of its stores are located in Europe, and over 80% of its sales are there. Its original FSA can be traced back to its introduction of the hypermarket concept to France, and then throughout Europe. French legislation protected small local stores in France, and this limited its expansion within France, forcing Carrefour to expand across Europe. Today it has 37% of its stores in France, another 53% across Europe, for a total of 90%. It also opened its first store in Latin America – in Brazil, 1975 and Asia, 1989 (in Taiwan). Yet its major growth has been in Europe, with French-based FSAs; so its FSAs and locational factors place it in cell 2.

Carrefour's growth was clearly determined by the deregulation and retail opportunities available throughout Europe as the EU became more integrated. This has allowed Carrefour to expand its French based supplier network and consumer hypermarket concept across Europe, with synergy in procurement and logistics. Eventually, Carrefour may move towards cell 1 with global scope in location. It will need to change its system for employee training which is still local. But, to become a true global cell 3 firm, Carrefour would need to reduce its regional dependence on Europe and greatly increase its diversification to Asia and North America. There is no sign of this, so we keep it in cell 2.

Gucci – While too small to be a top 500 firm, the Gucci group is a global business in cell 3. In 2002 it had 42% of its sales in Europe (its home region); 21% in the United States; and 32% in Asia (20% for Japan). By stores it had 34% in Europe; 19% in North America; and 47% in Asia (with 31% in Japan). It is global on sales but not on distribution of stores. Gucci is owned by the French retailer Pinault-Printemps-Redoute (which had 70% of its stock in 2003). While Gucci has its head office in the Netherlands, its controlling shareholder is French. Gucci is rather like LVMH (another truly global firm); both are in cell 3. Its FSAs are in its brand-name products, and its fashion and design abilities. It has a global geographic scope of locational advantage.

Pharmaceutical firms

Merck is a US based pharmaceutical company created in the 1960s when the German E. Merck Co. was transferred to the US government after the war, and traded publicly. In 2001, Merck had 83.6% of its sales of health products in the United States. The FSAs of Merck are location bound since its brand-name drugs are certified by the US FDA and are not able to be sold abroad, unless they are retested and recertified by each national authority. As healthcare systems vary country by country all pharmaceutical firms face host nation CSA regulatory disadvantages. Thus the drug companies, like Merck, are cell 2 firms. For Merck there are no regional healthcare advantages in NAFTA. Nor are there any within the EU, as local country distribution systems still predominate; e.g. the French and British systems are totally different. The pharmaceutical industry is far from being global; it is not even regional, except for possibly some European MNEs doing business in North America.

To overcome the location-bound nature of their FSAs, some drug firms become bi-regional in cell 4. Several European drug MNEs are now big players in the United States. It is necessary for them to invest in the large US market as their FSAs otherwise remain regional. For European drug firms to achieve a global reach of their FSAs in brand name and products, they need to become players in North America. An example is *AstraZeneca*. It has 32% of its sales in Europe but 52.8% in the United States as a host-region market. Other firms like this include *GlaxoSmithKline*. These European bi-regional firms are in cell 4. They have a geographic reach of drugs FSAs, but their own locational advantages are limited to Europe and one other triad region, i.e. in cell 4. They do not have global scope. By having a strategy to enter the large US market, making acquisitions and gaining both production and marketing presence in the United States, these European MNEs are aligning their global FSAs with host-regional locational factors in cell 4. Their organizational structures are now nationally responsive to their critical US market. In contrast, the US based drug companies are not investing in the same manner in the regional expansion of the EU and are still largely in the home region of cell 2.

Pharmaceutical firms rely on a strong FSA – their entire success usually depends upon a small portfolio of highly profitable brand-name drugs that are then marketed regionally or across the world. The firms need ongoing R&D and access to local clusters of research scientists and chemical engineers. An increasing amount of world R&D is being done in the United States, drawing in European drug firms to this leading edge regional market and research base. Thus the CSAs of US firms are usually local and are largely explained by the key elements of the single diamond framework of Porter (1990). In contrast, the European firms need to follow a "double diamond" approach of Rugman and Verbeke (1993a).

For pharmaceutical firms, the regional location of factors somewhat restricts the potential global locational advantage of a brand-name drug. Once the R&D in the home country has created a new drug there are obvious production-based FSAs that could be global. Yet the heavily regulated national health systems limit the firm's ability to distribute that branded product in a global manner. Indeed, certification and marketing by the local health user requires extreme national responsiveness. This constrains US pharmaceutical firms from moving from cell 2 into cells 4 or 3, where the FSAs in production and branding would otherwise be feasible.

Automobile firms

Toyota has 49.2% of its sales in Japan and 36.6% in North America; it only has 7.7% in Europe. Toyota is a bi-regional MNE in cell 4. It has strong FSAs with brand equity in high-quality cars, such as the Corolla sedans, and SUVs along with the high-end Lexus line. It also has one of the best production processes in the industry. These FSAs were first developed within the CSAs of the Japanese home diamond, with a highly skilled workforce, high and sophisticated demand, and good supplier networks. This CSA was strongly aligned to its FSA, such that Toyota has largely replicated it in the United States. It has built a network of highly skilled, nonunionized workers and suppliers in North America, and it has adapted to the host-region's regulatory environment. For example, Toyota has the most successful environmentally friendly car, the Prius hybrid; but, more to the point, its Lexus cars set new standards for the luxury car segment in North America.

Toyota can be placed in cell 4; it has a regional scope in location and a global reach for its FSAs. It is like the European pharmaceutical firms in that success in North America requires the adoption of a bi-regional policy and a double diamond strategy. In Toyota's case this means investing in nationally responsive products and localized production clusters in North America, rather than in a homogeneous export style from Japan. Toyota has taken its Japanese founder's philosophy of the "Toyota way" of consensus-style decision marketing, low-cost production, high quality, and consumer satisfaction introduced by Kiichiro Toyota but adapted it in a North American context in cell 4. Toyota is not in cell 3 as it has a minor presence in Europe with only 7.7% of its sales there; its geographic scope is not yet global.

In contrast to Toyota, most other Asian auto makers, such as *Hyundai*, have not yet become cell 4 players; Hyundai is still in cell 2. It has a local/regional geographic scope as it relies on the local CSAs of Korea, and its FSAs are still also aligned with these. In 2001, Hyundai had 81.6% of its sales in Asia and 18.1% in North America. Its European sales were insignificant. The carmaker does not adapt its models very much for North America and Europe, and still has an "exporting" mentality, although it is now building a production facility in North America, in Alabama. The reach of its FSAs are purely regional as the FSAs are in price competition with improving quality, but in North America there is still a weak image and poor distribution channels. In 1998, Hyundai, the largest automobile maker in Korea, merged with Kia Motors, the second largest. This enhanced its FSAs in scale and R&D, again on a regional level, and established broader platforms for vehicle construction.

The Korean government has protected the Korean car market by tariffs and discounted excise taxes, and this home-country regulatory CSA helps to limit Hyundai to cell 2. It is now attempting to develop international production networks, and the first efforts are in Asia and in North America. Hyundai now produces in China, India, and Turkey with its US plant at Alabama soon to be operational. Hyundai will need to improve its brand image producing better-quality cars and SUVs and being more nationally responsive in advertising and sponsorships to be able to move from cell 2 to cell 4 in the future.

Others

L'Oréal has 48.5% of its sales in Europe and 32% in North America – it is a bi-regional MNE. Only 10 years ago it had 75% of its sales in Europe. It has made overseas acquisitions and then improved their local brands, e.g. Maybelline in the United States. Its strong FSAs are built on high-quality brand names such as: L'Oréal, Maybelline, and Matrix. It also has: Vichy, Lancôme, Helena Rubinstein, and Armani perfumes. It has built on strong French CSAs in Parisian high-fashion and sophisticated consumers; it still has 68% of its workforce in France. However, these local CSAs have declined and been replaced by regional ones at the European level. With its global brand-name products, L'Oréal is now cell 4, having moved there from cell 2 some ten years ago when it's French FSAs were still predominant. L'Oréal is the industry leader in brand equity. It also has 3% R&D to sales, above the industry average of 2%.

The main US rival of L'Oréal is *Estee Lauder*. It is in cell 2 with a local/regional geographic scope where US based CSAs matter and match the regional reach of its brand-name FSAs, which include Tommy Hilfiger. Estee Lauder has 61% of its sales in the Americas and 26% in Europe.

Kraft has 72% of its sales in North America. It has only six truly "global" brands, as against being the US leader in twenty-one of twenty-five top food categories. Its main "global" brands include: Kraft; Maxwell House; and Philadelphia. These are all strongly US based suggesting a limited geographic scope to its locational factors. It is also clear that Kraft's main FSAs are aligned with strong local US sales, placing it in cell 2 of figure 3.1 While it seeks a global reach in its FSAs, such as in global scale economies and brands, these are still rare in the retail business, and Kraft has relatively few "global" brands to place it in cells 4 or 3. Neither has Kraft yet developed capabilities in national responsiveness, so it stays in cell 2. Kraft has recently acquired Nabisco, another cell 2 business. An additional problem for Kraft is that it is owned by Philip Morris through the Altria holding company. As Philip Morris faces litigation, this negative US CSA also restricts the geographic scope of Kraft to cell 2.

Nestlé, the world's largest food and beverage company, is better placed in cell 4 of figure 3.1, in contrast to Kraft, in cell 2. Nestlé has a global reach in its overall managerial FSAs with 70% of its sales from its six largest global brands: Nestlé, Nescafé, Nestea, Purina, Buitoni, and Maggi. Yet the geographic scope of Nestlé is still regional rather than global – it is a "near miss" global firm. It has 31.6% of its overall sales in Europe and 31.4% in North America. It has built on an administrative heritage of the local Swiss CSA in chocolate and efficient organization to expand across Europe, taking advantage of the EU internal market measures. Nestlé is still in cell 4 as the EU regulations alone cannot make it a global firm. In Asia and the Americas each country's direct regulations restrict distribution of retail food stuffs, and there persist local differences in tastes. Nestlé is partly a global firm on the reach of its brand-name FSAs, but it cannot be classified as fully global in scope; it is in cell 4.

We will revisit the analysis of other large firms, using this framework in later chapters, especially in chapter 10. In chapters 5–9 we have more detailed case studies of firms in a variety of industries: retail, banking, pharmaceuticals, autos, and others. Next, we develop a framework to analyze the actual strategies and structures of firms, and the changes in strategy required by the regional effect. This will allow us to take account of strategies of national responsiveness in a more detailed manner than the current framework allowed.

THE INTEGRATION/RESPONSIVENESS MATRIX

A major trend that has affected the thinking of corporate MNE strategists over the last twenty years is that of balancing a concern for economic integration with national responsiveness. Integration can be defined as

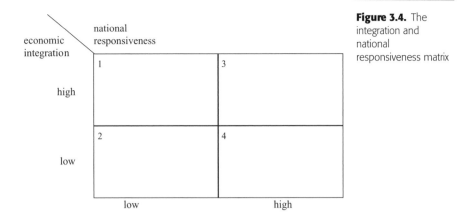

Figure 3.4. The integration and national responsiveness matrix

the production and distribution of products and services of a homogeneous type and quality on a worldwide basis. Sometimes integration is confused with globalization. It has been argued (by Yip 2002, and others) that to a large extent MNEs have homogenized tastes and helped to spread international consumerism. Yet while throughout the triad of North America, the wealthier nations of Europe and Japan, there has been a growing acceptance of standardized consumer electronic goods, automobiles, computers, calculators, and similar products; the data in this book indicate that sales are regional rather than global. Thus the goal of efficient economic performance through a universal integration strategy may be achieved regionally, not just globally. The vertical axis can thus represent either global or regional integration.

MNEs are open to the charge that they are overlooking the need to address local concerns. National responsiveness is the ability of MNEs to understand different consumer tastes in segmented regional or country markets and/or to respond to different national standards and regulations that are imposed by autonomous governments and agencies. This axis is driven by CSAs, but the firm makes the ability to deliver national responsiveness into a location-bound FSA. Multinationals continually have to deal with the twin goals of economic integration and national responsiveness. Both axes deliver FSA; the vertical has non-location-bound FSA while the horizontal has location-bound FSAs.

Conceptually, the twin issues of integration and national responsiveness can be analyzed through the use of figure 3.4, which has been adapted from Bartlett and Ghoshal (1998).

The vertical axis measures the benefits of economic integration. Movement up the axis results in a greater degree of economic integration; this generates economies of scale as a firm moves into international markets selling its products or services. These economies are captured as a result of centralizing specific activities in the value-added chain. They also occur by reaping the benefits of increased coordination and control of geographically dispersed activities.

The horizontal axis measures the benefits of corporations being nationally responsive. Companies can address local tastes and government regulations. This may result in a geographical dispersion of activities or a decentralization of coordination and control for individual firms. Firms with the ability to be nationally responsive have an organizational capability in the form of a location-bound FSA. It is location bound as the firms need a different strategy in each country or regional market.

On the basis of the two axes in figure 3.4, four situations can be distinguished. Cells 1 and 4 are the simplest cases. In cell 1 the benefits of integration are high, and the benefits of national responsiveness are low. This focus on economies of scale leads to competitive strategies that are based on price competition and/or brand-name recognition.

The opposite situation is represented by cell 4, where the benefits of national responsiveness are high, but the benefits of integration are low. In this case companies adapt products and services to satisfy the high demands of sovereign consumers and governments, and they can ignore economies of scale or other FSAs.

Cells 2 and 3 of figure 3.4 reflect opposite situations. Cell 2 incorporates those cases where the benefits of both integration and national responsiveness are low. Both the potential to obtain economies of scale and the benefits of being sensitive to country differences are of little value.

Many small and medium-sized firms (SMEs) are here. In cell 3 the benefits of integration and national responsiveness are both high. There is a strong need for integration in production, along with high requirements for country or regional adaptations in marketing. Cell 3 is the most challenging cell and one in which many successful "transnational" MNEs operate. Using this framework, we can analyze the impact of various exogenous policy shocks and trends on different industries, firms, banks, and other private sector institutions.

THE REGIONAL STRATEGY MATRIX

Figure 3.5 presents a new framework that distinguishes between global, regional, and national strategies for MNEs with geographically strongly dispersed sales, assets, and employees. The vertical axis represents the actual product characteristics (ex post) of an MNE at these three levels: world (or "global") product, regional (or triad) product; and nation-based product.

The extent to which products are standardized at the global, regional, or national level represents the "revealed preferences" of MNEs to institutionalize a particular approach at the world scale or to adapt to the

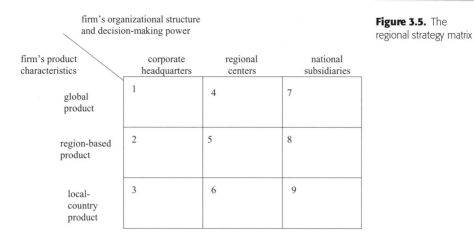

Figure 3.5. The regional strategy matrix

requirements of national/regional markets. In contrast, the horizontal axis is more a reflection of "stated preferences", i.e. the extent to which MNE managers view strategic decision making as a process concentrated in one home base or dispersed across regions or countries.

More specifically, the horizontal axis represents the location of decision-making power (ex ante) for corporate, business, or functional strategy issues. Here, the question to be answered is whether all of the MNE's key strategic decisions (e.g. choice of product/market niches, choice of strategic management tools to outperform rivals, key decisions made in each functional area, including R&D, production, marketing, distribution, human resources management), are taken in a single location, or whether at least a substantial portion of these decisions is taken in several "home bases" at the national or regional levels.

Figure 3.5 is an adaptation of Rugman and Verbeke's (1993b) framework on "global" strategies. They argued that the truly important decisions to be taken by MNEs are related to two parameters. First, the number of home bases with which they function, i.e. the number of locations where important strategic decisions are taken (equivalent to the horizontal axis of figure 3.5, where the number of home bases determines strategic decision making). Second, the use of non-location-bound versus location-bound firm specific advantages (FSAs), (equivalent to the vertical axis of figure 3.5, whereby the nature of the MNE's FSAs determines its product offering). The former allow various approaches to standardize the MNE's product offering across borders and to earn benefits of integration (related to scale, scope and benefits of exploiting national differences). The latter provide the potential to gain benefits of national responsiveness.

The difference with Rugman and Verbeke's (1993b) resource-based perspective on the integration-national responsiveness model is that figure 3.5 explicitly introduces a regional dimension to the analysis. This is now needed due to the emerging empirical work, Rugman (2000), which suggests that "global" strategies are not appropriate for most MNEs that actually operate on a triad/regional basis. More specifically, on the horizontal axis this regional dimension implies that a number of strategic decisions are left to region-based headquarters, rather than nation-based ones. The vertical axis implies the development of FSAs useful at the level of the set of nations that form the region. These are region-bound company strengths: they can contribute to survival, profitability, and growth beyond the geographic scope of a single nation, but these "regionally responsive" strategies are still location bound, in the sense that they cannot be deployed globally, Morrison, Ricks, and Roth (1991), Morrison and Roth (1991). In this context, Yip's (2002, p. 7) view that a global company "has the capability to go anywhere, deploy any assets, and access any resources; and it maximizes profits on a global basis" may be a useful normative message, but one that applies to very few, if any, MNEs in practice. Indeed, most MNEs rely largely on sets of location-bound and region-bound FSAs as the basis for their competitiveness.

Figure 3.5 helps identify some of the more important mistakes made by proponents of globalization and a global strategy for MNEs. They view as a reflection of a global strategy not only cell 1, but also cells 2, 3, 4, and 7 (where strategies other than globalization are required). In cells 2 and 3, they focus on the decisions and actions of corporate leaders, typically the CEO, the top management committee, and the MNE's board of directors. It is undoubtedly the case that most key financial decisions in MNEs are taken at that level. However, even if all major corporate strategy decisions are taken centrally, typically in the home country (left column of figure 3.5), as is the case for many companies in, e.g. the computer business (both hardware and software), cells 2 and 3 reflect respectively the existence of substantial regional and national responsiveness regarding the product offering (including its service component) that actually is provided to the market.

In other words, MNEs that tailor their product offering to regional and national circumstances do not pursue a simple global strategy as suggested by cell 1. Considerable resources must be allocated to allow for the required level of sub-global responsiveness in terms of what is being delivered to the market. In addition, even if the MNE's product offerings were largely global, this does not necessarily imply that all important decisions on market penetration, distribution, advertising, etc. can be taken centrally. Bounded rationality constraints are likely to force corporate management to delegate important decisions to the regional and national levels, thereby positioning the firm closer to cells 4 and 7 of figure 3.5.

This point is vitally important, as, at the other end of the academic and policy-oriented spectrum, many anti-globalization critics suffer from a similar misperception; they view MNEs as centrally directed, profit maximizing entities, eager to sell standardized products around the globe. Anti-globalization critics state that MNEs are insensitive to host-country and host-region demands, especially those of host-country governments. In fact, the presence of intense international rivalry and the liability of foreignness that every MNE faces in foreign regions of the world, forces MNEs to be particularly sensitive to the requirements of host-country governments and other salient stakeholders, Rugman and Verbeke (1998b).

Of course, this does not imply that MNEs can or should adopt an approach in cell 9, and be fully polycentric, with products carefully tailored to each national market and most strategy decisions left to host-country subsidiary managers. Much conceptual and empirical evidence suggests that a "multi-national" approach leads to overlapping efforts and duplication in innovation, inconsistent national strategies, opportunistic behavior by subsidiary managers, and more generally a waste of resources and lack of clear strategic direction, Bartlett and Ghoshal (2000). The great strength of an MNE is to overcome market imperfections characterizing national markets and to develop systemic, network-related rather than asset-based FSAs, see Dunning and Rugman (1985). Even for MNEs with a polycentric administrative heritage, cells 6 and 8 are likely much more relevant than cell 9 of figure 3.5. In cell 6, attempts are made to achieve decision-making synergies across markets, e.g. by developing pan-European or pan-American strategies in particular functional areas, Rugman and Verbeke (1992). In cell 8, economies of scale and scope are pursued by the national subsidiary managers themselves, through standardizing at the regional level their product offering across those national markets that have strong similarities in demand. In that case, subsidiary initiative is critical, Birkinshaw (2000), Rugman and Verbeke (2001a).

The strategy and international management literature has done a good job of distinguishing between cells 1 and 9, but it has not addressed most of the other cells. For example, the basic matrix of integration (cell 1) and national responsiveness (cell 9) popularized by Bartlett and Ghoshal (1989) distinguished between a pure global cell 1 strategy and the "act local" national responsiveness strategy of cell 9 of figure 3.5. In addition, the key contribution of their "transnational solution" framework was the prescription that MNEs should usefully combine strategies in cells 1 and 9. They should attempt to develop appropriate strategies for each separate business, for each function within that business, and for each task within that function, the capability to implement either a national or a global approach.

The Bartlett and Ghoshal (1989) framework thus can usefully explain cell 3 (centralized, global strategic decision making combined with local product offering), i.e. the global think-local act approach. It also allows the analysis of less common cases in cell 7, whereby rather powerful, national subsidiaries are responsible for delivering global products, but choose themselves which products have the most potential in their national markets and largely take responsibility for the delivery, an approach found in many global professional services companies. Yet, their framework cannot handle cell 5, triad-based strategies very well, nor the intermediate cases of cells 2, 4, 6 and 8, i.e. all cases whereby the regional level is important.

This book reports data suggesting that an increasing number of MNEs operate largely at the regional level. Therefore regional elements are becoming increasingly important in many MNEs, either in terms of strategic decision making, or actual product offering. If, as the empirical evidence provided in the next sections suggests, many MNEs are at least partially operating in cell 5 on a triad basis, then any strategy-related analysis of the MNE's functioning first needs to take into account the requirement to decompose its strategic decision-making processes and product offering along global, regional, and national lines building upon a more complex analytical tool than a conventional integration-national responsiveness matrix. Only then can a correct analysis be performed of the actual extent of triad-based decision-making power and can the rationale for region-based and/or adapted products and services from these MNEs be properly investigated. If the theoretical construct itself of a "regional solution" (cell 5 in figure 3.5) is neglected, little can be expected from empirical research on strategy and structure in MNEs to portray accurately the present importance and future potential of the regional approach.

Here, it is important to observe that the regional approach has sometimes been described as the mere outcome of a global strategy. The best-known articulation of this perspective can be found in Yip (2002), who argues, "Before deciding whether and how to do business in a region of the world, a company needs to have a clear global strategy [which includes] the core business strategy, the competitive objectives for the business, and the extent to which the business will be operated as one integrated business or a looser collection of geographically independent units. Next, a company needs to decide on the overall role of the region within the global strategy" (p. 222). Yip's (2002) view assumes a particular sequence and hierarchy in MNE strategic decision making. In practice, however, the global-regional sequence is unlikely to occur.

The regional solution of cell 5 of figure 3.5 should be viewed as an efficient, corporate response to several factors. First, internal information processing requirements are critical. If the "rules of engagement" are different in each region (different industry structure, different regulatory system, different competitive position of the firm, different optimal expansion pattern, different product scope, different strategy tools required to outperform rivals, etc.) intra-regional information processing must be sufficiently dense so as to permit affiliates to cope optimally with shared external circumstances and to develop regionally consistent strategies. Second, customer requirements may vastly differ across regions depending upon the level of economic development, culturally determined preferences, etc. Third, region-based cluster requirements may impose specific types of behavior on firms in order for these firms to be perceived as legitimate within the context of regional clusters, especially suppliers, related and supporting industries, the non-business infrastructure, etc. Here, region-based, isomorphic flexibility may be critical for firms to function effectively as true insiders in the region. Finally, political requirements at the regional level are increasingly important. It could be argued that regional cooperation agreements such as the North American Free Trade Agreement (NAFTA) and the European Union (EU) single-market measures mainly represent the elimination of trade and investment barriers, and therefore allow a reduced attention devoted by MNEs to government policy; in fact, regional agreements usually imply not merely the elimination of national regulation, but a shift of regulatory authority to the regional level, and thereby the need to allocate firm resources to monitor and manage relationships at that level.

The rigidity of the triad has been explored in Rugman (2000). As discussed in chapter 11, it is reinforced by the new trade regime of the World Trade Organization (WTO), which has to devote enormous managerial resources to arbitrate triad-based trade disputes and trade-remedy law type protectionism (as in the bananas, beef hormones, export subsidies, and steel cases). The new protectionism of health, safety, and environmental regulations is preventing an open world market and reinforcing triad markets. The NAFTA is being expanded into the Free Trade Agreement of the Americas (FTAA) and twenty countries are in negotiations to be added to the EU. These political developments reinforce the triad and the need for regional government policies and triad-based firm strategies.

EXAMPLES OF THE REGIONAL STRATEGY MATRIX

In the 3×3 matrix of figure 3.5 linking the locus of decision-making power to the product characteristics with local adaptation, the strategies of several MNEs can be positioned as follows:

AstraZeneca   Cell 5
Merck   Cell 2

AstraZeneca as a bi-regional firm has regional corporate governance and distribution systems (the US market is so important with 52.8% of its sales that it is now run separately from its head office in Europe where it has

32% of its sales). On the other hand, as a home-region firm, Merck, is in cell 2 with a strong corporate HQ despite needing to operate regionally in Europe as well as in the US home market. Probably Merck has a tension in this structure and does not perform as well in Europe as AstraZeneca does in the United States.

Kraft   Cell 6
Nestlé   Cell 9

   Kraft and Nestlé both have food products that are nationally regulated and supervised by country health and safety codes. Thus, they need to be aligned to local markets. Nestlé also has national units, whereas Kraft has regional centers (Nestlé is discussed in greater detail in Chapter 10). Kraft's product delivery and marketing are operated locally, but "back office" functions like HRM, accounting, auditing, legal, and treasury are more centralized and co-coordinated. Some production is also co-coordinated globally. Kraft has decision making at regional centers in North America and International (largely Europe) through co-CEOs.

L'Oréal   Cell 5
Estee Lauder   Cell 1

L'Oréal is in cell 5 of figure 3.5 as its US operations are administered by a regional office, to match its home European one. It has adapted its product line for North America, e.g. Maybelline, controlled from New York; and it is more mass marketed than some of its high-end French based cosmetics. L'Oréal says that its products are "culturally diverse global cosmetics brands" (see case study on L'Oréal in chapter 9). Estee Lauder is more centralized with a strong HQ, but global products which are not adapted to local needs, i.e. in cell 1.

Philip Morris   Cell 1
BAT   Cell 5

Philip Morris is in cell 1 of figure 3.5 as its strong corporate HQ produces global brands, Marlboro in particular, which are not adapted locally. It does not need to be as concerned with regulations in other countries as its main problem is class action litigation in its US home market. British owned BAT is in cell 5, as it runs its US operation with a large degree of autonomy through B&W, as a regional centre. It also has regional brands rather than the global ones of Philip Morris.

Toyota   Cell 2
Hyundai   Cell 1

Toyota has a strong, centralized, hierarchical organizational structure. This is based on Kiichriro Toyota's "the Toyota way" of consensus decision making and discipline. Yet Toyota's product characteristics are much more region based, especially with adaptation in the vital US host market.

Hyundai is also centralized, but its products are not adapted, i.e. it is in cell 1 of figure 3.5.

Wal-Mart   Cell 1
Carrefour   Cell 1

Both will be positioned in cell 3 of the matrix in figure 2.1. Both have centralized decision making, and both sell mainly in their home markets. Carrefour may be moving toward cell 2, but there is little evidence to support such regional adaptation of its production and services.

Similar analysis can be performed for the majority of other top 500 companies. Indeed, most MNEs need to be analyzed at the regional level, using figures 3.3 and 3.5. The examples discussed above illustrate the alignment of the new analytical frameworks with the basic data on regionalization of MNE activities. These frameworks will be used in the following chapters of the book as some fifty firms in total are analyzed in more detail, especially in chapters 5–9. Then in chapter 10 there is an extension of the theory of this chapter; in particular the individual business units of the firms are discussed in order to examine the upstream and downstream aspects of business activity.

Next in chapter 4 we discuss more advanced theoretical aspects of using regional sales data to analyze the strategies of firms. Some firms are outsourcing parts of their production and have international supply chains. Yet we do not have such data on production, value added R&D, and other necessary information for the 500 largest firms (or for smaller firms) as their annual reports only are required to report consolidated sales data. Thus we cannot test directly some alleged aspects of globalization – such as the outsourcing of production. Yet, it can be shown that production is likely to be much more localized than are sales. These, and related issues, are discussed in chapter 4.

APPENDIX TO CHAPTER 3

This is my unabridged review of Govindarajan and Gupta (2001) published in *Academy of Management Executive* 16:3 (August 2002): 157–59.

This book is a good example of the current state of analysis of "global strategy". It is a well-written managerial popularization of the academic research of two distinguished scholars on the current fad of how to develop a global strategy. The main insights in the book come from extensive analysis of the strategies and performance of multinational enterprises (MNEs) such as Dell, HP, ABB, IBM, Microsoft, Amazon.com., Yahoo, Canon, P&G, Tetra Pak, Nucor Steel, Ford, and some emerging Chinese and Indian MNEs. Some of these case examples suffer from unfortunate timing, e.g. the Enron story is doubly wrong – both the Indian investment discussed and the stock market value of the company fell apart. Also the

HP story predates the merger problem with Compaq. But most of the analysis is sound, e.g. that Amazon.com has been very slow to internationalize – the opposite of the so-called "born global" dot.coms who have mainly died in childbirth.

Perhaps of greatest utility is the choice of the unit of analysis, which is the strategic business unit (SBU) rather than the MNE as a whole. Today's giant MNEs have dozens of SBUs in scores of countries, and it is refreshing to have a focus on the decision making of these subsidiary managers rather than the parent firm alone. The authors also state that they have based their research on interviews with SBU level managers. Perhaps as a consequence of this exposure the authors pay more attention than usual in such global strategy books to the need for strategies of "national responsiveness". This is emphasized, for example, in chapter 4 on exploiting global presence. Of the six strategies discussed, the very first one is the national responsiveness one of "adapting to local market differences."

Eventually, in the key model of the book, the so-called "star framework" (p. 94), the authors plot a three-dimensional diagram of the drivers of global value. In this, "locational competencies" are placed equally with "global coordination" and "activity architecture." Academic readers will note that this is virtually identical to the well-known Bartlett and Ghoshal framework of "national responsiveness," "global integration," and "worldwide learning." It is the focus of their model on the SBU activity parts of the value chain that makes the Govindarajan and Gupta book relevant. There is also in-depth analysis of the strategies of major MNEs such as Wal-Mart, HP, Microsoft, Canon, etc. Yet the authors still manage to conclude with chapter 9 on "globalization in the digital age," although it is now pretty clear that neither of these phenomenon really exist in the simplistic forms first imagined and that management strategy based on such assumptions is not very useful, as I discuss in this book. The authors know the MNEs and other companies cited very well, and their enthusiasm for their global models is readily apparent. Yet this very enthusiasm blinds them to a fundamental flaw in their thinking.

The basic problem with the entire book is that the authors simply assume that "globalization" exists whereas their own data and examples keep demonstrating that it does not. Indeed, virtually all of the MNEs they study started operating on a regional basis in the three triad markets of the European Union (EU), North America (NAFTA – the US, Mexico and Canada), and Japan. In chapter 1 the authors claim that Chinese, Indian, and Mexican MNEs will make the top 500 "radically different in twenty years" (p. 17). Yet with just 12 MNEs from China and one each from Mexico and India, there is a long way to go! The authors use trade data to argue that there is "global integration". Yet 62% of all EU trade is intra-regional; 56% of NAFTA trade is intra-regional, as is Asia's trade (see chapter 11 data in this book). My data suggest that regional strategy matters, not global strategy, as is shown in this book. Indeed, global strategy is a myth. To solve the disconnect between global and regional strategy, readers need to substitute the word "international" for "global" wherever it appears in Govindarajan and Gupta and then think regional.

The very first example of "building global presence" is Wal-Mart, which takes up all of chapter 3. Yet the author's own data indicate that Wal-Mart is not a global business. It does have 1,004 "international" stores, but 624 of these are in Canada and Mexico, i.e. NAFTA explains the majority of Wal-Mart's "global" presence. As it has nearly 3,000 "domestic" stores, the ratio of foreign-to-total sales for Wal-Mart is only 13.8%. The global retail competitor to Wal-Mart used by the authors is French-based Carrefour. This business is even less global, having most of its sales in Europe, where there is an economic union with intra-regional free trade. Yet the authors argue that Carrefour's "international" profits are 62% of total profits without making any adjustment for home-based EU sites. My interpretation of these cases is that neither retail firm is truly global, as retail is local, or at least regionally located within the EU or NAFTA blocks.

The book proceeds along these lines – the need for global mindsets, global knowledge machines, global business teams, global strategy games, global this and that. While there is not too much harm that can come to managers in reading this book, as they have a remarkable capacity for reality and relevance, they will not learn as much as they could have because of the authors rather casual use of the data on globalization in chapter 1. This is a great pity as their basic model of SBU activities in the value chain is just as applicable at the triad/regional level as at their so-called "global" level. Today, it is necessary to be a bit more careful in using the "global" concept. It is not a useful takeaway for managers to read in this book that they need to develop a "global" presence, have a "global" mindset, and devise a "global" strategy to derive "global" competitive advantage. Yet this is a one-sentence summary of the book. In reality, the MNEs analyzed in this book are engaged in international business, not "global" business.

4

Regional and global strategies of multinational enterprises

Globalization, in the sense of increased economic interdependence among nations, is the issue of our times, but, like many great issues of history, it is poorly understood. In this chapter, looking at the business aspects of globalization, we discuss the key actors in the globalization process, namely the firms that drive this process. This chapter explains the fundamental impediments that prevent most of these firms from becoming truly "global" businesses, in the sense of having a broad and deep penetration of foreign markets across the world. This new view on "globalization" is very different from the conventional, mainstream perspective. The latter perspective focuses primarily on macro-level growth patterns in trade and FDI, and compares these data with national GDP growth rates, but without ever analyzing the equivalent domestic or home region growth data for the MNEs responsible for the trade and FDI flows, World Investment Report (2002).

THE TRIAD POWER CONCEPT

In 1985, Kenichi Ohmae, at that stage a leading McKinsey consultant in Japan, published his landmark study *Triad Power*, arguably one of the most insightful international management books of the last two decades. The triad, in Ohmae's work, is a geographic space consisting of the United States, the EU and Japan. (Rugman, 2000, presents data on this "core" triad.) This geographic space, according to Ohmae, shares a number of commonalities: low macro-economic growth; a similar techno-logical infrastructure; the presence of large, both capital and knowledge intensive firms in most industries; a relative homogenization of demand (with a convergence of required key product attributes) and protectionist pressures. The triad is home to most innovations in industry and also includes the three largest markets in the world for most new products. A useful indicator of the triad's enduring importance is the concentration of the world's largest MNEs in the United States, the EU and Japan, as reported in Rugman (2000). In 2000, of the world's largest 500 MNEs, 430 had their corporate headquarters in these core triad regions.

The problem faced by many of these MNEs, according to Ohmae, is that they sell "engineered commodities," i.e. innovative and differentiated products, resulting from high investments in capital-intensive produc-tion processes and knowledge development. Unfortunately, these prod-ucts rapidly lose their "monopoly status." In spite of patents and brand names, technology often diffuses more rapidly to rivals than the required distribution capabilities can be built in foreign markets, thereby making it difficult to recoup innovation costs. The dilemma for any company that has developed a new "superproduct" with large expected demand throughout the triad is as follows: setting up an extensive distribution capability for the product ex ante, throughout the triad, which may entail high, irreversible, fixed costs and therefore high risks, if the superprod-uct somehow does not deliver on its sales expectations. Conversely, if the superproduct is first marketed at home, rival companies in other legs of the triad are expected to rapidly create an equivalent product, capture their triad region market and dominate distribution in that market.

In this context, Ohmae introduces the concept of "global impasse" to describe the problems faced by even the largest companies to repeat their home-triad base market share performance in the two other triad markets. Only a limited number of firms, such as Coca-Cola and IBM, have, according to Ohmae, succeeded in becoming a "triad power." A triad power is defined as a company that has "(1) equal penetration and exploitation capabilities, and (2) no blind spots, in each of the triad regions," Ohmae (1985, p. 165). In Ohmae's view, the deep penetration into each triad market is critical to recover innovation costs. The absence of blind spots is important in order to "avoid surprises," i.e. unexpected strategic moves by foreign rivals or home country competitors setting up alliances with foreign firms. A triad power is thus an MNE that has been successful in "insiderization".

Given the global impasse challenge described above, Ohmae (1985, chapter 12) prescribes the use of consortia and joint ventures to capture the non-home triad markets. The relative non-transferability of the MNE's home region capabilities to greenfield affiliates may result from an inappropriate repertoire of routines to deal with host-region demands, in the spirit of Nelson and Winter (1982). Second, the tacit and socially embedded nature of capabilities deployed by host-region rivals may make it too expensive for the MNE to duplicate such capabilities in the short run. Finally, the firm may need access to resources that cannot be purchased in efficient factor markets. The above considerations imply that hybrid entry modes may be optimal in host regions. In case the MNE wishes to become a triad power on its own, through wholly owned operations, Ohmae prescribes an "Anchorage" perspective, i.e. a corporate center that is mentally located in Anchorage (Alaska), at an equidistance from the economic and political power bases in the United States, the EU and Japan. This is in line with Perlmutter's (1969) prescription of developing a geocentric mentality in MNEs. In practice, such a firm should operate with regional headquarters in each leg of the triad in order to capitalize on commonalities within each region at a lower cost and with more market knowledge than if corporate headquarters performed these activities.

The triad power MNE's operations in each region should exhibit nine organizational characteristics, Ohmae (1985, p. 206). These are clearly not grounded in theory, but reflect useful insights at McKinsey based on consulting assignments: the result, according to Ohmae (1985, p. 207) is that foreign firms can become "honorable incumbents" in host regions of the triad. Finally, Ohmae (1985) contains one last important insight, namely that MNEs from each triad region should identify a "fourth region", where it should be easy, relative to the rest of the world, to earn an important market share. This fourth region will depend on the industry and firm involved, but for Japan it would typically include Asian markets, for the United States, its neighboring trading partners, and for Europe, those countries with which much trade or trade potential exists.

However, Ohmae (1985) did not actually anticipate the extension of the core triad to the "broad" triad of today. The broad triad consists of NAFTA, the expanded EU and Asia. In parallel with the introduction of the Canada US Free Trade Agreement in 1989, NAFTA in 1994 and its expansion to the Free Trade Area of the Americas by 2005, the EU expanded to 25 countries on May 1st, 2004 (and perhaps more in the future). In Asia, in November 2002, China agreed to a free trade agreement with the ten members of the Association of South East Asian Nations (ASEAN), signaling a wide trade and investment agreement for Asia. Such institutional arrangements constitute the cooption of attractive, proximate foreign markets (from a geographical, cultural, economic, and administrative perspective) into a "broad" triad region. This will facilitate even deeper intra-regional market penetration. In some cases, when less developed countries are involved, this may accelerate location shifts of mature industry operations from highly-developed areas in the region toward lower cost sub-regions. Rugman (2000) provides data on the intra-regional trade and investment of these broad triad regions, with a majority of trade already being intra-regional in each part of the broad triad of NAFTA, the EU and Asia.

The present chapter tests whether the world's largest firms have been capable of implementing Kenichi Ohmae's visionary strategy and becoming (broad) triad powers during the two decades after his path-breaking book.

EMPIRICAL ANALYSIS OF TRIAD POWER

As discussed in chapter 2, the average intra-regional sales of the world's 500 MNEs is 71.9%. Of the 380 firms studied, over 80% (320) derive most of their sales in their home-region of the triad. This relative sales dominance in a specific regional market, rather than a very wide and evenly distributed spread of sales, reflects five underlying issues critical to the MNE's functioning. First, it demonstrates the fallacy of so-called "global" products. If most MNEs' sales are unevenly distributed across the globe, and mostly concentrated in just one geographic market, this means that products are not really global in the sense of being equally attractive to consumers all around the world.

Second, the lack of global market success reflects the limits to the non-location bound nature of the MNEs' knowledge base, i.e. its firm specific advantages (FSAs). Firms may have sophisticated and proprietary technological knowledge, brand names etc. but there appear to be severe limits to the joint international transferability of this knowledge and its acceptance by customers across regions, irrespective of whether this knowledge is embodied in final products and then exported, transferred as an intermediate product through licensing or used in foreign affiliates through FDI.

Third, the perceived lack of market performance across regions also points to a relative inability to access and deploy the required location bound FSAs, which would lead to benefits of regional and national responsiveness.

Fourth, if the MNE's market position is very different in the various regions of the world this indicates the need for very different competitive strategies; a leadership role in one market requires very different patterns of decisions and actions than the role of a (perhaps ambitious) junior player in another market. This should obviously be reflected in the deployment of specific combinations of non-location bound and location bound FSAs in each region. Unfortunately, in spite of much "think global, act local" rhetoric in both the academic and popular business press, there appears to be little empirical evidence that this approach has permitted host-region market penetration levels similar to the ones obtained in the home region.

Fifth, the four elements above have important implications for MNE governance. It might be incorrect to attribute the present relative lack of overseas market success of many firms to an inappropriate governance structure. The presence of multiple environmental circumstances may also be critical here (powerful foreign rivals in other triad regions; government shelter of domestic industries; buyer preferences for local products; cultural and administrative differences as compared to the home region, etc.). However, the need for regional strategies does suggest the parallel introduction of a regional component in the MNEs' governance structure to deal appropriately with the distinctive characteristics of each leg of the triad, and with the regions outside of it, much in line with Ohmae's (1985) prescriptions. This perspective is developed further in the later sections of the chapter.

This need for distinct regional strategies is an important observation as many well known strategy and international business (IB) scholars keep developing normative models that advocate simple globalization strategies as a set of purposive decisions and actions instrumental to a broad and deep penetration of foreign markets, i.e. extreme geographical fragmentation of sales. Authors who have recently argued in favor of a global strategy and ignore the realities of regionalization include: Vijay Govindarajan and Anil K. Gupta (2001), J. P. Jeannet (2000), and George Yip (2002). Regionalization should be viewed as an expression of semi-globalization, Ghemawat (2003). It implies that international markets are characterized neither by extreme geographical distribution of sales, nor complete integration. Incomplete integration means that location specificity, in this case regional specificity, matters. Only in a context of incomplete integration is there scope for international MNE strategy that is conceptually distinct from conventional domestic strategy.

THE MEANING OF REGIONAL STRATEGIES

The majority of the world's largest 500 companies are MNEs; i.e. they produce and/or distribute products and/or services across national borders. Yet, very few MNEs are "global" firms, with the ability to sell the same products and services around the world. The challenge of selling standardized products and services across borders, as originally advocated by Levitt (1983), has been dealt with appropriately in most of the main-stream IB literature. It is now widely recognized that benefits of integration resulting from global scale economies can only be reaped if accompanied by strategies of national responsiveness, guided by both external pressures for local adaptation and internal pressures for requisite variation. What is unfortunately not correctly understood is that, irrespective of MNEs' efforts to augment their alleged non-location bound FSAs with a location bound component, no *balanced* geographical dispersion of sales is achieved in most cases. Instead, the data indicate that most MNEs are regionally based in their home-triad market, of either North America, the EU, or Asia (principally Japan). An apparent paradox is that a very large MNE in terms of overall foreign sales volume can have a concentration of its international activities in its home-triad region and lack a truly global dimension. While it could be argued that there is more to globalization than sales dispersion, for example, foreign assets and foreign employment have sometimes been used together with foreign sales to compose a "transnationality index," it should be recognized that only sales dispersion constitutes a true performance measure at the output level.

If MNEs have exhausted their growth potential in the home-triad region and then decide to venture into other regions, they may face a liability of regional foreignness, including several additional risks that were absent in the host region and may be of an economic, cultural, administrative or geographic nature, in accordance with Ghemawat's (2001) recent observation that distance still matters. Given the size of each triad region, most of the advantages of standardization can often be achieved within the home-triad region, and this process is enhanced if governments in this region pursue policies that promote internal coherence via social, cultural and political harmonization (as in the EU) or even merely via economic integration (as in NAFTA and Asia).

A related point is that inter-block business is likely to be restricted relative to intra-regional sales by government imposed barriers to entry. For example, the EU and the United States are likely to fight trade wars and be responsive to domestic business lobbies seeking shelter in the form of subsidies and/or protection. Cultural and political differences among members of a single triad region may remain, but these will mostly be less significant than across triad regions, Rugman (2000). The end result is the persistence of MNEs that will continue to earn 80% or more of their income in their home triad region. There will only be a limited number of purely "global" MNEs in the top 500.

For 365 of the 380 firms included in our study, data were available that permitted a further decomposition of their foreign sales. It should be noted that many of the remaining 135 *Fortune* 500 companies are actually operating solely in their home region, with no sales elsewhere, and for others there are insufficient data. As reported earlier, in chapter 3, of the 365 with data, the vast majority (320) are home-region based, having few sales in the other two regions of the triad. A limited set (36) is "bi-regional", which we define as having at least 20% of sales in two legs of the triad. Only nine MNEs are truly "global," with at least 20% of their sales in all three regions of the triad.

The definitions adopted earlier in the book, and explained in chapter 2, are as follows:

(a) Home-region oriented: 320 firms have at least 50% of their sales in their home region of the triad. The threshold of 50% was chosen as we assume that a region representing more than 50% of total sales will systematically both shape and constrain most important decisions and actions taken by the MNE. It also implies a concentration of the MNE's customer-end related FSAs in that region. The concept of customer-end FSA is explained in the next section.

(b) Bi-regional: 25 MNEs are bi-regional, defined as firms with at least 20% of their sales in each of two regions, but less than 50% in any one region. This set includes 25 firms with sales ranging between 20% and 50% in the home region and 20% or over in a second region. The threshold of 20% was chosen because we assume that having two regional markets each representing at least one fifth of a "$10 + billion" firm's sales reflects impressive market success resulting from extensive "customer-end" FSAs in those two markets. The question could then be raised whether a particular absolute volume of sales, irrespective of the 20% threshold percentage, would make a firm bi-regional. In our framework, an absolute sales volume is, in itself, insufficient. We view the status of a region from a micro-level, corporate strategy perspective; here, this status is fully dependent on the relative sales achieved vis-à-vis market performance in other regions.

(c) Host-region oriented: eleven firms have more than 50% of their sales in a triad market other than the home region.

(d) Global: only nine of the MNEs included are global, defined as having sales of 20% or more in each of the three regions of the triad but less than 50% in any one region of the triad. The 20% figure is less than the one-third required for an equal triad distribution, and so is biased downwards in favor of finding global MNEs. Conceptually, it implies the successful deployment of customer-end FSAs in three distinct markets. The North American and European region of the broad triad are of approximate equal size, as measured by GDP. Asia is smaller than either as measured by GDP but is nearly equal in terms of purchasing power parity (PPP). In other words, weighing the broad triad by GDP or PPP will not generate more global firms.

Within each of the groups above, the home triad region sales weighted averages are as follows:

(a) Home-region oriented (320 firms): 80.3%
(b) Bi-regional (25 firms): 42%
(c) Host-region oriented (11 firms): 30.9%
(d) Global (9 firms): 38.3%

IMPLICATIONS FOR NEW ANALYSIS

In this section some of the implications of this lack of empirical evidence for globalization are considered across the field of IB research. Five research areas of particular relevance are selected. (There is further discussion of associated issues in chapters 11 and 12.) The first two areas deal with the foundations of MNE competitive advantage, namely FSAs and location advantages respectively. The next three areas are related to MNE strategy, structure and performance. Finally, the sixth area assesses the broader societal implications of regional MNEs.

Implications for the relevance of the internalization and internationalization models of international expansion

The internalization model of foreign expansion, Buckley and Casson (1976), Rugman (1981), and especially its "eclectic paradigm" version has been the dominant conceptual model in IB research during the past two decades. It suggests that firms will establish foreign affiliates in the case of strong FSAs, location advantages in host countries and internalization advantages, Dunning (1981). The model assumes that MNEs systematically engage in a cost/benefit calculus of all possible entry modes, namely exports, licensing, FDI (including, more recently, hybrid modes). Here, FDI may be the preferred mode from the outset if government-imposed and natural market imperfections make exports and licensing impossible or comparatively more expensive, and if the firm has already been operating abroad, Buckley and Casson (1981). In contrast, the internationalization model of the Scandinavian school argues that firms will incrementally build foreign operations, starting with low resource commitments in culturally proximate countries, and then expand these commitments and geographic scope. Here, experiential learning is critical and path dependencies can be observed in the growth of the MNE's experiential knowledge base, especially as regards knowledge of the markets involved, Johansson and Vahlne (1977) (1990), Barkema et al. (1996). Little integration has occurred between the two schools, which have largely flourished on their own without much cross-fertilization, and each has a loyal following of researchers. The internalization school focuses at the outset on market imperfections involving "business/usage" specificity, whereas the internationalization school starts from imperfections arising from "location specificity," in the spirit of Ghemawat (2003). The data presented in this chapter suggest that the two approaches may actually be closer to each other than usually thought.

The relative lack of market success in host-triad regions can be interpreted, at least partly, as a reflection of the limited customer value attributed to home-triad region FSAs, whether transferred through exports (FSAs embodied in final products), licensing (FSAs transferred to foreign licensees) or FDI (FSAs transferred to foreign affiliates, whether subsidiaries or hybrid units). It also suggests that the nine conditions proposed by Ohmae (1985) to become a performing insider in host triad regions are beyond the reach of most MNEs. If only limited customer value is attributed to the MNE's FSAs, exports become impossible and location advantages abroad cannot be used to leverage these FSAs. In those cases, the internalization question of optimal entry mode choice becomes redundant. In other words, it is only in locations (typically in the home region of the triad) where the MNE's home-region FSAs are valued by customers, as compared to relevant rivals, and for which minimum sales volumes can be expected, that conventional internalization theory is fully relevant. In this case of easy market penetration, there is no need for a lengthy learning process, in the sense of an incremental accumulation of host-region experience, to compensate for the liability of foreignness. The case of easy market penetration is consistent with Vernon's (1966) product life cycle and the findings in Rugman (1981) that R&D (at that time) was centralized in the parent firm, and would constitute the basis for a relatively easy international expansion, but with the entry mode choice contingent upon transaction cost considerations. Interestingly, the Scandinavian school internationalization model may be useful in determining the locations where MNEs have the luxury of such an extensive entry mode choice menu and, where they do not, as a function of location-driven learning requirements (as opposed to mere business/usage transaction cost reduction considerations). The data suggest that extensive choice options occur in the home triad region only, for most companies. Future research should therefore explore in more depth the complementarities, rather than the differences, between the internalization and internationalization perspectives on international expansion.

Implications for research on the diamond of international competitiveness

Porter (1990) has suggested that international competitiveness at the level of specific industries critically depends on a favorable configuration of home-country diamond conditions. Here, four determinants have been viewed as critical: factor conditions (with a focus on created and advanced production factors); demand conditions (with a focus on total demand and sophistication of demand, based on precursor status); related and supporting industries (with a focus on the presence of world class firms with which cluster type linkages exist); and strategy, structure and rivalry (whereby strong rivalry and benchmarking against the toughest competitors are critical to innovation). Porter's perspective has led to several follow-up studies, some of them applying the diamond framework, Cartwright (1993), Dunning (1996), and other ones providing extensions and suggestions to ameliorate the model, Rugman and D'Cruz (1993), Rugman and Verbeke (1993a), Rugman, Van den Broeck, and Verbeke (1995), and Moon et al. (1998).

The data in this chapter suggest two important extensions of research building upon the diamond concept.

First, the diamond is useful primarily to expand internationally in the home triad region, meaning that "favorable diamond conditions" in the home country do not appear sufficient in most cases to permit a truly global expansion. IB research should focus on the reasons for this lack of relevance of the home-country diamond in host-triad regions.

Second, the reduction in geographic scope of the national diamond's significance for international competitiveness has asymmetric implications for large economies such as the United States, Japan, and Germany and small open economies such as Canada, Belgium, and Singapore. For MNEs originating in large countries, it means reassessing the market attractiveness of so-called small markets in the home-triad region. The presence of FSAs instrumental to achieving a high market share in geographically proximate markets, but that are region bound, should refocus these MNEs' efforts from assessing foreign market attractiveness through using macro-economic data toward developing and using data that better indicate the firm's real market penetration potential, as illustrated by the Tricon case discussed in Ghemawat (2001). Regarding MNEs from small open economies, the data suggest that it makes sense to focus on demand in adjacent, large economies that are part of the home region. This confirms the need to adopt double diamond thinking in IB research that focuses on MNEs in these small open economies, much in line with Rugman and Verbeke (1993a), Rugman et al. (1995) and Moon et al. (1998). Here, it should be emphasized that regional integration not only benefits MNEs in the form of creating supply side efficiencies, but also improves market integration at the demand side, for example in terms of positively influencing buyers' confidence, attitudes and purchase intentions vis-à-vis products from foreign countries inside the triad region, Agarwal et al. (2002). Here, it would appear that, within one triad region, "country-of-origin" effects in purchasing decisions are complemented with "region-of-origin" preferences.

Figure 4.1. a. A resource-based re-interpretation of the integration-responsiveness framework

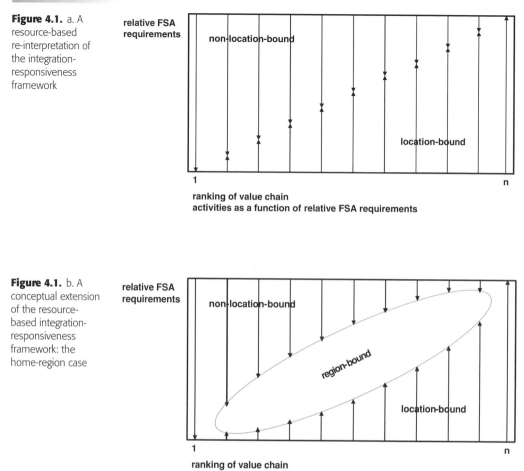

Figure 4.1. b. A conceptual extension of the resource-based integration-responsiveness framework: the home-region case

Implications for research adopting a resource based perspective on the integration / national responsiveness framework

Perhaps the most important implications of the empirical data on triad-based MNE activities are for research adopting a resource-based approach to MNE functioning. The integration/national responsiveness framework developed by Bartlett and Ghoshal (1989) was given a resource-based interpretation by Rugman and Verbeke (1992). The latter authors have argued that benefits of integration, in the form of scale economies, scope economies and benefits of exploiting national differences require non-location bound FSAs. In contrast, benefits of national responsiveness require location bound FSAs. The data presented in this chapter, however, suggest the need for a radical extension of the framework, as suggested in figure 4.1 (a, b, c).

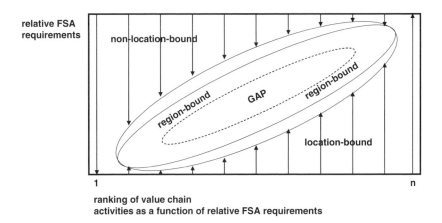

relative FSA requirements

non-location-bound

region-bound

GAP

region-bound

location-bound

1

n

ranking of value chain
activities as a function of relative FSA requirements

Figure 4.1a provides a stylized, alternative representation of the conventional integration/national responsiveness framework. Here, the horizontal axis describes the discrete set of critical activities (elements of the various value chain functions) to be performed by MNEs in order to be successful in foreign markets in terms of effectively selling a particular product in those foreign markets. The tasks, numbered from 1 to n, are arranged as a function of the relative needs for non-location bound FSAs (area NLB) and location bound FSAs (area LB), with an increasing need for the latter. Bartlett and Ghoshal's (1989) "transnational solution" case can then simply be interpreted as a firm that can effectively access and deploy the required dual knowledge bundles (of NLB and LB areas) for each activity to be performed for each product within each strategic business unit. In addition, each "generic" subsidiary type (namely strategic leaders, contributors, implementers and black holes), receives access to an idiosyncratic set of FSA bundles or resources to create such bundles, thereby guaranteeing appropriate selectivity in resource allocation. The basic framework described in Figure 4.1a does not take into account the learning imperative, the resource-based implications of which have been discussed elsewhere, Rugman and Verbeke (2001a).

The conventional framework needs to be augmented since operating in the *home*-triad region may be associated with new needs for the development of *region-bound* FSAs, imposed by regional integration, see e.g. the nine cases discussed by Rugman and Verbeke (1991), especially the Volvo Trucks case. This situation is represented in Figure 4.1b, where many activities require a set of region-bound FSAs. Hence, regional integration creates both a threat and an opportunity for MNEs as they need to complement the conventional bundles of non-location bound FSAs and location bound FSAs with a set of region-bound FSAs. The data in this chapter suggest that many of the world's largest and most international MNEs have been quite successful in doing so.

Figure 4.1. c. A conceptual extension of the resource-based integration-responsiveness framework: the host-region case

Finally for the case of MNEs in *host*-triad regions, few of these firms are capable of developing and deploying the required set of region-bound FSAs. Instead, a too limited set of region-bound FSAs is usually created, leading to a competence gap. This is represented by the area within the dotted lines in figure 4.1c. Here, the decay of the non-location bound FSAs occurs at a much faster rate (depending upon the differences between the regions involved) than in the home-triad region, and it also becomes much more difficult to access and deploy the required conventional location bound FSAs. This is compounded by the fact that region-bound FSAs cannot be simply created to fill the competence gap. This is in contrast with the home-triad leg case, whereby the reach of conventional location bound FSAs is extended across borders or non-location bound FSAs are "regionally sharpened," and a competence gap can be avoided. This explains why many MNE operations in host regions are primarily sensing instruments with little real effectiveness in market terms, thus giving these operations a "black hole" status.

In this context of two generic FSA types, it is interesting to observe that many large MNEs are much less home-region based in terms of their sourcing, both in resource industries and manufacturing, but appear incapable of capitalizing on this broader geographical sourcing to achieve global sales penetration. This has two critical implications. First, it means that the concept of location bound versus non-location bound FSAs needs to be extended. The former concept usually implies that profitable deployment is possible only in the home country. The latter concept assumes global transferability. The data suggest that many MNEs have FSAs that are region bound, i.e. they can be deployed across national borders, but only in a limited geographic region. Here, value added through aggregation, in the sense of exploiting similarities across countries, Ghemawat (2003), can be achieved in the home region but appears difficult across regions. Second, the required MNEs' FSAs in "back-end" activities to achieve broad geographic sourcing (of R&D outputs, raw materials, intermediate inputs, labor and capital) and production, may be very different from the FSAs required in "customer-end" activities to achieve a global distribution of sales. Here, value added through arbitrage, Ghemawat (2003), i.e. exploiting differences among countries, appears to be achievable more often across regions. Customer-end activities that require specific FSA bundles are defined here as all activities included in the interface with the firm's customers and that are significant to the customer's decision to purchase goods and services from the firm, irrespective of the value chain function to which these activities belong. The back-end activities requiring specific FSA bundles include all activities outside this critical interface with customers, but which are also significant to the firm's success, again irrespective of the value chain function in which these activities occur.

In this context, figure 4.2 shows two hypothetical accumulation patterns over time, of the MNE's FSAs at the back end (sourcing/production)

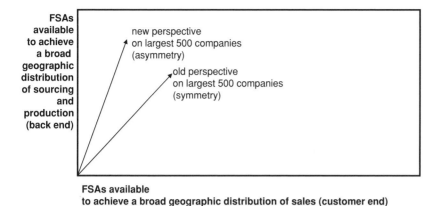

and the front end (sales). At either end of the value chain, these resource bundles consist of non-location bound FSAs, conventional location (read country) bound FSAs and region bound FSAs. The poor market performance achieved in host-triad regions suggests that most firms are not capable of accessing and deploying the required knowledge bundles at the customer-end side, because these bundles are likely to be quite different from the knowledge combinations effective in the home-triad region, whereas this does not necessarily hold for back-end activities. In broader terms, national and home region organizing principles adopted by MNEs, and engrained in their FSAs, appear to limit most MNEs' repertoire of customer-end strategies required to be effective in the host-region market. This is particularly interesting given that many markets, especially for commodity products, are characterized by "global" (uniform) prices, driven by "global" competition. In contrast, it appears much easier to adopt effective sourcing (and manufacturing) strategies associated with a broad geographical coverage. The liability of foreignness faced by the MNE, Hymer (1976) Zaheer (1995) thus needs to be unbundled into customer-end and back-end components.

The diagonal arrow in figure 4.2 shows a hypothetical expansion path over time, whereby the FSAs available for effective global sourcing/production (here, in the sense of broad geographical coverage, but not necessarily limited to a triad context, since the most optimal geographical configuration of sourcing and production is firm and industry specific) and those for global market penetration grow in very similar ways.

In contrast, the arrow on the left hand side of the diagonal in figure 4.2 reflects a new perspective on the typical large top-500 MNE, which is trapped in its home-triad region as far as market penetration is concerned. Here, the development of customer-end FSAs seriously lags behind the growth in back-end FSAs. It may thus be potentially easy to achieve a global distribution of sourcing/production, whereas a global distribution of sales may be more difficult to accomplish. This observation implies,

Figure 4.2. Old and new perspectives on the largest 500 companies

in terms of institutional theory, that most MNEs are not capable at the customer end, of effectively coping with either (or both) the internal iso-morphic pressures arising from headquarters or home-region units and isomorphic pressures arising from host region, external organizations, Campbell and Verbeke (2001). In fact, having an origin in one region may have negative legitimacy spill-over impacts on the MNE's operations in host regions. In contrast, at the back end, best practices and legit-imate behavior in industry can be more readily emulated, namely by observational learning and selective imitation, even without strong prior network ties in host regions.

The new perspective suggested in figure 4.2 implies that IB research should perhaps be redirected from trying to analyze an MNE's FSAs through conventional measures (such as R&D expenditures, advertising expenditures etc.) towards finding appropriate proxies for these firms back-end and front-end FSAs. This requires making a distinction between those that are truly transferable globally and those that are location (country) bound and region bound, meaning that they are character-ized by a rapid decay once attempts are made to deploy them outside the home region. To a large extent, much of the recent work on the globalization of particular value chain functions, such as finance, R&D, purchasing and logistics, production etc. has focused solely on the back-end portion of the MNE's FSA bundles. This largely reflects an arbitra-tion issue, with the MNE taking advantage of the incomplete integration of factor markets, Ghemawat (2003). This may reflect a "global logic" in the minds of managers, but is distinct from a strong global market performance.

The most extreme case of this perspective is Porter's (1986) focus on the MNE's configuration, i.e. the concentration versus dispersion of its value-added activities, and the coordination thereof. The limited rel-evance of the configuration/coordination framework for international business strategy has already been explained elsewhere, Rugman and Verbeke (1993b). It is also useful to note that the important issue of comparative market share performance in different regions, irrespec-tive of how value-added activities are distributed and coordinated across borders, is not taken into account by Porter. In practice, any value chain function can have substantial back-end and customer-end com-ponents. The back-end/customer-end dichotomy can therefore not be reduced to the simple distinction between upstream and downstream activities.

Implications for research on MNE structure

A large body of work has been written on the need for a fit between strategy and structure in MNEs, as a precondition for survival, profitabil-ity and growth, much in line with mainstream work in strategy and industrial organization on domestic firms. In this particular case, the strategic importance of each triad region, combined with the different market characteristics faced by MNEs in each of these regions, would suggest the introduction of geographic components in the MNEs' structure.

Some of the more grounded work on MNE strategy/structure interfaces can be attributed to Egelhoff (1982) and his follow-up work, including Wolf and Egelhoff (2002). Egelhoff adopted an information processing model to study the strategy-structure fit. He viewed the use of geographic divisions in MNEs as appropriate in cases whereby, "operations within a region are relatively large, complex and sufficiently different from other regions that opportunities for specialization and economies of scale are greater within a region than they are along worldwide product lines." His empirical work suggested that three variables are critical to choose geographical divisions: relatively large operations (measured as F/T sales), foreign manufacturing (share of foreign manufacturing in foreign sales) and a large number of foreign subsidiaries.

Two comments can be made here. First, although the mean foreign sales percentage of the 34 *Fortune* 500 firms included in his initial research was 50%, no distinction was made between intra-regional and inter-regional sales. Second, the research assumed that one particular organizational structure always dominates the MNE (functional structure, international division, product divisions, geographic divisions, and a matrix structure) and can be readily identified based upon statements made by managers and the analysis of publicly available information. However, the data in this chapter suggest that the geographical distribution of foreign sales does matter and that a strong discrepancy between intra-regional and inter-regional sales has important implications for MNE structure. More specifically, the differentiation between back-end and customer-end building upon different sets of FSAs should be reflected in the MNE's organizational structure, systems and perhaps even culture.

Interestingly, several chapters have been written on regional components in MNE organizational structure, such as regional headquarters, Heenan (1979), Grosse (1981), D'Cruz (1986), Daniels (1987), Dunning and Norman (1987), Morrison et al. (1991), Lasserre (1996), Yeung et al. (2001). To the extent that these chapters discuss customer-end related structural elements, these appear to be largely of a normative nature, i.e. intended to improve the firm's market position, without much empirical evidence that such structural elements are actually effective in practice. For example, Lasserre (1996) has argued that Western MNEs' regional headquarters in Asia serve entrepreneurship enhancing roles (scouting out new business opportunities, processing and distributing relevant information on the region, and signaling commitment to regional stakeholders) and integrative roles (exploitation of synergies across national subsidiaries, executing activities in areas where regional resource allocation should occur). However, little, if any, evidence is provided that any of these roles fundamentally improved the MNEs' effectiveness in bringing their products to the Asian customer. Yeung et al.'s (2001) analysis of such regional headquarters in Singapore, building on Lasserre (1996) argues that their roles will depend on a number of parameters, which include geographical distance, familiarity with the host region, commitment to the host region, and regional integration, etc., thus implicitly suggesting the importance of using the regional headquarters to complement in an idiosyncratic way each MNE's existing FSA bundles.

More research is needed that links the required knowledge bundles for each critical value added activity in host-triad regions with specific structural elements, that may also include elements of organizational physiology and psychology, Bartlett and Ghoshal (2000). Here, it should be recognized that such regional elements may increase the difficulty of managing multidivisional (M-form) companies since performance evaluation should be differentiated for units operating in the various regions, even within similar businesses, given the enormous differences in environmental circumstances faced by the affiliates in each region. In other words, even at a single point in time, MNEs may adopt both participative decentralization and administrative centralization simultaneously.

These two approaches have traditionally been viewed as inefficient corruptions of the M-form, Williamson (1975), Freeland (1996), but may in reality constitute a pre-condition for the effective governance of MNEs with regional strategies. Here, participative decentralization reflects the involvement of regional divisions in corporate strategic planning, and this may be critical for successfully conducting customer-end activities in host regions, given both the relative lack of appropriate information at the corporate headquarters' level on host regions, and the need to preserve subsidiary commitment and initiative in those host regions. In contrast, administrative centralization may be more appropriate for the management of back-end activities across regions, given the relative availability of information at corporate headquarters on these activities and the possibility of reducing both production and coordination costs through optimally exploiting imperfections in national and regional factor markets.

Implications for research on the performance effects of geographical diversification

Much of the literature on geographical diversification has attempted to evaluate the linkage between diversification and profit performance, e.g. Rugman (1976), Buckley et al. (1977) (1984), Geringer et al. (1989), Morck and Yeung (1991), Hitt et al. (1997). Usually some proxy is adopted for the share of foreign sales in total sales (or in some cases, a more back-end related measure, such as the number of subsidiaries abroad) to assess the degree of geographical diversification. Recent research has established the importance of the home-country environment, i.e. the *locus of origin* of geographic diversification efforts, for the scope and financial performance effects of geographic diversification, Wan and Hoskisson (2003).

In this chapter, however, we emphasize the importance of the *locus of destination*. The relative sales in host-triad regions, vis-à-vis the home-triad region, are themselves a critical performance parameter. Perhaps the mixed results in past research on the profit impact of geographical diversification, may be partly explained by: (1) a lack of investigation of the *locus of destination* of the diversification efforts (intra-regional versus inter-regional) and (2) the fact that market share success in non-home triad markets may be at the expense of profit performance. Thus, future research on the impacts of geographic diversification should study explicitly the regional patterns and scope of MNE sales growth. In addition, it could include relative sales in host-region markets as a performance parameter (dependent variable), rather than as a mere independent variable affecting financial profitability. Recent work by Vermeulen and Barkema (2002) correctly points out that some benefits of international expansion (such as tax benefits, common purchasing, and improved access to inexpensive labor) are easier to accomplish than other benefits, which require learning. Although these authors do not view host-region market penetration performance relative to home-region performance as a proxy for international success, their work does suggest that a broader geographic scope of the expansion process negatively moderates the impact of a firm's foreign subsidiaries on its profitability. More specifically, they demonstrate that a broader geographic scope strains the MNE's absorptive capacity, Cohen and Levinthal (1990), particularly in the short run, leading to time compression diseconomies. They also show that foreign expansion is easier to absorb for MNEs if it occurs in "related" countries, following the classification of countries into clusters developed by Ronan and Shenkar (1985).

Another recent chapter by Ruigrok and Wagner (2003) with a focus on back-end FSAs confirms this perspective. Ruigrok and Wagner suggest that US firms are usually characterized by an inverted J-curve, in terms of an internationalization impact on performance (measured by return on assets).

Internationalization is associated with performance improvements, until a threshold is reached, when performance starts to decline. The reason is that US firms can usually expand (from a back-end perspective) in a first stage to culturally proximate countries such as Canada, the United Kingdom and Australia. In contrast, German firms face a U-curve in terms of performance effects of internationalization. A low psychic distance is found in only two small economies, namely Austria and Switzerland, which implies that German firms are required to target a much wider and varied market (the EU) from the outset, thereby incurring higher learning costs. Ruigrok and Wagner's (2003) perspective on back-end internationalization suggests that even there, the linkages between country-of-origin and country-of-destination are critical in determining the optimal route of internationalization and organizational learning.

This is an important observation as influential work in IB has argued that the operational flexibility of MNEs, resulting from their internationally dispersed network of affiliates confers arbitraging advantages, information-related network externalities etc., Kogut (1983), Kogut and Kulatilaka (1994). However, the analysis above suggests that location determines the extent to which such benefits can be earned. More specifically, a lower (cultural, administrative, geographic and economic) distance, although reducing the hypothetical, maximum arbitraging and network externality benefits, will facilitate earning such benefits in practice.

A question to be answered by future research is whether the prior existence of a strong internal network in the home region (and the related proven ability to learn and to manage risks) is critical for subsequent positive performance effects associated with interregional expansion. The creation of a strong competitive position in the home region may reflect one step in an evolutionary strategy of resource re-combinations, that follows a clear sequential pattern, and creates platforms for future investments, Kogut and Zander (1993). However, it is unclear whether such platforms are themselves truly non-location bound, or can only be applied in a limited geographic space.

CONCLUSIONS

The evidence is that of the world's largest MNEs, the vast majority have an average of 80% of total sales in its home region of the triad. There are as few as 10 triad-based global companies among the largest 500 companies. What are the normative implications of this observation? It could be argued that these few examples of global corporate success should be viewed as best practices and benchmarks to be carefully studied and emulated by other large MNEs, most of them are characterized by a much more narrow and shallow penetration of host-region markets. However, the observed weak market position in host regions, as compared to the home-triad market, may also be interpreted as the outcome of a rational preference for regionally-based activities, resulting from a careful cost benefit calculation. Here, strategic interactions among large players, taking the form of interregional chess, may influence international sales patterns and the selection of target markets.

More generally, it could be argued, from a co-evolutionary perspective, that regional strategies of MNEs are embedded in – and co-evolve with – the broader competitive, organizational, and institutional contexts at the regional level, in the spirit of Koza and Lewin (1998). In this situation, MNE regional strategy choices evolve interdependently with changes in prevailing industry practices, legitimate organizational forms, government regulations, etc. It should be recognized that regions themselves may change over time (as with the inclusion of the Americas in NAFTA and further EU expansion), and therefore provide new opportunities for MNE growth. The triad perspective developed in this chapter should therefore be viewed as a starting point for future empirical analyses, recognizing that regionalization is open-ended over time.

Where globalization does occur, it is only at the back end of the value chain. Some of the world's largest MNEs master the art of connecting globally dispersed inputs. These can be in the form of financial capital, human capital, R&D knowledge, components, etc., and can be integrated to better serve home-region clients. Hence, it appears possible to be global at the back end of the value chain, and much can undoubtedly be learned from observing and imitating the routines of global leaders in this portion of the value chain.

Does this imply that large MNEs should be complacent as far as the customer end is concerned and solely focus on their home region of the triad? Probably not, but senior MNE management should understand that widespread geographic diversification may well have managerial pitfalls similar to the conventional drawbacks of product diversification. A clear focus is required in terms of scope of geographic expansion, and the economic evaluation of international growth plans must take into account the costs of inter-regional "distance" and the liability of inter-regional foreignness.

The recognition of the fallacy of customer end, global strategies may go a long way to improving the ability of the world's largest MNEs to profitably exploit international growth opportunities. Perhaps it is time for "global strategy" scholars to recognize the limited usefulness of simple messages advocating the globalization of MNE strategy and structure. Such globalization is not being achieved by the vast majority of MNEs, which operate mainly in their home region of the triad.

Finally, this chapter has uncovered two fundamental paradoxes of IB, which so far have eluded most, if not all, scholars in the field. First, at the customer end, national responsiveness and localized adaptation are almost universally advocated as a panacea for penetrating international markets, but in reality most MNEs attempt to add value primarily by capitalizing on similarities across markets. This is an aggregation strategy often met with success in the home region. Second, at the back end (including FDI-driven foreign manufacturing), opportunities for scale and scope are usually considered abundant. Yet, in reality, MNEs add value primarily through arbitrage, i.e. exploiting differences across nations and regions. Successful integration thus reflects locational specificities. We live in a world of semi-globalization, where IB research needs to fundamentally rethink the substance of aggregation and arbitrage opportunities; this chapter has suggested that the region may be a good starting point for such an endeavor.

5

Retail multinationals and globalization

Contents

In an astonishing development, the largest corporation in the world in 2002, measured by sales, was Wal-Mart. The sales of the world's largest retailer exceeded that of former world leaders such as General Motors and Exxon. Retail companies represent 10% of the top 500 MNEs. This indicates that much more analytical attention needs to be directed to retail and other service-related business rather than just to manufacturing multinational enterprises (MNEs). In this chapter, the international dimension of retail organizations is discussed. Are these "global" businesses? If so, do they have a "global" strategy?

In the case of Wal-Mart, the answer to both questions is no. The data indicates that, while Wal-Mart has 26.5% of its stores outside of the United States, most of these are located in Canada and Mexico, its NAFTA partners. That is, Wal-Mart is a North American business, with only 9.6% of its stores being outside of its home region. In terms of revenue, only 16.3% of Wal-Mart's revenue is international, and, again most of this is in the North American region.

Yet, even otherwise well-informed analysts have discussed the nature of Wal-Mart's globalization and its use of global strategy. In a representative book, Govindarajan and Gupta (2001), devote all of chapter 3 (their first detailed case study) to an analysis of the "global" strategy of Wal-Mart. This type of approach is misguided. Wal-Mart is a regional business and has a regional strategy; it is a regional MNE, not a global MNE. It turns out that virtually all retailers are in the same position as Wal-Mart. As the data in this paper show, only one retailer, out of the world's largest forty-nine retail MNEs, is truly global – most are either home-country based or operate, at best, in neighboring regions. A few operate in two parts of the "triad" of North America, the EU, and Japan. But most of the European retailers have nearly all the business in the EU, the US retailers in North America, the Asians in Asia. In short, retail MNEs are not global but regional, especially if we consider the term "global" in its two different meanings: a global sales presence on the one hand, and a global strategy on the other hand. Many scholars have misused the "global" concept, and this chapter confronts this misunderstanding in terms of the empirical reality of regional retailing.

Case 5.1

The Wal-Mart case: A NAFTA-based retailer

In 2001, Wal-Mart became the world's biggest company in terms of sales revenues; a breathtaking achievement for the company that Sam Walton started in Arkansas as recently as 1962. Indeed, with revenues of $217.8 billion for the year ending in 2002, Wal-Mart is now ahead of General Motors and Exxon Mobil. Wal-Mart's success can be attributed to a scale strategy based on reduction of costs to generate steadily its "always low prices" formula and physical growth or market coverage.

Wal-Mart's international expansion began in 1992 when it entered into a joint venture with Cifra SA, a successful Mexican retailer, in which it held 50% interest in its partner's retail operations. In 1998, Wal-Mart acquired a controlling interest in Cifra and officially changed the company's name to Wal-Mart of Mexico. Since 1992, Wal-Mart has also expanded into eight other international markets: Argentina, Brazil, Canada, China, Germany, South Korea, Puerto Rico, and the UK.

A more careful analysis shows that "international" expansion does not necessarily mean "global" expansion. Wal-Mart is a regional but not a global business. For example, Wal-Mart only has 10% of its stores outside of North America as indicated in table 1. At the beginning of 2002 Wal-Mart had a total of 3,989 stores. It reported that 1,004 of its stores were "international," and the remaining 2,985 were in the domestic US market. An additional 458 were in Mexico and another 166 in Canada. Thus a total of 3,609 of its stores are in the NAFTA region. Only 380 stores are truly "international," i.e. outside of Wal-Mart's home triad. In other words, Wal-Mart is

still a North American business. The locus of its business model strategy and structure is regional and triad based.

In addition, although international sales are estimated to be 16.3% of total sales, extra-regional sales represent just 5.9% of total sales, and the North American Free Trade Agreement (NAFTA) market stands at an estimated 94.1% of its total sales. This means that the home triad is still its locus for strategy. There is still a very long way to go for Wal-Mart to become a truly global retailer. Indeed, Wal-Mart only has 4.8% of total sales in Europe and 0.4% in Asia. It does not have a "global" strategy. The UN *World Investment Report 2001* reported that Wal-Mart has one of the lowest scores of any of the 100 largest MNEs. On a transnational index Wal-Mart has a "network spread index" (a measure of actual to possible foreign direct investment – of which there were a possible 187 in 1999) of under 5%.

Table 1. Wal-mart's "globalization"		
total stores		3,989
United States	2,985	
Mexico	458	
Canada	166	
NAFTA		3,609
international		380

Sources: Wal-Mart, Annual Report.

In Asia, Wal-Mart operates nineteen stores in China and nine in South Korea. The company is carefully entering Japan. In March 2002, it bought a 6.1% minority share in The Seiyu Ltd. company with an option right to buy up to 66.7% over time.

The group entered Europe in the late 1990s, by purchasing the Wertkauf and Interspar supermarkets in Germany. It then entered the British market by acquiring ASDA. In 2002, Wal-Mart operated nearly 350 locations in these two European markets, but in Germany the company is still losing money. There are a number of factors that explain this. First, Wal-Mart is not well known in Europe. This is why the company has chosen to retain the ASDA name in England. The European customer is also more quality oriented, and a strategy that relies on just low prices is not as successful. A notable exception is British Asda, which had adopted Wal-Mart's focus on low prices. Even in this case, however, a low-cost strategy was secondary to developing long-term relationships with suppliers of well-known, quality-oriented, differentiated brands. Second, European competitors have emulated the company's most successful strategies in cost reduction and supply-chain management, reducing Wal-Mart's relative competitive advantage in their local markets. Third, Europe has a different cost structure. Real estate development, when possible, is more costly and wages are also higher. Finally, the scale effect does not work in Europe. When the company must source 90% of its offer locally, which bargain or logistics savings can it cash in with so few stores? In Germany, local competitors offer very low prices, and Wal-Mart is not big enough to achieve the local economies of scale required to compete on price alone.

This being said, the Latin American and NAFTA (especially Mexican) operations are much more successful. The higher success in its regional market can be attributed to a number of factors. One is that it can rely on suppliers for their US stores to deliver products for the Canadian and Mexican market. Another factor is the lack of substantial competition in many Latin American markets. In Mexico, Wal-Mart purchased the most successful local retailer, gaining local expertise and avoiding local competition.

Time, patient investment, and key expertise in each foreign market may help Wal-Mart to enlarge successfully its international operations to become a global player or at least a bi-regional player in the next decade.

Sources: www.walmart.com; Wal-Mart, *Annual Report 2002*; The Fortune Global 500, *Fortune*, July 2002; Alan M. Rugman and Stephane Girod, (2003) "Retail Multinationals and Globalization: The Evidence is Regional," *European Management Journal*, 21:1, 24–37.

Questions for discussion

1. Is Wal-Mart a multinational enterprise? Why?
2. Is Wal-Mart a "global" or a "regional" business? Why?
3. What is the business model of Wal-Mart? How does sourcing in China affect it, if at all?
4. What is Wal-Mart's basic strategy?
5. What is Wal-Mart's basic structure?
6. Why can't Wal-Mart simply export its strategy to the European market?
7. How can Wal-Mart compete with local retailers in Mexico, the EU, and Asia?
8. What strategy does Wal-Mart need to succeed in Europe? In Asia?

THEORY

The theoretical basis of this chapter is that of Rugman (2000), where it was demonstrated that, today, most economic activity (both in manufacturing and services) is location bound, taking place in clusters in the "triad" of the EU, North America, and Japan. The geography of location and the drawing power of nearby markets lead to rigidities that influence the strategic management decisions of firms, including multinational enterprises (MNEs). In fact, the choice of entry mode and choice of location are complementary strategic management decisions of profound importance to MNEs.

The key theoretical driver behind this paper is the insight from MNE scholars such as Dunning (2001), Enright (2000), Rugman and Verbeke (2001), and Dunning and Mucchielli (2002), that in most triad clusters of value-added activities the MNEs are embedded as leading participants. The most extreme version of this viewpoint is that of Rugman and D'Cruz (2000) who argue that MNEs act as "flagships" to lead, direct, coordinate, and manage strategically the value added activities of partner organizations in a business network, including key suppliers, key customers, and the non-business infrastructure. While Dunning (2001) refers to flagships as leaders only of vertical clusters (as in autos), Rugman and D'Cruz (2000) also include horizontal clusters (as in textiles, financial services, etc.).

The new thinking explored in this paper is the extent to which MNEs are "regionally" based, in the spirit of Rugman (2000). Examples will be examined from the retail MNEs based in North America (US – Canadian), from within the EU, and from Japan. Coupled with this regional focus will be an analysis of the past, present, and future role of retail MNEs in such regional/triad geographical spaces. The nature of regional business and case studies of failures of global strategy are discussed in Rugman and Hodgetts (2001).

There is abundant empirical support for the Rugman (2000) proposition that large retailers operate on a triad rather than a global basis. The old-fashioned view of "global" MNEs operating in an integrated and homogenous world market with globalization as the predominant form of international business needs to be replaced. The world's largest retailers are mainly triad-based regional players, not global ones. They operate on a strongly segmented regional/triad basis, and a relevant framework to analyze MNE strategy needs to recognize this. In short, management strategy as taught in business schools today needs to refocus from a global strategy and globalization perspective to a more empirically accurate focus on triad market activity and the regional MNEs.

Our findings are partially confirmed in work on the triad-based nature of the automobile sector by Schlie and Yip (2000). However, they argue that most MNEs first follow a global strategy, and then some selectively regionalize, i.e. regionalization is a sequential process. We have not observed this; rather the triad strategies of MNEs in 2002 are very similar to the nature of triad strategies in the 1970s.

The chapter provides empirical evidence which demonstrates that all the major retailers in reality operate on a triad/regional basis. Only one MNE is truly "global," with a global strategy; the rest are home-triad based and need regional strategies. Methodologically speaking, this evidence is obtained by relying on two criteria: the ratio of foreign sales to total sales, which triggers the distinction between intra-regional sales and inter-regional sales, and the ratio of foreign stores to total stores. Other criteria, such as the number of countries where MNEs run operations or international market shares were discarded as not sufficiently accurate.

Table 5.1.	The largest US retailers, number of stores, 2001						
company	US	Canada	Mexico	North American triad%	international	%	total
Kroger	3,634	–	–	100.0	–	–	3,634
Wal-Mart	3,118	174	499	90.5	398	9.5	4,189
Albertsons	2,300	–	–	100.0			2,300
Sears	2,167	511	–	100.0	–	–	2,678
K-Mart	2,105	–	–	100.0	–	–	2,105
Target	1,381	–	–	100.0	–	–	1,381
JC Penney	4,060	–	–	100.0	–	–	4,060

Source: Wal-Mart, Annual Report 2001; Sears, Annual Report 2001; www.sears.com; K-Mart, Annual Report 2001.
Note: In addition to Sears' Canadian retail stores, the company has over 2,157 Sears catalogue stores. These are independently owned catalogue stands that operate mostly in remote areas across Canada.

EMPIRICAL EVIDENCE

The Templeton Global Index, Gestrin, Knight, and Rugman (2000), showed that the ratio of foreign assets to total assets of the largest multinationals in the retail industry stood at 26% in 2000, far behind industries such as tobacco (78%), soaps (56%), or chemicals (50%). This is a clear sign of the non-existence of global retail MNEs.

The evidence shows that the large retail organizations are completely triad based, whatever the segment they specialize in: general merchandise, grocery, specialty retail, mail-order retail, or department stores. Table 5.1 reports data showing that the large US retailers like Kroger, Wal-Mart, Albertsons, Sears, K-Mart, and Target are all North American based. All but Wal-Mart have no stores outside the United States, and Wal-Mart only has 10% of its stores outside of the NAFTA region. This and other examples of retailers illustrate the key point of a lack of global presence. In the following section a more comprehensive test of globalization is reported.

Wal-Mart has 4,414 stores of which 3,244 are in the United States, 196 are in Canada, and 551 are in Mexico. Only 423 are in international markets, i.e. 9.6% of the total stores, see table 5.2. Nonetheless, Wal-Mart is the most international large-scale retailer from the United States. In 2001, foreign revenue as a percentage of total revenues was 16.26% ($35.4 billion of a total of $217.7 billion).

Kroger, Albertsons, Target, and JC Penney operate in the United States only. Sears operates only in Canada and the United States. K-Mart recently divested itself of its operations in Canada and

Table 5.2.	Wal-Mart's "globalization" is really regionalization	
country/region	no. of stores 2001	% of total
US	3,244	73.5
Mexico	551	12.5
Canada	196	4.4
NAFTA	3,991	90.4
other international	423	9.6
total stores	4,414	100.0

Source: Wal-Mart, Annual Report, 2002.
Note: Wal-Mart's Annual Report has international stores at 1,170, which is 26.5% of the total.

Table 5.3. Kingfisher's international operations		
country/region	no. of stores	% of total
United Kingdom	2,164	73.1
France	420	14.2
Germany	194	6.6
Belgium	55	1.9
The Netherlands	23	0.8
Italy	12	0.4
Austria	3	0.1
Luxembourg	2	0.1
European Union	2,873	97.2
Eastern Europe	56	1.9
Total Europe	2,929	99.1
Canada	13	0.4
Brazil	3	0.1
Turkey	5	0.2
China	2	0.1
Taiwan	8	0.3
Total	2,960	100.0

Source: Kingfisher, Annual Report 2001.

Mexico. Its stores are all in the United States. There is a K-Mart Australia, but this is owned by an Australian company, Coles Myer.

Outside the United States, Daiei has 4,028 stores (which includes 1,566 specialty stores). It is mainly a Japanese operation, but the company also has fifteen stores in China and four in the United States.

Groupe Pinault-Printemps of France makes 54.7% of its revenues outside of France. However, it only makes 30.9% of its revenues outside of Europe.

Kingfisher of the UK operates in sixteen countries around the world, especially in France and Germany, but 97% of its stores are in Europe. An additional 2% are in Eastern Europe and only 1% outside of Europe, see table 5.3.

Carrefour of France has 9,200 stores in thirty countries. Yet, only 19% of Carrefour's revenues originate from outside of Europe. See attached table 5.4. Clearly Carrefour, and all other retail MNEs, need to be analyzed on a European regional level; they are not global organizations.

Metro AG, a German cash and carry general merchandise retailer, has 70.2% of its 1,788 stores in Germany and 98.9% in Europe. Otherwise it has fifteen stores in China and five in Morocco, for a world total of 1,788.

THE HOME-TRIAD BASE OF MNE RETAIL ACTIVITY

In the following pages, several of these three key types of MNEs identified earlier in this book are examined:

(i) home-region based retail MNEs;
(ii) MNEs in two parts of the triad: these are labeled "bi-regional" MNEs;
(iii) MNEs in all three parts of the triad: these are labeled "global" MNEs.

There are several viable alternative ways to evaluate international business activity. The most useful, across all the 500 largest MNEs, is by looking at sales revenues. It is possible to calculate the ratio of foreign-to-total sales, (F/T) sales. Ideally, only sales by for-eign affiliates should be included, but often the exports of the home firm are also included as "foreign" sales in the consolidated accounts of many of the companies listed.

To conduct a definitive test of the true nature of the international business of the world's largest retailers we evaluate the sales and assets of all retail firms listed in the *Fortune* Global 500. This is an annual ranking (by sales) of the world's 500 largest MNEs. For the latest year of data available (2000), the *Fortune* 500 list for 2001 includes forty-nine retailers. Of these, the "triad" breakdown was:

NAFTA   26
Europe   16 (of which 15 are from the EU)
Asia   7 (of which 5 are from Japan)

These forty-nine retail firms are listed by decreasing order of sales revenue (i.e. by the *Fortune* 500 ranking) in table 5.5. There are missing data for one of the forty-nine MNEs.

Many of these firms have no inter-national sales at all (Kroger, Target, Albertsons, Walgreen, CVS, Lowes, Fed-erated, George Weston, Best Buy, Publix, Rite Aid, May, Winn Dixie, Circuit City, and Safeway). Of the allegedly forty-nine "global" retailers, eighteen are purely domestic firms, leaving thirty-one with international sales. Of these, only two are bi-regional, with less than 50% of their sales in their home region and more than 20% of their sales in another region, and both of these are host-region oriented. These firms are Royal Ahold, a Dutch MNE, with 59% of its total sales in NAFTA (see Ahold box) and Delhaize Le Lion, a Belgian MNE, with 77% of its sales in NAFTA. In addition, there are only three other MNEs with substantial sales over 20%, in a foreign region. These are: Ito Yokado, a Japanese MNE with 39% of its sales in NAFTA; Otto Versand, a German MNE, with 27% of its sales in NAFTA; and Pinault Printemps Redoute, a French MNE, with 21% of its sales in NAFTA. Yet, these last three firms have over 50% of their sales in their home region of the triad and are therefore classified as home-region oriented.

Table 5.4.   Carrefour's international locations

country/region	no. of stores	% of total
France	3,367	36.6
Europe (excl. France)	4,870	52.9
Spain	2,719	29.6
Italy	918	10.0
Belgium	442	4.8
Greece	375	4.1
Portugal	332	3.6
Poland	62	0.7
Switzerland	11	0.1
Czech Rep.	11	0.1
Total Europe	8,237	89.5
Americas	645	7.0
Argentina	391	4.3
Brazil	226	2.5
Mexico	19	0.2
Colombia	5	0.1
Chile	4	0.0
Asia	109	1.2
China	27	0.3
Japan	3	0.0
South Korea	22	0.2
Taiwan	27	0.3
Thailand	15	0.2
Malaysia	6	0.1
Indonesia	8	0.1
Singapore	1	0.0
other and non specified	209	2.3
Total	9,200	100.0

Source: www.carrefour.com.

Table 5.5. The world's largest retail companies by sales

companies	origin	rank in Global 500	sales in bn $	int'l sales in bn $	int'l sales in % of TOT SALES	sales Nafta in bn $	in % of tot sales	sales EUROPE in bn $	in % of tot sales	sales ASIA PACIFIC in bn $	in % of tot sales
Wal-Mart	NAFTA/US	1	219.8	35.486	16.3	204.9e	94.1e	10.439e	4.8e	0.846e	0.4e
Itochu	ASPAC/JP	17	91.2	0.218	15	0	0	0	0	1.460	100
Marubeni	ASPAC/JP	25	71.8	na	na	na	na	na	na	na	na
Carrefour	Eur/Fr	35	62.2	31.639	50.8	n/s	na	50.830	81.3	4.111	6.6
Royal Ahold	Eur/NL	38	59.6	50.931	85	35.3	59.2	19.621	32.8	354	0.6
Home Depot	NAFTA/US	46	53.6	3,323e	6.2	53.6	100	0	0	0	0
Kroger	NAFTA/US	56	50.1	0	0	50.1	100	0	0	0	0
Metro AG	Eur/Ger	72	44.3	18.9	42.7	0	0	43.1	97.3	1.0	2.25
Sears Roebuck	NAFTA/US	83	41.1	5.179	12.6	41.1	100	0	0	0	0
Target	NAFTA/US	89	39.9	0	0	39.9	100	0	0	0	0
Albertsons	NAFTA/US	100	37.9	0	0	37.9	100	0	0	0	0
Kmart	NAFTA/US	104	36.1	0	0	36.2	100	0	0	0	0
Safeway	NAFTA/US	113	34.3	4,116e	12	34.3	100	0	0	0	0
Tesco	Eur/UK	114	33.9	5.208	15.4	0	0	31.73	93.6	2.17	6.4
JC Penney	NAFTA/US	124	32.6	498	1.6	31.6	98.6	0	0	0	0
Ito Yokado	ASPAC/JP	161	26.8	9.962	40	9.8	39	0	0	15.087	61
Pinault Printemps Redoute	Eur/FR	181	24.9	13.678	54.7	5.31	21.2	17.289	69.1	1.381	5.6
Walgreen	NAFTA/US	183	24.6	0	0	24.6	100	0	0	0	0
J Sainsbury	Eur/UK	184	24.6	4.100	16.7	4.1	16.7	20.500	83.3	0	0
Aeon	ASPAC/JP	196	23.6	2.596	11	1.7	7e	0	0	21.948	93
Groupe Auchan	Eur/FR	199	23.4	8.4	35.5	na	na	23.462e	99.5e	na	na
CVS	NAFTA/US	215	22.2	0	0	22.2	100	0	0	0	0
Lowes	NAFTA/US	216	22.1	0	0	22.1	100	0	0	0	0
Groupe Casino	Eur/FR	231	20.5	5.088	25	2.1	10.2	16.118	78.8	1.065	5.2
Daiei	ASPAC/JP	237	20.1	0.2	1	0.1	0.5	0	0	20	99.5
Delhaize le Lion	Eur/BE	245	19.6	16.161	84	14.9	77	4.214	22	183	1

Company	Region										
Best Buy	NAFTA/US	247	19.6	0	0	19.6	100	0	0	0	0
Federated Dpt Sto	NAFTA/US	292	16.9	0	0	16.9	100	0	0	0	0
Kingfisher	Eur/GB	314	16.1	6.601	40.2	0.13[e]	0.8[e]	16.377[e]	98.3[e]	0.09[e]	0.6[e]
George Weston	NAFTA/CA	318	15.9	0	0	15.900	100	0	0	0	0
Publix Supermark	NAFTA/US	328	15.3	0	0	15.300	100	0	0	0	0
Rite Aid	NAFTA/US	331	15.2	0	0	15.200	100	0	0	0	0
Karstadt Quelle	Eur/Ger	347	14.4	1.621	11	0	0	14.4	100	0	0
May Dpt Stores	NAFTA/US	351	14.2	0	0	14.200	100	0	0	0	0
Gap Inc.	NAFTA/US	363	13.8	2.349	17[e]	12.200	88.4	1.0[e]	7.7[e]	0.54[e]	3.9[e]
Otto Versand	Eur/Ger	372	13.6	7.5	55	3.7	27.4	9.33[e]	68.6[e]	0.5[e]	4[e]
Winn Dixie Stores	NAFTA/US	398	12.9	0	0	12.900	100	0	0	0	0
Circuit City Stores	NAFTA/US	403	12.8	0	0	12.800	100	0	0	0	0
Coles Myer	ASPAC/AU	406	12.6	0	0	0	0	0	0	12.600	100
Safeway	Eur/GB	418	12.3	0	0	0	0	12.300	100	0	0
Migros	Eur/CH	427	12	1.08	9	0	0	12	100	0	0
Marks and Spencer	Eur/GB	439	11.7	2.7	13.7	0	0	10.26[e]	87.7[e]	1[e]	8.6[e]
Woolworths	ASPAC/AU	442	11.5	0	0	0	0	0	0	11.5	100
C Dior/LVMH	Eur/FR	446	11.2	10	83.4	3.13	26	4.222	35	3.739	31
Office Depot	NAFTA/US	450	11.1	1.552	21	5.843[e]	79[e]	n/s	n/s	n/s	n/s
Toys R Us	NAFTA/US	457	11	1.900	17	9.100	83	n/s	n/s	n/s	n/s
Great Atlantic and Pacific Tea	NAFTA/US	458	11	3,127[e]	28.5	11.000	100	0	0	0	0
Staples	NAFTA/US	469	10.7	2.265	21.2	9.900	92.5	800	7.5	0	0
TJX	NAFTA/US	470	10.7	1,220[e]	11.4	10.179	95	521	5	0	0

Notes: Data are from 2000 in US $.

Itochu: Conglomerate – For Int'l Sales, we take into account their grocery-stores operation only: "Family Mart," 3rd largest grocery retailer in Japan.

Case 5.2

Ahold: a bi-regional retailer

The US market has been a difficult one for retailers from other triad regions. Carrefour, the French retail giant withdrew its efforts at expanding there and groups like Auchan, Sainsbury, or Casino have barely a symbolic presence. Yet Ahold, the largest European food retailer, has become such a major retailer in the United States that it is the fifth largest food distributor. Indeed, Royal Ahold derives a higher percentage (60%) of its revenues from the US market than the EU.

Confined to a very tiny Netherlands market, Ahold's management was looking for new areas of growth in the 1970s. Careful analysis was given to several countries and areas to avoid direct conflicts with local giants and seize significant market shares. Germany, France, and the UK already had their emerging retail giants. The North American, Spanish, and Scandinavian markets seemed more promising. Today, Ahold is successfully rooted in the United States.

In the United States, the company operates five main banners: *"Stop and Shop"* is the leading one in New England where it holds a 40% market share, a very valuable asset as, due to severe zoning restrictions, big discounters like Wal-Mart can barely expand in this territory; *"Giant"* holds a significant position around the Washington DC area; *"Bi-Lo"* is positioned in the central eastern states and was the first chain the group purchased in 1977; *"Tops"* is based in New York, while the last acquisition, *"Brunos"*, operates in and around Florida. In addition, a third of the US revenues come from the food service operations that provide sub-contract services to 250,000 accounts.

All these firms are independent but share experience and a common means to generate synergies. In 1999, to focus on the maximum global integration of the group's backward side of the value chain, the CEO, Cees van der Hoeven, implemented the "Ahold Network". Today, US subsidiaries have completed the joint integration of their fresh food supply. The savings at stake are, of course, critical in an industry where margins are salami thin.

As far as the downstream side of the supply chain is concerned, however, the group intentionally acts as a local: local firm with local banners, local communication or community involvement, and local product ranges.

Ahold faces severe competition in the United States, where Bi-Lo is somewhat hit by Wal-Mart's aggressive strategy, (today the price gap between the two chains is 12%). Ahold's goal is to focus on this critical region and consolidate. With its remaining 8.2% sales revenues coming from Asia and Latin America, Ahold is clearly not a global player. In Europe the retailer is absent from the leading four economies; it is very weak in Asia after it left China in 1999 (after closing its joint venture with its partner from Shangai). The company's self-proclaimed goal to "be no.1 in every region in which it has presence" is not yet realistic.

Sources: www.ahold.com; Ahold, *Annual Report 2001;* "Ahold: Tougher Times" – *BNPParibas Equities* – February 2002; Richard Tomlison "The biggest Grocer you have never heard of" – *Fortune* – July 8, 2002.

Questions for discussion

1. Is Ahold a multinational enterprise? Why?
2. Is Ahold a "global" or a "regional" business? Why?
3. What is Ahold's basic strategy?
4. What is Ahold's basic structure?
5. What strategy does Ahold need to succeed in the United States?
6. How can Ahold compete with local retailers in the United States?
7. What is the most likely entry mode for a company like Ahold into the United States?
8. How does the structure of Ahold's operations in the United States reflect its entry mode into the market?

Only one retailer is "global". This is Christian Dior/LVMH which has 83.4% international sales. Of these, 35% are in its home base in the EU; another 31.3% are in Asia; and another 26% are in NAFTA. Thus Christian Dior/LVMH operates across all three parts of the triad; in this sense it is a unique retailer with a triad, global presence. We discuss this MNE in more detail in the box "LVMH: The only global retailer."

As shown in table 5.6, there are eleven retail MNEs with the vast majority of their international sales in their home region of the triad of NAFTA; twelve with most of their international sales in their home EU market; and four Japanese-based MNEs. Interestingly, Wal-Mart, so often praised as global, belongs to this group of home-based MNEs. As our approach is to categorize main retail operators and to illustrate each type of strategy, we provide more analysis on Wal-Mart in a box above. It is an example of a home-region based MNE, not a global one.

The breakdown of the forty-nine retail MNEs is as follows and details appear on table 5.6:

domestic	18
home-region oriented	27
bi-regional	2
global	1
no data available	*1*
total	49

The following five points emerge from this empirical analysis:

(i) First, we find that 77.7% of domestic firms are from the United States. They belong to the world's top 100 firms but have no sales overseas. This is not surprising, as the US market is so powerful and integrated that most firms do not even have to go abroad to generate growth. In the grocery segment, several companies are even only present in sub-national regions of the country, i.e. the west or the north east.

(ii) Second, the NAFTA and European MNEs are almost equal as far as home-region oriented firms are concerned. This reflects the positive impact of regional trade agreements like the EU and NAFTA.

(iii) Third, the two bi-regional MNEs are European, from smaller countries like Belgium and Holland. Ahold and Delhaize have larger sales in NAFTA than in Europe. This was a strategic choice carried on through acquisitions since the 1960s. These companies acted as locals as much as possible, not using their European names in North America. Both these companies are host-region oriented. That is, they continue to concentrate primarily in one regional market. In this case, however, it is not its home-region market.

(iv) Fourth, the only firm in the truly global category is the leading world retailer of luxury goods, LVMH. Luxury goods fulfill people's self-achievement and not their basic needs like many of the other segments of the general or specialty retail industry. Marketing matters for LVMH, and it has a strong set of brand images, internationally recognized style, and quality standards. Luxury travels well and this makes LVMH more global than Carrefour or Wal-Mart.

Table 5.6. The world's largest retail companies by nature of international operations

companies	origin	rank in Global 500	sales in bn $	int'l sales in bn $	int'l sales in % of tot sales	sales Nafta in bn $	in % of tot sales	sales EUROPE in bn $	in % of tot sales	sales ASIA PACIFIC in bn $	in % of tot sales
domestic firms											
Kroger	NAFTA/US	56	50.1	0	0	50.1	100	0	0	0	0
Target	NAFTA/US	89	39.9	0	0	39.9	100	0	0	0	0
Albertsons	NAFTA/US	100	37.9	0	0	37.9	100	0	0	0	0
Kmart	NAFTA/US	104	36.1	0	0	36.2	100	0	0	0	0
Walgreen	NAFTA/US	183	24.6	0	0	24.6	100	0	0	0	0
CVS	NAFTA/US	215	22.2	0	0	22.2	100	0	0	0	0
Lowes	NAFTA/US	216	22.1	0	0	22.1	100	0	0	0	0
Best Buy	NAFTA/US	247	19.6	0	0	19.6	100	0	0	0	0
Federated DPT STO	NAFTA/US	292	16.9	0	0	16.9	100	0	0	0	0
George Weston	NAFTA/CA	318	15.9	0	0	15.900	100	0	0	0	0
Publix Supermark	NAFTA/US	328	15.3	0	0	15.300	100	0	0	0	0
Rite Aid	NAFTA/US	331	15.2	0	0	15.200	100	0	0	0	0
May Dpt Stores	NAFTA/US	351	14.2	0	0	14.200	100	0	0	0	0
Winn Dixie Stores	NAFTA/US	398	12.9	0	0	12.900	100	0	0	0	0
Circuit City Stores	NAFTA/US	403	12.8	0	0	12.800	100	0	0	0	0
Coles Myer	ASPAC/AU	406	12.6	0	0	0	0	0	0	12.600	100
Safeway	Eur/GB	418	12.3	0	0	0	0	12.300	100	0	0
Woolworths	ASPAC/AU	442	11.5	0	0	0	0	0	0	11.5	100
Home-based firms											
Carrefour	Eur/FR	35	62.2	31.639	50.8	n/s	n/s	50.830	81.3	4.111	6.6
Metro AG	Eur/Ger	72	44.3	18.937	42.7	0	0	43.106	97.3	1.000	2.25
Kingfisher	Eur/GB	314	16.1	6.601	40.2	0.13[e]	0.8[e]	16.377[e]	98.3[e]	0.09[e]	0.6[e]
Groupe Auchan	Eur/FR	199	23.4	8.4	35.5	na	na	23.462[e]	99.5[e]	na	na
Great Atlantic and Pacific Tea	NAFTA/US	458	11	3,127[e]	28.5	11.000	100	0	0	0	0
Groupe Casino	Eur/FR	231	20.5	5.088	25	2.1	10.2	16.118	78.8	1.065	5.2
Staples	NAFTA/US	469	10.7	2.265	21.2	9.900	92.5	800	7.5	0	0
Office Depot	NAFTA/US	450	11.1	1.552	21	5.843[e]	79[e]	n/s	n/s	n/s	n/s

Gap Inc.	NAFTA/US	363	13.8	2.349	17[e]	12.200	88.4	1.0[e]	7.7[e]	0.54[e]	3.9[e]
Toys R Us	NAFTA/US	457	11	1.900	17	9.100	83	n/s	n/s	n/s	n/s
J Sainsbury	Eur/UK	184	24.6	4.100	16.7	4.1	16.7	20.500	83.3	0	0
Wal-Mart	NAFTA/US	1	219.8	35.486	16.3	204.9[e]	94.1[e]	10.439[e]	4.8[e]	0.846[e]	0.4[e]
Tesco	Eur/UK	114	33.9	5.208	15.4	0	0	31.73	93.6	2.17	6.4
Itochu	ASPAC/JP	17	91.2	0.218	15	0	0	0	0	1.460	100
Marks and Spencer	Eur/GB	439	11.7	2.7	13.7	0	0	10.26[e]	87.7[e]	1[e]	8.6[e]
Sears Roebuck	NAFTA/US	83	41.1	5.179	12.6	41.1	100	0	0	0	0
Safeway	NAFTA/US	113	34.3	4.116[e]	12	34.3	100	0	0	0	0
TJX	NAFTA/US	470	10.7	1.220[e]	11.4	10.179	95	521	5	0	0
Aeon	ASPAC/JP	196	23.6	2.596	11	1.7	7[e]	0	0	21.948	93
Karstadt Quelle	Eur/Ger	347	14.4	1.621	11	0	0	14.4	100	0	0
Migros	Eur/CH	427	12	1.08	9	0	0	12	100	0	0
Home Depot	NAFTA/US	46	53.6	3.323[e]	6.2	53.6	100	0	0	0	0
JC Penney	NAFTA/US	124	32.6	498	1.6	31.6	98.6	0	0	0	0
Daiei	ASPAC/JP	237	20.1	0.2	1	0.1	0.5	0	0	20	99.5
Otto Versand	Eur/Ger	372	13.6	7.5	55	3.7	27.4	9.33[e]	68.6[e]	0.5[e]	4[e]
Pinault Printemps											
Redoute	Eur/FR	181	24.9	13.678	54.7	5.31	21.2	17.289	69.1	1.381	5.6
Ito Yokado	ASPAC/JP	161	26.8	9.962	40	9.8	39	0	0	15.087	61
Bi-regional firms											
Royal Ahold	Eur/NL	38	59.6	50.931	85	35.3	59.2	19.621	32.8	354	0.6
Delhaize le Lion	Eur/BE	245	19.6	16.161	84	14.9	77	4.214	22	183	1
Global											
C Dior/LVMH	Eur/FR	446	11.2	10	83.4	3.13	26	4.222	35	3.739	31
No data available											
Marubeni	ASPAC/JP	25	71.8	na	na	na	na	na	na	na	na

Note: The home-based and bi-regional firms are ranked in decreasing order of ratio international sales/total sales.

Case 5.3

LVMH: the only global retailer

LVMH is the French-based world leading luxury goods group that was founded in 1987 through the merger of Louis Vuitton and Moët Hennessy. In 2000 the group had sales of 11.6 billion euros – up from 8.5 billion euros in 1999 – and captured 15% of the world market share of luxury items (including wines). LVMH currently employs around 53,000 people, most of whom work outside of France, and the company generates the bulk of its sales in foreign markets. Indeed, only 16% of all revenues are earned in France and an additional 18% originate in the rest of Europe. The United States accounts for 26% of sales, while Japan accounts for another 15%. The remaining 25% is generated primarily in Asia and Latin America. In other words, the group fits the definition of a global company with a balance of sales in each part of the triad.

One benefit of this global presence is a more diversified market risk. This helped the group as a whole to overcome the Asian crisis in 1998, as this recession severely affected its retail division in the region.

Customers everywhere recognize LVMH's famous brand names such as Christian Dior, Dom Perignon, Givenchy, and Moët and Chandon. And LVMH's wide array of international products are so successful that it currently holds 15% of the world market for luxury goods. This market grows by about 10% annually, and it attracts strong competitors, including star brand names like Gucci, owned by PPR; Richemont, the Cartier's owner; and Bulgari.

To be successful in this industry, it is very important to have an effective organizing strategy. In 1990, the four fashion houses of the group operated ten wholly-owned stores in the ten largest cities of the world. Today Christian Dior alone runs 116 stores. The group left a pure manufacturing and marketing strategy to also integrate a retail dynamic that totally changed its organization and the structure of its margins.

LVMH's organizational arrangement is much more than that of a typical conglomerate. The whole organization focuses on shared costs and synergies, both backward and forward of its value chain. It has organized itself around its five main lines of business. These groups, which are really strategic business units

(SBUs), are set up so that they can sell nationally known, high-quality products in a way that both addresses local cultural tastes and takes local rules and regulations into consideration. These five SBUs include:

(1) *The LVMH Fashion and Leather Goods* SBU which owns such world-famous brand names as Louis Vuitton, Loewe, Celine, Berluti, Kenzo, Givenchy, Christian Lacroix, Marc Jacobs, Fendi, StefanoBi, Emilio Pucci, and Thomas Pink.
(2) *The Wines and Spirits* SBU which markets such offerings as Moët and Chandon, Dom Pérignon, Veuve Clicquot, Krug, Pommery, Mercier, Ruinart, Canard Duchêne, Château d'Yquem, Chandon Estates, Cloudy Bay, Cape Mentelle, Hennessy, Hine, Newton, and MountAdam.
(3) *The Perfumes and Cosmetics* SBU which sells Parfums Christian Dior, Guerlain, Parfums Givenchy, Parfums Kenzo, Bliss, Hard Candy, BeneFit Cosmetics, Urban Decay, Fresh, and Make Up For Ever.
(4) *The Watches and Jewelry* SBU which markets such brands as TAG Heuer, Ebel, Zenith, Benedom, Fred, Chaumet, and Omas.
(5) *The Selective Retailing* SBU which includes a wide variety of operations including Duty Free Shops, Miami Cruiseline, Sephora Europe, Sephora AAP, Le Bon Marché, La Samaritaine, and Solstice.

The profit margin on luxury goods is very high so control over production, distribution, and advertising are central to profitability. In the manufacture of its high-quality merchandise, for example, LVMH ensures that production standards are the highest, and the use of its "Made in France" label is used appropriately to appeal to its market niches. The country-specific advantage is obvious, and it materializes globally entailing so little adaptation in the group's forward strategy. Because it only sources in France, Italy, and Switzerland, LVMH products have the appeal to quality and luxury of these countries. To source in third world countries would create a number of problems, including a decrease in status and the potential loss of intellectual property through opportunistic suppliers or copy cats. The company also markets its brand names internationally so that buyers everywhere are familiar with them. One way it does this is by setting aside 11% of all sales to be used exclusively for advertising. On a centralized basis, LVMH also uses a common laboratory for cosmetics research, purchases bulk media products – to receive the most value for its promotion dollar – and integrates the operations for all of the branch offices in each group to ensure maximum efficiency.

By carefully overseeing major operations from the top while allowing the individual SBUs to make those decisions that directly affect their own local markets, it has maximized its international presence and become the most global retail company. This international presence has come at a cost but may well pay off in the longer run. The key indicator is a 100% drop in the group's profitability between 1997 and 2001 that coincides with the boost given in the retailing direction through the acquisition of the US-based Duty Free Shops (DFS). When the deal was settled in 1997, the goal was to grab the hefty Asia-Pacific travel market, as DFS had 180 airport concessions in this area. The timing was bad, however, and when the Asian crisis and a persistent Japanese recession hit the Japanese travel business, the investment became a burden. Furthermore, some customers were put off by new DFS-LVMH-products – only types of "luxury supermarkets." Some competitors were reluctant to sell through the LVMH network. To compensate for lost sales revenues in the Pacific, and after closing down fifteen concessions and firing 3,000 employees, the management decided in 1999 to launch the DFS Galleria in major US tourist centers. These are small downtown shopping malls for luxury items. In addition, Sephora Inc, LVMH's beauty retail chain, was started. The main US department stores, JC Penney or Federated Department Stores, however, perceived these steps as a declaration of war; all of a sudden, their supplier became their competitor. Some cosmetic vendors like Chanel or Estée Lauder even refused to sell at Sephora.

Although LVMH is a global company in terms of sales, it takes on a different strategy in two of its most important host-nations: the United States and Japan. Approximately half of its US and Japanese distribution is achieved through concessions at key department stores such as Neiman Marcus, Saks, Mitsukoshi, and Seibu. In non-triad areas, such as in the Gulf Region, franchizing is a key strategy.

Bernard Arnault's vision of a totally integrated group is necessary to become an industry leader, which also requires innovative management and new international alliances. By internalizing the new multi-brand retail business, the management made some mistakes and maybe went too fast. But LVMH has benefited from this experience to become a true global retailer.

Sources: Adapted from http://www.lvmh.com; "The Sweet Smell of Success," *Business Week*, July 16, 2001; Carol Matlack, "Identity Crisis at LVMH?" *Business Week*, December 11, 2000; "European Luxury Goods" *Merrill Lynch Equities*, May 2001

Questions for discussion

1. Is LVMH a multinational enterprise? Why?
2. Is LVMH a "global" or a "regional" business? Why?
3. What type of firm-specific advantages and country-specific advantages does LVMH possess? Are they "global," "regional," or "local"? Why?
4. What is LVMH's basic strategy?
5. What is LVMH'S basic structure?
6. Can LVMH compete successfully with local retailers in North America, Europe, and Asia?
7. How does LVMH's home-country affect its competitiveness?
8. How would outsourcing to less developed countries affect LVMH?
9. What are some of the LVMH's CSAs that are listed in this case? Can you think of any others?
10. What are some of the LVMH's FSAs that are listed in this case?
11. Can you think of a way in which LVMH can be argued to not be a global company?

CONCLUSION

The empirical data show no evidence of globalization in the retail sector. Of the forty-nine retailers regarded as "global" in the *Fortune* 500 list, eighteen are purely domestic; twenty-seven are very concentrated in

Case 5.4

Carrefour: a regional retailer in Europe

Anyone observing French retail giant Carrefour over the last three decades must concede that international expansion is a key part of its strategic plan. Today, it has 9,200 stores in thirty countries. Despite this, only 18.7% of Carrefour's revenues originate outside of Europe. Of these, 6.6% are derived from Asia, with the rest being unclassified.

In 1996, the French government introduced the "Raffarin Law" restricting the expansion of hypermarkets. The aim was to maintain the French countryside from turning into large warehouse style retail structures and to protect urban shopkeepers. This was also a regulation to protect the French way of life in which local food farmers supply small local shops. For Carrefour, this meant that growth of its hypermarket business could only come from acquisitions in its local market or from expanding into foreign markets.

In the United States, Carrefour opened three hypermarkets in Pennsylvania and closed them as a result of local competition. In its home region of Europe, however, Carrefour is the number one retailer in Spain, Portugal, and Greece, and the second largest retailer in Italy.

Carrefour was the first western hypermarket company to expand into the Asian market in the mid 1990s. By 2001, it was the third largest retailer in China and had operations in Thailand and Japan. The company bet that Asian customers would be willing to move from their traditional outdoor markets to purchase at air-conditioned and "all in one roof" hypermarkets. Its hypermarkets relied on local suppliers that can offer products at the same price level as those that supply the local competition. For their part, local suppliers were all too ready to enter contracts with Carrefour, which promises to put its products in shelves across the Asian region. Moreover, where local contacts are not readily available, Carrefour's competitive advantage comes from centralized purchasing and other logistics.

Since products are offered in a comfortable environment at competitive prices, the local competition is nothing to worry about. In fact, Carrefour is more concerned about competition from other western retailers such as Wal-Mart and Tesco. Both Tesco and Carrefour raced to open the first hypermarket in the Thai market and basically tied. Now both their hypermarkets face each other in a busy Bangkok street. If they want to survive on the long haul, however, western companies should always be wary of potential local or regional competitors. In Hong Kong, where Jardine Matheson and Li Ka-shing dominate the market, Carrefour was forced to close operations.

The benefits of international expansion are not clear. While Carrefour's operating margins in France were about 6% in 1999, its Asian and Latin American hypermarkets, as well as some of its European operations, were losing money. In particular, the company was hit by the Asian crisis, which also contributed to a Latin American recession.

The promise of scale economies is unlikely to materialize at a global basis. This is because to cater to local tastes, hypermarkets must purchase from local producers. This tying into the local economy also helps protect their investment from nationalist factions who might risk the collapsing of local suppliers with the ousting of a foreign company.

Sources: www.carrefour.com; Carrefour, Annual Report, 2001; "French fusion," The Economist, September 2, 1999; "A hypermarket," The Economist, April 5, 2001.

Questions for discussion

1. Is Carrefour a multinational enterprise? Why?
2. Is Carrefour a "global" or a "regional" business? Why?
3. What is Carrefour's basic structure?
4. What is Carrefour's basic strategy?
5. What strategy does Carrefour need to succeed in Europe?
6. How did the domestic and home-region environment influence Carrefour to expand internationally?
7. How can Carrefour compete with local retailers in North America?
8. How can Carrefour compete with local retailers in Asia?

their home region of the triad; only two are bi-regional; and only one is global. This is not evidence of globalization but of regional business, indeed mainly localized retail business. While the retail industry is becoming more "international", and there is a new need for firms to expand abroad to generate new growth, this is not "global" activity. Most of the international expansion is within the local home region of the retail MNE. International business is not synonymous with global business. Instead a regional solution to strategy is required.

6 Banking multinationals

Contents

Over the last twenty years, a trend to open domestic markets to competition has propelled a number of financial services firms to expand internationally. This has mainly been accomplished through cross-border mergers and acquisitions. Despite this liberalization, financial services continue to be highly localized in their home region. Not only are financial companies more localized than manufacturing companies, but they are also less likely to expand within their own region than are most industries in the manufacturing sector.

Nonetheless, more than ever, financial firms have now diversified their activities across many business lines. As a result of liberalization within markets, financial firms now offer commercial banking, investment banking, and insurance services. This makes an examination of a firm's global scope even more difficult as some business lines exhibit more international diversification than others.

The data offered in this chapter show that financial institutions continue to be localized in their revenue generation, and that this is true for most of their business lines. Larger banks, the data also show, are more likely to engage in significant operations across regions.

Of the 200 service MNEs for which information is available, there are forty in the banking industry and twenty-seven in other financial industries, see table 6.1.

Table 6.1. The top 500 MNEs, by industry			
industry category	no. of firms in the fortune 500	no. of firms in the RNGMA	% of total
manufacturing	206	180	87.4
1 aerospace and defense	11	11	100.0
2 chemicals and pharmaceuticals	19	18	94.7
3 computer, office and electronics	39	36	92.3
4 construction, building materials and glass	12	11	91.7
5 energy, petroleum and refining	43	31	72.1
6 food, drug and tobacco	18	14	77.8
7 motor vehicle and parts	31	29	93.5
8 other manufacturing	13	13	100.0
9 natural resource manufacturing	20	17	85.0
Services	294	200	68.0
1 banks	62	40	64.5
2 entertainment, printing and publishing	9	9	100.0
3 merchandisers	77	63	81.8
4 other financial services	58	27	46.6
5 other services	25	21	84.0
6 telecommunications and utilities	43	27	62.8
7 transportation services	20	13	65.0
Total	500	380	76.0

As shown in table 6.2, none of the forty banks for which data are available in the top 500 are global; indeed, thirty-nine are classified as "home-region oriented," with a majority of their sales in their home region of the triad. Of these, five banks derive all their revenues from within their home region. One bank is "host-region oriented," as the European bank, Santander, has 55.7% of its sales in the Americas, mainly Latin America. Across all the 40 banks, the average home-region sales figure is 78.3%.

Figure 6.1 shows the distribution of the forty banks in terms of extra-regional sales and revenues. Higher percentages of extra-regional sales are associated with higher revenues. Thus a large degree of resources is necessary to significantly access foreign regions. Among the largest banks, European banks have a higher level of extra-regional sales than North American banks.

There are data for another twenty-seven financial services companies in the top 500. These include diversified financials, insurance, and securities companies. Again, all but one of these are home-region oriented. But ING, a European insurance company, has 51.4% of its sales in North America. Across all twenty-seven financial institutions the average home-region sales figure is 71.9%, see table 6.3.

Figure 6.2 shows the relationship between size and global scope for the twenty-seven financial service companies not classified as banks. As

Table 6.2. The regional nature of the banking industry

	500 rank	company	region	revenues in bn US$	F/T sales	% intra regional	North America % of total sales	Europe % of total sales	Asia-Pacific % of total sales
host-region oriented									
1	136	Santander Central Hispano Group	Europe	30.4	66.1	44.3	55.7[l]	44.3	na
home-region oriented									
1	27	Deutsche Bank	Europe	66.8	69.0	63.1	29.3	63.1	6.5
2	31	Credit Suisse	Europe	64.2	73.3	60.9	34.9[l]	60.9	4.1
3	47	Bank of America Corp.	North America	52.6	na	92.9	92.9[a]	3.5[m]	2.7
4	54	JP Morgan Chase and Co	North America	50.4	na	67.7	67.7[z]	23.2[m]	6.7
5	59	UBS(q)	Europe	48.5	62.0	58.0	37.0[l]	58.0	5.0
6	82	Mizuho Holdings	Asia-Pacific	41.5	30.3	74.4	19.7	5.8	74.4
7	85	Fortis (q)	Europe	40.5	na	64.3	21.4[z]	64.3	na
8	115	Royal Bank of Scotland	Europe	33.8	19.0	81.0	12.0[z]	81.0[u]	na
9	137	Sumitomo Mitsui Banking	Asia-Pacific	30.2	22.4	83.4	11.1[l]	5.6	83.4
10	150	HBOS	Europe	27.8	7.9	92.1	na	92.1[u]	na
11	154	Barclays	Europe	27.6	na	88.0	6.0[z]	88.0	na
12	165	Mitsubishi Tokyo Financial Group	Asia-Pacific	26.1	na	64.4	23.6	7.0	64.4
13	168	DZ Bank	Europe	26.0	na	85.6	na	85.6	na
14	174	UFJ Holdings (q)	Asia-Pacific	25.3	29.4	78.5	15.5	6.1	78.5
15	186	Bank One Corp.	North America	24.5	na	100.0	100.0	na	na
16	191	Société Générale	Europe	23.9	na	77.3	15.6	77.3	3.6
17	193	Commerzbank	Europe	23.8	na	85.5	8.5	85.5	3.0
18	201	Westdeutsche Landesbank	Europe	23.1	na	80.0	12.8	80.0	5.1
19	206	Lloyds TSB Group	Europe	22.8	na	81.2	na	81.2[u]	na
20	211	Wachovia Corp.	North America	22.4	na	100.0	100.0	–	–

21	242	IntesaBci	Europe	19.9	31.6	80.4	na	80.4	na
22	259	Crédit Lyonnais	Europe	18.8	28.0	82.0	8.0	82.0	7.0
23	272	Almanij	Europe	18.1	21.0	97.9	1.9	97.9	–
24	280	Abbey National	Europe	17.8	4.0	99.5	0.5	99.5	–
25	283	Washington Mutual	North America	17.7	na	100.0	100.0	na	na
26	294	Landesbank Baden-Wurtemberg	Europe	16.9	na	94.8	2.7	94.8	2.5
27	299	Royal Bank of Canada (q)	North America	16.5	28.3	71.7	71.7[c]	na	na
28	304	US Bancorp	North America	16.4	na	100.0	100.0	–	–
29	320	Bayerische Landesbank	Europe	15.8	na	82.1	12.9[z]	82.1	5.2
30	361	CIBC	North America	13.9	39.8	79.7	79.7[a]	na	na
31	366	Bank of Nova Scotia (q)	North America	13.7	35.9	71.2	71.2[a]	na	na
32	370	Toronto-Dominion Bank	North America	13.6	28.5	86.6	86.6[a]	na	na
33	395	Norinchukin Bank	Asia-Pacific	12.9	na	90.6	2.2	7.2	90.6
34	419	Nordea	Europe	12.2	na	100.0	na	100.0	na
35	449	Bank of Montreal (q)	North America	11.2	46.5	70.7	70.7[a]	na	na
36	461	Danske Bank Group (q)	Europe	10.9	27.5	94.3	5.1	94.3	0.6
37	463	Daiwa Bank Holdings	Asia	10.9	<10	>90	na	na	>90[j]
38	473	Bankgesellschaft Berlin (q)	Europe	10.6	22.2	77.8	na	77.8	na
39	475	Norddeutsche Landesb. (q)	Europe	10.6	18.9	94.8	2.9	94.8	2.3
Weighted Average*				25.3		78.3			
Total				1,010.9					

Notes: [q] UBS: Calculated using data on operating income from the Annual Report; Fortis: Europe is Belgium, The Netherlands and Luxembourg. Numbers are estimates using total revenues, net of interest expense; UFI: Estimated using ordinary income figures from the Annual Report; Royal Bank of Canada: Revenues are estimated using gross revenues as reported in the Annual Report; Bank of Montreal: Estimated using net income business as reported in the Annual Report; Bank of Nova Scotia: Revenues are estimated using income figures as reported in the Annual Report; Bankgesellschaft Berlin: Estimated using income data as reported in the Annual Report. Data for Europe only include Germany; Norddeutsche Landesb: Data are calculated using income figures as reported in the Annual Report. [a] refers to Canada and the United States; [c] refers to Canada only; [z] refers to the United States only; [l] refers to the Americas; [u] refers to the United Kingdom only; [m] refers to Europe, the Middle East and Africa; [j] refers to Japan only. Weighted intra-regional sales average is weighted according to revenues. Data are for 2001.

Figure 6.1. Size and international scope in the banking industry

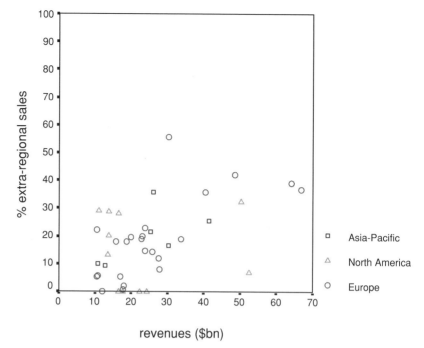

revenues ($bn)

is the case with banks, larger firms are more likely to exhibit a higher percentage of extra-regional sales. In addition, European firms once again show higher levels of extra-regional sales than their North American and Asian counterparts.

The issue of transfer pricing – the artificial reporting of profit across taxation jurisdictions that is prevalent in financial services – puts in doubt the integrity of our conclusions. Unfortunately, other financial indicators of a firm's global scope, such as profit, are exposed to the same problem. Non-financial indicators, such as the number of employees, may also not represent the true importance of a given region if some of the international operations are processed in another region. Similarly, other indicators might not provide a full picture of a firm's expansion because they are only relevant to a line of business. Bank branches might provide insight into the regional retail operations of a bank but might not represent other lines of business, such a credit cards, securities, or insurance. This chapter uses revenues for all cases except for Citigroup, which reports income.

BARRIERS TO GLOBAL EXPANSION IN THE BANKING INDUSTRY

The banking and other financial services industry does not export material goods, and for that reason, tariff barriers to trade have no direct

Table 6.3. The regional nature of other financial services industries

	500 rank	company	region	revenues in bn US$	F/T sales	% intra regional	North America % of total sales	Europe % of total sales	Asia-Pacific % of total sales
host-region oriented									
1	20	ING Group	Europe	83.0	77.3	35.1	51.4	35.1	3.4
home-region oriented									
1	9	General Electric	North America	125.9	40.9	59.1	59.1[z]	19.0	9.1
2	18	Allianz	Europe	85.9	69.4	78.0	17.6[l]	78.0	4.4[f]
3	30	AXA (q)	Europe	65.6	77.3	51.2	24.1[z]	51.2	19.9
4	34	American International Group	North America	62.4	na	59.0	59.0[a]	na	na
5	50	Assicurazioni Generali (q)	Europe	51.4	67.2	91.4	1.7[a]	91.4	na
6	52	Fannie Mae	North America	50.8	–	100.0	100.0[z]	–	–
7	63	State Farm Insurance Cos.	North America	46.7	–	100.0	100.0	–	–
8	73	Morgan Stanley (q)	North America	43.7	25.0	75.0	75.0[z]	17.9	6.3
9	79	Munich Re Group (q)	Europe	41.9	54.7	72.3	19.3	72.3	4.1
10	95	Merrill Lynch (q)	North America	38.8	31.0	73.0	73.0	16.6[m]	8.7
11	96	Zurich Financial Services	Europe	38.7	na	51.0	38.3	51.0	na
12	132	Goldman Sachs Group	North America	31.1	35.6	65.9	65.9[l]	25.0	9.1
13	144	Allstate	North America	28.9	na	100.0	100.0[a]	na	na
14	157	Prudential Financial	North America	27.2	17.0	83.0	83.0[z]	na	13.3[j]
15	209	American Express	North America	22.6	24.7	75.3	75.3	11.0	6.5
16	212	Lehman Brothers Hldgs.	North America	22.4	37.0	63.0	63.0[z]	29.0	na

(cont.)

Table 6.3. Continued

	500 rank	company	region	revenues in bn US$	F/T sales	% intra regional	North America % of total sales	Europe % of total sales	Asia-Pacific % of total sales
17	222	Royal and Sun Alliance	Europe	21.5	55.1	64.8	27.1[l]	64.8	na
18	260	Loews	North America	18.8	–	100.0	100.0[a]	na	na
19	330	Mitsui Sumitomo Insurance	Asia-Pacific	15.2	2.0	98.0	na	na	98.0[j]
20	359	Household International	North America	13.9	9.2	92.5	92.5[a]	na	na
21	432	Power Corp. of Canada	North America	11.9	32.4	100.0	100.0[a]	–	–
22	440	Cathay Life	Asia	11.6	–	100.0	–	–	100.0
23	445	Yasuda Fire and Marine Insurance (q)	Asia	11.3	–	100.0	–	–	100.0
24	453	Old Mutual (q)	Europe/Other	11.1	6.6	93.4	na	na	na
25	465	Sun Life Financial Services	North America	10.9	76.9	83.5	83.5[a]	12.4	2.8
26	483	Manulife Financial (q)	North America	10.5	70.3	71.1	71.1[a]	na	20.1
Weighted Average*				37.2		71.9			
Total				1,003.6					

Notes: [a] AXA: Europe represents France, the UK, Germany and Belgium. An additional category "other countries" might include other European nations; Assicurazioni Generali: Used premium income (€45.6 billion) to estimate geographic distribution of revenues; Morgan Stanley: Estimated using geographic information on premiums (totaling €36.1 billion). This represents 84% of revenues; Merrill Lynch: Estimated using net revenues from Annual Report; Yasuda Fire and Marine Insurance: Now part of Sompo, the Annual Report describes overseas sales as immaterial and does not report them; Manulife Financial: The data are estimated using sales by division (US, Canada and Asia) as reported in the Annual Report. [a] refers to Canada and the United States; [z] refers to the United States only. [l] refers to the Americas; [f] includes Africa; [m] refers to Europe, the Middle East and Africa; [j] refers to Japan only. Weighted intra-regional sales average is weighted according to revenues. Data are for 2001.

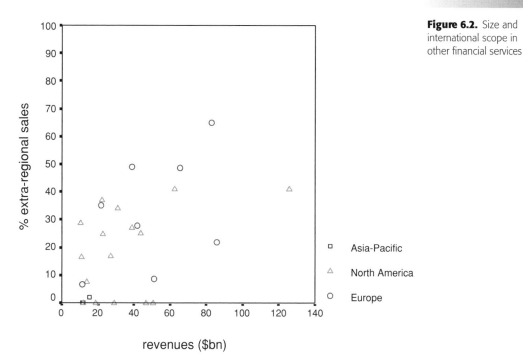

Figure 6.2. Size and international scope in other financial services

impact on the industry. Non-tariff barriers to trade, such as government regulations and the domestic environment (including business, cultural, and language differences) are the relevant issues for an analysis of international expansion. These non-tariff barriers to trade make foreign direct investment the primary means of international expansion in the banking and financial services industry.

Around the world, all governments heavily regulate their banking and financial services industries. Some of these regulations are uniform to all banks while others specifically target foreign banks. Restrictions on licensing, for instance, might make the emergence of a new, domestic, or foreign bank very difficult while limitations on branch expansion by foreign banks target non-domestic banks. Similarly, some nations limit the share of the equity in a bank that can be held by any one shareholder, regardless of nationality, while other nations specifically limit the amount of foreign ownership allowed in a bank. Interstate banking restrictions in the United States, which have now been overturned, made a large presence by a foreign bank difficult across state lines. Restrictions on the types of services that a bank may provide also limit the ability of foreign banks to expand across all its business lines. These restrictions have at times been extra-territorial, as was the case pre-1999 in the United States when a foreign bank could not merge with a securities or insurance firm in its own region and continue to operate in the United States. Some countries specifically restrict the types of services a foreign bank might provide in preference to its domestic banks. China, for example, restricts foreign banks' participation in local currency operations. There are many layers of regulations that may affect the ability of a bank to expand into foreign regions, and this is one factor that undermines the possibility of attaining economies of scale in foreign regions.

A related issue is whether a service company, depending on key human resources and capital, can effectively compete in a foreign country in the long run. In developing countries, access to capital is particularly scarce, and domestic banks in these countries may be unstable and lack the trust of citizens. In this case, a trusted foreign bank might have a competitive advantage over its domestic counterparts. This advantage can allow the foreign bank to expand in the country's development years to become a large player with good knowledge of the market at future stages of development. An example of this advantage can be seen in Citibank's acquisition of Banamex in Mexico. Shortly after the merger, the company gained 1.5 million client accounts. Similarly, the previously state-run banks of Brazil gained credibility after being auctioned to large foreign banks with stable reputations.

Across triad regions, however, international expansion in the financial sector is less likely. The United States and EU both have trusted domestic banks and human resources personnel that tailor products to their domestic market. Organic growth is unlikely to be a successful entry strategy because of the established domestic competition. Foreign banks are more likely to undertake acquisitions of already established banks in the market. This is still a risky strategy. The success of the acquired subsidiary depends on the human resources within it. Foreign banks must be cautious and provide enough autonomy to the subsidiary to continue providing competitive locally-responsive products. Corporate cultural clashes have seen much of an acquisition evaporate in terms of human resources.

Still in question is whether the inter-triad exchange of ownership brings with it any economies of scale that cannot be achieved through expanding intra-regionally. Traditionally, an assumption is made that diversifying into foreign markets decreases risk. It is highly probable, however, that this benefit is outweighed by the burden of overcoming regulations and information costs, including cultural and language differences. In addition, most firm-specific advantages are not transferable to other triad regions which have competitive financial industries of their own. Only in developing countries, where fiscal instability has led many consumers to distrust local financial institutions, can the reputation of these companies provide a true competitive advantage. Even here, banks are restricted from entering some business lines or are unwilling to enter risky businesses. The relative size of these markets with respect to the foreign bank's home-region market makes the significance of these developing regions small in drafting overall strategy.

SIZE AND INTERNATIONAL SCOPE

Figure 6.1 and figure 6.2 map the relationship between revenues and extra-regional sales for triad firms in the banking and other financial services industries, respectively. European firms are represented by a circle. Triangles represent North American firms. Asian firms are marked by a square. In Figure 6.1, based on the 40 banks of Table 6.2, higher percentages of extra-regional sales are associated with higher revenues signaling that a large degree of resources is necessary to significantly access foreign regions in the banking industry. Among the largest banks, European banks have a higher level of extra-regional sales than North American banks. Indeed, all banks with over 40% of their sales in foreign regions are European.

Figure 6.2 shows the relationship between size and global scope for the 27 financial service companies in Table 6.3 not classified as banks. As is the case for banks, larger firms are more likely to exhibit a higher percentage of extra-regional sales. In addition, European firms once again show higher levels of extra-regional sales than their North American and Asian counterparts.

CASES

We now discuss five cases: Citigroup, Deutsche Bank, Bank of America, Crédit Suisse, and JP Morgan Chase. These are the five largest banks in the top 500 list.

Citigroup

Overcoming cultural barriers, different regulations, and financial systems makes establishing a truly global bank very difficult. No one has done it as well as Citigroup's Citibank. Formed in 1998 by the merger of Citicorp and Travellers Group, in 2001 Citigroup was the largest financial MNE, and it had a presence in over 100 countries around the world.

Citigroup is a financial services holding company whose activities are conducted through four business segments: global consumer, global corporate and investment bank, private client services, global investment management, and proprietary investment activities. In turn, each of these business units is further segmented. The global consumer unit, for instance, includes cards, consumer finance, and retail banking (including Citibank) while the global investment management arm includes life insurance and annuities, private bank, and asset management.

Despite its global scope, Citigroup is a very home-region based North American business, and this is true in virtually every line of business.

Table 6.4. International operations of Citigroup: consumer banking division (% of total)

country/region	revenue	no. of accounts	deposits
NAFTA	72.7	77.1	45.5
Japan	8.9	3.3	10.2
other Asia	5.8	6.2	24.2
Western Europe	6.8	6.4	9.1
Latin America	3.6	4.5	7.1
other	2.2	2.5	4.0
Total	100.0	100.0	100.0

Source: Citigroup, Annual Report, 2001.

Indeed, Citibank became less global after the merger with Travellers in 1999 as the latter's insurance business was very localized, and this offset much of Citibank's banking diversification in South America and Asia. In 2002, Citigroup also acquired Banamex, one of the largest banks in Mexico, further strengthening its position within the NAFTA region. Today, 69% of the group's income is derived from within the North American free trade area. Within Citigroup's largest segment, Global Consumer, 73.1% of income is derived from North America. Similarly, 88% of all global investment management income was derived from Citigroup's home region. Together, 51.9% of the income derived from its global corporate and investment bank and its private client services was intra-regional.

Table 6.4 displays data on Citigroup's regional indicators for its consumer banking division. Over 70% of the company's revenue is derived from its home region of the triad. NAFTA also accounts for 77.1% of all accounts, but only for 45.5% of all deposits.

In 2002, Citigroup International (which reports revenues outside of North America) had revenues of $21.5 million, or slightly over 30% of total revenues. Customer accounts outside of North America total $50 million. No region outside of North America accounts for a significantly large portion of revenues.

Table 6.5 shows the foreign-to-total ratio of a number of Citigroup's business lines. In all areas, except for commercial loans, the United States accounts for over 50% of the group's operations.

Prior to the merger with Travellers, Citibank's presence in developing countries was relatively more important. The success of that line of business should be analyzed with particular reference to the company's ability to capture market share in developing countries, as opposed to other countries in the triad. Table 6.4 above reports that 24% of Citibank's consumer banking deposits originate in non-industrialized countries in Asia. This is a higher percentage than for Western Europe or Japan. In addition, Citigroup has almost twice as many branches and offices outside the core triad markets as it does in its own home region.

Citibank enters a developing country with its own marketing strategy. In the first stage of development, the bank caters to the global customer (usually a large corporation) by providing short-term loans, cash management, and foreign exchange services. During a country's second stage of development, as demand grows in the face of a burgeoning middle class, Citibank begins to offer personal financial products.

Table 6.5. Selected indicators of Citigroup's international scope average volume in millions of dollars

indicator	US	foreign	US as a% of total
investments	95,781	38,822	71.2
brokerage receivables	25,058	2,517	90.9
trading account assets	81,241	37,304	68.5
trading of federal funds and securities	104,150	34,087	75.3
consumer loans	151,837	79,782	65.6
commercial loans	53,834	91,867	36.9
employees	149,000	123,000	54.8

Source: Citigroup, Annual Report, 2001.

Citibank's experience in China illustrates the political risk of foreign expansion and the company's international expansion strategy. Citibank opened its first office in China in 1902 but was thrown out by the new Chinese communist government of Chairman Mao in 1949. Even after Citibank was allowed back into the country, its business was mainly restricted to foreign currency. China's market potential, however, always attracted the bank, and when the country began to show interest in opening its borders and joining the WTO, Citibank stepped in as a key broker in negotiations with the US government. The bank's efforts are paying off. In the 1990s, the Chinese began to open their economy and make commitments for further reforms. By 2001, import tariffs had been decreased to an average of 15% from 44% in 1992. Import tariffs are expected to continue to decrease and average 9% by 2006.

Today, the bank's revenue from corporate business in China is still one-fifth of that of South Korea. Deregulation will not only allow Citibank to open fully functional branches, it will also attract the burgeoning MNEs market and local clients. Citibank can also benefit from large local companies who seek to do international business. Among these is Legend, a Chinese PC manufacturer, that today controls over 25% of the domestic market and is yet unknown outside the mainland.

Citibank's second marketing stage for emerging markets is expanding into personal banking. Though personal banking has not yet been deregulated, Citibank is already applying for a license in China. In early 2003, Citibank was the first foreign bank to be granted a license to offer internet banking to foreign and local companies as well as consumers. A significant portion of Citibank's income comes from credit cards. Citibank is hoping that increases in disposable income among middle-class Chinese will prove profitable. Once the credit card market becomes saturated, the bank is likely to move consumers into mortgages, personal loans, pension funds, and other financial products.

Though Citibank has a definite first-mover advantage in the Chinese market, it still faces competition from domestic banks, such as the Industrial and Commercial Bank of China and other large foreign competitors, such as the HSBC, which also has extensive experience in the region. As of 2000, there were seventy-one foreign financial institutions operating in some form in Shanghai.

Citigroup's international expansion into triad markets and non-triad markets is highly dependent on the expansion of MNEs. These MNEs have created a market for a bank that can handle their financial needs across national borders, and this then leads to a stable income generation stream for the bank. Citigroup offers stability and tailored know-how for MNEs that might not be replicated by more locally-focused banks. In fact, only HSBC can claim to have as large a scope of operations in this market niche. Market entry into this niche is blocked by the relatively large investments required for international expansion; know-how and building a reputation must be undertaken to compete successfully. Citigroup and HSBC both entered this market at an early stage, and this first-mover advantage creates a further barrier for more localized banks.

Questions for discussion

1. Is Citigroup an MNE? Why?
2. Does Citigroup's global consumer banking (GCB) sub-segment operate as a multinational business unit? Is it global?
3. What is Citigroup's basic structure?
4. What is Citigroup's basic strategy?
5. What kind of barriers does Citigroup face in the development of a global strategy?
6. How does Citigroup seek to enter developing nations and does this constitute a global strategy?
7. Is Citigroup able to implement all stages of its entry strategy for developing countries in China? Why?
8. List Citigroup's FSAs as described in the case.

Deutsche Bank

In 2002, Deutsche Bank derived 66.9% of its revenues from its home-region market of Europe, half of which was derived from Germany. North America accounted for 24.2% of total revenues. The remainder originated in Asia-Pacific, Africa, and South America. Similarly, although over 60% of the bank's employees reside in foreign countries, 71% are located in Europe. Although Deutsche Bank has customers from seventy-six countries, has aspirations to become a global lending provider and labels itself a "universal bank," it is not a global company, but a home-region company with a significant presence in the United States.

In 1999, Deutsche Bank acquired Bankers Trust for $9.2 billion, more than twice its book value. The move was meant to support global ambitions and improve the group's investment banking arm. At the time, Bankers Trust was the eighth largest US bank, assuring a significant, if not major, presence for Deutsche Bank in the American market. In addition, Deutsche Bank incorporated Bankers Trust's skills in equity underwriting and high-yield debt to its portfolio while strengthening some of its own operations.

Deutsche's drive to become a global bank with strong investment banking capabilities has been supported by other acquisitions. In 1989, Deutsche purchased Morgan Grenfell, a UK based merchant bank. Spain's Banco de Madrid was acquired in 1993, and in 1998 Crédit Lyonnais of Belgium was added to its portfolio. The fall of the USSR also meant that Deutsche could expand not only into East Germany but also into other Eastern European countries. In 1995, Deutsche opened a branch in Warsaw, and a year later a subsidiary was established in Hungary. In Asia, Deutsche Bank acquired a Japanese trust bank and an Australian fund-management company in 1997. More recently, it acquired Scudder, a US asset-management firm in 2002.

Deutsche Bank has 1,711 branches worldwide. In 2002, 936 of these banks were in Germany. Yet, Deutsche is not looking to become a global retail bank. Instead, the firm wants to get out of small-scale banking in Germany altogether and become a global investment power house.

Germany's retail banking system is heavily regulated and fragmented, and despite its size Deutsche accounts for a fraction of domestic deposits. Deutsche Bank is one of four large private German banks that compete with state-owned banks. Competition from mutual and savings banks is likely to result in losses in this market. Meanwhile, guaranteed state-owned regional banks can access funds in capital markets at lower interest rates. With reported costs of 80% of their income, compared to 60% by other European competitors, German banks are continuously ranked at the bottom of the stack. To add to its national complaints, Germany's labor laws make hiring and firing personnel very difficult and costly. This explains the bank's creating of Bank 24 in 1994 to combine its branch network and online banking. This can potentially allow the divestiture of all retail banking operations.

Deutsche is also highly susceptible to the German market and the broader European market. The recent collapse of German companies, including Philipp Holzmann, the Kirch Group, and Fairchild Dornier cost German banks millions.

Deutsche's international ambitions and move into investment banking are heavily driven by regulations in its domestic market. Its past acquisitions and new strategy do not guarantee a carving of this market. Other banks, such as UBS, attempted similar strategies only to find themselves in dire straits. Nonetheless, Deutsche Bank is successful in securities, foreign exchange, and asset management which might provide an edge against competitors. Mergers and acquisitions, however, are a profitable area the bank is hoping to strengthen but has not yet successfully done so. In addition, the acquisition of other localized banks, such as Banker's Trust, does not provide the necessary know-how for global expansion. At best, the bank can hope to gain a bi-regional scope with its European and US arms acquiring know-how in inter-regional transactions across two regions of the triad. Deutsche is now best positioned to become a bi-regional bank with the potential for luring the business of European firms doing business in the United States. Whether or not Deutsche will be able to successfully compete in the US investment banking market, where domestic companies are already world leaders, or to lure US MNEs with operations in Europe, has yet to be seen.

Bank of America

A leading financial services firm, Bank of America's strength is primarily its home-region retail and corporate banking expertise. The bank's thirty international offices, which serve customers in over 150 countries, do not translate into a significant international presence. In 2002, Europe, the Middle East, and Africa accounted for 3.4% of Bank of America's revenues. Asia, Latin America, and the Caribbean accounted for 3.1%. The United States and Canada accounted for 93.5% of all revenues; this represents an increase from 92.9% in 2001. In terms of total assets, 92.5% are located in the United States and Canada.

Between 1986 and 1998, NationsBank negotiated a series of acquisitions to strengthen its domestic position, including Bankers Trust of South Carolina (1986), First Republic Bank of Texas (1988), Missouri's Boatman's Bancshares (1996), Florida's Barnett Banks (1996), and Montgomery Securities (1997). In 1998, the bank's major expansion plans concluded with the purchase of Bank of America, and the new entity took on that name. The timing was right. Regulations that had prevented banks from operating across state borders were completely eliminated in 1994. By 2002, Bank of America was ranked as the largest US bank in terms of branches. Consolidation, however, did not turn into a competitive advantage. The new Bank of America was riddled with bad loans and a cost-cutting strategy to justify the price of acquisitions that jeopardized the quality of its customer service and hampered attempts to expand internationally.

A home-region based company with a national strategy, Bank of America, has a competitive edge in the extremely competitive US retail banking market, but not a significant presence in any foreign market. To further broaden its scale and scope, large investments to diversify its revenue generation and customer base have been undertaken. Nonetheless, significant competition within the related markets has led to only minor penetration by the bank into institutional and investment markets. A growing expertise in asset management and investment banking may play a pivotal role if the bank seeks to become a major global competitor. However, it will be difficult for a product-oriented, low-cost player to compete in the higher-end services that will allow for such growth.

Crédit Suisse Group

Crédit Suisse Group (CSG) origins date back to 1856 when the Schweizerische Kreditanstalt was founded to help finance railway construction and industrialization in Switzerland. CSG rose from being a Swiss railway finance company to one of the world's most revered banks by developing products that meet the diverse needs of corporate, private, and retail customers.

The Swiss banking group utilized its home country's stringent banking/secrecy laws to position itself as an international banking power. While CSG has significant operations in twenty-three countries, based on the distribution of its revenues and assets across the global triad (North America, Europe, and Asia-Pacific), it remains a home-region firm. Europe accounts for 64.5% of CSG's revenues while the Americas account for an additional 28.0%.

The group entered the US market in 1940 by opening a branch in New York. In 1978, CSG began to cooperate with First Boston, Inc. of the United States, and in 1990 it acquired a controlling position in the firm. CSG acquired Donaldson, Lufkin and Jenrette, a US investment bank in 2000. Crédit Suisse First Boston (CSFB), as the US subsidiary of CSG is known, was considered one of the most successful firms in Wall Street during the booming 1990s.

However, by the early 2000s, the company was running into trouble. Along with other banks, it was being investigated over the advice and financing it provided to Enron. CSFB had entered a partnership with Enron that was used to hold unprofitable assets and eventually contributed to the company's bankruptcy. In 2002, the state of Massachusetts brought a civil case against CSFB for fraud, accusing the bank of intentionally giving bad advice to small investors.

In 1999, the Japanese Financial Supervisory Agency (FSA) ordered Crédit Suisse Financial Products (CSFP), the derivatives arm of CSFB, to halt all business in Japan. CSFP combined investment and commercial banking disregarding Japanese law, destroyed documents, and obstructed the FSA investigation. However, the FSA did not order CSFP to indefinitely stop operations as a result of any of these things, but because it deemed the products the CSFP offered were "inappropriate." In 2002, the United Kingdom Financial Services Authority fined Crédit Suisse First Boston International (CSFBI), formerly CSFP, £4 million for attempting to mislead Japanese authorities about the extent of its Japanese operations between 1995 and 1998 and for destroying documents. At the time, this was the highest fine the UK authority had imposed on a firm.

The CSG has had to come to the rescue of its international operations, setting aside hundred of millions of dollars to help CSFB through legal suits. CSG is perhaps one of the best examples of how government regulations and political risk can hinder the banking industry from expanding into foreign markets.

JP Morgan Chase

With $29.6 billion and $1.6 billion in revenues and net income, respectively, JP Morgan Chase is a dominant player in the financial services industry. Today, JP Morgan Chase is globally recognized for its retail and investment banking, a combination of the competitive market position in credit cards, home finance, and auto finance that Chase brought to JP Morgan when the companies merged in 2002. Despite this global reputation, its operations are mainly North American based. In 2002, 73% of its revenues originated in the United States, an increase from 67.7% the year before. Europe, the Middle East, and Africa, on the other hand, only accounted for 17.3%. Asia accounted for a measly 6.4%. The remaining 2.5% of revenues were derived from other regions, including Latin America. In 2001, consumer and commercial loans were 99% and 63% domestic, respectively. The broadened Americas account for 63% of JP Morgan's treasury and security service. Finally, 73% of both investment management and private banking is based in the Americas, mainly in the United States. JP Morgan Chase is another North American regional bank. The group is currently a home-triad based firm that, while recognized for its global expertise, remains locally focused.

Recently, JP Morgan has been attempting to pioneer geographic diversification into developing countries of the financial industry's downstream knowledge base. In 2003, JP Morgan transferred its economic research work to Mumbai, India. By hiring abundant, and underpaid, local financial services workers, JP Morgan hopes to decrease costs while attracting the best graduate economists. Their jobs would consist of providing analysis of companies and research reports for investors. JP Morgan insists that the quality of the work will not deteriorate even if the research is being performed by workers in a foreign region with very different circumstances. Nonetheless, to ensure quality, principal analysts in major triad markets will collect information from Indian researchers to produce final reports. Whether JP Morgan will be able to transfer a substantial amount of its production to international offices is yet to be seen.

JP Morgan Chase is predominantly an investment bank that is in the process of diversifying itself through a growing retail and consumer financial services business. In 2002, the group's acquired position via Chase Manhattan in credit cards, home finance, and auto finance buoyed its financial performance in a weak capital market. However, the firm continues to be focused largely on North America, and it will struggle to grow into a global company unless it acquires a largely foreign firm in the future.

7

Pharmaceutical and chemical multinationals

Contents

A set of stringent local and regional regulations prevents pharmaceutical companies from adopting a global strategy. R&D and sales are more concentrated within North America and Europe than in Asia. In addition, the relative size of the US market for pharmaceuticals creates a significant imbalance that shapes the industry and defines international strategy. In chemicals, a lower dependency on patents, the existence of multiple substitutes, and the less essential nature of products results in lower R&D spending and more geographically spread sales.

Of the world's 500 largest multinational enterprises (MNEs), the sector which is consistently one of the most innovative is chemicals and pharmaceuticals. In this chapter we examine the R&D of the eighteen MNEs in this sector and relate this to the regional nature of their sales. Of the 500 largest companies in the world, it is possible to find data on their geographic sales in the "broad" triad regions of Europe, North America, and Asia. As was discussed in table 6.1 these data exist for 380 of the 500 firms. Of these 380, 200 are in services, leaving 180 in manufacturing. Of the 180 manufacturing MNEs, there are eighteen in the chemicals and pharmaceuticals sector.

company	region	revenues in bn US$	F/T sales	% intra regional	North America (%)	Europe (%)	Asia Pacific (%)
bi-regional							
1 Bayer	Europe	27.5	na	41.3	30.6	41.3	16.6
2 Aventis (q)	Europe	21.6	91.2	36.4	44.8	36.4	6.4
3 Novartis	Europe	20.9	98.0	47.0	47.0	33.0	17.0^f
4 Roche Group	Europe	19.2	98.2	37.1	38.0^z	37.1	13.6
host-region oriented							
1 GlaxoSmithKline	Europe	42.6	95.7	28.6	50.9^z	28.6	na
2 AstraZeneca	Europe	17.8	na	31.9	55.6	31.9	5.5^j
home-region oriented							
1 Merck	North America	51.8	16.0	84.0	84.0^z	na	na
2 Johnson & Johnson	North America	36.3	38.1	61.9	61.9^z	21.0	11.5^f
3 Pfizer	North America	32.4	35.9	64.1	64.1^z	na	29.8^j
4 BASF	Europe	30.6	78.4	58.9	24.2	58.9	15.7^f
5 DuPont de Nemours (E.I.)	North America	24.0	52.4	53.4	53.4	26.3^m	7.3
6 Bristol-Myers Squibb	North America	18.2	37.6	62.4	62.4	22.2^m	na
7 Abbott Laboratories	North America	17.7	37.8	65.1	65.1^a	na	na
8 Wyeth	North America	14.6	36.7	63.3	63.3	5.1^u	na
9 Mitsubishi Chemical	Asia-Pacific	13.4	16.0	85.5	na	na	85.5
10 Akzo Nobel	Europe	13.3	94.0	52.0	27.0^a	52.0	11.0
11 Eli Lilly	North America	11.1	41.0	59.0	59.0^z	19.5^w	na
insufficient information							
1 Dow Chemical	North America	27.6	59.2	40.8	40.8^z	33.4	na
Other							
1 Pharmacia	(acquired by Pfizer July 2002)						
weighted average*		24.47		54.5			
Total		440.5					

Table 7.1. The regional nature of the chemical and pharmaceutical MNEs

Data are for 2002.
Note: ^{z} refers to the US only; ^{a} refers to Canada and the US; ^{m} refers to Europe, the Middle East and Africa; ^{j} refers to Japan only; ^{f} includes figures for Africa. ^{q} Regional data on Aventis are calculated using data for its core business, which represents 85% of revenues. To calculate revenues in US dollars, where the company did not provide a figure, the following exchange rates were used: euro (0.9495); Swiss franc (0.64505) and pound (1.50377). * Weighted intra-regional sales average is weighted according to revenues. Numbers might not add up due to rounding.

Of these eighteen MNEs in the chemicals sector, data are available for all eighteen (one company, Pharmacia, was acquired by Pfizer in 2002), and these can be classified as shown in table 7.1:

Global	0
Bi-regional	5
Host bi-regional	2
Home region	11

Table 7.2.   Research and development in the chemical and pharmaceutical industries

company	industry	region	revenues in bn US$	R&D in bn US$	R&D % of sales
1 Merck	pharmaceutical	North America	51.8	2.7	5.2
2 GlaxoSmithKline	pharmaceutical	Europe	42.6	4.4	10.2
3 Johnson & Jonhson	pharmaceutical	North America	36.3	4.0	10.9
4 Pfizer	pharmaceutical	North America	32.4	5.2	16.0
5 BASE	chemical	Europe	30.6	1.1	3.5
6 Dow Chemical	chemical	North America	27.6	1.1	3.9
7 Bayer	chemical	Europe	27.5	2.4	8.7
8 DuPont de Nemours (E.I)	chemical	North America	24.0	1.3	5.3
9 Aventis	pharmaceutical	Europe	21.6	3.6	16.6
10 Novartis	pharmaceutical	Europe	20.9	2.8	13.4
11 Roche Group	pharmaceutical	Europe	19.2	2.7	14.3
12 Bristol-Mysers Squibb	pharmaceutical	North America	18.2	2.2	12.2
13 Astra Zeneca	pharmaceutical	Europe	17.8	3.1	17.2
14 Abott Laboratories	pharmaceutical	north America	17.7	1.6	8.8
15 Wyeth	pharmaceutical	North America	14.6	2.1	14.3
16 Mitsubishi Chemical	chemical	Asia-Pacific	13.4	0.6	4.8
17 Akzo Nobel	chemical	Europe	13.3	0.9	6.5
18 Eli Lilly	pharmaceutical	North America	11.1	2.1	19.4
19 Pharmacia	(acquired by Pfizer July 2002)				
weighted average*			24.5	2.4	9.9
Total			440.5	43.7	

Data are for 2002.
* Average R&D% of sales is weighted using revenues.

The regional sales of these eighteen MNEs, across the triad, are also reported in table 7.1. Their average home-region sales are 54.5%, while for all 180 MNEs in manufacturing it is 62%.

Table 7.2 examines the R&D of these MNEs. The average R&D to sales percent for these chemical and pharmaceutical MNEs is 9.9%. Eli Lilly had the highest R&D to sales expenditures at 19.4%, followed by other pharmaceutical companies such as: AstraZeneca at 17.2%, Aventis at 16.6%, and Pfizer at 16%. In contrast, there were relatively low R&D expenditures by chemical firms: BASF at 3.5%, Dow Chemicals at 3.9%, DuPont at 5.3%. These data suggest that pharmaceutical companies conduct greater R&D than chemical MNEs.

In this chapter we analyze such innovation differences in the chemicals sector, especially in pharmaceuticals which records consistently higher R&D expenditures than pure chemical MNEs. Once a drug has been developed and patented, few substitutes, if any, can compete with it over a prescribed period of time. Patients suffering from disease, especially those that are terminal or which produce discomfort, have a significantly inelastic demand for drugs as do the doctors working with health insurance schemes. Since the cost of manufacturing a drug is often marginal, pharmaceutical firms depend on national patent protection for their discovery to generate profits. Over the last decade, the development of drugs has become more and more expensive and produced lower profits than in previous decades. Yet, as a pharmaceutical's survival is dependent on new drug development, R&D expenditures are the only way of assuring the long-term survival of the company.

The products of chemical companies, on the other hand, are often not necessities and have many substitutes. Marketing a differentiated product to the consumer is often the only way to obtain a premium price. R&D investment might produce a better paint, textile, pesticide, or plastic but many chemical products are now commodities, with low returns to R&D.

It is often difficult to disentangle chemical companies and pharmaceutical companies as they tend to engage in similar businesses. For instance, companies in both sectors engage in biotechnology, and some chemical companies have pharmaceutical operations. It is no surprise that Bayer, which has a large pharmaceutical arm, is the company with the highest R&D to sales ratio. In table 7.3, the R&D to sales ratios of the six chemical and twelve pharmaceutical MNEs are reported. On average, pharmaceutical companies spend 12% of revenues on R&D, more than twice that spent by chemical companies.

Pharmaceutical companies also tend to be slightly more intra-regionally oriented with regards to revenue. This might reflect a relatively tougher set of regulations for pharmaceutical companies. At nearly twice the size of the European market, the United States is the largest world market for pharmaceuticals. It is also the fastest growing and not surprisingly, where most large pharmaceutical companies prefer to operate. The Boston Consulting Group estimates that 40% of all research facilities of large pharmaceutical companies in the world are located in the United States. While a major reason for this is the large size of the US market, most importantly, on average, US residents pay more than twice as much as Europeans for pharmaceutical products. Price controls in European countries can influence upwards the extra-regional percentage of sales for European pharmaceutical MNEs while decreasing the extra-regional percentage sales of US pharmaceutical MNEs.

Most firms tend to have a larger portion of their R&D facilities in their home region of the triad. Indeed, looking at table 7.4, which shows the distribution of R&D facilities across the triad for a selected number of pharmaceuticals, all of the firms show over 50% of their R&D facilities to be in their home region. This, however, understates the significance of home-region based R&D. The number of facilities tells us little about the particular importance, or of the resources devoted to research, in a given geographic region. A more telling statistic would be the amount of R&D expenditure in each region. This information is generally not available. R&D is highly centralized in the home region of the triad, even when sales are more spread across regions. For instance, host-region oriented European-based firms, like AstraZeneca and GSK, continue to have over

Table 7.3. The chemical and pharmaceutical industries, a comparison

company	region	revenues in bn US$	F/T sales	% intra regional	R&D % of sales
chemical industry					
1 BASF	Europe	30.6	78.4	58.9	3.5
2 Dow Chemical	North America	27.6	59.2	40.8[z]	3.9
3 Bayer	Europe	27.5	na	41.3	8.7
4 DuPont de Nemours (E.I.)	North America	24.0	52.4	53.4	5.3
5 Mitsubishi Chemical	Asia-Pacific	13.4	16.0	85.5[f]	4.8
6 Akzo Nobel	Europe	13.3	94.0	52.0	6.5
average*		22.7	62.4	52.7	5.4
Total		136.4			
pharmaceutical industry					
1 Merck	North America	51.8	16.0	84.0[z]	5.2
2 GlaxoSmithKline	Europe	42.6	95.7	28.6	10.2
3 Johnson & Johnson	North America	36.3	38.1	61.9[z]	10.9
4 Pfizer	North America	32.4	35.9	64.1[z]	16.0
5 Aventis (q)	Europe	21.6	91.2	36.4	16.6
6 Novartis	Europe	20.9	98.0	47.0	13.4
7 Roche Group	Europe	19.2	98.2	37.1	14.3
8 Bristol-Myers Squibb	North America	18.2	37.6	62.4	12.2
9 AstraZeneca	Europe	17.8	na	31.9	17.2
10 Abbott Laboratories	North America	17.7	37.8	65.1[a]	8.8
11 Wyeth	North America	14.6	36.7	63.3	14.3
12 Eli Lilly	North America	11.1	41.0	59.0[z]	19.4
weighted average*		25.3	54.8	55.3	12.0
Total		304.17			

Data are for 2002.
Notes: [z] refers to the US only; [a] refers to Canada and the US; [f] includes figures for Africa. [q] Regional data on Aventis are calculated using data for its core business, which represents 85% of revenues.
Averages for F/T Sales exclude companies for which data are not available. If the same companies were excluded from the % intra-regional column, the averages would be 55.5% for chemicals and 56.7 % for pharmaceuticals. If the same companies are excluded from R&D as % of sales, the averages are 4.5% for chemicals and 11.6% for pharmaceuticals. * Weighted intra-regional sales average is weighted according to revenues.

50% of their R&D facilities in Europe. Bayer, the bi-regional chemical company, allocates over 70% of its R&D budget to Europe even though this region accounts for only 41.3% of total revenues.

BARRIERS TO GLOBAL STRATEGY IN THE PHARMACEUTICAL INDUSTRY

A set of stringent local and regional regulations prevent pharmaceutical companies from adopting a global strategy. R&D and sales are more con-centrated within North America and Europe than in Asia. In addition, the relative size of the US market for pharmaceuticals creates a significant imbalance that shapes the industry and defines international strategy. In chemicals, a lower dependency on patents, the existence of multiple

Table 7.4. Chemical multinationals' distribution of R&D facilities across the triad					
company	country	region	North America % of total	Europe % of total	Asia Pacific % of total
1 AstraZeneca	Sweden	Europe	33.3	55.6	11.1
2 Merck	United States	North America	50.0	41.7	8.3
3 Pfizer	United States	North America	54.5	27.3	18.2
4 DuPont	United States	North America	53.3[z]	na	na
5 Aventis	France	Europe	25.0	50.0	25.0
6 GlaxoSmithKline	United Kingdom	Europe	25.0	70.0	5.0
7 Roche Group	Switzerland	Europe	36.8	52.6	10.5

Source: Individual Annual Reports, 2002.
Source: Company documents.
Note: [z] United States only.

substitutes, and the commodity nature of products results in lower R&D spending and more geographically spread sales.

The pharmaceutical industry is heavily regulated by national and regional governments. The first set of regulations that pharmaceutical firms must overcome is the drug approval process. Presently, this approval is attained at a national level, so pharmaceuticals must test their products and follow the procedures in each jurisdiction. The EU, however, is moving towards a regional approval process to take effect in 2004 or later (FDA News, 2003). The liability for damage caused for drugs also varies across nations and must be taken into account when introducing a new drug.

Another set of regulations is price controls. Some countries have price controls for pharmaceuticals in the form of fixed pricing, reference price lists, or volunteer agreements with the pharmaceutical sector. The United States, the largest pharmaceutical market in the world accounting for nearly half of the world's market for pharmaceuticals, takes a more *laissez-faire* approach to pharmaceutical pricing; thus there is more R&D in the United States than in Europe.

In Germany, the government has adopted regulations to decrease the overall expenditure on pharmaceuticals. A reference price system forces patients to pay the difference between the reference price and the market price. Since most patients are not willing to pay this difference for many drugs, pharmaceutical companies are forced to bring their prices down to the reference price or face a huge decrease in sales of prescription drugs. The French government encourages the use of generics and directly regulates prices of prescription drugs. In 2003, the Italian government implemented a pharmaceutical-reimbursement policy that would only offer refund to a level set by the Health Ministry. The Department of Health of the UK has the power to regulate prices for pharmaceutical products and control the profits of pharmaceutical companies. As a result, a voluntary agreement was reached in which manufacturers can set initial prices for their drugs, but price increases are regulated.

Figure 7.1. Size and international scope in the chemical and pharmaceutical industry

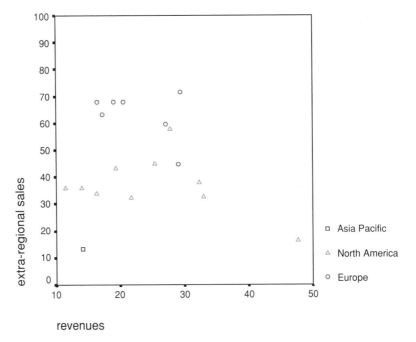

Marketing is done at a national level. This is because governments not only approve a drug and might set prices, but they also regulate distribution and advertising. The type of packaging and labeling that is permitted and whether a drug is sold only with a prescription is the decision of each government. Some governments even force pharmaceuticals to license the rights to produce their patented drugs. Some governments allow pharmaceuticals to market directly to consumers; others restrict this practice while others ban it altogether.

Many pharmaceutical (and chemical) companies are also in the crop-science business and must plan their strategies to conform to individual government regulations and customer perceptions about genetically modified crops.

Despite such barriers to trade, pharmaceutical products have some of the lowest percentage of intra-regional sales among manufacturing industries. A number of factors explain this: (1) Most pharmaceutical products need not be heavily adapted (in some cases only the packaging and labeling is different) for each geographic market. (2) Large pharmaceutical companies own the rights to brand-name drugs that are essential for healthcare across the world. (3) Once research and development costs are sunk, pharmaceutical companies will continue to sell the drug despite government price control as long as a profit on production costs is made. What governments are doing is basically regulating monopolies on patented drugs which may have very inelastic demand curves.

Figure 7.1 plots all the firms listed in table 7.1, showing revenues against extra-regional sales. It illustrates the significant difference in extra-regional sales determined by the region of the triad in which the firm's headquarters are located. European firms are more likely to be extra-regional than North American firms. Indeed, all European firms derive over 40% of their sales outside of their home-region. If we exclude BASF, the seven other European firms have over 59% of their sales extra-regionally. In contrast, extra-regional sales for most North American firms are between 32% and 45%. Only Dow Chemical has a higher level of extra-regional sales at 57.9%, though this number might decrease if Canadian and Mexican sales are included. Merck is another exception with extra-regional sales of 16.4%. Once again, this number might be lower if data on NAFTA partners were included. Only one Asian firm was included in the sample, very domestic Mitsubishi Chemical. The three largest firms, all North American, exhibit low extra-regional sales (high levels of intra-regional sales). This is consistent with an industry in which one market, the North American market, is significantly larger than other markets.

CASE STUDIES

We now examine the strategies of six pharmaceutical MNEs in a set of case studies. In these case studies we analyze the strategy and structure of the MNE, especially in relation to its R&D. We use frameworks from international business strategy, such as Rugman and Verbeke (1990) with their focus on firm-specific advantages (FSAs) and country-specific advantages (CSAs). The MNEs to be examined are:

bi-regionals	Aventis
	GlaxoSmithKline
	AstraZeneca
	Bayer
home region	Merck
	Pfizer-Pharmacia
	Eli Lilly
	Dupont

Aventis

In 1999, Hoechst of Germany and Rhône-Poulenc of France combined their businesses to create Aventis – a bi-regional pharmaceutical company that researches, develops, manufactures, and markets branded prescription drugs. In 2002, Aventis employed 71,000 people in 100 countries around the world. Although 91.2% of its revenues are derived from sales in foreign markets, the European region accounts for 36.4% of revenues. The most important market for Aventis is North America, where it derives 44.8% of its revenues. Asia-Pacific accounts for approximately 6.4% of sales.

　　Aventis is organized across business lines. Its core businesses include: prescription drugs, human vaccines, and animal health. The company markets its products through its commercial subsidiaries. The most important of these are located in the United States, Japan, France, and Germany, which together account for 64% of Aventis' core business sales. Presently, Aventis is aggressively seeking expansion in the US market. The company currently derives just below 40% of its sales from this country, significantly less than other large European pharmaceuticals. Aventis' structure is centralized in terms of drug development and is decentralized in terms of marketing. The company is divided into three core businesses, and its commercial operations are nationally responsive units in major markets. Its North American marketing operations are just as important as the European ones.

Aventis' strategy is one of low levels of economic integration in terms of marketing and high levels of national responsiveness. Once a drug has been developed, it must be approved by each national government in which it operates. Marketing must also be done in accordance with local legislation, the structure of the healthcare system which influences the distribution of drugs, price controls, and individual cultures and preferences of clients. The locally based structure of the pharmaceutical industry makes high levels of economic integration in distribution and marketing impossible and forces firms to be nationally responsive. Even in terms of manufacturing, whether a drug will be produced locally or imported across national borders is highly dependent on the regulations of the nation and regional trade treaties.

R&D centers for Aventis are located across the triad. Two research centers are based in Europe; there is one in North America and one in Asia-Pacific. Thus R&D shows high levels of economic integration. Indeed, Aventis' development of a drug can take place in any of its R&D labs across the world and lead to a drug product that can be sold in all jurisdictions. Like all other pharmaceuticals, Aventis is faced with the increasing cost of production and marketing new drugs. The development of new and expensive R&D technology and the increasing layers of regulation in each national market increase the cost of bringing new drugs to market. On the revenue side, governments at all levels and other bulk clients are seeking to reduce healthcare expenditure. At the same time, a growing population with higher life expectancy is increasing the demand for pharmaceuticals. In industrialized countries the aging population seeks to live healthier lives by ensuring access to medication.

One major FSA that Aventis possesses is its drug portfolio and the R&D for its continued development. This is potentially a global advantage if a drug could be sold across the world. Unfortunately, individual national regulations prevent such global production and sales. Its pipeline of drugs in development and its researchers constitute FSAs that are potentially global but not in practice. The expertise of each individual marketing subsidiary is also an FSA. The CSAs are regional. The intellectual hubs that foster the ability of researchers have allowed Aventis to expand its R&D

capabilities across the triad. There is one R&D facility in North America, one in Asia-Pacific, and two in Europe. For the firm, each region has a set of regulations that it must adhere to. In the case of North America, its most important market, those regulations are dominated by those of the United States. The United States takes a more favorable stance on genetically modified foods than the EU, and this is echoed by the population. Thus, Aventis would have a much easier time marketing GM products in the United States than in Europe.

Questions for discussion

1. What is Aventis' basic strategy?
2. What is Aventis' basic structure?
3. Is Aventis a multinational enterprise? Why?
4. Is Aventis a global business?
5. Why is Aventis seeking to expand aggressively in North America?
6. What type of firm-specific advantages and country-specific advantages does Aventis possess? Are they "global," "regional," or local? Why?
7. How was Aventis' crop-science division affected by cultural differences?
8. How do regional demographics affect Aventis' marketing operations across the world?

GlaxoSmithKline

With £28.3 billion in revenues, and 100,000 employees, GlaxoSmithKline (GSK) is one of the largest pharmaceutical companies in the world. The company markets over seventy prescription drugs and a variety of consumer healthcare products. Although incorporated in the UK, over half of its sales originate in the United States. It is a host-region, bi-regional company.

Approximately thirty years ago, British Glaxo was a small company in the dry milk, antibiotics, respiratory drugs, and nutritional businesses. The discovery of Zantac, a drug to treat stomach ulcers, catapulted the company into the mainstream pharmaceuticals market and financed its expansion into the US market. As the patent for Zantac was about to expire, Glaxo found itself in a sticky situation. Up to that point, the company had relied on internal R&D, but this had failed to develop the R&D capabilities for sustainable long-term growth. In 1995, the company merged with Wellcome, a company known for its strength in R&D and its lack of marketing capabilities. The merger was successful in that the new company produced a stream of new drugs that could be marketed using Glaxo's expertise. In 2000, Glaxo Wellcome merged with SmithKline Beecham. According to Sir Richard Sykes, then chairman of Glaxo Wellcome, the deciphering of the human genome would transform the industry, and only large companies who can afford to invest to work with this new information would succeed. Together, these two companies are immune to the problem of losing a major blockbuster drug; no one drug accounts for more than 12% of the company's revenues.

Based on location of consumers, the United States is GSK's largest market accounting for 50.9% of revenues. If we consider only pharmaceuticals, the US market becomes even more significant accounting for 54.4% of revenues. With Canada, this number increases to 56.8%. GSK derives 28.6% of its sales from its home-market region of Europe. In the heavily-regulated pharmaceutical market alone, GSK derives an even lower portion of its sales from the region, at 26.1%. The European market accounts for 25% of the world market for pharmaceuticals.

GSK's strategy is one of low economic integration in terms of marketing and high levels of national responsiveness. Government regulations, the structure of the local healthcare system, and cultural differences, make high levels of economic integration in distribution and marketing impossible for pharmaceutical firms and require firms to be nationally responsive. Even in terms of manufacturing, whether a drug will be produced locally or imported across national borders is highly dependent on the regulations of the nation and regional trade treaties. GSK must be significantly more responsive to its host region of North America as it is its primary market. Nonetheless, R&D shows high levels of economic integration. Indeed, GSK's development of a drug can take place in any of its R&D labs across the world and lead to a drug product that can be sold across all regions. It has developed a network where "best practice" in its R&D labs can be used anywhere in the network.

The first step in the development of a drug is research and development. GSK spends over £2.6 billion in R&D and has over 15,000 researchers in twenty-eight major R&D sites around the world. Of these, fourteen are located in Europe: ten in the UK, and one in each of Belgium, France, Italy, and Spain. In North America, the United States houses five R&D facilities and Canada one. In Japan, the company has R&D operations in the Tsukuba Science City in Takasaki.

GSK spreads R&D around the world to take advantage of CSAs in terms of human resources and institutional infrastructure that might help it develop a new drug. For instance, it links to an academic department in a major research university with a teaching medical center that is exploring a new drug treatment. Another reason is to monitor more closely the research progress of its competitors, most of which also have R&D facilities in all areas of the world. Finally, R&D facilities might be better able to respond to the particular needs of regional communities.

Once GSK has developed a new drug, it must obtain government approval. This must be done for each individual nation in which the company markets the product, and the process can be significantly different in each jurisdiction.

Production and marketing are the next steps for a new drug. GSK's supply chain is divided into a primary supply chain and a secondary supply chain. The primary supply chain manufactures active ingredients for its products and ships them to the secondary supply chain, which manufactures the end product. There are six primary supply chain sites: Australia, India, Ireland, Singapore, the United States, and the UK in Europe, there are seventeen secondary supply chain sites. North America houses an additional six secondary supply chains. The rest of the world houses thirty-two secondary sites in nineteen countries (the Middle East and Africa houses five sites, twenty-two sites are located in Asia-Pacific, and Latin America accounts for the remaining five sites).

Proximity and regional regulations prevent multinationals from segmenting national markets. As a result, GSK was not able to continue selling drugs to Spain under a two-price system, one for local consumption and one for exports into the EU. Similarly, the integration of the North American market under NAFTA makes preventing the importation of Canadian pharmaceuticals into the United States difficult despite the health section having been exempted from the national treatment provisions of NAFTA. Indeed, pharmaceutical companies are struggling with supplying drugs to the Canadian market that erode their profits in the US market. Beneficiaries from this intra-regional trade of drugs are considering whether to challenge the US government and GSK under NAFTA to continue to trade in pharmaceuticals.

Although the United States and Europe account for nearly 80% of GSK's sales, developing countries took center stage over AIDS medications. In 2000, Cipla of India offered to produce generic versions of AIDS drugs to underdeveloped countries at a 90% markdown. GSK and other pharmaceuticals sued the South African government to stop the drug from being imported, but this sparked a public relations nightmare. Oxfam, a development NGO, accused the pharmaceuticals of waging war on the world's poor. The companies had a difficult time explaining to their developed-country consumers how they could potentially let millions die of AIDS when a cure was readily available. Under a storm of criticism, the drug companies withdrew the suit and paid the South African government's legal costs.

Questions for discussion

1. Is GSK a multinational enterprise? Why?
2. Is GSK a bi-regional company? Why?
3. What is GSK's basic strategy?
4. How is GSK's production organized?
5. Is GSK's secondary supply chain structure global, regional or local? Why?
6. Why does GSK spread R&D around the world?
7. What factors have made North America the primary market for GSK? Would the situation be different if we measured units sold? Why?
8. Why must GSK see the North American and European markets as regional?
9. Why must GSK be careful about its operations in non-triad regions?

AstraZeneca

In 1999, British Zeneca merged with Swedish Astra to create what at the time was the third largest pharmaceutical company in the world. The merger was considered a union of equals. Astra was a leader in the ulcer market, with Prilosec, at the time the world's best selling drug. Yet the dependency on this one drug made the company highly vulnerable as its patent was projected to expire in 2001. Today, 55.6% of European AstraZeneca's $17.8 billion in revenues is derived from North America. Its home region of Europe accounts for only 31.9% of revenues. Japan accounts for a mere 5.5%, and the remaining 7% is derived from other markets. It is a host-region oriented firm.

In 1999, Imperial Chemical Industries (ICI) divested its pharmaceutical business under the name Zeneca. ICI, the world's largest producer of paint, remained a chemical manufacturer. While Zeneca continued to prosper independently, the separation proved devastating for ICI. In the four years that followed, ICI's shares were significantly undervalued, and the company sought acquisitions, including companies it had divested to strengthen its position.

AstraZeneca is a good example of the marketing difficulties pharmaceuticals face even after they have cleared drug regulatory bodies. Each national jurisdiction has its own rules for marketing drugs, forcing companies to structure their marketing strategies to fit the local environment and preventing the development of a global strategy.

Aventis' strategy is one of low levels of economic integration in terms of marketing and high levels of national responsiveness. The nationally based structure of the pharmaceutical industry makes high levels of economic integration in distribution and marketing impossible and forces firms to be nationally responsive. Even in terms of manufacturing, whether a drug will be produced locally or imported across national borders is highly dependent on the regulations of the nation and regional trade treaties. Nonetheless, R&D shows high levels of economic integration. Indeed, Aventis' development of a drug can take place in any of its R&D labs across the world and lead to a drug product that can be sold in all jurisdictions.

For AstraZeneca to develop a global strategy, the weight of the safety and marketing regulations in each national jurisdiction is too large relative to overall operations. The emergence of regional blocks means another set of regulations and barriers that AstraZeneca must take into account. Therefore, the company cannot have a uniform global strategy. Governments are nationally responsive to the demands of their citizens. Drugs are perceived differently across national borders. In addition, local communities may react differently to drugs. There is also an entire industry around the approval process that governments have an interest in maintaining.

A significant risk for pharmaceutical companies is the discovery of new or more dramatic side effects that were not discovered during clinical testing. In late 2002, the Japanese government restricted the use of Iressa, a drug aimed at patients with lung cancer, after over 100 deaths were reported linked to taking the drug. Clinical trials showed that lung-cancer patients showed significant improvement after taking the drug. The Japanese Ministry of Health did not ban the drug as it considered the benefits to late-stage cancer patients outweighed the risks. However, the discovery prompted AstraZeneca to change its labeling to reflect the risks and the Japanese Ministry of Health to require that patients taking the drug be hospitalized for four weeks to monitor side effects. In clinical trials, Japanese patients taking Iressa benefited significantly more from the drug than other patients. However, it turned out that they were also far more likely to suffer from interstitial lung disease (ILD), a side effect of the drug. ILD, the cause of all Iressa-related Japanese deaths, occurs in all cancer treatments. Yet, a media panic in Japan made international news and threatened to jeopardize Iressa's approval in the United States and Europe.

In the case of Iressa, AstraZeneca made the decision to launch the drug in the Japanese market first. The panic that ensued compromised drug approval in its two largest markets of Europe and North America. Although a regional strategy is required for drug marketing, the strategic launching of pharmaceuticals must be thought of on a global basis. Panics in the media do not remain regional. AstraZeneca's mistake was to launch Iressa without examining or taking into consideration that the Japanese were more likely to suffer interstitial lung disease. Even though they were also more likely to benefit from the drug, the risks associated with it were far higher than for other regions.

In conclusion, while AstraZeneca has to be careful in its European domestic market, it also faces regulations in its large North American market and in the Asian market. These prevent the company from adopting a worldwide strategy. At the same time, it can be argued that regional effects might have worldwide repercussions. It needs to think regionally rather than globally, but continue to consider the intra-regional effects of its regional actions.

Questions for discussion

1. What is AstraZeneca's basic strategy?
2. Is AztraZeneca a multinational enterprise? Why?
3. Is AstraZeneca a home-region oriented business? Why?
4. Can AstraZeneca develop a global strategy?
5. What kinds of barriers are there to the development of a global regulatory body?
6. Regarding the Iressa incident, how does national responsiveness become at issue?

7. If you were a manager at AstraZeneca, can you think of situations in which you might have to plan a global strategy?

8. What main factors contribute to AstraZeneca's reliance on the North American market for most of its revenues?

Bayer

Established in 1863, Bayer had its beginnings as a dyestuff factory in Barmen, Germany. Since 1899 it has produced Aspirin. In 1965 the company expanded internationally by purchasing an interest in a US factory and began exporting supplies. The first European manufacturing expansion outside of Germany occurred in 1976, when a dyestuff factory was opened in Moscow. Today, the company operates in almost every country in the world.

In 2002, Bayer's revenues totaled $27.5 billion. Two regions, Europe and North America, accounted for 41.3% and 30.6% of sales respectively. Another 16.6% originated in the Asia-Pacific market. Latin America, where the company has had a marketing presence for over a century, accounts for most of the remaining revenues, with the Middle East accounting for the rest. It is a bi-regional company on sales.

In terms of employees, Europe and North America, which account for 57.6% and 20.1% respectively, are Bayer's two largest workforces. Europe also accounts for the largest portion of Bayer's capital expenditures, 60%. It is home-region based on employees.

All research and development labs are integrated into Bayer's worldwide research network. Europe accounts for 70.1% of worldwide R&D spending. The second largest recipient of R&D expenditure is North America, accounting for 27.4%. Japan receives a mere 2.5%. Again, this is home-region based on R&D. Although Bayer has an R&D network that includes the three triad regions, its expenditures are highly concentrated in its home region. Just over 70% of all R&D expenditure goes to Europe. This does not show a relatively even distribution of R&D across regions. North America accounts for a significant 27.4% of R&D spending, but Japan receives barely any R&D funding. Nonetheless, the results of R&D spending become an FSA that can be transferred across regions. This is particularly true for its non healthcare businesses. Its healthcare business is significantly more hindered by regulatory barriers.

Today, Bayer is one of only a handful of firms that combines pharmaceutical production with other businesses: chemicals, polymers, and agrochemicals. Investors have been pressuring the company to follow the example of ICI, which divested its pharmaceutical arm, Zeneca. The move, investors and analysts hoped, would strengthen the company's drug business and free it from the cyclical nature of Bayer's other chemical businesses. Instead, in 2002, the Bayer Group acquired a new corporate structure. Bayer is now the holding company of four product-oriented companies: Bayer CropScience, Bayer Healthcare, Bayer Polymers, and Bayer Chemicals; and three service oriented companies: Bayer Technology Services, Bayer Business Services, and Bayer Industry Services. Each business has its own management team, which is expected to strengthen its individual core competencies.

Bayer supports the activity of its new businesses through Bayer organizations across the world. These assess the needs of their market and promote and distribute the product. Many of these geographic units are relevant to only one of Bayer's businesses. In the future, Bayer expects to restructure some of its geographic support business into legal entities with their own mandate and management team. Bayer is structured across product/service lines. Future plans to restructure its geographic businesses will not change their main role, which is to support the product lines. This is because Bayer depends on the synergies it can attain from its product oriented lines, not on the benefits of a geographic structure.

Bayer's FSAs include the thirty-two drugs in pre-clinical trials. Its R&D labs are an FSA. Finally, its new structure is an FSA that might prove favorable. Bayer's home-country CSAs stem from a home country that is a hub for innovation. Germany has a well-educated workforce and institutional support system, such as good universities and business resources. There is also significant competition that pushes domestic companies to excel internationally. For Bayer, patented products constitute an FSA. Changes in patent legislation might change the length of life of that FSA or the benefits that Bayer may accrue as a result of this FSA. These changes in the FSA result from government regulations; i.e. they are a CSA. Patent legislation is a CSA. Bayer's basic strategy in its pharmaceutical arm is one of high economic integration and high national responsiveness. Other business segments are less subject to regulation and so may exhibit a lower level of national responsiveness.

Bayer's healthcare faces the same challenges as pharmaceutical companies. It had to withdraw its cholesterol-lowering drug, Lipobay, in 2001, after a crisis of public confidence. It now has thirty drugs in pre-clinical development, but may have little to show in terms of revenues until at least 2006. Generic brand companies infringe its patent rights. For instance, in October 2001, generic manufacturer, Apotex, accepted an order from the Canadian government to supply Cipro, an anthrax fighting drug.

In August 2001, Bayer withdrew its blockbuster cholesterol-lowering drug, Baycol from the market. The drug had been prescribed to six million people worldwide before it was discovered that it could cause rhabdomyolysis, a muscle disorder that can result in kidney and other organ failure and that can lead to death in some patients. Although the drug was distributed worldwide, the ramifications varied widely across jurisdictions, which all have different judicial environments. Of the 100 deaths believed to be linked with Baycol, thirty-one occurred in the United States.

This prompted 8,400 lawsuits from patients who claimed to have suffered health deterioration as a result of taking the drug. The company could not estimate the cost of settling these cases.

In collaboration with GlaxoSmithKline, Bayer is marketing Levitra to compete with Viagra in the erectile dysfunction market. This market is particularly sensitive to the local culture and marketing must be done to conform to local traditions and sexual taboos. The pill is vibrant orange in the hopes of bringing to mind energy and vitality. Market studies on sexual difference across cultures lead Bayer to believe that its drug, which takes less time to take effect, would compete effectively in the US market, where men tend to engage in sexual intercourse soon after taking erectile dysfunction pills.

This example of the marketing of an erectile dysfunctioning drug shows that cultures do not share a homogeneous perception of sexuality or, indeed, of acceptable sexual behaviors. Marketing to promote drugs must be sensitive to local cultures and religions to avoid offending the local audience.

Questions for discussion

1. What is Bayer's basic strategy?
2. What is Bayer's basic structure? Is this expected to change?
3. Is Bayer a home-region oriented firm?
4. In terms of R&D, is Bayer a regional or global company?
5. Why are cultural differences important when marketing drugs?
6. What are some of Bayer's FSAs?
7. What are some of Bayer's home-country CSAs?
8. How are Bayer's "FSAs" and "CSAs" affected by changes in patent legislation?

Merck

Merck is a US based firm deriving 83.6% of its revenues from its home-national market. That Merck derives most of its profits from the United States is no surprise. This is the case for most large pharmaceutical companies. After all, the United States is the largest market, and it has the least price regulation among all industrialized countries. Most of Merck's research is conducted in North America, where the company has six research facilities (five in the United States and one in Canada). Yet, despite the dominance of the North American region, the company also has five R&D facilities in Europe and one in Japan.

Merck's strategy is one of high economic integration and low national responsiveness. Although the company is facing different market conditions in Europe which would require developing a nationally responsive strategy, this only accounts for a small fraction of its operations.

The company is organized on the basis of products and services. Merck's revenues are derived from prescription therapeutic and preventive products. Medco Health revenues are derived from the sale of prescription drugs in the United States through managed prescription drug programs. Merck has "global" product lines (i.e. run in a uniform manner from head office). The firm is basically divided across business lines. There is no significant geographic segmentation in terms of business units. A product/service based structure that includes nationally based Medco Health gives Merck a competitive advantage against other competitors in the US market, but it does nothing to help it compete in other regions of the world. Merck's strategy is based on centralized product/service lines, not regional ones. That is, there is no European SBU to integrate all European operations. In addition, the European market is fractured in terms of language, culture, and healthcare structure, making a regional strategy more difficult to achieve.

Ray Gilmartin, Chairman of Merck, stands by the motto, "Medicine is for the people. It is not for the profits. The profits follow." This is why the company stood aside while the pharmaceutical industry restructured through a wave of mergers in the late 1990s. At the time, Merck faced the same problems plaguing the entire industry: (1) the patent expiry of some of its most important drugs; (2) competition from generic companies; (3) increased price regulation by national and sub-national governments; (4) increased costs of developing a drug; and most importantly (5) a slow-down in the number of successful new products that it develops. Yet, while competitors rushed to buy rivals to increase overall R&D expending, Merck chose to go at it alone relying on the strength of its research force. This strength is undisputed. Between 1996 and 2000, the company patented 1,933 new compounds, the highest in the industry. That this is done with a lower R&D budget than that of other large pharmaceuticals only increases the reputation of Merck as a research-oriented company. The benefit of such a vision is that the company can lure some of the best scientists, or, at the very least, some of the more dedicated to their research.

One of Merck's FSAs is the caliber of its researchers. Indeed, Merck is considered to have a very research-focused organization, and this attracts the best scientists to its ranks. Other FSAs include its patented compounds, its pipeline of drugs in progress, and its portfolio of current drugs in the market. Merck's reputation is also an FSA. Not only is the quality of its research well regarded by the public, but also by being the first company to realize the mistake the industry was making in South Africa, and being key to brokering a deal that included cheap drugs, Merck has come to be well regarded in terms of corporate responsibility.

As a US based firm, Merck is located in the largest pharmaceutical market in the world, where most R&D is performed, so it is a hub of innovation that Merck can use to improve its competitive position. R&D facilities are often built to take advantage of specific human resources in an area or region, to take account of government incentives, or institutional infrastructure as well as to monitor competitors.

Merck has also had to take a different stance in poorer countries where the cost of medication is prohibitive for many patients. In 2001, together with other large pharmaceutical companies, Merck, in collaboration with other large pharmaceuticals, launched a lawsuit against the South African government. At the time, the country was switching to generic drugs to combat AIDS, which was affecting 10% of its population. Drug costs were often higher than salaries, and, like Brazil, the country had to decide to either honor the patents of large MNEs to produce its own or to import it from countries that already legalized generics and produced them at a fraction of the cost. Throughout the world, protestors rose up against the lawsuit, forcing pharmaceutical companies to justify letting 250,000 people die every year. Merck was the quickest to realize the public relations hole which it had dug, and it acted to broker an agreement between the industry and developing countries. Merck no longer makes a profit from selling HIV drugs in the poorest of countries. Others in the industry complain that this inhibits future research, but Merck was quick to point out that as long as pharmaceuticals can continue to make significant profits in the developed world, research will continue at the same pace.

Questions for discussion

1. Is Merck a regional or global business?
2. What is Merck's basic strategy?
3. What is Merck's basic structure?
4. Does Merck choose product-based strategic business units or regionally based strategic business units?
5. How does Merck's structure affect its competitiveness across the world?
6. Are Merck's European operations regionally integrated?
7. Given that Merck derives over 80% of its sales from the United States, why has it opened research facilities in the other two regions of the triad?
8. What are some of Merck's FSAs?
9. What are some of Merck's CSAs?

Pfizer Pharmacia

In 2000, Pfizer offered $90 billion to Warner-Lambert shareholders to win a hostile takeover and snatch the company from American Home Products, which was already negotiating a friendly merger with Warner-Lambert. Only two years later the company offered $60 billion for Pharmacia. These acquisitions turned Pfizer into the largest pharmaceutical company in the world with an estimated $37.5 billion in revenues and a $7 billion R&D budget.

Pfizer is a home-region oriented company with 64.1% of its sales in the United States. Its R&D is headquartered in its home region of the United States. Excluding Pharmacia, six of the pre-merger company's R&D

facilities are in the North American region (one in Canada and five in the United States). Europe hosts three Pfizer R&D facilities and Japan two labs.

The company operates in two business segments: pharmaceuticals and consumer products. The pharmaceutical segment is the largest, accounting for 92% of Pfizer's business and includes human and health pharmaceuticals and capsugel, a capsule-making sub-segment. Pfizer's Consumer Healthcare business manufactures over the counter healthcare products, including Listerine, Rolaids, Vizine, and BenGay. International operations include both the pharmaceutical and consumer product segments. Marketing is conducted through subsidiaries and through distributors.

In an industry where constant innovation is the most valuable long-term predictor of wealth creation, Pfizer is better known for the capabilities of its sales force. To date, its competitive advantage has been marketing. Pfizer's 11% world market can be attributed to the company's sales force of 35,000 representatives.

Even if Pfizer cannot compete as an innovator, it is well positioned to profit from the innovations of others. This might be the company's saving grace since a large R&D budget has produced very little relative to the industry. It costs Pfizer more than three times as much to discover a compound that can be patented than it costs its largest US competitor, Merck. Between 1996 and 2001, Pfizer patented 1,217 compounds at a cost of $17.5 million each. For the same period, Merck patented 1,933 compounds at a cost of $6 million each. One of the most compelling reasons given for mergers and acquisitions, a large R&D budget, has not yet proven fruitful. For a discussion of the international expansion of Pfizer, see Fina and Rugman (1995).

Small pharmaceuticals that can produce a prize drug are willing to partner up with Pfizer to have the product pitched through their marketing machine. Lipitor was produced by Warner-Lambert and marketed through a joint venture with Pfizer. This drug alone justified Pfizer's hostile takeover. Celebrex and Aricept, two other best-selling drugs in Pfizer's portfolio, were also discovered by smaller players, Searly and Eisai of Japan.

Eli Lilly

Eli Lilly, the Indiana-based pharmaceutical company, is a home-region oriented company with 59% of its sales derived from within the United States. Western Europe accounts for an additional 19.5% of sales. The remaining 21.5% of sales originate in non-specified foreign countries. In terms of assets Eli Lilly is even more intra-regional. Nearly 74% of all long-lived assets are located in the United States. Western Europe accounts for an additional 15.6%. One main explanation for the relative importance of the US market is that prices in the United States are significantly higher than in the rest of the industrialized countries. As a result, revenues in Eli Lilly's home region tend to be higher regardless of similar unit sales in other regions.

Eli Lilly only operates in one industry segment, pharmaceuticals. Its business units are divided according to product lines which are defined by the type of ailment they target. In the United States, Lilly markets its products through thirty-five wholesale distributors, three of which account for nearly 50% of domestic sales. Although the government and managed care institutions account for a large portion of sales, direct sales by Lilly are not material; it is the wholesalers who process these orders. Lilly takes a more direct role in marketing its drugs. This is done through sales representatives who contact physicians, wholesalers, hospitals, managed-card organizations, and governments. These representatives are divided in terms of product lines, neurosciences, endocrinology, cardiovascular, etc. A special force is dedicated to marketing targetted managed care organizations and the government. The efforts of sales representatives are complemented with advertising in medical journals, distribution of pamphlets, and samples to physicians and, in the United States and Canada, advertising targeted directly to customers.

Eli Lilly products are sold internationally despite different regulatory environments because it is to the benefit of each country to approve a new medicine. Internationally, promotion, distribution, and marketing are highly dependent on national regulation. Most products are marketed through sales representatives. In the majority of foreign countries, Lilly has its own sales force, but in others, it uses independent distributors. In 2002, Lilly's R&D budget was $2.1 billion, or 19.4% of total revenue. In the United States, R&D facilities are located in Indiana and Greenfield. There are also four European based R&D facilities and three Asia-Pacific based R&D facilities.

Lilly's strategy is one of high economic integration and low national responsiveness. Although the company faces different market conditions in Western Europe that require developing a nationally responsive marketing strategy, this only accounts for about 20% of its operations. In its home region, Lilly requires a high degree of economic integration. Eli Lilly's FSAs include its portfolio of patented drugs, its pipeline of new drugs, its biotechnology competencies, and its R&D centers. In terms of marketing, FSAs are its distribution routes and its sales representatives, both in the US market and internationally. A firm specific disadvantage is the loss of reputation from some quality control problems. Changes in patent legislation that allow generic firms and large pharmaceuticals to produce a competing drug reduce Lilly's FSAs. Its biotechnology competencies and its R&D centers all contribute to developing drugs that can one day be patented drugs that can be sold across borders. FSAs relating to marketing, however, are not transferable to other countries or regions. This is because of differences in regulations not only in each country, but also because of cultural differences, including language.

Lilly lost the rights of Prozac, the company's best known drug, to a generics maker, Barr Laboratories. Prozac accounted for approximately

30% of Eli Lilly's revenues, and while management expected the patent to expire within a few years, they were taken by surprise by two court decisions that ended their patent in 2000. The results were devastating. The company lost about 30% of its share value while generic producers captured 70% of the market for Prozac in the first month.

Questions for discussion

1. Is Eli Lilly a bi-regional company? Why?
2. What is Eli Lilly's basic strategy?
3. What is Eli Lilly's basic structure?
4. Is Eli Lilly a "global" or "regional" company?
5. Which of Eli Lilly's FSAs, if any, are listed in this case?
6. Which of Eli Lilly's CSAs, if any, are listed in this case?
7. The case illustrates a factor that affects the stability of Eli Lilly's FSAs. What is this factor and how does it affect FSAs?
8. Which, if any, of the company's FSAs are transferable to other regions/ countries? Which are not?

DuPont

In 1802, a French immigrant, E.I. du Pont de Nemours, founded an explosives firm in the United States. By the end of the century, the company began to move to other chemical products, and in 1902, three du Pont cousins purchased the company and began to transform it into a global chemical company producing paints, plastics and dyes. Today, DuPont's revenues reach $24 billion and the company products include: Lycra for the production of garments, seeds for agriculture, auto-paints, a Kevlar fiber that is used to make bullet-proof vests and inputs for electronic companies, among others.

DuPont has operations in seventy-five countries around the world, but derives 47.6% of its revenues from its home market of the United States. Its home-region market, which, in addition to the United States, includes Canada, Mexico, and a number of Caribbean countries accounts for 53.4% of DuPont's revenues. Europe, the Middle East, and Africa account for an additional 26.3% of sales. Asia only accounts for 7.3% of sales. The remaining 13% of sales is derived from South America.

There are more than seventy-five DuPont R&D labs across the world. The United States is home to about forty of these. The remaining thirty-five are located in eleven countries around the world.

DuPont used to be a chemical and pharmaceutical company, but in 2001 it divested itself of its pharmaceutical arm by selling it to Bristol-Myers Squibb. The company retains interests in some of its previous pharmaceutical products. In 2002, DuPont restructured itself into five business units: agriculture and nutrition; coatings and color technologies; electronic and communications technologies; performance materials; and safety and protection. In addition, the company created INVISTA, which administers its textiles business. In progress are plans for INVISTA to be spun off from the company when the market conditions become appropriate.

DuPont's business units face competition on price, quality, performance, and specifications from a variety of companies. In the paint business, for instance, DuPont competes with ICI of Britain, and its agricultural division must compete with Monsanto.

In the textile business, Lycra is DuPont's stellar product. Today Lycra is used in bras, cycling shorts, and it is even mixed with leather. Products bearing the Lycra sticker are sold at a 20–25% premium above the same products using spandex, the generic name for the product. The company's grip on over 50% of the spandex market is the direct result of an aggressive and innovative marketing strategy. Yet, Lycra is still highly susceptible to substitutes, new inventions, and even a better marketing campaign by a competitor. Lycra is also a luxury good. That it sells at a premium means it suffers a loss of market share during regional recessions.

Refusal by the US government to ratify the Kyoto Protocol and the ensuing media coverage has made consumers inside and outside the United States more vigilant about the environment. Furthermore, American corporations understand that in the future, a new elected government might ratify the treaty, and they cannot fall behind foreign companies in their environmental record. This is one reason why CCX, a voluntary project by twenty-eight large companies, including DuPont, has been developed to modestly decrease emissions by about 1% per year from the 1999 level. Yet DuPont has gone a bit further than most corporations. In 1999 it promised that by 2010 it would derive 25% of its revenues from renewable inputs, as opposed to the petroleum-based products that are the norm in the chemical industry, and to decrease emission of greenhouse gases by 45% of the 1990 level.

CONCLUSION

Innovation in the chemicals and pharmaceuticals industry occurs largely within the home-region bases of the large MNEs. There are two distinctive markets in North America and Europe for pharmaceuticals; these markets are segmented by strong regulations and different institutional frameworks for distribution and marketing. Even within the EU, there are strong national differences in regulatory regimes. These segmented national and regional markets deny MNEs the potential R&D and marketing global scale economies in production that they might achieve. Pharmaceuticals, in particular, are not global. Chemicals can be more global, but these MNEs are much less innovative. Both trends lead to regional, rather than global, strategies.

8 Automotive multinationals

In this book it has been demonstrated that the vast majority of international business activity is conducted on a regional basis, rather than globally, see also Rugman and Brain (2003), Rugman and Verbeke (2004). The large "triad" markets of the European Union (EU), the United States (or, more broadly, NAFTA) and Japan (or, more broadly, all of Asia) also account for most of the sales of the world's largest automobile companies. Of the 180 manufacturing MNEs in the world's top 500, the motor vehicle and parts industry accounts for twenty-nine of these manufacturing MNEs.

As shown in table 8.1, none of the twenty-nine automotive MNEs in the two largest 500 are global; in fact, twenty-three are classified as "home-region oriented", with a majority of their sales in their home region of the triad. Two automakers and two parts makers are bi-regional, with over 20% of their sales in two parts of the triad and less than 50% in any region. DaimlerChrysler and Honda derive more than 50% of their revenue from a host region and are labeled "host-region oriented." The weighted average of intra-regional sales in the automotive sector is 60.6%, just below the manufacturing sector's average of 61.8%.

The automotive sector is concentrated in the three triad regions of the United States (North America), Europe and Japan (Asia). In each of these regions, domestic producers are significantly more competitive than foreign producers. General Motors, Ford, and the Chrysler Group of

Table 8.1. The regional nature of the motor vehicles and parts industries

500 rank		company	region	revenues in bn US$	F/T sales	% intra regional	North American % of total sales	Europe % of total sales	Asia-Pacific % of total sales
bi-regional									
1	10	Toyota Motor	Asia-Pacific	120.8	50.8	49.2	36.6	7.7	49.2[j]
2	58	Nissan Motor	Asia-Pacific	49.6	50.3	49.7	34.6	11.0	49.7[j]
3	285	Bridgestone	Asia-Pacific	17.6	61.2	38.8	43.0[j]	10.1	38.8[j]
4	342	Michelin	Europe	14.6	na	47.0	40.0	47.0	na
host-region oriented									
1	7	Daimler Chrysler	Europe	136.9	na	29.9	60.1	29.9	na
2	41	Honda Motor	Asia-Pacific	58.9	73.1	26.9	53.9	8.1	26.9[j]
home-region oriented									
1	3	General Motors	North America	177.3	25.5	81.1	81.1	14.6	na
2	5	Ford Motor	North America	162.4	33.3	66.7	66.7[z]	21.9	na
3	21	Volkswagen	Europe	79.3	72.3	68.2	20.1	68.2	5.3
4	49	Fiat	Europe	51.9	65.6	73.3	13.0	73.3	na
5	112	BMW	Europe	34.4	73.4	57.3	31.7[l]	57.3	na
6	125	Renault	Europe	32.6	60.8	89.1	na	89.1	na
7	133	Hyundai Motor	Asia-Pacific	30.9	20.9	81.6	18.1	0.3	81.6
8	166	Delphi	North America	26.1	na	77.7	77.7	18.4	na
9	171	Mitsubishi Motors	Asia-Pacific	25.6	40.9	62.8	22.1	12.1	62.8
10	252	Denso	Asia-Pacific	19.2	32.4	73.1	20.0[l]	6.8	73.1
11	264	Johnson Controls	North America	18.4	na	62.9	62.9	25.6	na
12	267	Volvo	Europe	18.3	na	51.6	30.2	51.6	6.0
13	278	Visteon	North America	17.8	29.0	71.0	71.0[z]	15.6	na
14	296	Mazda Motor	Asia-Pacific	16.8	34.3	65.7	24.4	7.0	65.7[j]
15	306	TRW	North America	16.4	40.7	59.3	59.3[z]	na	na
16	343	Man Group	Europe	14.6	72.6	68.7	15.6	68.7	12.7
17	352	Goodyear Tire and Rubber (q)	North America	14.1	45.9	54.1	54.1[z]	na	na
18	369	Lear	North America	13.6	51.4	58.2	58.2	31.6	na
19	381	Suzuki Motor	Asia-Pacific	13.3	31.6	68.4	13.3	14.9	68.4[j]
20	404	Isuzu Motors	Asia	12.8	30.8	69.2	39.6	na	69.2[j]
21	456	Magna International	North America	11.0	67.2	67.7	67.7	31.4	na
22	462	Fuji Heavy Industries	Asia	10.9	34.0	66.0	33.7	na	66.0[j]
23	484	Dana	North America	10.5	na	74.8	74.8	17.4	3.2
weighted average*				42.3		60.6			
Total				1,226.5					

Notes: [q] Goodyear Tire and Rubber: Based on the location of the selling subsidiary (i.e. exports are not included). [z] US only; [l] Americas; [j] refers to Japan only.

* Weighted intra-regional sales average is weighted according to revenues.

DaimlerChrysler (a US company prior to the merger with Daimler Benz) each have 28.3%, 21.1%, and 12.9% of the US market for motor vehicles. Together, the largest three domestic automakers in the United States have 62.3% of the US market. Imports account for approximately 15% of the United States market and do not include locally made Japanese brands, Morris (2000).

In general, the European market is more fragmented than the North American market. In 2002, Renault had 11.3% of the European market for passenger cars and light commercial vehicles. Volkswagen and Opel (a GM subsidiary) followed with 10% and 9% of this market respectively. The five largest European brands, Renault, Volkswagen, Peugeot, Fiat and Citroen, accounted for 43.6% of the European market. Ford, the fourth largest competitor in Europe, had 8.9% of the market. Japanese and South Korean firms accounted for approximately 12.2% and 3.1% respectively.

The Japanese market is the most consolidated of all triad markets. Toyota alone has 38.3% of the automobile market, Henderson, 2003. Honda, the second largest Japanese automaker, accounts for 15.6%. Together, Honda, Toyota, Renault-Nissan, and Suzuki-Maruti, the four largest Japanese automakers, have 78.4% of the Japanese market. Ford, which acquired domestic Mazda, accounts for 5%. General Motors, the US leader, has a mere 0.4% of this market. VW, the European leader, has 1.2%. Imports are a mere 4.5% of the Japanese market and include imports by Japanese companies manufacturing abroad.

Excluding Japan, Toyota is the market leader in two of the six largest countries in Asia-Pacific: Malaysia and Thailand. South Korea is dominated by Hyundai, which controls 72.9% of that market. Suzuki-Maruti is the leader in India, with 36.8% market share. Indeed, only Australia and China have western-based market leaders. In Australia, GM controls 22% of the market, followed closely by Japan, which holds 20.6% of the market. Including Japan, the top six Asian automakers control 69.5% of the Asian market. This includes Renault-Nissan (8.1%) and Ford-Mazda (4.4%), Japanese companies which were purchased by western firms, Henderson, 2003.

Although the majority of the market in each of the three triad regions is controlled by home-region oriented companies, foreign companies continue to play a major role in each region. A number of these companies attained a competitive position by acquiring the operations of a local producer, such as GM's Opel subsidiary and others, through organic growth in foreign markets, such as Toyota and Honda in North America. In Europe, however, Ford holds 10.9% of the market and is the fourth largest competitor.

Figure 8.1 displays the relationship between extra-regional sales of the world's largest firms in the motor vehicle industry and their revenues. These are all of the firms listed in table 8.1. The largest firms are North American, General Motors, and Ford, and these are relatively more intra-regional than the next two largest firms: Toyota and

Figure 8.1. Size and international scope in the motor vehicle industry

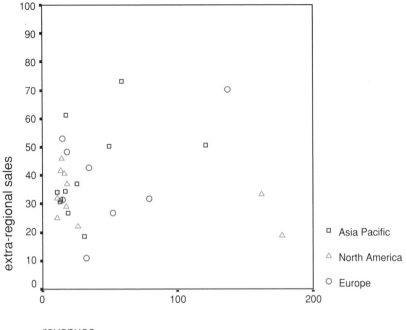

DaimlerChrysler, the first being shown as Asia Pacific and the second as European controlled.

BARRIERS TO GLOBAL EXPANSION IN THE AUTOMOTIVE INDUSTRY

The auto industry operates largely in "clusters" of localized activity within each major triad region, as discussed in Rugman and D'Cruz (2000). There are networks of key supplies, other suppliers, key distributors, other partners, and the OEMs assemble cars from imports of literally thousands of suppliers, all location bound.

Another persistent barrier to a global strategy or a global car is cultural barriers across regions. European consumers prefer performance cars with good engines while in the United States large comfortable cars are the norm. Even within NAFTA, while the United States and Canada prefer automatic transmissions, most cars in Mexico have manual transmissions. In terms of customer tastes, it is impossible to market the same car across regions, and usually all of the economies of scale for a model are achieved within each major region.

Another factor is fuel. Diesel continues to be popular in Europe but is being phased out in the United States because of its environmental implications. Rather than phase out the less expensive fuel, European automakers are seeking ways of making it a cleaner alternative.

Table 8.2. General Motors, by region, 2002					
country	sales units (000)	sales units (%)	sales $ (%)	assets (%)	production capacity (000)	capacity (%)
United States	4,859	57.0	74.3	70.9	4,839	51.3
North America	5,623	66.0	82.3	80.5	6,213	65.8
Other Americas	635	7.4	2.5	1.5	794	8.4
Total Americas	6,258	73.4	84.8	82.0	7,007	74.2
Europe	1,662	19.5	14.2	14.7	2,123	22.5
Asia-Pacific	605	7.1	na	na	311	3.3
Other	na	na	1.0	3.3	na	na
Total	8,525	100.0	100.0	100.0	9,441	100.0

Source: Adapted from General Motors, Annual Report, 2002.

CASES

We now discuss five cases with their top 500 ranking in parenthesis: General Motors (3), Honda (4), Toyota (10), DaimlerChrysler (7), and Volkswagen (21).

General Motors

The world's largest manufacturer of automobiles is General Motors (GM). In 2002, the company's revenues totaled $187 billion; GM accounted for nearly 15% of the world's market for trucks and automobiles. General Motors produces and manufactures vehicles in all three triad markets. Nonetheless, 74.3% of its sales originate in the United States, its home national market. Including Canada, Mexico, Puerto Rico, and Caribbean markets in North America, this number rises to 82.3% of total sales. On the production side, its network of North American factories – which exist partly as a result of NAFTA – accounts for 65.8% of production capacity. An international company yes, but by no means a global company; see table 8.2.

General Motors is primarily an automotive company, but it also operates communications services businesses and has a financing and insurance arm. Its automotive business is segmented geographically: GM North America, GM Europe, GM Latin America/Africa/Mid-East, and GM Asia Pacific. Each of these regions has a set of brands it promotes. In North America, for example, these are Chevrolet, Pontiac, Saturn, etc. In Europe, GM's brands include Opel, Vauxhall and Holden, among others. The GM Daewoo and Suzuki brands are marketed throughout Asia-Pacific.

Each regional market in which GM operates has its own set of environmental regulations. In the United States, GM must design its vehicles to conform to the Environmental Protection Agency's (EPA) regulations and the environmental regulations of individual states. Other regulations that relate to automotive design include noise control and fuel economy.

The company's industrial processes are also heavily regulated with laws relating to water discharges, air emissions, waste management and environmental cleanup. European and Asia-Pacific markets have similar laws to which GM's operations must comply. For instance, the European Union is making all carmakers financially responsible for dismantling and recycling its own vehicles.

The company is most successful in the North American market, where it holds 28% of the market compared to 8.7% of the European market and 3.4% of the Asia-Pacific market. In North America, GM has a competitive advantage in that it is already well situated in the market and has a loyal consumer base. In other regions, however, it faces competition from local automakers that know their home regions very well. In Europe, Volkswagen, BMW, and DaimlerChrysler build high performance cars. In Asia, competitors build smaller, more fuel efficient cars that cater to local preferences. Each region has a particular competitive environment in which the major world players compete for market share. There are regional clusters of auto production and assembly in each of the triad regions, Rugman and D'Cruz (2000). Local competitors are more adept at meeting the demands of their regional markets because they possess know-how on consumer preferences, government regulations, and market trends. While foreign companies might hire local personnel, purchase local car manufacturers, and do extensive market research, companies headquartered in that region are more capable of responding to changing circumstances of their primary market.

General Motors' primary market is North America, in particular the United States. It derives most of its revenue and most of its profits from its home-region operations. GM's strategy must balance the benefit of investing in foreign regions to the benefits of investing in its home-region market. Foreign markets, though potentially profitable, do not offer the consolidated GM company sufficient incentive to switch the focus of its strategy. GM has plans to expand in China, but this is a country where rival MNEs are already active and where local Chinese producers are adapt at appropriating the intellectual property of western firms. In other words, China offers potentially high returns, but has great risks.

Questions for discussion

1. Is GM a multinational enterprise? Why?
2. What is GM's basic strategy?
3. How does this strategy accommodate its international operations?
4. What is GM's basic structure?
5. What factors prevent GM from adopting a global strategy?
6. What are some of GM's CSAs listed in this case?
7. What are some of GM's FSAs listed in this case?
8. How would you describe GM's regional production network in terms of FSAs/CSAs?

Volkswagen

In March 1998, Germany's Volkswagen revamped its strategy in the US market by introducing the New Beetle. The car appeal is the sixties and seventies nostalgia of the VW Beetle. In 2002, Volkswagen delivered over 420,000 vehicles to the United States market and accounted for approximately 10.1% of the passenger car import market.

Although the Volkswagen comeback into the US market has been a success, the North American market is still a minor part of the company's operations.

Table 8.3. Volkswagen, 2002

country	delivered units (000)	delivered units* (%)	sales $ (%)	assets (%)
Germany	940	18.9	27.5	50.0
rest of Europe	2,210	44.3	41.8	28.7
total Europe	3,150	63.2	69.3	78.6
North America	663	13.3	19.9	16.4
South America	421	8.5	3.8	2.9
Africa	na	na	1.1	0.3
Asia/Oceania	621	12.5	5.9	1.8
other	128.9	2.6	1.1	0.3
Total	4,984	100.0	100.0	100.0

Source: Adapted from Volkswagen, Annual Report, 2002.
* Delivered units include unsold inventory.

In 2002, only 19.9% of total revenues originated in North America. It is the European market that Volkswagen depends on for the vast majority of its revenue. Like GM, which concentrates on the US market, VW's primary market is Europe. Its cars reflect the European taste for performance, safety and durability. Germany accounted for 27.5% of total sales. Including other European countries, the intra-regional sales of VW rise to 69.3%. In addition, Europe accounts for over three-fourths of all assets. This is a highly regional company, and while success in other regions is significant, the company's main strategic market continues to be its home region, see table 8.3.

Over the last few years, Volkswagen has increasingly relied on foreign markets for its revenue and production. Between 1993 and 2002, production outside of Germany rose from 53.3% of all units to 64.5%, and its foreign workforce rose from 40.7% to 48.1% of the total. However, many of these factories and workers are located in Eastern Europe. Similarly, unit sales in foreign markets increased from 69.1% to 81.8%, but a large portion of these units are actually sold in the European regional market. Units delivered to Europe accounted for 63.2% of total deliveries in 2002.

Volkswagen also has a larger share of the passenger car market in its home region. The company holds 30% of its domestic market and 17.9% of the European market (including Germany). This is well above its market share in the other two triad regions. Although the company has had some success in developing countries, with 25.1% of the Mexican market and 20.2% of the South American market, its revenues from these regions account for a very small fraction of total revenues because of the small size of these economies and their automobile markets.

Toyota

In 2002, two regional markets accounted for well over 80% of Toyota's revenues: Asia (with Japan at 45% of revenues) and North America, at

Table 8.4. Toyota's regional breakdown in 2002					
country	sales units	sales units (%)	sales $ (%)	assets (%)	production (000) units	production (%)
Japan	2,217	38.3	45.0	52.8	4,029	75.9
Asia-Pacific	2,675	46.2	na	na	na	na
North America	1,780	30.8	38.8	35.8	793	14.9
Europe	866	15.0	8.8	6.7	258	4.9
Other	463	8.0	7.4	4.7	225	4.2
Total	5,785	100.0	100.0	100.0	5,306	100.0

Source: Toyota, Annual Report, 2002.
Notes: Production% is calculated using units.
Unit sales shows percentage of units sold in each region.
Sales $ shows percentage of revenues generated in each region.
Asia-Pacific includes Japan.

38.8% of revenues. Europe was only at 8.8% of revenues. In terms of units sold, the geographic distribution is similar: Asia and Oceania account for 46.2% of unit sales (Japan at 38%); North America for 30.8%; and Europe for 15%. Thus, in terms of revenue and units sold, Toyota is a bi-regional company. Market share shows a slightly different picture. Toyota holds approximately 40% of the Japanese market but only 10% of the North American market. Moreover, production is not as dispersed around the world; 75.9% of all Toyota cars are still produced in Japan. Only 14.9% are produced in North America. Other regions account for less than 10% of production.

Over the last 10 years, Toyota's intra-regional percentage of sales has decreased from 57.1% to 46.2%. One major reason for this is the Japanese market itself, where sales decreased from 48.4% of total revenues in 1993 to 38.3% in 2002. In contrast, North America, European, and non-triad sales have steadily increased in importance. In 1993, Toyota derived 25.4% of its sales from North America. This rose to 30.8% in 2002; EU restrictions on imports of Japanese cars were one reason why Toyota historically has been unable to be successful in the European market. European sales accounted for a mere 9.9% of total sales in 1993, but by 2002 Toyota almost doubled the number of units sold so that, in this year, the region accounted for 15% of total sales. This is partly a result of more local production but also of Toyota learning to cater to the European market.

The Asian economies have been in a slump since the 1990s, and Europe has been growing slowly. This is why the North American market is very important for all Japanese manufacturers. Japanese carmakers began to manufacture in the United States, the largest North American national market, in the 1980s to protect themselves from import restrictions. North America is Toyota's second largest regional market in terms of revenues. It is also highly profitable. In 2002, one-fourth of Toyota's profits originated in this region.

Table 8.5.	Toyota vehicle sales, 1993–2002					
Year	Total	Japan	Asia-Pacific	North America	Europe	other
			units sold			
1993	4,466,218	2,159,474	2,548,736	1,134,006	442,291	341,185
1994	4,130,846	2,010,130	2,372,598	1,105,447	384,249	268,552
1995	3,260,670	1,560,970	1,857,920	911,578	288,065	203,107
1996	4,148,641	2,058,457	2,422,167	1,117,248	360,003	249,223
1997	4,559,515	2,216,072	2,659,759	1,201,309	415,580	282,867
1998	4,456,344	1,907,059	2,300,369	1,293,121	500,668	362,186
1999	4,695,147	1,929,279	2,244,982	1,485,095	557,506	407,564
2000	5,182,774	2,177,524	2,517,465	1,689,483	633,879	341,947
2001	5,526,863	2,322,838	2,726,131	1,733,569	691,135	376,028
2002	5,784,917	2,217,002	2,675,493	1,780,133	866,351	462,940
			% of units sold			
1993	100.0	48.4	57.1	25.4	9.9	7.6
1994	100.0	48.7	57.4	26.8	9.3	6.5
1995	100.0	47.9	57.0	28.0	8.8	6.2
1996	100.0	49.6	58.4	26.9	8.7	6.0
1997	100.0	48.6	58.3	26.3	9.1	6.2
1998	100.0	42.8	51.6	29.0	11.2	8.1
1999	100.0	41.1	47.8	31.6	11.9	8.7
2000	100.0	42.0	48.6	32.6	12.2	6.6
2001	100.0	42.0	49.3	31.4	12.5	6.8
2002	100.0	38.3	46.2	30.8	15.0	8.0

Source: Adapted from Toyota, *Annual Report, 2002.*
Note: 1995 is calculated using 9 months instead of 12.

Toyota manufactures locally over two-thirds of the cars it sells in the United States. The company's Canadian plant also serves this regional market, and a Mexican plant in Tijuana is expected to increase local production when it opens in 2005. Local responsiveness is important. Toyota introduced its luxury models to accommodate the aging and wealthier North American baby boomers in the 1990s. Today, the company is introducing cars to target the young American customer, the demographic echo of the baby boomers. Sixty percent of US car buyers remain loyal to the brand of their first car. It is thus imperative to service this young market.

American consumers, for their part, have been responsive to the company's reputation for quality and in particular for the lower price at which Toyota's cars are sold. In fact, during economic downturns in which consumers seek more value for their money Toyota does better in the United States. The company's cars are not only less expensive, but they also consume less gasoline than American cars. The resale value is also higher for Toyota cars. One major advantage for Toyota is that it has some of the best manufacturing facilities in the world, and it combines this with excellent relationships with its suppliers. The company is so efficient that, despite the lower price of its cars, it makes an average profit of $1,000 on each car sold compared to $330 for GM.

Toyota's European operations are money losers, but the company continues to try to access this market and increase its market share from its 3.8% level in 2002. To boost its image for performance in the region, the company recently began to compete in Formula One races. To protect itself from currency risk, Toyota will now produce a higher percentage of its cars within the region. That also means more local procurement. To this end, Porsche was asked to produce engines for its European models. Porsche already produces transmissions for the company. The company expects to increase its market share to 5% by 2005.

Always a pioneer, Toyota is one of the most efficient companies at outsourcing production to suppliers with whom it enjoys an amicable long-term relationship. If the auto industry is to become more like the electronics industry (as many believe may occur), vehicle brand owners (VBOs), such as Toyota, GM, VW, will be the equivalent of original equipment manufacturers (OEMs) in the electronics industry, such as Nokia, IBM, and Microsoft, and will concentrate on designing, engineering and marketing vehicles to be sold under their brand while others take care of the petty details of manufacturing. Toyota is well ahead of other triad automakers in the way to outsourcing manufacturing.

DaimlerChrysler

When German Daimler-Benz merged with US Chrysler, the aim of the German company was to secure a share in the large US economy-class car market. Synergies (for instance in the area of purchasing), it argued, would reduce costs across all operations. At first glance, one can argue that the merger achieved its goal. In 2002, 58.7% of the company's revenues originated in North America, a trend that has remained relatively stable since 2000, see table 8.6. The numbers can be deceiving though; soon after the merger the Chrysler group was plagued by management defections and decreasing profits.

Two things help explain the troubles of this merger. The first is that these companies were producing very different products. Mercedes Benz, Daimler-Benz' brand, had a competitive edge in the luxury market. Chrysler produced popular cars for the US market. Although the expensive parts of Daimler's vehicles could be used for more affordable Chrysler cars and the cheaper Chrysler parts be used on Daimler vehicles; both these moves were likely to reduce the competitive advantage on each of the markets in which the original companies operated. Chrysler cars could have become less affordable while Daimler's brand might have lost its reputation for quality. In effect, while some parts can be shared and

Table 8.6.   DaimlerChrysler, 2002

country/region	revenues $USbn	% of total	production locations	% of total	employees	% of total
Europe	53.4	34.1	29	27.9	216,300	59.2
of which Germany	24.2	15.5	na	na	na	na
				–		
North America	92.1	58.7	58	55.8	127,064	34.8
of which United States	81.5	51.9	na	na	na	na
				–		
South America	1.9	1.2	6	5.8	12,776	3.5
				–		
Asia Pacific	7.6	4.9	7	6.7	4,143	1.1
Asia	6.3	4.0	7	6.7	2,665	0.7
Australia and Oceania	1.4	0.9	–	–	1,478	0.4
Africa	1.8	1.2	4	3.8	5,288	1.4
Total	156.8	100.0	104	100.0	365,571	100.0

Source: DaimlerChrysler, Annual Report, 2002.
Note: Numbers might not add up due to rounding.

suppliers can manufacture different products for both vehicle brands at lower prices, the benefits from the merger were limited by the different product lines of each company.

The second, and perhaps most important barrier to overcome, was the cross-cultural differences between the German and US companies. From the beginning, Daimler's management dominated the merged company, which resulted in an outflow of key US personnel from management positions and the designer ranks. The Germans tended to be bureaucratic while US managers made decisions on the spot. Many US managers left unable to deal with the imposed management style. Capable designers went to rivals General Motors and Ford. Over time, the company has improved its cultural management of the US operations, and this is improving the company's overall position in the motor vehicle market.

DaimlerChrysler is undoubtedly a host-region based company, but a closer look at the organization shows, not a cohesive organization with a bi-regional market span, but two internal groups with individual global standings. Table 8.7 shows revenues for the company's groups. The Mercedes Car Group, the non-commercial vehicle successor to the German part of the merger, derives 63% of its revenues from the European

Table 8.7.   Daimler Chrysler revenues, 2000–2002

country/region	2002	2001	2000
(in percentages of total)			
European Union	31.1	29.9	31.0
of which Germany	15.5	15.9	16.0
North America	58.7	60.1	59.1
of which United States	51.9	53.1	52.0
other markets	10.2	10.0	9.9
Total revenues	100.0	100.0	100.0

Source: DaimlerChrysler, Key Figures, 2002.

Table 8.8. Honda, 2002		
country	sales $ (%)	assets (%)
Japan	23.3	31.4
North America	55.6	53.0
Europe	11.2	7.4
other	9.9	8.2
Total	100.0	100.0

Source: Adapted from Honda, *Annual Report*, 2003.

market. The Chrysler Group, on the other hand, continues to derive over 90% of its revenues from the North American market.

In terms of production, the Mercedes Group has eight production locations in Europe while the Chrysler Group has none. In the NAFTA region, the Chrysler Group has thirty-eight production locations while the Mercedes Group only has one. This reflects two separate entities each trying to capitalize on their own knowledge of its home region, not a truly bi-regional or host-region oriented company.

Honda

Toyota may be the largest Japanese automaker in the world, but in the United States, it is Honda that rules the road. In 2002, the Honda Accord was the best-selling passenger car in the United States. Not surprisingly, given the size of the US market, the company generates over half its revenues (55.6%) in North America. Its home market of Japan accounts for only 23.3% of sales. European sales account for 11.2% of sales while sales to other account for the remaining 9.9%. Most of the company's long-lived assets are also in its host region of North America, 53%. See table 8.8.

This unusual dependence on the North American market is the result of Toyota's dominance of the Japanese market. The relative spread of revenues across the triad is not only influenced by the ability of a company to penetrate a foreign market, but also by how much of the domestic market it can attain. A small car manufacturer might have better opportunities for growth, despite the liability of foreignness, in another region of the triad than in its own home region.

Honda's future success is expected to rely on the company's three strategic directions: to create value, "glocalization" a term the company coined to mean localized global operations and a commitment to the future. To increase value, the company relies on continued innovation. Honda's modular production methods are giving it an edge against the competition. Around the world the company is known for its smaller, less expensive, more efficient and environmentally friendly cars.

Glocalization is the company's commitment to a global supply chain that is responsive to local customers. "Made by Global Honda" has already been chosen as the expression that will represent this global supply network that will link facilities in different regions. Honda divides its business into five regional operations: its domestic market of Japan; North America, Latin America, Europe, the Middle East, and Africa; and Asia and Oceania. The Japanese market is expected to be served through imports from China, Thailand, Malaysia and Indonesia. To maintain its local responsiveness, the company has R&D facilities in each of the triad markets.

Questions for discussion

1. Is Honda a multinational enterprise? Why?
2. Is Honda a global multinational enterprise? Why?
3. If Honda's plan for "Made by Global Honda" is successful, what would this imply in terms of regionalization? What barriers to a true global supply network is the company likely to face?
4. What is Honda's basic strategy?
5. What is Honda's basic structure?
6. What are some of Honda's CSAs listed in this case? Can you think of any others?
7. What some of Honda's FSAs listed in this case?
8. What is the relationship between geographic revenues and assets for Honda? What does this signal about the company's worldwide strategy?

CONCLUSIONS

The world's automobile sector has no companies producing globally. Instead, most production occurs in sub-regional clusters within the broad triad economies of the EU, North America, and Asia. GM is a very home-region oriented firm, as is VW. Only Toyota and Honda are "bi-regionals," able to create significant sales presence in the host region United States, as well as in their home-region market of Japan and Asia. There is no evidence of a global car; just regional production as well as intra-regional sales. It's a regional world, not a global one.

9

Profiles of leading
multinational enterprises

Contents

The last four chapters have examined leading firms in four sectors: retail; banking; chemicals; and automobiles. In total, a set of twenty-three firms has been considered across these four sectors. Only one of these firms

(LVMH) is global; seven are bi-regional, and the remaining thirteen are home based. In this chapter another twenty-two firms will be profiled. These firms come from all these three major classifications: there are ten home-region firms; six bi-regionals; three global; plus two "near miss" global firms; and one host-region case. In this chapter, corporate strategy and structure of these well-known firms, as well as the performance of these firms, will be analyzed using publicly available information.

We are particularly interested in the extent to which each firm has a regional or global scope in its geographic sales (as shown by its classification in chapter 2) and the extent to which its FSAs have a home-region or global reach. We will later analyze each of these twenty-two firms (plus the twenty-three from the preceding four chapters) in terms of the regional matrix of figure 10.2 in the next chapter. Chapter 10, indeed, will serve as a summary chapter with the strategic positioning of each of the forty-five firms studied in detail in this book, plus a further five, for a total of fifty detailed case studies.

This chapter now examines a series of cases from each major category.

(a) Home-region cases: AOL Time Warner; Cisco Systems; TotalFinaElf; NEC; Starbucks; General Electric; Siemens; Haier; Procter and Gamble; Marubeni and Ashai Glass.
(b) Bi-regional cases: Kodak; McDonald's; L'Oréal Paris; LaFarge; Motorola; and British Petroleum.
(c) Global cases include: IBM; Flextronics; and Canon.
(d) "Near miss" global cases: Nestlé; Royal Dutch/Shell Group.
(e) Host-region cases: News Corp.

In this particular chapter, data for 2002 are used wherever possible. In other chapters, data for 2001 were used, reworked from the *Fortune* 500 for 2002. In practice, updating data makes very little difference; indeed none of the firms described here would be reclassified using the latest data for 2002. (This point is discussed further in chapter 12).

HOME-REGION CASES

AOL Time Warner

In 2001, America Online and Time Warner merged to create a massive multinational media and entertainment company with stakes in the internet connectivity, cable services, filmed entertainment, networks, music, and publishing industries. Yet, the AOL part of the name was dropped in mid 2003, as the stock market capitalization of the firm was then less than half of its value at the time of the merger. AOL Time Warner, ranked 98 in the *Fortune* Global 500, advertises itself as "a truly global company, with millions of readers, viewers, listeners, members, and subscribers – and thousands of employees – in every corner of the world." This seems credible; the firm has subsidiaries in thirty-four countries. Yet, a closer examination of the company's revenues in 2002 reveals that 80.7% of its revenues are derived from NAFTA countries. Assets outside the United States are minimal, and over 90% of all employees are located in the United States. This is clearly not a global company but one heavily dependent on its home-region market.

Market expansion in the media and entertainment industry is driven by mergers and acquisitions. The AOL and Time Warner merger is only the largest of many strategic alliances and acquisitions in the North American region that highlight an intra regional strategy. Acquisitions and strategic alliances within North America significantly outnumber those with European firms.

In its 2003 European Fact Book, AOL Time Warner claims that it is nationally responsive as it uses local European operators and services; employs local management and workers; develops local talent in journalism, film, television, and music; and has local partnerships for licensing, distribution, and production. Despite these statements, a significant portion of its European programming is provided by the North American home-region base, in order to achieve economies of scale. The local adaptation is less important than its FSAs in integration and brands.

Indeed, AOL Time Warner's marketing and distribution operations in Europe are insignificant. The limited success it has achieved in the region can be attributed to the company's successful brands, including: Time Inc., CNN, HBO, Warner Bros., Warner Music, New Line Cinema, and America Online. Some of these brands have been servicing Europe since the early twentieth century. This core competency enables the company to partner with strong regional firms to expand its international network.

Turner Broadcasting System, a subsidiary company which delivers CNN, has a number of joint ventures that allow it to offer targeted, locally responsive programming in markets in foreign countries, including Spain, Turkey, and Germany. Warner Bros. Pictures, another AOL Time Warner subsidiary, achieves international success in marketing and distributing its films through alliances with local companies and those which operate internationally. To be more locally responsive, Warner Bros. Pictures also purchases, produces, and distributes local films, but these are only a small fraction of total production.

North America is the most important market for AOL Time Warner for total revenues, total assets, and employees. The firm's second largest region, Europe, is significantly less important comprising less than 20% of total revenues and a smaller percentage of assets and employment. A large portion of the firm's programming continues to be produced in North America and distributed throughout its international operations with the help of subsidiaries and strategic alliance partners. Whether AOL Time Warner will be able to become a global company (or even needs to) depends on its ability to free its foreign subsidiaries from strong ties to US operations, providing more local programming that can compete effectively in other regions of the triad.

Cisco Systems

Ranked 213 in the *Fortune* Global 500, Cisco Systems is one of the largest networking firms in the world. It markets routers, switches, network access equipment, and network consulting services to customers in all three regions of the triad. Cisco is a home-region oriented company with 58.6% of its sales in North America in 2002. Revenues from Europe account for 25.6% of sales. Asia is responsible for only 15.8% of revenues.

Cisco's value chain includes design, development, manufacture, marketing, and technical support of networking products and services. Manufacturing itself has been outsourced to global contract manufacturers such as Flextronics and Solectron, which have manufacturing facilities across the world. While downstream, Cisco is North American oriented, upstream the firm is more geographically diversified.

Except in the telecommunications gear market, which is dominated by Nortel, Alcatel and Lucent, Cisco is the largest competitor in the corporate networking market. This focus on the corporate networking industry, as opposed to telecommunications, may be the reason why it remained profitable during the telecom downturn of the early 2000s. Cisco's market domination is based on the firms it acquires. These smaller firms bring innovative technology that is then incorporated into Cisco products, allowing Cisco to develop and market products that are superior to competitors' offerings in terms of quality, performance, and reliability. This FSA allows Cisco to sell its products at a premium price to its corporate consumers.

Cisco routers and switches are primary components of the internet and follow a universal standard that is compatible with all other components. This allows the company to achieve economies of scale by producing a relatively standard product for all its markets. By utilizing outsourcing companies to manufacture its products, Cisco also takes advantage of the economies of scale in large-scale manufacturing that these can provide.

In fibre-optics, Cisco's products compete with those of smaller firms such as Ciena, Corvis, and Sycamore. These companies have switching technology that is different from Cisco's, is compatible with present relevant technology, and is accepted by the market place. Moreover, the technology used by competitors is arguably better at conserving the original light signal, and this might become relevant in those markets that are already dominated by other competitors. It might also eventually, as both technologies further develop, affect Cisco's domestic market.

In the evolving IP telephony market, which is essentially the migration of voice data information onto the backbone of the internet, Cisco might also have to become more locally responsive. Presently, voice and telecommunications networks are highly regulated across the world. This is partly because land lines have traditionally been natural monopolies, but even wireless technology must be licensed and regulated. Whether this will extend to IP telephony is still to be seen. The internet, after all, has remained relatively free from regulation, and whatever IP telephony already exists has not yet been significantly regulated. Nonetheless, whatever type of regulation might be imposed on IP telephony is likely to be at the national/regional level and not at a global level. Such regulation might force Cisco, directly or indirectly – through companies that use their products – to be more locally responsive.

As technology continues to evolve, reducing costs, the wireless market is expected to grow dramatically. Yet, wireless telecommunications is a highly regulated industry that has not been technologically standardized. As a result, Cisco must ensure that its switching technology adheres to the standards of each nation or region if it is to effectively compete in the long term.

Cisco's growth to become a major player in the networking business was the result of serving the networking needs of businesses and the internet – an unregulated environment, but with standard technology needs. Whether Cisco can continue to provide the same products across the world with little differentiation will depend on how the markets for its business lines evolve over time. The firm has strong product quality and reliable FSAs as well as a recognized and respected brand name. Country-specific factors, however, are yet to be defined in many of its business lines.

TotalFinaElf

Ranked 15 in the *Fortune* Global 500, TotalFinaElf is one of the five largest oil companies in the world. In 2002, the company derived 54.8% of its sales from its home-region market of Europe. Another 11.7% was derived from North America, while the remaining 33.5% was accounted for by other non-specified regions. In terms of employment, TotalFinaElf is even more concentrated, with 75% in its home region.

Low oil prices in 1998 threatened to wipe out smaller oil companies, driving the world's largest companies into a frenzy of mergers that saw the number of players decrease from ten to five mega-oil companies by 2003. The largest mergers were BP and Amoco, Exxon and Mobil, Texaco and Chevron, and Total and Elf Aquitaine of France, to say nothing of the smaller players who were also acquired by these newly formed firms. Many were friendly mergers sold to management in each company as a marriage of equals. The takeover of Elf Aquitaine by Total, however, was a messy battle.

In 1995, Thiery Desmarest, a French civil worker turned petroleum explorer, became Total's CEO. At the time, the company was a middle-size European player; but in 1999, Total acquired Belgian Petrofina, outbidding and dethroning Elf Aquitaine as France's largest oil company. Days after completing the Petrofina deal, the CEO of Elf Aquitaine, Philippe Jaffre, received an unexpected all-stock offer from Totalfina worth $43 billion. Elf Aquitaine counter attacked with its own offer of $50.97 billion for Totalfina. Two months after the initial offer, shareholders handed the reins of the new company to Total.

A major reason for national regulatory approval of the merger was that it involved no foreign companies. Also, at a time of industry consolidation in an industry highly dependent on the ability of securing exploration contracts, one large French company could remain world competitive, but few thought two smaller companies could compete.

Trouble in the Middle East after the World Trade Center attacks of 9–11, created much uncertainty for the French oil company. One-fourth of the company's oil and gas production is located in the Middle East. When the United States attacked Iraq in 2003, French President, Jacques Chirac, stood firm in opposition. TotalFinaElf had for a long time seen Iraq as strategically important for long-term operations. But, political differences between France and the United States, which was to occupy Iraq, undermined TotalFinalElf's plans in the region.

In terms of FSAs, the consolidated TotalFinaElf now has the required size to bid for international contracts. This is a resource-based firm, however, and CSAs are extremely important. In the case of petroleum, where newer reserves are found in non-industrialized countries, international politics might become an important determinant of success. Thus, home-country and host-country CSAs are relevant, as well as the CSAs of third party countries.

NEC

In 1899, the first Japanese joint venture with foreign capital was established when Western Electric Company of the United States became a partner on the creation of Nippon Electric Company (NEC), a telephone and switching systems manufacturer. NEC, ranked 84 in the *Fortune Global 500*, now produces computer products, networking, semiconductors, industrial systems, and home appliances.

NEC's first international excursion was an export contract with Korea in 1951 to supply radio equipment. Taiwan Telecommunication Company became NEC's first post-war FDI venture. By the early seventies the company had additional operations in the United States, Mexico, Brazil, China, and Australia. Despite over fifty years of international expansion, Japan still accounts for about 83% of the company's revenues in 2002. North America accounts for an additional 5% while the remaining 12%

are sales in other parts of the world. In terms of long-lived assets, 90% are in its home market of Japan. Clearly, NEC is a home-region based company.

In the early 2000s, the company began to experience heavy losses as a result of the US recession. Heavy competition, as well as the world-wide effect of the US slowdown, forced the company into $415 million in losses in 2002. The heaviest losses were in North America ($237 million), but the company's home market also lost significantly ($126 million). The remaining $52 million in losses were in other markets. The company is now seeking to restructure to avoid further losses and become profitable again. Among the hurdles it has had to overcome is the Japanese aversion to cutting jobs, exporting production, and selling plants to foreign companies. This last one has already started to happen. In the first eight months of 2002, contract manufacturers took over a NEC workstation plant in Ibaraki and two optical-communications equipment factories in Miyagi and Yamanashi. The transfer of companies to contract manufacturers, which are better positioned to take advantage of economies of scale, often comes with long-term contracts to supply the same products that were originally manufactured to the seller.

NEC is also following other manufacturers on the road to China. In 2002, NEC announced plans to raise Chinese manufacture and assembly of PCs destined for the Japanese from 10% to 70%. The company already outsourced parts to these cheaper regions, but up to that point had continued to retain most assembly operations in Japan. In the upstream, NECs strategy will remain intra-regional.

In the plummeting DRAM market, however, it is unlike that any type of reform will help NEC against competitors from countries with lower costs. Not surprisingly then, NEC teamed up with Toshiba, Hitachi, and Mitsubishi to build an anti-dumping case against cheap foreign competitors. If this CSA is achieved, Japanese consumers will have to pay more for DRAM than consumers in other parts of the world. Korean companies are more likely to be affected and have established that they will consider legal action against any trade barrier. Hynix Semiconductor, one of the companies likely to be affected, claims that the decrease in price has been caused by a decrease in worldwide demand, not dumping. Samsung claims to be selling at the most expensive prices in the world.

NEC depends significantly on the Japanese market for its revenue and a large portion of its production. The firm's CSAs are extremely important for this firm, and as foreign competition undermines their national advantage, the firm might seek to create artificial CSAs to maintain market share in its home market. The firm's FSAs are location bound despite producing standardized products and having a global brand name. This is because management is not globally minded and has not created a globally diversified firm whose products and brand appeal to the other

Table 9.1. The distribution of Starbucks' stores, 2002				
Region	company operated	licensed	total	% of total
North America	3,496	1,110	4,606	78.25
Asia and Oceania	62	783	845	14.36
Europe, the Middle East and Africa	322	113	435	7.39
Total	3,880	2,006	5,886	100.00

Source: Adapted from Starbucks, Annual Report, 2002.

two regions of the triad. Compared to other firms in the industry, it is likely that NEC will continue to be home-region oriented expanding its market and production to nearby countries in Asia.

Starbucks

From its first location in Seattle's Pike Place Market in 1971, Starbucks has grown into one of the largest coffee chains with 5,886 locations in markets across the world. Although championed as a global company, Starbucks is highly home-region oriented. As shown in table 9.1, the company directly operates 3,496 coffee houses in forty-three US states, the District of Columbia, and five Canadian provinces. It also licenses 1,110 stores in North America, including thirty in Hawaii, one in Mexico, and one in Puerto Rico. While Starbucks might have licensed operations in far away countries like Oman and China, it is not global in its scope of operations; 78.25% of all its stores are located in its home region of North America. Most of its stores in Asia are licensed to other operators, and about half are located in Japan.

Since about 70% of its foreign stores are operated by others under licensing agreements, Starbucks derives an even lower percentage of its revenues from foreign regions. As shown in table 9.2, 86.1% of the company's net revenues are derived domestically. Including Canada, its second largest market, 91% of revenues are derived from North America. Only 9% of the company's revenues are derived from foreign regions – not exactly a global coffee giant. It also operates with an international division, which is a primitive type of global organizational structure.

Starbucks purchases and roasts high-quality coffee beans that are then brewed and retailed in coffee shops that cater to a loyal following. The corporate coffee culture, as it has been labeled, caters mostly to young urban professionals that appreciate the distinct taste of Starbucks' coffee. In addition, the company relies on outside retailers, such as supermarket

Table 9.2. Starbucks' net revenues by region, 2002		
region/country	net revenues	% of total
North America	2,993,225	91
of which, United States	2,830,650	86.1
other	295,683	9
Total	3,288,908	100

Source: Adapted from Starbucks, Annual Report, 2002.

chains, to sell ground coffee and cold drinks, such as the Frappuccino, which it markets in partnership with Kraft foods.

With coffee houses in twenty-five countries, Starbucks is to coffee what McDonald's is to hamburgers, and not surprisingly this has also made it a target of anti-globalization protesters. Coffee prices fell considerably in the late 1990s and led to the displacement of thousands of farmers. The main reason for a fall in the price of coffee was the oversupply that arose from improved production techniques and from a crop boom in the 1990s. Though Starbucks only purchases approximately 1% of the global supply of coffee, its high-profile has made it a main target for protestors who accuse the coffee giant of not providing a fair price to coffee growers. This is despite Starbucks' policy of purchasing high-quality beans at premium market prices. To address the concerns of protestors, Starbucks introduced Fairtrade endorsed coffee to its coffee houses. While the amount of Fairtrade coffee sold by the company is insignificant, at 1% of total sales, it is enough to portray the company as progressive and avert a consumer boycott.

Starbucks' FSAs include a brand name that is associated with a high-end corporate coffee culture. The distinctive taste of its coffee is also an FSA, as is the firm's relationship with its suppliers, to which the firm pays a premium price for high-quality beans. Cultural CSAs are the most important for Starbucks as they are the basis on which its niche market can succeed as a premium marketer of services of what is otherwise a staple product.

General Electric

General Electric (GE) is a multibillion dollar, multinational enterprise whose products range from 65-cent light bulbs to billion-dollar power plants. In terms of revenue, GE ranks as number nine in the *Fortune Global 500*. The company derives approximately 59.8% of its revenues from the United States. Adding revenues from Canadian and Latin American operations, this number rises to 63.7%. GE is a home-region oriented firm. Europe, its largest foreign regional market, only accounts for 18.5% of its revenues while countries in the Pacific Basin account for a mere 9.1% of revenues. The remaining 8.7% of revenues are accounted for by other regions (3%) and non-segmented US exports to other countries (5.7% of revenues).

The firm's ability to manage a diverse multiproduct-line operation and a range of services is the main reason for the company's revenue totaling over $130 billion. GE's advantage over generally failing conglomerates is its ability to transfer knowledge over the whole company. This can be attributed to the successful leadership of former CEO Jack Welsh who oversaw GE's transformation from a mainly manufacturing company to a service-oriented knowledge-based company. He defined the company's culture by creating a workforce that can identify opportunities and implement changes. Product–related concepts, such as Six Sigma, are the basis of the firm's success. Indeed, GE pioneered production practices that encourage employee innovation, process improvement, and best practices under the Six Sigma banner, which emphasizes near-zero defects in all parts of the company's operation.

In October 2000, General Electric, the world's largest producer of jet engines, and Honeywell, a manufacturer of aircraft electronics, agreed to a $42 billion merger. The two US based companies secured antitrust authorities approval in the United States and Canada, but the deal came to a halt as a result of the EU. This was the first time the EU blocked a merger between two US companies. The European competition commissioner claimed that such a merger would have closed the market to competitors and asked GE to divest itself of GE Capital Aviation Services by selling it to one of its main rivals. General Electric offered to sell the company privately, but the EU countered that a friendly transaction might not result in true divestiture. US politicians, frustrated by the European stand, threatened to retaliate if the EU did not approve the merger. Republican Senator Phil Gramm went so far as to accuse the EU of enacting policies to protect their companies. The EU rejected US government intervention in the matter, and the merger did not materialize.

The nature of a diversified conglomerate makes the recognition of FSAs and CSAs more difficult. In its product segment, integration strategies might translate into an FSA if R&D and knowledge could be coordinated across its product lines. In all areas of the organization, an FSA for GE lies in its implementation of Six Sigma which is said to make it a learning organization. Indeed, the firm owns a structure and workforce with a unique capability to innovate and disseminate knowledge of best practices. At the same time, it is difficult to assess the degree to which a diversified product line affects economies of scale and the competitive advantage of each product against those of firms dedicated to more specific product lines.

CSAs are also difficult to assess because a large portion of the firm's operations are in diversified financials, which are heavily regulated. Its product offerings, on the other hand, have virtual free access across national borders.

Despite the company's firm-specific advantage (FSAs) in production, knowledge, and best practices, its competitive edge has not been transferred equally to other parts of the world, especially not to other triad nations which have significant domestic competitors. Its strategy, moreover, is subject to regulatory approval in more than one region.

Siemens

Ranked at 395 in the top 500, Siemens of Germany is a home-region oriented company with 53% of its sales in Europe (21% of its total in Germany); 29% in the Americas (24% is in the United States); and 12% in

	500 rank	company	region	revenues in bn US$ 2001
1	19	Intl. Business Machines	North America	85.9
2	22	Siemens	Europe	77.4
3	32	Hitachi	Asia-Pacific	63.9
4	37	Sony	Asia-Pacific	60.6
5	45	Matsushita Electric Industrial	Asia-Pacific	55.0
6	70	Hewlett Packard	North America	45.2
7	77	Toshiba	Asia-Pacific	43.1
8	84	NEC	Asia-Pacific	40.8
9	88	Fujitsu	Asia-Pacific	40.0
10	103	Tyco International	North America	36.4
11	117	Compaq Computer	North America	33.6
12	131	Dell Computer	North America	31.2
13	138	Motorola	North America	30.0
14	141	Mitsubishi Electric	Asia-Pacific	29.2
15	143	Royal Philips Electronics	Europe	29.0
16	147	Nokia	Europe	27.9
17	162	Intel	North America	26.5
18	180	Lucent Technologies	North America	25.1
19	190	Canon	Asia-Pacific	23.9
20	194	ABB	Europe	23.7
21	210	L. M. Ericsson	Europe	22.4
22	213	Cisco Systems	North America	22.3
23	261	Solectron	North America	18.7
24	263	Nortel Networks	North America	18.5
25	268	Sun Microsystems	North America	18.3
26	293	Sanyo Electric	Asia-Pacific	16.9
27	300	Xerox	North America	16.5
28	326	Emerson Electric	North America	15.5
29	327	Onex	North America	15.4
30	346	Sharp	Asia-Pacific	14.4
31	379	Ricoh	Asia-Pacific	13.4
32	386	Electrolux	Europe	13.1
33	388	Flextronics International	Asia-Pacific	13.1
34	431	Sumitomo Electric Industries	Asia	11.9
35	464	Oracle	North America	10.9
36	491	Whirlpool	North America	10.3

Table 9.3.   World's largest computer, office and electronics industries

the Asia Pacific region (3% in Japan). Of its 417,000 workforce, 41% are located in its home base of Germany. Siemens is the third largest firm in the electronics category, see table 9.3.

The firm's structure is to use decentralized product line SBUs. Yet it co-ordinates groups and divisions to realize synergies across R&D, procurement, process development, shared services, etc. But as Siemens had 1220 subsidiaries in 2002, it is difficult to generalize about their degree of autonomy versus centralized co-ordination. There are consolidated subsidiaries reporting to head office in Munich on a monthly basis whereas non-consolidated report quarterly. Operating groups and subsidiaries are independent profit centers with regional units supporting their activities. Its strategy is based on development of a set of strongly-branded product lines; these are its FSAs. To an extent Siemens builds on the technological and human capital CSAs of Germany. Siemens has strong global brand name products and a strong home base in Germany for its R&D and strategic development.

Haier

With revenues of $8.7 billion in 2001, Haier of China does not rank as a top 500 firm. Like most Chinese firms, the bulk of its sales are intra-regional. Haier has 88.4% of its sales in Asia; 10.4% in North America; and only 1.2% in the EU.

Haier produces electrical appliances such as refrigerators, microwaves, and small appliances. Its subsidiaries in North America and Europe are responsible for distribution and after-sales service, and they are also consulted for design and production modifications. The firm's major advantage against competitors comes from China's abundant and inexpensive labor. This CSA, combined with new product development, has allowed Haier to become a major player in Asia but not yet globally.

Haier is a supplier to Wal-Mart, Target, and other leading US retailers and is now attempting to turn itself into a well-known North American name. In New York, the firm has purchased the Haier building to house corporate offices, showrooms, and R&D labs. In South Carolina, the firm has an industrial park that produces refrigerators and is expected to produce air conditioners and washing machines in the future. These major investments show that Haier seeks to create a bi-regional infrastructure in which localized research, design, and local production in the US are complemented with China's abundant-labor production.

Haier competes with GE, Siemens, Samsung, Philips, Whirlpool, Hitachi, and other large MNEs. Few major technological advances are expected in household appliances, a mature business segment. Inputs such as plastic and steel are commodities. Therefore, scale economies and production-cost efficiencies are critical for commercial success. Here, Haier's low wage Chinese home market CSA is critical. Haier is in cell 2 of the regional matrix of figure 3.2; it has strong local cheap labor home-country advantages giving it a regional geographic scope, and it now sells regionally across Asia, but not much elsewhere, meaning that it lacks global scope in its FSAs.

Procter and Gamble

Home-region oriented Procter and Gamble has the working of a global company. The firm structure is comprised of four interactive parts, whose subsidiaries are strategically placed around the world to best achieve cost-effectiveness, marketing and production, and design quality. At the front end, seven Market Development Organizations (MDOs) are responsible for marketing products in the following regions: North America; ASEAN, India, Australia; China; Northeast Asia; Central and Eastern Europe, the Middle East and Africa; Western Europe and Latin America. In turn, these MDOs collaborate with any one of five product-based Global Business Units (GBUs) responsible for R&D, design and the manufacturing processes. Global Business Services (GBSs), mainly located in developing countries, provide accounting, human resource management, logistic and system operations to all operations in a given region. A Corporate Functions (CF) segment oversees operations.

This global structure, however, has not resulted in an even distribution of sales across all three regions of the triad, or across P&G's seven-region segmentation. North America accounts for 55% of the firms revenues. Europe accounts for a significant 27%, but no other region accounts for more than 20% of the firm's sales.

The firm's most important FSA is its ability to market products in multiple regions. It does this through product adaptation, marketing, and packaging to the needs of customers in diverse regions and by creating successful brands. Indeed, the firm managed thirteen brands with revenues of over 1 billion dollars in 2003. Some of its most famous brands include Tide, Ariel, Pantene, and Crest.

P&G's strategy does not necessarily include developing global brands like Pringles, its most globally diversified brand. Instead, the firm might choose locally trusted brands to channel new products to multiple regions. Blendax, a European brand, is now the portal by which P&G markets Whitestrips that are sold in North America under the Crest brand. Many successful brands were carefully picked up through acquisitions and then revamped with new marketing. Between 1980 and 2000, P&G acquired Cover Girl, Noxzema, Clarion, Oil of Olay, Blendax, Old Spice, Max Factor, and Pantene, among others. That is, the firm finds regional brands to develop regionally.

Another FSA is that its portfolio of products allows the diffusion of the firm's R&D to different product lines in all regions. For example, a fabric detergent discovery may create improved versions of Tide and Cheer in North America, Ariel in Latin America, and Bold in Japan. It might also spill over to non-fabric cleaners such as Salvo. This, and the GBUs ability to coordinate production across the world, translates into scale economies that are difficult to rival in the industry.

P&G has gone further than most companies in creating a global structure that incorporates non-industrialized countries. For example, the GBS for the Americas is located in Costa Rica, while the Philippines GBS provides services to the Asian region. Factories are located in Asia and Eastern

Europe and Latin America, as well as in more developed countries. R&D, usually reserved for developed nations, has also seen its way to developing countries like China.

Despite a highly diversified geographic structure and the use of local brands to market products, P&G continues to derive the majority of its sales from its home region. In addition, there are no regulatory barriers to marketing the majority of its products across national borders. Its strategy of acquiring successful local brands to expand internationally allows it to evade local cultural resistance to a foreign brand while eliminating a major competitor. P&G may be preparing itself to become a truly global firm.

Marubeni

The five large Japanese keiretsus are all represented in the top 500 list: Mitsubishi at 12; Mitsu at 13; Ichikan at 17; Sumitomo at 23; and Marubeni at 25. All of these are home-region based organizations. For example, Marubeni has 70% of its sales in Japan; 14% in the United States, and 4% in Europe. It is responsible for Nissan's sales, and the Nissan Sales Corporation has 68% of its sales in Europe; 19% in the United States; and 10% in Latin America (it has more sales in Japan – a separate firm sells for Nissan in its home market).

Marubeni attempts to use a horizontal organizational structure to be locally responsive, but its product decisions are centralized and report to Japanese head office. The Japanese keiretsus like Marubeni are placed in cell 9 where its global FSAs are matched by local CSAs in quality and cost, building on the Japanese single diamond of highly skilled human capital.

Ashai Glass

Ashai Glass, 499 in the *Fortune* Global 500, produces a diverse range of glass products, electronics and display equipment, as well as chemical products. In 2002, the firm had sales of $11 billion. Of this, 69% were derived in Asia; 18% in Europe and 13% in North America. It is the market leader with 30% of the world's auto glass sales. Across all its SBUs in glass, its main rivals are Pilkington; Saint Gobain; Corning; Nippon Electric Elan; and DuPont. One of its firm SBUs is Automotive Glass.

In the glass segment, most of Ashai's revenues are derived from the construction industry, and the firm is a major competitor in most business lines. In the automotive industry the firm commands 30% of the world's market. This is a business-to-business industry and Ashai is a key supplier of glass to the major automobile OEMs.

Ashai Glass has 60% of the auto glass market in Japan and supplies all the Japanese OEMs. In the United States it has only 13% of the market, but it supplies the Japanese OEMs, Mercedes, and even the US big three. In Europe it supplies Renault and PSA, but not Mercedes. Asahi is a centralized company with a focus on high-quality standards, integration, and a common strategy. It is located in cell 5 where its Japanese CSAs have become regional in Asia; it has global FSAs in high quality, and it has developed regional FSAs in management to supply OEMs in Europe and North America.

BI-REGIONAL CASES

Kodak

Kodak, ranked 383 in the *Fortune* Global 500, is a bi-regional company. Approximately 46.8% of its sales are in the United States. Europe (including the Middle East and Africa) and Asia-Pacific are also important regions accounting for 26.2% and 17.5% of total sales, respectively. If Canada and Mexico account for a mere 3.2% of sales, it might be categorized as home-region oriented, but the firm does not provide this information.

"You press the button, and we do the rest," was Eastman Kodak's slogan when it introduced the Kodak Brownie in 1900. The user-friendly camera put photography at the reach of the average person. The company is today recycling the slogan to promote its easy-to-use digital photography cameras. Kodak pioneered digital cameras in 1976, but unlike Kodak's early innovations, which mostly went unchallenged, digital photography is turning out to be a battle ground for competitors, including electronics and computer manufacturers who have access to digital technology.

Slowly, but surely, digital photography will become the most popular form of recording images. Consumer reaction to this new technology will define the revenue generation model, but the significance of this is yet to be seen. Traditionally, photographic companies derived revenues from selling cameras, but most importantly, from selling film and developing and printing photographs. Today, the digital camera user has a number of alternative printing methods, if he or she wants to print at all.

Consumers might choose to use one of two external printing options: take their memory chip to an internet kiosk to have prints developed, or send their picture files over the internet to be printed and mailed back to them. Kodak's retail network might give it a competitive advantage if consumers can be convinced to drop by and use full service or self-serve printing machines at their locations. If, however, consumers choose to do everything from home, sending photographs to a virtual kiosk that would then mail prints, upstarts might gain a hold in the better part of the market.

Kodak's brand name, however, is likely to provide a significant advantage even on the internet. If a customer wants to develop photos, one might just try www.kodak.com. That is, if Windows will allow it. Collaboration with Microsoft turned confrontational when Microsoft developed its own photo software that popped up automatically when a camera chip was inserted. The windows software directed users to photo developers who paid fees to Microsoft. For Kodak, the consequences could be devastating. The company needs to be able to enter the web-based printing market to make up for losing profits in its traditional film business. To add insult to injury Microsoft teamed up with Kodak's archrival Fuji, listing it as one of the photo-developing service providers. Kodak complained to anti-trust regulators. How the battle for web-based developing will turn out, no one yet knows.

Another consumer alternative is to print photographs at home using a regular color printer or a more specialized photograph printer available at many computer and office supplies stores. While the concept of consumers having their own developing stations seems unlikely at the moment, CD writing was once only considered for the most enthusiastic of computer users and is now a standard feature in most computers sold. If something similar were to happen in the photographic industry, it would probably take revenues from traditional photographic companies to manufacturers of printer-friendly photographic paper, ink, cartridges, and toner. Will there be a spot left for Kodak to contribute in this market? The company certainly hopes so and is teaming up with computer companies such as HP and Lexmark to position itself should the market go this way. Yet, even this type of revenue generation is at risk since the European Commission began to investigate whether printer companies were illegally forcing consumers to purchase their ink, toners, and cartridges.

Perhaps the bleakest prediction for this industry is the near extinction of printing and developing revenue. Research shows that most people never print their digital photographs. Why would a consumer print her photographs if she can store them inside her computer, save them on disks, and share them with family and friends around the world at a negligible price? It is likely that only a select few photographs will ever make it to paper.

Other types of revenue generation include the manufacturing and selling of cameras, digital camera software, and compatible computer software, and photographic printing machines. Kodak has entered all of these markets, but whether it can be successful in all of them for the long run is still being decided.

Outside the digital wars, Kodak is consistently challenged by competitors in many other of its business lines. In 1997, Kodak and Fuji participated in a price war on traditional film that threatened to make film

Table 9.4. McDonald's revenues

country/region	revenues	% of total
United States	5,423	35.2
Canada	633	4.1
Total United States and Canada	6,056	39.3
Latin America	814	5.3
Europe	5,136	33.3
APMEA	2,368	15.4
Partner brands	1,032	6.7
Total	15,406	100.0

Source: McDonald's, Annual Report, 2002.
APMEA = Asia Pacific, Middle East, and Africa.

into a commodity. In the mid-1990s, Kodak pushed forth a case in the WTO claiming Japan's trade regulations did not allow it to enter the Japanese market. This, it claimed, allowed Fuji to reduce profit margins in the US market, effectively dumping products. The WTO dismissed all charges.

Kodak's traditional FSAs are being challenged by innovations that have increased the number of competitors and changed the rules of the game. Its brand name in photography now competes with other well-known brand names in the electronics industry for a market and revenue stream that are yet to be defined.

McDonald's

Data show that McDonald's has not expanded equally across the globe. In 2002, 72.6% of the company's revenues originated in two regions, North America with 39.3% of total sales (excluding Mexico) and Europe with 33.3% (see table 9.4). Asia Pacific, the Middle East and Africa, on the other hand, account for only 15.4% of revenues. This is not a global company, but a bi-regional company.

The company's spread of locations tells a slightly different story. North America accounts for nearly half (47.6%) of all outlets and Europe only for 19.3%. Asia-Pacific, the Middle East, and Africa, account for a small percentage of revenue but 24.3% of all locations are in this market (see table 9.5). That is, the company derives less revenue per location in Asia-Pacific, the Middle East, and Africa than in its two major regional markets.

When José Bové, a self-proclaimed leader of France's anti-globalization movement, was sentenced for vandalizing a McDonald's restaurant in 1999, he claimed to have the support of the French people. Although that might have been an overstatement, he is not the only one that equates McDonald's restaurants with a drive towards global cultural homogeneity.

Yet, McDonald's bends over backwards to blend into local cultures. In the land of José Bové, Asterix, a French comic-strip character who stands for individuality and ironically symbolizes local resistance to imperial forces, has replaced the goofy Ronald McDonald. In India, where local tastes are very different than those in America, the company crafted an entirely different menu that does not use beef, pork, or animal flavoring due to the mostly vegetarian population. In Israel, locally owned

McDonald's purchases over 80% of its ingredients from local producers, including 100% kosher hamburger meat, potatoes, lettuce, buns, and milkshake mix.

On the other hand, McDonald's does bring its own brand to its foreign operations. In China, where children's birthdays are not traditionally celebrated, a successful McDonald's marketing strategy encouraged birthday parties at their establishment. Not a bad deal for children, but still a cultural effect from a foreign multinational. More mundane things, such as "combo meals," are popularized through McDonald's expansion. The company's presence creates a cultural exchange, not a one-sided cultural takeover.

Table 9.5. McDonald's locations

country/region	no. of stores	% of total
United States	13,491	43.4
Canada	1,304	4.2
Total United States and Canada	14,795	47.6
Latin America	1,605	5.2
Europe	6,070	19.5
APMEA	7,555	24.3
Partner brands	1,083	3.5
Total	31,108	100.0

Source: McDonald's, Annual Report, 2002.
APMEA = Asia Pacific, Middle East, and Africa.

L'Oréal Paris

Like many other French companies, L'Oréal Paris, ranked 415 in the top 500, capitalizes on its country's reputation for fine luxury beauty products. A multinational cosmetics manufacturer, L'Oréal has 238 subsidiaries and a presence in 130 countries. Sixty-eight percent of L'Oréal's 50,000 employees work outside of France. L'Oréal is a bi-regional company with 49.9% of its sales in Western Europe. The North American market is an additional 30.3%. Operations in Japan, Latin America, Eastern Europe, and other Asia account for less than 20% of the company's revenues.

Much of the firm's expansion into international markets, as well as its movement into niche markets at home and abroad, was the result of acquisition of already established brands. In 1996, L'Oréal purchased US cosmetic giant Maybelline, and in 2001 purchased both Japan's Shu Uemura and Kiehl's of the United States. L'Oréal also owns Cacharel, Garnier, Helena Rubinstein, Lancôme, and Vichy, among others.

The bi-regional nature of L'Oréal's operations make government regulations in the United States and the EU very important, and the company might get caught up in the cross fire. In 2001, the EU proposed a ban on all new products that were developed using animal experiments, which L'Oréal performs, even if the animal testing was not done in the EU. This negatively threatened the firm's CSAs in its two main regions. It meant that it may not be able to develop new products involving animal testing to be sold in its home region. It also meant that if the United States decided to retaliate against this extra-territorial regulation, L'Oréal could see its ability to import and export freely from its two main regions jeopardized.

As a western company, L'Oréal has sought to enter the growing Chinese market. This could potentially lead to global scope. Today, the cosmetics company manufactures locally and has made Maybelline, a traditionally US product, China's top-seller make up line. Sales in China are growing at about 25% per year; a combination of several factors, including the opening up of the Chinese market, has increased the individual expectations of the young urban population and the company's ability to adapt to the local market.

Not all cosmetic products are created alike. Shampoos and hair coloring products for the Chinese market have different recipes from in the United States and Europe because Chinese hair is stronger, and color preferences are different. In marketing, L'Oréal has signed up Zhang Ziyi, from the movie Crouching Tiger, Hidden Dragon to model Maybelline lipstick, a move that has helped the company achieve 33% of the Chinese lipstick market. Marketing decisions are made under the philosophy that no one knows a target group better than the target group itself. Only eight of L'Oréal's 3,000 employees in China are foreigners. The average age of employees is twenty-eight years, the same age as the customers the company is trying to attract.

Entering the Chinese market has not been an easy task for L'Oréal, and the country is unlikely to become an easy win. L'Oréal and other western companies are under heavy pressure from Chinese start-ups who have shown an incredible ability to become competitive in a very short span of time. Another problem facing foreign companies in China is the wide range of counterfeit products sold under their name. This has several implications, including the loss of product and the loss of reputation that may come from under-performing clones. While the Chinese market offers much promise to L'Oréal, the company's operations there are insignificant.

LaFarge

One of the world's largest cement firms is French MNE, LaFarge. The firm offers more than 5,000 products ranging from ultra-high performance concrete, ready-mix concrete, improved roofing material, plasterboard insulation systems, etc. It has a presence in seventy-five countries, and while it operates from its European base it is expanding in North America and Asia. In 2001, LaFarge derived 40% of its sales from Western Europe, 32% North America, and 8% from Australia. The remaining 20% of revenues originate in Central and Eastern Europe, Africa, the Indian Ocean, the Mediterranean Basin, and Latin America. In an industry that is essentially location bound, this is an extraordinary market presence.

Cement is very costly to transport, so virtually all production is local and close to large urban areas. Only sea transportation is at all viable (e.g. across the great lakes, where Canadian firms export to the United

States). However, even then most cement plants are not near ports as they need to be near limestone deposits. Since trade is so costly, firms engage in foreign direct investment, buying up local cement firms, and thereby becoming MNEs.

In 2001 LaFarge acquired Blue Circle industries, a UK cement and building company bringing its total production capacity from 107 million tons to 150 million tons, or 10% of world capacity. The merger reinforced LaFarge's position as top dog in Europe and was a big shot in the arm for its international business in Asia. In North America, LaFarge was forced to sell part of Blue Circle's concrete business to satisfy regulators.

In the United States, foreign companies account for a large portion of cement production; for example, two of the major cement companies are foreign-owned Cemex and Holnam. The US cement firms are generally smaller than the European and other foreign-owned firms. LaFarge's North American subsidiary is also a big player in the region with revenues of $2.8 billion. The company is the largest supplier in Canada and the third largest in the United States after Holnam and Cemex.

In the third part of the triad, the largest cement MNEs are also moving to acquire assets in Asia where the market is dominated by independent suppliers. Lafarge has a capacity of thirty million tons in Asia and is the market leader in the Philippines and Malaysia, where the company acquired local companies. China is the largest producer of cement in the world with over 576 million tons of capacity, or a third of world production. The country has thousands of cement manufacturers working with different levels of technology. Lafarge, Heidelberger, Zement, and Italcementi are already in China.

India is the fourth largest cement producer in the world with 110 million tons of capacity. There are 120 large cement plants owned by fifty-seven companies throughout the country. LaFarge is slowly entering the Indian market but is still a relatively small player with capacity totaling 1.43 million tons in 2001. Italcementi has capacity of six million tons in India.

As shown in table 9.6, the world's concrete industry is dominated by triad-based MNEs, in which European and Mexican firms are competing in both the rich markets of the EU and North America and also in the new markets of Asia. These firms bring their FSAs in management and logistics to domestic cement operations.

Motorola

Ranked 138 in the *Fortune* Global 500, Motorola is a bi-regional company. In 2002, 45% of its sales were in the United States. Asia-Pacific is the second most important market for the company accounting for 28% of sales. In Europe, stiff competition has stymied the firm, which only derives 14% of its revenues from this region.

Table 9.6.	World production capacity of the largest five cement producers, 2001				
	home country	cement production capacity (mln of tons)	% of world capacity	scope of operations (in countries)	revenues (in billions of US $)
LaFarge	France	150	10.0%	75	11.3
Holcim	Switzerland	109.8	7.3%	70	8.3
CEMEX	Mexico	78	5.2%	Over 30	5.6
Heidelberg Zement	Germany	55	3.7%	50	6.3
Italcementi	Italy	39	2.6%	14	3.5
Others		1068.2	71.2%	na	na
Total		1500	100%	na	na

Note: to calculate figures in US $ an average exchange rate over the year 2000 was used.

Motorola had its beginning when Paul Galvin began manufacturing car radios at affordable prices in 1929. At the time, skeptics wondered if anyone would be interested in a car radio. The Motorola, a name derived from motor and Victrola, dominated the car radio market for several years and became a springboard from which Galvin's company expanded into communication equipment for the military, the "walkie-talkie" was developed by a Motorola engineer, and consumer goods like televisions.

In the 1970s, increased competition from the Japanese forced Motorola to abandon the car radio and to sell its television business to Matsushita. Instead, the company was to focus on two-way pagers and other types of communication technology. In 1983, the company introduced the first cell phone. Today, Motorola is the second largest cell phone company after Nokia, and it has become the leader in cable modems and set-top terminals. Not a surprising ending considering the route.

The battle has just begun though. The company faces stiff competition from Nokia and Ericsson in its cell phone market and has recently reported heavy losses. There are many reasons for this. Its home market has low market penetration of wireless phones. Only 30% of Americans own a mobile cell phone, while 60% of Britons do. Europeans use their cell phones in a different way also, relying heavily on text-messaging as a principal means of communicating. Some of the differences have to do with the fact that local calls through land lines are basically free in the United States and are billed by the minute in Europe. Another factor is that the EU adopted a common wireless platform while the United States chose to let the market decide. This type of fragmentation impeded market-wide economies of scale from materializing.

Yet, others blame Motorola itself for its economic troubles. Approximately 70% of wireless phones are purchased by network providers who then sell them to their subscribers. Market research shows that someone who buys a Nokia phone is likely to spend more on phone calls than one with a Motorola. Also, satisfied Nokia customers are likely to retain their plans and phones while Motorola customers are likely to look for other options. The company has also been criticized for not being responsive to the European market, including the wireless crazy youth market. This is not surprising since it still has all its phones designed in Chicago.

At a time when plants were being closed in Europe and the company was reporting company-wide losses – partly as a result of a worldwide economic slowdown – Motorola was expanding aggressively in China. By 2001, the country had the largest number of cell phone subscribers in the world. In the PC market, where the company is also active, Motorola planned to open at least ten semi-conductor wafer fabrication plants to increase its output by $10 billion by 2006.

In China, Motorola faces stiff competition from other western companies. Ericsson and Nokia both have healthy shares of this market. Yet, in 2002, the company reached $3.7 billion in revenues, making China its largest market in the Asian region. Motorola's advantage in this market stems from a first-mover advantage in wireless and PC technology. For years, the company was the biggest US investor in China. Another advantage comes from its reliance on the Mac OS, which is better able to handle Chinese characters. It takes between 7,000 and 10,000 Chinese characters to be basically literate, making a western-style keyboard unfeasible. Motorola's subsidiary, Lexicus, owns voice- and handwriting-recognition technology that might also help overcome the language barrier. Motorola is also struggling against local start ups which might eventually threaten its home market.

Motorola is significant not only because US companies are less likely to be bi-regional than their European and Asian counterparts, but also because it is the only US company in the sample whose foreign regional market is Asia-Pacific.

British Petroleum (BP)

Ranked the fourth largest company in the top 500, with $178.7 billion in revenues, BP has 45.4% of its sales in Europe; 38.3% in North America; but well under the 20% required in Asia to make it a "global" firm. Instead, it is classified as a bi-regional firm. Its (F/T) is 76.8%, making it a very international firm, but one with a major presence in only two regions of the triad.

The merger of British Petroleum and Amoco on December 31, 1998, and the company's subsequent purchase of Atlantic Richfield Company (i.e. ARCO) in 2000, significantly increased the company's operations in the US market as well as facilitating two of the firm's long-term strategic goals: to cut costs through greater efficiency and economies of scale and to diversify its operations away from crude oil exploration, production and retail sales. The recent mergers have increased BP's natural gas production to 34% of overall company production – from 20% in 1998.

Like most large oil companies, BP faces declining oil reserves. This has forced the company to find new sources of production both inside and outside the triad. Outlined as a five-year initiative, BP plans to focus over half of its upstream investment activities on five specific areas: Angola, the Asia-Pacific, Azerbaijan, the Gulf of Mexico and Trinidad.

BP is aiming to make solar power a $1 billion revenue stream by 2007, driven primarily by its standing as a leading producer of solar power cells. Although company revenues from alternative energy sources (i.e. solar, wind, etc.) remain small at about $240 million in 2002, BP ranks highly with environmentalists; it was at the top of the Financial Times World's Most Respected Companies rankings, see Rugman and Hodgetts (2003). For the short term, BP's exploration into alternative energy sources will not drastically alter its production and sales structure. Though its usage will be primarily confined to the most developed economies due to the expensive nature of the technology, the projected market size will have little impact.

BP has developed into a bi-regional company, but this is due to the recent merger activity centered in linking its European base with the US market. With current exploration and production facilities maturing and slowly declining in the North Sea and Alaska, BP is being forced to use better technology to continue its presence in North America and to find new sources of crude oil in Asia and Europe. Increasingly, the firm will have to develop FSAs in alternative energy.

GLOBAL CASES

International business machines

In 1911, four recording and processing equipment manufacturers in the United States merged to form the Computer-Tabulating-Recording Company (C-T-R). C-T-R opened an office in Canada six years later under the name of International Business Machines Company. This name was adopted by all the company's operations in 1924, and today most people simply recognize this firm, which is the world's nineteenth largest, as IBM.

A pioneer of the personal computer (PC), IBM is also well known for leading the way to globalization. Its operations span over 160 countries, and it has research laboratories in six countries across the triad. Indeed, IBM is the largest of only nine global companies in the *Fortune* 500. For the year 2002, IBM derived 44.9% of all its revenue from the Americas (40.4% in the United States) compared to 24.3% in Europe, the Middle East and Africa, and 21.1% in Asia-Pacific (13.5% in Japan). The remaining 9.7% of its revenue derives from IBM's uncategorized global operations.

IBM was an international company at its conception. C-T-R had brought together the international operations of all its predecessors. IBM Canada, for example, was founded to consolidate the Canadian operations of three of the companies that had been merged under C-T-R. Over the following decades, the company pursued international expansion across the world.

In Latin America, an office was opened in Brazil in 1917. Within the next twenty years, IBM secured contracts with governments and corporations in Argentina, Mexico, Ecuador, Chile, Cuba, Uruguay, and Peru.

In Asia, the company opened its first office in Bombay, India in 1920. The Philippine market was entered in 1925, and this was followed in 1926 by the first IBM equipment being installed in Osaka, Japan, for the Nippon Mutual Life Insurance Company. In China, the first IBM machines were installed at the Peking Union Medical College in 1934.

IBM's entry into the European market started when a branch of the International Time Recording Company, an IBM forerunner, opened in France in 1914. It was only in 1919 that a consolidated IBM was introduced in Europe. In the 1920s and 1930s, IBM manufacturing facilities sprang up in Germany, France, England, and Italy.

Production is also spread around the world. Product lines are clustered in regions that offer plentiful labor or specialized technology, depending on the nature of the product. ThinkPads are manufactured in Shenzhen, China, and desktops in Guadalajara, Mexico. This reliance on developing countries allows the company to take advantage of low-labor costs while placing it inside some of the fastest-growing markets in the world.

IBM's highest commitment to globalizing production is its increasing reliance on electronic-manufacturing service providers. More than two-thirds of the company's Intel-based products are manufactured in worldwide factories by contract manufacturers, including Sanmina-SCI and Solectron, (see Flextronics Case Study).

IBM is one of only a few companies that have been able to successfully penetrate foreign regional markets in terms of revenues and production. One main reason is that the computer, office, and electronics industry in which IBM operates is one of the most global, with average intra-regional sales of 56.2%. Seven of the nine global firms are from this industry. This extra-regionality is the result of standardized components that can be transported cheaply across the world, allowing for a global supply chain.

In terms of assets, however, IBM is highly intra-regional. In 2002, 63.8% of long-lived assets were located in the United States. There are a number of reasons for this, including: (1) foreign production facilities are often owned by contract manufacturers; (2) the cost of land and equipment is higher in the United States than in many of the developing countries in which the company manufactures; and (3) the United States remains the most important market for IBM. Indeed, while IBM has over 20% of its sales in each triad market, the Americas continue to account for the largest portion of sales. It is difficult to argue that this is merely the result of a home-region advantage. The United States is after all the largest triad economy and the largest market for technology products.

Flextronics

The emergence of "electronics-manufacturing service providers" (EMS) has led corporate rivals such as Sony and Philips, or Ericsson, Alcatel and Motorola, to share the same factories to manufacture their competing products. Indeed, companies unknown to the public, such as Flextronics, Solectron, Sanmina-SCI, Celestica, and Jabil, among others, produce such well-known products as IBM PCs, the Microsoft Xbox video console, Web TV set-top boxes for Phillips and Sony and portable phones for Ericsson, Alcatel, and Motorola. In 2002, EMS industry revenues were estimated at $134 billion. The two largest EMS companies, Flextronics and Solectron, account for 9.7% and 9.2% of this market, respectively.

Flextronics has design, engineering, and manufacturing operations in 28 countries across the world. Its revenues totaled $13.4 billion in 2002, of which only 24.4% originated in its home-region market of Asia. North America accounted for 30.1% while Europe accounted for an additional 45.5% of total sales. Yet, a closer look at the data reveals that Flextronics' regional sales segmentation cannot be compared to those of original equipment manufacturers. In North America, over half of all sales are reported as deriving from Mexico. Malaysia accounts for 18% of Flextronic's total sales, or over 70% of all sales in Asia. Finally, Hungary accounts for 12%, or 28% of all European sales. Flextronics does not deal with end customers. Its clients are all original equipment manufacturers who then sell their products mainly in the large, industrialized countries. Flextronics might be recording its sales in Hungary, but this is not where most of its products are used by end customers.

The predominance of the North American market in terms of revenues is explained by strong ties to US businesses. Most of its contracts are with US companies, and most of its senior executives are graduates from North American universities. This is a surprising fact for a company that is headquartered in an Asian country. Flextronics was incorporated in Singapore in 1990 with the purpose of becoming a global manufacturer with operations in Asia, but the company has the vision of US entrepreneurs.

Flextronics specializes in handheld electronics devices: IT infrastructure, communications infrastructure, computer and office automation, and consumer electronics. Over the last few years Flextronics has expanded by purchasing smaller EMS contractors and factories from its brand-name customers. In 2001, Flextronics purchased half of Xerox's office equipment making operations for $220 million. The deal came with a five-year outsourcing contract for Flextronics to manufacture Xerox products. A similar deal was accomplished in 2000 when Casio sold a Japanese factory to Flextronics.

Transporting electronics by air is cost efficient, whereas cars are always transported by sea, allowing contract manufacturing to be successful in this industry, where parts might travel the world over before the finished product is delivered. In terms of floor space, 42.8% of the company's manufacturing square footage is in Europe. This compares to 32.5% in Asia and 22.0% in the Americas. Flextronics has six industrial parks in low-cost regions near each large triad market. In Asia, two industrial parks in China and a network of regional manufacturing facilities supply printers, cell phones, telephone switching boards, and PDAs, among other products. In the Americas, products from its two industrial parks, one in Mexico and one in Brazil, and its network of manufacturing facilities include: automotive, telecommunications, networking equipment, and hardware products, among others. In Eastern Europe, Poland and Hungary host two industrial parks that are also supported by nearby manufacturing facilities and which produce telecommunications infrastructure, electronics for automotives, printers and disposable cameras, among others.

The choice of location for production facilities is determined by the quality of the labor force, the cost of producing in the country, and the proximity to a triad market. Mexico, for example, is the low-cost region within the North American market. Brazil has the best industrial capabilities among countries in South America and strong ties to large international firms from Europe and North America. China has abundant labor, high expected economic growth, and is near the large Japanese market where international firms like Canon, NEC, and Sony are headquartered. Eastern Europe is the low-cost production area for Western European markets. It is no surprise that Flextronics' industrial park in Poland is located near a university from which it can acquire skilled labor.

Contract manufacturing accounts for less than one-fourth of electronic manufacturing, but due to their manufacturing specialization and lower costs, EMS companies might dominate the industry in the future. This process will redefine the role of OEMs in the electronics industry to that of design and marketers.

EMS do much more than providing cost-effective manufacturing; they also help in the design of products to make them easier to manufacture. They provide logistics services, such as material procurement, inventory management, vendor management, packaging, and distribution, and automation of key components of the supply chain through advanced IT. In addition, EMS offer after-market services such as repair and warranty services.

Today's electronic manufacturers have come a long way from the cheap labor-based contractors that used to dominate the industry. Robotic automation is now a significant part of the production process and is mostly handled by specialists. It is their manufacturing expertise that makes for lower cost, but EMS provide many more advantages to OEMs. They decrease the risk of manufacturing because OEMs no longer need to make large investments on a new factory to produce a new product that might or might not be successful. EMS can also purchase inputs at lower prices because they are not only making cell phones for Alcatel, but also those for Motorola and Ericsson, increasing their purchasing power.

Canon Group (Global)

Few companies can claim to be truly global multinationals, but with sales, revenues, production, and employees distributed across the world, the Canon Group of Japan, ranked 190 in the *Fortune* Global 500, comes as close as any to fitting that title. In 2002, 71.5% of Canon's revenues originated outside of Japan. The Americas accounted for 33.8% of total revenues, Asia accounted for 28.5%, and Western Europe for 20.8%. The remaining 16.9% of revenues were generated in other areas, including Eastern Europe.

Canon develops, manufactures, and markets cameras, business machines, and optical products. The company had its beginnings in 1933, when Precision Optical Instruments Laboratory was established to conduct research into cameras in Roppongi, Minato-ku, Tokyo. In 1947 the company changed its name to Canon Camera Co., and only in 1969 the company took on the name Canon Inc. In 2001, the company had revenues totaling $23.9 billion with 93,620 employees.

Canon's international expansion started in 1955 with the opening of a New York branch. Initially, the company relied on sole distributors and established some in Europe and Latin America in the late 1950s and early 1960s. The sole distributor system was abolished in 1963 to make way for company-owned subsidiaries under the direct control of the Japanese headquarters.

International expansion goes beyond marketing to include production, research, and development. Taiwan became the site of Canon's first foreign-production facility in 1970. Two years later the company opened a manufacturing plant in Germany. By 2001, the company had production facilities in all parts of the triad – Western Europe, the Asia Pacific region, and North America. Nevertheless, the vast majority of Canon's production facilities remain in Asia, including Japan.

In 1990, R&D centers were opened in the USA, Australia, France, Thailand, and the People's Republic of China. Each R&D facility specializes in a specific product line and is coordinated by a centralized R&D lab in Japan. Approximately 8% of Canon's revenues are spent in R&D. Together with its R&D strategy, this has made Canon one of the best world innovators and the largest holder of patents after IBM.

Canon is organized regionally. Canon USA oversees operations in the Americas. The subsidiary employs 10,908 people and has its own marketing, R&D, and production facilities. Two companies oversee

European operations. Together, Canon's European operations direct 12,875 employees, two manufacturing plants in Germany and France, and R&D centers in the UK and France. Canon's operations in Asia and Oceania, excluding Japan, account for the largest number of employees in foreign countries. Region-wide activities for the Asian market are overseen by the Canon Asia Marketing Group, but marketing operations in this region are sub-fragmented into sub-regional or national markets. The Southeast Asia region is the responsibility of Canon Singapore. Hong Kong has its own subsidiary that is also responsible for Taiwan and part of South Korea. The mainland Chinese market is the responsibility of Canon (China) Co. Japan's home market is still very important. Nearly half of Canon's employees are still working in Japan and company-wide R&D is still centralized there. Canon Australia is responsible for operations in the Oceania region.

Over the last few years, Canon has been re-organizing its production facilities to take advantage of its global scope, selecting suppliers and production facilities across the world to minimize costs and decrease production time. As a result product design data can now be sent to plants around the world via computer. Information is translated through an automatic translation system allowing faster communication between subsidiaries.

Canon realizes that a global company must do more than just spread sales, production, and R&D facilities across the world. It must also participate actively in local communities. The company does this by involving itself in local matters, such as funding environmental programs and local sports.

HOST-REGION CASES

News Corp.

In 1952, Rupert Murdoch inherited a small newspaper company from his father called the *Adelaide News* that he transformed into the world's 364th largest company, News Corp., a news empire that includes newspapers, magazines, books, TV networks, satellite networks, and movies. Murdoch's media empire includes such well-known names as the Fox Network, Fox News, National Geographic cable network, *TV Guide* and *The New York Post* in the United States, the *Sun* newspaper, *The Times* in the UK, and *The Australian* in Australia.

In 2002, the company had revenues of $16 billion that originated in the United States, the UK, and Australia. The United States is the largest market for News Corp. accounting for 80.3% of total revenues in 2002. The UK, its second largest market, accounts for only 12.5% of revenues. Australia, its home-region market, accounts for 7.2%.

In the 1980s Murdoch became a United States citizen to circumvent laws that prevented foreigners from owning TV stations. This saw the beginning of the Fox network from which its US media empire grew. One of Murdoch's main ambitions has been to build a worldwide satellite platform. These efforts have been hampered by News Corp.'s failed attempts at acquiring a satellite company in the United States. In fact, while News Corp.'s satellites cover 100% of the Asia and Australia and 80% of the Latin America TV households, it has no coverage in the United States or Canada and only covers 20% of the European TV households.

News Corp.'s TV service, Star, distributes thirty-eight channels to 300 million viewers in eight different languages viewers the Asia region. Star Plus channel is the dominant cable channel in India where the company has produced Hindi versions of popular shows, such as "Who Wants to Be a Millionaire?"

In 1993, Murdoch's statement that satellite dishes would become an "unambiguous threat to totalitarian regimes everywhere" led the Chinese government to ban private ownership of satellite dishes. Since then, the media baron has been trying to repair his relationship with the Chinese government. News Corp. initially entered the Chinese market through a joint venture with the People's Daily newspaper and the internet portal Netease. The company moved to a better strategic spot when in 2001, after long courting with the communist government, News Corp. secured a stake in Netcom, a state-owned company that owns an 8,500 kilometer high-speed fiber-optic cable network connecting seventeen cities. The acquisition paved a relationship with Beijing and planted a seed for the company's expansion into China's untapped market.

Programming for the Chinese market targets young audiences in much the same way as Fox does for the North American market. A program "Women in Control" is a male beauty contest in which a displeased female audience may drop a contestant into cold water. "Wanted!" is an adaptation of the United States' "America's Most Wanted" in which the audience help the police solve crimes.

In the late 1990s, News Corp. was criticized because of its tax practices by the UK media. The company has a complex infrastructure of loosely woven companies across the world. The group lists 800 subsidiaries of which sixty are incorporated in tax havens such as the Cayman Islands, Bermuda, the Netherlands Antilles, and the British Virgin Islands. Of all its British operations, News Publishers, incorporated in Bermuda, was the most profitable in the 1990s, this despite the lack of any significant employees at the subsidiary, a company that seems to derive all of its income from other News Corp. group companies. The company was incorporated in Australia, which has the least accountable of all accounting standards among developed nations. In the United States, News Corp. lists its subsidiaries in Delaware, which does not force companies to file publicly available accounts. In 1998, News Corp.'s effective corporate taxes worldwide amounted to 6% of pre-tax profits. This compares to 31% for Disney, another competitor in the same industry. What the media has not claimed was that there was any actual wrongdoing. Murdoch's company was simply taking advantage of tax loopholes in the different jurisdictions in which it operates. Nonetheless, the lack of transparency has had some negative effect for the company, especially after the Enron scandal.

"NEAR MISS" GLOBAL CASES

Nestlé

With 260,000 employees, 6,000 brands, and eighty-four factories spread around the world, Nestlé is the world's largest food company. Nescafé instant coffee, Perrier water, and KitKat chocolates are just some of the products that the company produces and markets around the world. The company is as much a household name in some parts of Africa, Asia, and Latin America, as it is in Europe and North America.

In 2002, Nestlé derived 32.2% of its sales from the European region. North America (excluding Mexico) accounts for an additional 21.7% of sales. An additional 12.3% of revenues originated in Asia-Pacific. The remaining 33.7% of sales are derived from non-triad nations in Latin America, Africa, and the Middle East. This is not a global company in the traditional triad definition, but one that spans the entire world.

Nestlé's international growth strategy is heavily dependent on acquisitions. Between 1985 and 2000 acquisitions amounted to $26 billion and included the acquisition of Carnation in 1985, the largest takeover outside the oil industry at the time. There is no sign of a merger slowdown. Between 2001 and 2002, Nestlé's acquisitions amounted to over $18 billion.

In August 2002, Nestlé sought to acquire Hershey, the 108-year-old chocolate US firm. This pinned Nestlé against government regulators, politicians, and employees, not to mention Kraft and Cadbury, rivals who also wanted to snatch the company. Government regulators warned that if Nestlé purchased Hershey, the company would be forced to sell many of its brands to satisfy antitrust concerns. Politicians rose to support local towns that depended on Hershey. Public pressure led the board of Hershey's largest shareholder, Hershey Trust, to take the company off the market.

Nestlé has been particularly successful in non-triad nations where its strategy consists of purchasing successful local brands, keeping their original names and adding its own brand. In Peru, for instance, the company purchased ice cream and chocolate maker, D'Onofrio, and continued to market its products under the D'Onofrio brand, capitalizing on the reputation of this brand while adding the Nestlé logo as a parent brand to all packaging. Not a bad analogy to the entire Nestlé business where a "think local" philosophy is meshed together at the multinational level.

Entering third-world countries can be risky and unrewarding. Nestlé is known for thinking in the long term. In South Korea and China, the company lost money for ten years, but both these markets have turned around and are now highly profitable. In Russia, Nestlé endured Russia's currency crisis of the late 1990s while other investors fled the country. During this time, the company doubled its market share in chocolate, coffee, and ice cream at the expense of those who left.

Dealings with third-world countries may also affect a company's reputation in its large industrialized markets. In 2002, Nestlé demanded that the Ethiopian government deliver $6 million for a company that was expropriated in 1975 under a communist regime. NGOs and concerned citizens were outraged. At the time, Ethiopia was undergoing a famine that threatened as many as eleven million citizens with starvation. The Ethiopian government offered $1 million, but Nestlé rejected the offer. Oxfam decried the company's stance claiming that one of the richest companies in the world was trying to squeeze out as much as it could from one of the poorest countries in the world. A spokesperson for the World Bank, which was brokering the deal, stated that the $1 million offer seemed reasonable and accused Nestlé of trying to get as much as it could. The backlash led Nestlé to accept $1.5 million in compensation and to donate the entire amount for famine relief in the country.

Royal Dutch / Shell Group

The Royal Dutch/Shell Group is the third largest oil and gas group with $135.2 billion in revenues in 2001. The majority of the company's revenues are derived from oil products, but it also makes chemicals, gas and power, and develops renewable energy (such as "green" electricity). The company's proven oil reserves are 9.5 billion, and it has control of 55.8 trillion cubic feet of gas.

Most of Royal Dutch/Shell's crude oil is produced in Nigeria, Oman, the UK, and the United States. The company's exploration and production spans forty countries and employs 15,000 people. The group has interests in roughly fifty refineries worldwide and owns about 56,000 service stations around the world. In 2001, 46.1% of the company's revenues originated in its home market of Europe. The United States accounted for an additional 15.6% of sales.

The group had its origins in 1907 when Royal Dutch of the Netherlands and Shell Transport of the UK agreed to an unusual joint venture to create Royal Dutch/Shell. Under the terms of the agreement, the two companies would remain independent parent companies of the new group with Royal Dutch holding 60% equity and Shell Transport the remaining 40%.

Royal Dutch's organizational structure is among the most complicated in the world with over 100 subsidiaries in nearly 150 countries. For years, country-based subsidiaries have been loosely tied to headquarters, but now Shell is in the midst of a large company culture transformation. The increased competitiveness of its major rivals has led Shell to re-evaluate its organizational structure and to move away from the matrix-style structure that it adopted in 1959. Based on the local networks developed in each individual country of operations, this structure had led to a power struggle in recent years between headquarters and the powerful country managers scattered across the globe. These managers forged close relationships with local government and corporate personnel that sometimes did not meet overall policies of the organization. Another concern is that long-term profitability might not be sustainable in the wake of regional consolidation.

Shell is now taking part in what it calls a "globalization" process. One of its priorities includes the elimination of country manager positions in the company's Far East Exploration and Production operations. By replacing this localized strategy with operational alignment in five regional centers (America, Europe, Africa, Middle East, the former Soviet Union, and Asia-Pacific), the company aims to save over $500 million per year.

On the environmental front, negligent behavior toward downstream processes has resulted in the company operating four of the seven worst refineries in the industry. Criticized for this and other environmental abuses, the company has struggled in recent years to maintain its market position, particularly in Europe. Its image was severely tarnished in the 1990s as a result of the political and environmental actions of country managers in Nigeria. In 1995, Nine Ogoni protestors were killed for protesting against Shell, leading to international protests and boycotts. Since then, the company has made strides to increase communication with local communities in the countries from which it extracts oil.

Over the last few years, the company has outlined a socially oriented platform it must follow for the coming years: (1) to provide access to modern energy to poor countries; (2) to meet the increased demand for fossil fuels but also reducing its adverse environmental and social affect; and (3) to shift to a low-carbon energy system in the near future. Shell is widely regarded as the technological innovator in the oil and gas industry through its research and development of a variety of renewable energy sources, including wind, solar, nuclear, wave, and biomass technologies.

Some of its harshest critics in the 1990s now admit that the company has made a lot of progress. In fact, Royal Dutch/Shell is one of only a few industry leaders to endorse the Kyoto Protocol. In the United States, its subsidiary, Shell Oil Company, won the Keep America Beautiful Award for a combination of volunteer work by its employees and retirees, and its financial support for environmental organizations. Shell Global, produces photovoltaic cells, panels, and systems that provide solar energy for buildings and the company is focusing on developing wind farms to market its energy.

Still, Shell is initiating a worldwide expansion to maintain its positions globally. The company began in 2001 with purchasing ChevronTexaco's downstream Equilon interests and also partnered with Saudi Aramco to buy similar Motiva interests from the same company. Valued at well over $2 billion, the transactions bolstered Shell's presence significantly in the United States. In addition, the company completed a $1.2 billion transaction in April 2002 for Enterprise Oil. Though considered overpriced by industry analysts, Shell further strengthened in refinery capacity in the United States. The recent approval in 2003 by the Indian government to open two thousand stations in India in the near future is a significant breakthrough for the company, as well. Dominated by domestic oil companies through protectionist economic policies, Shell is positioning itself to become a strong foreign brand in India.

While Shell is a bi-regional company, it is still searching for innovative ways to leverage its technology with alternative energy sources. By expanding its natural gas business through a joint venture called Inter-Gen with Bechtel, Shell is taking the lead on the Russian Pacific coast with a $10 billion development project. In addition, the company opened its first hydrogen service stations, targeting Iceland in April 2003 and Japan in June 2003. Currently, Shell is planning to open one at the end of 2003 in Washington, DC, for market evaluation, as well. Regardless of the current company culture transition or questionable environmental practices, Shell will continue to pioneer alternative fuels to have a more diverse product base.

CONCLUSIONS

In this chapter it was found that a group of well-known firms from each of the major classifications defined in chapter 1 adopt the same strategies as the firms studied in the four industries of chapters 5–8. There are very few truly global firms with both a global geographic locus in sales and also a global reach in their FSAs. Instead, the great majority of firms are home-region based in both their geographic scope and in the reach of their FSAs. An interesting, but relatively limited, set of bi-regionals represent partially globalized firms with a global reach of FSAs but still a regional scope of operations and location. In the next chapter, the firms profiled in this chapter will be analyzed in relation to all others studied in detail in this book. Then the analytical framework will be pushed further, beyond corporate level, into the business units of the firms.

10 Analysis of the regional and global strategies of large firms

Contents

In order to delve deeper into the actual nature of regional or global strategy, there are some fifty firms studied in detail in one part or another of this book. The first half of this chapter provides a summary of this more detailed case work derived from the overall data analysis of the 380 large firms for which data or regional sales are available. Table 10.1 lists fifty of these firms. There are five global firms; nine bi-regional firms; six host-region oriented firms; twenty-one home-region firms; and two near miss global firms. In addition seven firms outside of the top 500, but discussed in this book, are included at the end of table 10.1. To illustrate the profound lack of globalization and the reality of regionalization, and in order to derive useful lessons for managers and scholars of international business, we analyze the strategies of these fifty firms. We also discuss rival firms and when appropriate attempt to analyze their strategy.

We now discuss the basic strategic positioning of these fifty firms in the first major theoretical framework developed earlier in the book. This is the regional matrix of the first half of chapter 3. This chapter serves both to summarize previous discussion of these firms and to help provide a synthesis across all the major cases. The second half of the chapter further develops analysis of the strategy and structure of large firms operating regionally, with a special focus on Nestlé and its lines of business.

	Table 10.1. Classification of leading multinational firms		
rank in top 500	firm	category in ch. 2	cell in fig. 10.1
1	Wal-Mart	home-region	2
3	General Motors	home-region	2
5	Ford	home-region	2
9	General Electric	home-region	2
11	Citigroup	home-region	2
15	Total Fina Elf	home-region	2
21	Volkswagen	home-region	2
22	Siemens	home-region	2
27	Deutsche Bank	home-region	2
31	Credit Suisse	home-region	2
35	Carrefour	home-region	2
47	Bank of America	home-region	2
54	JP Morgan	home-region	2
62	Merck	home-region	2
84	NEC	home-region	2
98	AOL Time Warner	home-region	2
127	Pfizer	home-region	2
172	DuPont	home-region	4
213	Cisco Systems	home-region	2
356	Procter & Gamble	home-region	2
441	Eli Lilly	home-region	2
19	Intl. Business Machines	global	3
190	Canon	global	3
230	Coca-Cola	global	3
388	Flextronics International	global	3
459	LVMH	global	3
8	Royal Dutch/Shell Group	near miss global	4
55	Nestlé	near miss global	4
4	BP	bi-regional	4
10	Toyota Motor	bi-regional	4
138	Motorola	bi-regional	4
158	Bayer	bi-regional	4
230	Aventis	bi-regional	4
340	McDonald's	bi-regional	4
383	Eastman Kodak	bi-regional	4
415	L'Oréal	bi-regional	4
416	Lafarge	bi-regional	4
7	DaimlerChrysler	host-region	4
38	Royal Ahold	host-region	4
41	Honda Motor	host-region	4
140	GlaxoSmithKline	host-region	4
301	AstraZeneca	host-region	4
364	News Corp.	host-region	4
	non-500 firm	category	cell
na	Starbucks	home-region	2
na	Nike	home-region	1
na	Adidas	bi-regional	4
na	Puma	home-region	2
na	Footlocker	home-region	2
na	Gucci	global	3
na	Haier	home-region	2

THE REGIONAL MATRIX AND THE LARGE FIRMS

Global Firms

LVMH – cell 3. LVMH has global reach in brand name recognition for its set of luxury products (FSAs). This strategic positioning has built on its original French/Parisian reputation for producing high-end products. LVMH also has a locational advantage that is global in scope: the relative homogeneity of tastes among the wealthy consumers for its high-end products across all the three regions of the triad. High-quality champagne, brandy, and fashion products can be thought of as similar to semi-conductors and other high-value added electronics components. None of these are subject to the location constraints of geography. It has global geographic scope as local (French) or regional (EU) regulations no longer affect the majority of its operations, which are mainly outside of its home region.

IBM – cell 3. This electronic and computer firm is global both in the reach of FSAs and also in the scope of its locational advantages. It no longer has any home-country or regional geographic scope. Its products are regarded as standardized and its brand name is universally recognized, giving it global reach in its FSAs.

Canon – cell 3. Canon has developed a global reach for its brand name, and while its global operations are coordinated through regional offices, it has global scope in its location advantages. Each regional office has control over manufacturing facilities, R&D facilities, marketing, and distribution, but its FSAs are the same in each region, leading to a cell 3 positioning. The industry in which it operates is also highly mobile across geographic space, so it is global in scope.

Flextronics – cell 3. Flextronics is now a key supplier of electronics and components to large OEMs headquartered in each region of the triad. Its clients include Microsoft from North America; Canon from Japan; and Nokia from Europe. Its products have global reach in FSAs, and they are customized for these major firms. The high value per unit of weight means that there are no locational constraints on production, yielding a global scope in locational advantages.

Coca-Cola – cell 3. In terms of FSAs, Coca-Cola has a globally recognized brand name, but it is somewhat subject to local tastes and regulations in terms of the geographic scope of its locational factors. According to CEO Douglas Daft, it is a global/local company with Coca-Cola adapting its product line to each of the host countries in which it operates. Even the sacred formula for the Coca-Cola soda is adapted to compete successfully in each region. Yet, its wide geographic scope of sales is consistent with its statistical classification as a "global" company in cell 3. Later we will analyze the fact that, for purposes of strategy, it is partly nationally responsive in its FSAs; it has an ability to adapt its product lines, distribution, and marketing to local needs and tastes.

Figure 10.1. The positioning of firms in the regional matrix

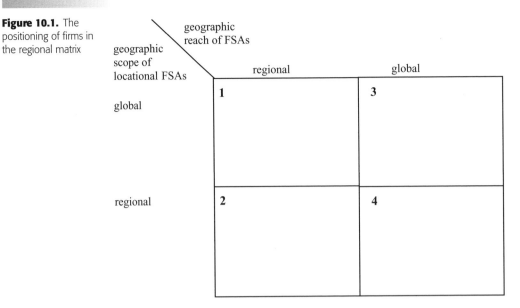

The five global firms analyzed above are positioned in cell 3 of figure 10.1. We now turn to analysis of the vast majority of large firms outside of cell 3, the firms which are not purely global.

Home-region oriented firms

Most of the firms studied in this book are classified as home-region firms, and they will be natural candidates for cell 2. We shall now analyze some key firms in the set of home-region based banks, pharmaceuticals, autos, and retailers outlined in chapters 5–8. Finally, we examine a group of home-region based firms unclassified by sector, as in chapter 9.

Retail

Most of the forty-nine retail firms in the top 500 would be positioned in cell 2 as local/local. *LVMH* is the global exception in cell 3, as discussed above. Another is a non 500 firm, *Gucci*, as discussed earlier, in chapter 2.

Wal-Mart is in cell 2. It is still a prisoner of the huge US domestic market and the local US business environment. While its business model and FSAs have moved from local to regional, by expanding to Canada and Mexico, it still has 94% of its sales in NAFTA, so its geographic scope is regional. The next challenge for Wal-Mart is to move to cell 4, where it would develop a global reach in its FSAs by adapting its business model to Europe and Asia. If it succeeds in adapting its FSAs to these other parts of the triad and achieves a global reach in its FSAs, it eventually could be positioned in cell 3, as the locational advantages can become global in scope. However, it is unlikely to be there for at least another 10 years. The local US home-region geographic scope of Wal-Mart currently anchors it more in cell 2 than cell 4.

Like Wal-Mart, large European retailers, such as *Carrefour*, are in cell 2. Like Wal-Mart, these firms have expanded across the EU, but remain regional in scope. In particular, over the last twenty years the growth of Carrefour matched the expansion of the EU, and it continues to grow mainly across the region. Old-fashioned French regulations restricting the growth of large retailers still affect its geographic scope of operations.

Royal Ahold is a cell 4 bi-regional. Recently it has made huge losses on its North American operations, apparently due to inadequate accounting and reporting standards. This illustrates the dangers of insufficient investment in understanding a foreign region. Companies should not be opportunistic in the large US market without a strategy and structure to fully understand its institutional environment. Royal Ahold had host-regional geographic scope with 59.2% of its sales in North America, but the global reach of its FSAs was not sustainable, as it had not invested enough in understanding the emerging corporate governance issues of North America. European-based firms need to invest more in overcoming the liability of foreignness of the large US retail market, with its different accounting standards, transparency, political system, and other peculiarities, than do US firms which benefit from their home US market in an asymmetric manner. Currently it is less important for US retail firms to go to Europe and Asia for market growth than it is for European and Asian firms to succeed in North America. The failure of the global reach of its FSAs has pushed Royal Ahold back to cell 2 subsequent to the 2001 data which helped position it in cell 4.

Banks

Across the top 500 firms all but one of the banks and most financial institutions are home-region based. The exception is Santander Central Hispano which is a host-region firm. The large US banks, such as *Bank of America*, *JP Morgan*, and *Citigroup* can be positioned in cell 2. All these banks are subject to historically rigorous US local financial regulations. The strongly-regulated US financial environment shows that local CSAs constrain the geographic scope of these US banks. US regulations have also historically created barriers to entry for foreign banks, although recent deregulation has weakened these barriers. As a consequence of strong regulation, the US banks have developed local FSAs that are difficult to exploit abroad. They only have a regional reach to their FSAs. US banks find it unnecessary and difficult to go abroad because of the magnetic pull of the US market. This is especially true for retail banking but less so for investment banking. However, across all these product lines the large US banks average over 80% of sales and assets in their home region; they are very home-region based.

The European banks are also positioned in cell 2. They benefit from regional financial regulations across the EU which have led to growth and expansion in that region of the triad. Despite this, few of these banks have moved to North America in a big way. Indeed, the reach of their FSAs still appears to be local or regional. The leading European banks, *Deutsche Bank* and *Crédit Suisse* have limited geographic scope and, are mainly operating in Europe with 63% and 61% of sales there respectively.

Pharmaceuticals

The major US based pharmaceutical firms are positioned in cell 2. These include *Merck*, *Pfizer-Pharmacia*, and *Eli Lilly*. These firms have patents which defend their products against generic producers only within the United States. In other regions of the triad the pharmaceutical patents, even when enforced, do not guarantee local success. Indeed, marketing in other regions of the triad by US firms needs to be extremely nationally responsive. In other words, the pharmaceutical markets are segmented by triad region. Even within regions there are strong national differences affecting regulation, marketing, and distribution. As a consequence of the segmented markets, the US firms have limited geographic scope with most of their sales in the United States. Even Canada has different regulations affecting pharmaceutical sales and products. US firms' penetration of other regions is mainly through merger and acquisitions.

In contrast, European pharmaceutical firms are positioned in the bi-regional cell 4. These include *AstraZeneca*, *GlaxoSmithKline*, and *Aventis*, the first of which is a host-region firm, as AstraZeneca has 52.8% of its sales in North America. GlaxoSmithKline has 49.2%; and Aventis has 38.8%, so these two are bi-regional. All of these firms have built on their success on European markets and have now entered the large US market. All have decentralized organizational structures whereby the US operations are run semi-autonomously from the European home office. Bi-regional organizational structures are required due to the large and dominating size of the US market in which there are strong established competitors. Again, there is asymmetry in markets and strategy between European and US firms. Perhaps due to complacency based on their success in their home-region market, US pharmaceutical firms have not developed similar bi-regional structures in Europe or Asia.

Some of the European chemical firms are also positioned in cell 4. Firms like *Bayer* benefit from the regional scope of EU integration but have a global reach in their FSA brands. Bayer is bi-regional with 40.3% of its sales in Europe and 32.7% in North America, so it has a regional geographic scope but a global reach in its brand name FSAs. *DuPont* is the only US multinational with a global reach in its brands, including Lycra, but it is still subject to regional scope, given the large size of the US base market. DuPont is a more global firm in its FSAs than its US competitors, but its geographic scope is still home-region based (with 55% of sales in North America), placing it in cell 4, despite being a home-region firm. *Pfizer-Pharmacia* (at 56.5% North America sales) and *Eli Lilly* (at 63.8%) are still strictly in cell 2. They have a strong home-region locational scope and rely on the US products which mainly have a local/regional reach in FSAs. They may move to cell 4 when they have a global reach to these FSAs and are less dependent on US brand patents for their FSAs.

Autos

The Japanese car producers, *Toyota* and *Honda Motors*, are bi-regional firms. They are positioned in cell 4. These firms produce triad recognized vehicles of high quality and reputations. They are subject to regulations such as NAFTA rules of origin and labor immobility. These lead to regionalized clusters of hundreds of auto parts suppliers selling most of their output to the regionally-based OEMs. Auto firms produce most of their output in distinctive regional clusters. Each cluster has independent sets of suppliers operating in regional networks.

Similarly, European auto firm *DaimlerChrysler* is in cell 4 as it can access the US market as effectively as its European home-region market. This has given a global reach to its FSAs, which otherwise were originally regional before the two companies merged and developed a controlling organizational structure with German efficiency in production FSAs improving the quality of Chrysler cars. DaimlerChrysler derives over 50% of its sales from North America. *Volkswagen* is in cell 2 as it has 68% of its sales in Europe; its scope is regional, not global.

In contrast, *General Motors* is better positioned in cell 2. Like the other auto firms it benefits from the regional regulations of NAFTA, yet the reach of its FSAs are still local. GM has a US based business model that is difficult to take elsewhere, especially to Asia. It has limited geographic scope with 81% of its sales in North America. While General Motors has a long presence in Europe, its sales there are still under 15%. This contrasts with *Ford*, whose sales there are about 22%. Ford has more European reach than GM, but it is still a home-region based firm (with 66.7% of the sales there) unlike some of its European and Asian competitors who are clearly bi-regional.

Others

LaFarge – cell 4. This is a concrete example of a bi-regional firm in cell 4. It is the largest cement producer in North America, and it has brought its successful European business model to this region without having to modify its strategy. The success of this cement firm has been achieved with a global reach in its FSAs despite the commodity nature of the product. Managerial skills in winning contracts, minimizing labor, transportation costs, and being close to the large urban markets have given the company a competitive advantage against rivals. Its geographic scope is still regional with 40% of its sales in Europe but 32% in North America.

British Petroleum/Royal Shell Group – cell 4. These European firms are in the bi-regional cell because of their success in the North American market. Both of these firms are sensitive to green/environmental concerns that have become important across the EU as the stakeholder approach to business strategy has dominated thinking. BP is the highest-ranking firm in the *Financial Times* "Survey of the World's Most Respected Companies." Royal Dutch/Shell comes in fifth. Both of these firms could be in cell 3 if their presence in Asia were to increase in the future. These European energy firms have a regional scope as they have built on regional economic integration across the EU, where they have approximately 40% of their sales.

TotalFinaElf – cell 2. In contrast, also has a regional geographic scope as it benefits from the EU, but the limited reach of its FSAs keeps it in cell 2. It is very local in the reach of its negative French-based FSAs, which have been affected by a public perception of scandal and corruption.

Haier – cell 2. In chapter 9 the Chinese firm, Haier, was discussed. Although Haier is too small to be included in the 500, there are now 11 Chinese firms in the top 500. Haier has 88.36% of its sales in Asia and 10.36% in North America. Indeed, all the large Chinese firms are very home-region based, and all would be positioned in cell 2 of figure 10.1. All have regional geographic scope, and all lack global reach in their FSAs.

Procter & Gamble – cell 2. With overall sales of nearly $40b, Procter & Gamble is a home-region firm with 55% of its sales in North America. It has a regional geographic scope, and its FSAs have a regional reach. It has the potential to move to quadrant 4 when its brand name products are recognized as having a global reach. It has established an organizational structure to move this way, and its ultimate target is to be a cell 4 firm, which will be dependent upon greatly increased sales in Asia.

AOLTime Warner – cell 2. The entertainment, media, and communications sector is subject to strong national regulations which limit its geographic scope. To be a successful player in the United States requires a large US presence. However, AOL Time Warner has developed regional FSAs as it distributes its products to Canada as well as the United States, despite failed attempts by Canadian protectionists to restrict entry.

News Corp. – cell 4. Australian-owned News Corp. has a global reach to its FSAs (unlike AOL Time Warner), but it is in cell 4 as it generates the majority of its sales (75%) in the US market through Fox and CNN. It is host-region oriented with limited geographic scope. The Fox and Sky segments of its portfolio are successful in North America and Europe respectively. But Fox and Sky follow a similar business model with a global reach in FSAs which transcend local regulations. One area, which is not global in reach of FSAs in Fox and Sky, is in coverage of cricket which is not shown in North America. However, North American consumers can watch as many soccer games on Fox as Europeans. Europeans can watch American football, baseball, and ice hockey on Sky, but only in the middle of the night.

L'Oréal – cell 4. L'Oréal is in cell 4 as it builds on the EU regional market and has now taken its successful business model to the North American region of the triad. It now has global FSAs and operates the North American part of its business in a nationally responsive manner. If it fails to grow in North America it will retreat from cell 4 to cell 2.

Nestlé – cell 4. Nestlé has globally recognized brand-name products, such as Nescafé and Perrier. It has a global reach in its FSAs in the overall management of these brands, as discussed later in this chapter. While it is a Swiss company and it is not formally part of the EU, it still benefits from the efficiencies of European economic integration and is regional in geographic scope. It has grown its brands throughout Europe, North America, and Asia, as well as in non-triad markets, including Africa. With continuous growth in Asia, it will move from cell 4 to cell 3, but currently is a "near miss" global firm in cell 4.

Starbucks – cell 2. Starbucks has moved rapidly from its origins with local Seattle coffee houses to operate across the world. Currently it is in cell 2 where it benefits from NAFTA regional integration, with 91% of its sales in the NAFTA region. But it has already established a potential global brand name, and may eventually move to cell 4, once it achieves global reach in its FSAs. While introductory textbooks of international business talk of Starbucks as a global firm, it cannot currently be classified as global because of its lack of geographic scope with a vast predominance of its sales in North America.

McDonald's – cell 4. McDonald's is a "near miss" global firm due to its universally recognized brand name and substantial presence of all three triad markets. It has successfully overcome local and regional regulations. Indeed, some might argue that McDonald's has overcome the segmentation due to local tastes because its business model allows its franchisees to adapt its menu to each market. Unfortunately, in this book McDonald's is not classified as truly global in cell 3 but is bi-regional in cell 4 due to an inadequate sales performance in Asia, where it is below the 20% cut off. If McDonald's were to increase its percentage of sales in Asia its statistical classification would be consistent with a possible strategic positioning in cell 3.

Cisco Systems – cell 2. This company produces and markets universal networking equipment for major multinationals. Although it operates in an industry with very little regulation and with global standards, its home sales are still 58%, with 25% in Europe, and 15.5% in Asia. With a majority of sales in its home region Cisco has so far failed to become global in scope, and it remains in cell 2 of figure 10.1. Its FSAs should have a global reach, yet it is still a local, centralized US firm. Cisco still lacks the managerial FSAs required to give it a global reach although the standardized nature of the electronics industry should give it a global scope in locational activities.

Kodak – cell 4. Unlike Cisco, Eastman Kodak has reduced reliance on its geographic base in the US region of the triad. It is bi-regional with 68.5% of its sales in North America, and 24.7% in Europe, the Middle East, and Africa. It also has 17.2% in Asia. It faces a dominant rival in Asia, Fuji Film, and a combination of rivals in Europe. Until it increases its geographic scope, Kodak is unlikely to sustain the past global reach in its FSAs in photo-optical equipment. In particular, it is not at all clear that it can achieve a global reach of FSAs in digital photography and associated products.

General Electric – cell 2. General Electric is a conglomerate with a wide variety of successful "global" products, but it still relies on its home-nation market for the majority of its product development and for its revenue (59%). Another reason to classify GE in cell 2 is that its financial arm is now a major part of the business and is subject to local US regulations. GE's primary success is through an integration strategy, with quality processes like six sigma, investment in employees, etc., all built up in its strong US home base. This has led to economies of scale; centralized R&D; brand-name products; but mainly based on the home market. GE has centralized control over functional (product lines) profit and loss centers.

Motorola – cell 4. This is another bi-regional firm with a global brand name and with a strong presence in two regions of the market. Motorola derives 44% of its revenues from North America and 26% from Asia, but it has not been able to match this success in the European market. It is in cell 4, as the company must align its designs to each regional, if not national, market as a result of local tastes, with regional clusters and production platforms.

NEC – cell 2. This firm remains very Japanese. Unlike its US rivals in electronics, NEC has not succeeded in diversifying sales to the other two regions of the triad. It has 80% of its sales in Asia. To an extent this reflects the disadvantage of being an Asian firm which is the smallest region of the triad. Yet it did not develop bi-regional strategies like Honda, Toyota, or GlaxoSmithKline. To become more global it needs to focus on the large US market. There is more to becoming a global firm than changing its name from Nippon Electronic Company to NEC. It also requires a change in internal management and organizational capabilities. The centralized hierarchical structure of a typical Japanese company like NEC is incompatible with success in the US market. Honda and Toyota have been exceptions as their products have been developed on a bi-regional basis by investing in an understanding of the North American market. For example, they have avoided unionized labor areas and developed vehicles responsive to US needs.

Nike – cell 4 of figure 10.1. It has a brand (the swoosh) which is globally recognized; yet it has the majority of its sales in North America. It has a limited regional rather than global geographic sales scope, despite outsourcing 99% of its production of shoes and clothing to cheap labor-driven independent contractors in Southeast Asia. Nike is not a "global" firm, however, as this cheap labor is an exogenous CSA, and its key strategy is to promote the global reach of its brand. Indeed, the threat of boycotts against Nike due to the perceived labor abuses of firms in the outsourced supply chain has required that Nike assume corporate responsibility for the labor practice of its independent suppliers. This has hit Nike's FSA in its home-region market of North America, and also in Europe. Its sales in Asia are still less than 20%, preventing it from becoming global in scope.

Adidas – cell 4. A major rival to Nike is Adidas, founded by Adi Dassler in Germany in 1948. It is a bi-regional cell 4 firm. It has used sport stars like English soccer captain David Beckham and boxing champion Muhammad Ali in the past. Adidas became famous when it supplied new screw-in studs in the soccer shoes of the German team that won the World Cup in 1954. In 1997 Adidas acquired the Salomon Group of sportswear and golf products. Sales for Adidas-Salomon in 2002 were 49% in Europe; 30% in North America; and 18% in Asia, making it a bi-regional company (indeed nearly global). For just the Adidas shoe division sales were 53% in Europe; 27% in North America, and 17% in Asia. In terms of employees for Adidas-Salomon, 51% are in Europe; 23% in North America; 21% in Asia; and 5% in Latin America. It has 14,700 people employed and had sales of $6.5b. in 2002. The Adidas part of the company employs 60% of all the people.

Like Nike, Adidas has outsourced most of its supply chain to low-wage producers in Asia, where it has 372 supplier factories; to Latin America where it has 169; but with still 201 supplier factories in Europe. Of the 742 supplier factories to Adidas, it only owns two. In order to safeguard its brand-name equity better than Nike, Adidas has a strict code of social and environmental corporate responsibility to be followed along its supply chain of independent contractors. Despite being statistically bi-regional, Adidas is a very centralized, ethnocentric, home-country based business, with a limited geographic scope. It does not adapt its shoes to local tastes, and it has a hierarchical product division structure. Adidas has become the number two player in North America, after Nike, and is the market leader in Europe. Like Nike, Adidas is a cell 4 firm in figure 10.1.

Puma – cell 2. A third athletic shoe and leisurewear company is Puma, also founded in Herzogenaurach, Germany by Rudolf Dassler (brother of Adi Dassler) in 1948. It is a cell 2 firm. It had sales of 910 million

Euros in 2002. Of these, 70% are in Europe; 23% in North America; and 5% in Asia. There are additional licensing agreements in Asia, especially in Japan.

Puma has triad-based "virtual" headquarters in Germany, the United States, and Hong Kong, which are its so-called core competency centers. These serve as regional hubs, along with Austria and Australia. They oversee Puma distributions, licensees, and subsidiaries within each region. Unlike Adidas, Puma has not yet moved on from being a home-region firm towards becoming a bi-regional or global firm. Puma is a cell 2 firm in figure 10.1.

Foot Locker – cell 2 was originally bought by Woolworth in 1974, but Woolworth closed its chain and became Venator Group in 1998. In 2001 Venator became Foot Locker and had sales of $4.5 b in 2002 – 80.7% of these were in North America. It has 3,625 stores, again mostly in North America. It has little presence in Asia. It is a sporting goods retailer, focused on sports shoes and apparel. Foot Locker is a cell 2 firm in figure 10.1.

This concludes our summary analysis of the strategies of an illustrative set of forty-two top 500 firms and an additional six non 500 firms across all the classifications used in this book. We should recall that 320 of the 380 firms with data are home-region based, and perhaps even more of this set of firms should have been analyzed than the cases for which detailed work could be undertaken. Most of these home-region firms will not have any global dimensions and may well remain in cell 2 or close by. We now turn to discussion of the issue of upstream production and lines of business.

A MODEL OF MULTI-REGIONAL STRATEGY AND STRUCTURE

The mainstream literature on globalization and global strategies has consistently prescribed a broader geographic scope of activities in order to reap the multiple benefits from operating in international markets. These benefits include higher growth rates than achievable in the domestic market, higher efficiency and profitability of current operations, improved opportunities for learning, and risk reduction advantages, see Bartlett (1986) and Tallman and Yip (2001) for insightful descriptions.

It has been suggested, while adopting a joint internalization and resource-based perspective, that multinational enterprises (MNEs) should use specific combinations of non-location bound firm-specific advantages (FSAs) and location-bound FSAs, as strategies to achieve an optimal resource deployment across borders, see Rugman and Verbeke (2001a) (2003c) for a synthesis. Non-location bound or internationally transferable

FSAs lead to scale economies, scope economies, and benefits of exploiting national differences. In contrast, location-bound FSAs, which have limited exploitation potential across geographic space, generate benefits of national responsiveness.

This stylized version of reality is able to explain the geographic expansion of three types of companies, using the terminology adopted by Bartlett and Ghoshal (1989). First, are the "multinational" firms; these companies derive their strengths mainly from the location-bound FSAs embedded in their subsidiaries, and are very nationally responsive in the various countries where they operate. An example of this archetype is the Dutch electronics company Philips. Second, are the "international" firms; these MNEs build competitive advantage through knowledge transfer across borders, i.e. the transfer of non-location-bound FSAs, and the subsequent production in host-country subsidiaries. An example is Procter & Gamble, the US based producer of consumer goods. Third, are the so-called "global" companies; those firms engage in the worldwide exports of their goods, and are supported by downstream-oriented subsidiaries abroad. The non-location-bound FSAs are mainly embodied in the final products themselves. Those products are typically produced in the home country and then sold across borders. An example is the Japanese electronics firm Matsushita.

Bartlett and Ghoshal (1989) have also advocated the adoption of the "transnational" solution, as the optimal combination of strengths derived from the three original archetypes. The transnational MNE deploys a mix of location bound and non-location-bound FSAs, whereby the latter can also be derived, at least in part, from host-country subsidiaries, Rugman and Verbeke, (1992) (2001b). ABB (Asea Brown Bovery) has often been identified as the quintessential transnational company, Bartlett and Ghoshal (1998, pp. 259–72).

However, in order to evolve toward the transnational solution, it is argued that managers should pursue an incremental, path-dependent trajectory of change. The selectivity required to manage the transformation toward a transnational company has three facets. First, respect for the firm's specific administrative heritage, i.e. each MNE should build upon its existing strengths responsible for the initial stages of international success. Second, extensive socialization, meaning substantial attention devoted to the physiology and psychology of the organization, rather than merely to sweeping changes in anatomy or organizational structure. Third, selectivity in terms of the roles assigned to national subsidiaries, given the strategic nature of their location (or lack thereof), and their contribution (or lack thereof) to new, non-location-bound knowledge development.

The feasibility of implementing the transnational solution builds upon three conditions that were not made explicit by Bartlett and Ghoshal (1989). Those conditions suggest that the transnational solution, as developed by these authors, may need to be adapted somewhat, in order to be effective in practice. The three conditions are the following: first, that new transnational strengths can be built to complement existing, more uni-dimensional FSAs, without much need to focus on the differential requirements for *organizational structure*, faced by each of the three MNE archetypes; second, that *socialization* can be achieved throughout the company at a rather low cost; third, that the MNE can be simply decomposed into a *portfolio of interdependent national units*, each of which can be assigned a specific role in the firm.

Given the above, this part of the chapter makes two points. First, difficulties in building transnational capabilities may prevent MNEs from replicating the market success achieved at home in other markets. This is especially true if markets require a different FSA–CSA configuration than the one that proved successful in the home market. Second, introducing a regional component in strategy and structure may go a long way toward addressing the managerial challenges expected, if the three conditions above do not hold. Indeed, relative ease to access/create complementary FSAs (building upon the MNE's administrative heritage), low costs of extensive socialization, and the easy decomposition of MNE in sets of subsidiaries with different assigned roles are not self-evident, as demonstrated below. Interestingly, when describing the evolution of ABB toward a transnational, Bartlett and Ghoshal (1998, p. 260 and p. 266) twice mention the importance of regional managers.

REGIONAL ORGANIZATIONS: STRATEGY AND STRUCTURE

The data of chapter 2 have four implications. First, most large MNEs appear incapable of emulating their home-region market success in the two other legs of the triad. Second, where market presence in host regions is much weaker than in the home region, or insignificant as a percentage of total company sales, this is likely associated with different managerial attention devoted to the various regions. Host regions will therefore not be treated in the same way as the home region, nor should they be, given their continued limited importance in terms of company sales and overall cash inflows. Third, if host-triad regions are potentially very important to competitiveness, but difficult to penetrate, they receive differential managerial treatment; such differentiation should include the adaptation of the MNE's market-strategy approach to host-region requirements and the creation of region-based components in the MNE's coordination and control structure to address the specific managerial challenges in those regions. Fourth, if we assume that the two tools above, namely regional market strategy adaptation and a regional component in the organizational structure, can improve host-region market penetration, then it is questionable whether the normative messages contained in the transnational solution are consistent with this approach.

Here, three complexities should be noted. The first complexity is that the administrative heritage of most MNEs, undoubtedly conducive to home-region market success, may well constitute an administrative rigidity when attempting to penetrate host regions. More specifically, an "institutionalization" approach, whereby home-region success recipes (i.e. the firm's administrative heritage) are replicated in host regions, and complemented incrementally with additional routines, as advocated by Bartlett and Ghoshal (1989) may be the wrong path to achieve market success. Perhaps regional adaptation is the key to achieving an optimal mix between global integration and national responsiveness, rather than attempts by each MNE archetype to take on board the strengths of the two other archetypes? Unfortunately, even Bartlett and Ghoshal's most recently published work does not recognize in conceptual terms this potential of regional adaptation, although a number of their cases do provide evidence of a substantial regional adaptation component, Bartlett, Ghoshal, and Birkinshaw (2003). A second, and related complexity, is that changes in regional strategy and structure, addressing requirements imposed by the regional host environment, may be more conducive to market success than attempts to increase socialization within the company. Socialization again reflects an institutionalization approach, which may be ill suited to penetrate distant markets in an effective and timely fashion, Van Den Bulcke and Verbeke (2001, ch. 10).

Finally, a third complexity is that the MNE cannot be simply decomposed into *national* units, dependent upon the *national* environment in which they operate and the knowledge base embedded in each *national* unit. Here, each of the triad market regions is, by definition, of critical importance to most large MNEs because of market size and the potential competitive benefits derived from being a dominant player in each of those markets, Rugman (2000). The knowledge base includes at least two FSA components, namely upstream and downstream FSAs. This decomposition may make it difficult to simply classify individual units in the firm as having a weak or strong knowledge base. *Downstream FSAs* or customer-end FSAs, refer to knowledge strengths deployed in activities with a direct interface with the customers, and are required to achieve successful market penetration. In contrast, *upstream FSAs* are deployed in activities that lack this direct interface, but are critical to creating an efficient internal production system.

An asymmetry may exist between a unit's downstream and upstream FSAs, mirrored in the MNE's organizational design, whereby many tasks within R&D, sourcing, manufacturing, and logistics operations are structurally divorced from customer-related subunits. This asymmetry explains why many MNEs have been able to develop internally efficient global operations, with a wide geographic dispersion across units of the upstream

Figure 10.2. Generic
roles of strategic
business units (SBUs)
in MNEs

geographic scope of SBU FSAs

		1 country	1 triad region	2 triad regions	All triad regions
FSAs type	down-stream FSAs	1	3	5	7
	upstream FSAs	2	4	6	8

activities (and FSAs) involved, but have simultaneously been incapable of capitalizing on such strengths at the downstream end, in terms of sales achieved.

Figure 10.2 constitutes a re-conceptualization of Bartlett and Ghoshal's (1989) framework on the "generic roles of national organizations" in the MNE, using these empirical and analytical insights on the pervasive nature of "regional" activities of MNEs. (The integration-responsiveness matrix was discussed earlier, in chapter 3.)

In line with the analysis above, figure 10.2 makes a distinction among the various generic roles of strategic business units within the company. The horizontal axis measures the strength of the FSAs, embedded in each strategic business unit, which may consist of either a single national affili-ate, or a set of affiliates, possibly located in various nations and bundled into a geographic or product division. MNEs evaluate business operations at various levels; here, the relevant level is the one at which performance is assessed as the basis of company-wide capital budget allocation. The strategic business unit's FSAs may be deployable at the national level, in one triad region, in two triad regions, or in all triad regions, as reflected by business performance. In reality, other regional sub-divisions than the triad-based one could be more relevant to particular MNEs, with typically a "rest of the world division" as critical to success, but in this book we focus solely on the triad. Figure 10.2 also makes a distinction, on the vertical axis, between downstream or customer-end, and upstream FSAs. Strong upstream FSAs are required to create an efficient internal pro-duction system within the nation, one region, or inter-regionally. Strong downstream FSAs are necessary to achieve market success in the market considered, again at the national, regional, or inter-regional level. Con-ceptually, individual strategic business units may have both upstream and downstream FSAs, which would make them span two vertical cells in figure 10.2.

When using figure 10.2, we can identify the business units in MNEs that perform the role of global market leaders in the firm, as measured, not by their location inside a large national market per se, but by their ability to achieve a satisfactory market penetration in each of the three legs of the triad. This is a reflection of strong downstream FSAs (cell 7). The reality for most MNEs is that they may lack even a single global market leader. In contrast, many MNEs have global production units, with upstream activities spread across continents, especially to take advantage of market imperfections in markets for raw materials, labor, components and other intermediate goods, and even to source final goods, but without an equivalent geographic distribution of sales (cells 6 and 8). In addition, most of the large firms have units with the status of national or intra-regional market leaders (cells 1 and 3), but usually confined to the home region. Where interregional market success is achieved, namely by a strong position in at least a second triad market, this often occurs through a distinct strategic business unit (to be located in cell 5 rather than cell 3). The strong market position in the second leg of the triad then usually reflects cooperative behavior, such as joint venture activity, mergers and acquisitions, etc.

The relevance of figure 10.2, in terms of the distinct roles of SBUs within the MNE, can be illustrated with the example of the food industry giant, *Nestlé*. Although Nestlé as a whole fits into the bi-regional (Europe and Americas) MNE profile, according to Rugman and Verbeke (2004), important variations exist regarding the roles of the different SBUs (tables 10.2 and 10.3). At the *downstream FSA* end, table 10.2 has a classification of the different SBUs of figure 10.2. The beverages SBU, as well as the milk products, nutrition, and ice cream SBU are positioned in cell 7 with a strong, balanced performance in all triad regions. The chocolate, confectionery, and biscuits SBU, as well as the Nestlé Waters SBU, can be positioned in cell 5. The PetCare SBU, still strong in Europe, is dominated by the Americas and can be positioned in cell 3. The prepared dishes and cooking aids SBU falls in cell 3. But a unit such as Trinks in Germany, mentioned as part of other activities in Nestlé's Annual Reports, should be positioned in cell 1. Thus, from the customer-end perspective, only two SBUs in Nestlé are truly global leaders.

At the *upstream FSA end*, we use as a proxy for Nestlé's FSAs, the distribution of plants across the world. This distribution is shown in table 10.3. The geographic distribution of plants is only an indicative parameter, as nothing is said about the relative size of the plants, or about the logistical linkages among them. With the exception of two SBUs (PetCare and Nestlé Waters), the other four SBUs have a substantial number of plants in all triad regions and are therefore global players in cell 8. The PetCare SBU is strongly represented in two regions, but has only three plants in the Asia, Oceania and Africa region (one in Australia, one in New Zealand,

Table 10.2. Geographic distribution of sales in SBUs of Nestlé

	Europe		Americas		Asia		
SBU	sales	%	sales	%	sales	%	total
beverages	4,623	35	3,646	27	5,110	38	13,379
milk products, nutrition, and ice cream	7,639	34	8,690	39	5,995	27	22,324
prepared dishes and cooking aids	8,206	52	5,725	36	1,791	11	15,722
chocolate, confectionery and biscuits	5,102	48	4,164	39	1,441	13	10,707
pet care	3,108	29	7,068	66	543	5	10,719
Nestlé waters	3,504	45	3,739	48	477	6	7,720
Overall*	32,182	40	33,032	41	15,357	19	80,571

Note: * Averages are weighted averages according to the revenue size of each business unit. Some activities by Nestlé, including pharmaceutical products, joint ventures and "Trinks" of Germany, are not included in the geographic distributions of overall sales. Numbers for Asia include Oceania and Africa
Source: Nestlé, 2002 Management Report.

Table 10.3. Geographic distribution of plants in Nestlé SBUs

	Europe		Americas		Asia, Oceania, and Africa		
	number	%	number	%	number	%	total
beverages	16	25	16	25	33	50	65
milk products, nutrition, and ice cream	18	27	17	26	31	47	66
prepared dishes and cooking aids	15	26	13	23	29	51	57
chocolate, confectionery and biscuits	16	39	10	24	15	37	41
pet care	6	38	7	44	3	19	16
Nestlé waters	na		na		na		
overall	71	29.0	63	25.7	111	45.3	245

and one in South Africa), with no plants in Japan, a triad nation, positioning the SBU in cell 6.

The normative message of figure 10.2 is threefold. *First*, it may not always make sense to classify MNE operations solely in terms of national units, nor to view their location in a specific nation as necessarily critical. From a triad perspective, regional and inter-regional success are also important, not only the size of a particular national market. Especially in the EU and the NAFTA area, the region is becoming an increasingly relevant unit of analysis to determine market performance. This signifies the need to augment location-bound FSAs, in order to make them more regionally deployable. It often also signifies the limited geographic deployability of so-called non-location-bound FSAs. Especially at the downstream end, there is little empirical evidence that non-location boundedness would systematically transcend all three regions of the triad, let alone the rest of the world. *Second*, the relative lack of market success across regions for most MNEs implies that decision making at the "global" level may not always be appropriate to address region-specific challenges. These may be better handled through region-based strategies and organizational structures. *Third*, interregional success in distributing and integrating upstream activities, especially through exploiting imperfections in markets for several types of intermediate goods, may lead to a global product organization, but this does not automatically translate into global market success, nor in the normative implication that downstream strategy and structure should emulate upstream strategy and structure.

A REGIONAL, NOT A TRANSNATIONAL SOLUTION

Bartlett and Ghoshal's (1989) work likely represents the single most influential international management book of the past 15 years, Bartlett and Ghoshal (2002). The "transnational solution" concept, meaning the simultaneous pursuit of "global" scale economies, "worldwide" innovation and "national" responsiveness is now described extensively in most modern international business (IB) textbooks, as the panacea for success in the "global market place." Westney and Zaheer (2001) argue that the transnational solution framework has de facto replaced the IB-literature's earlier focus on the Stopford and Wells (1972) inspired natural evolution of the MNE organizational structure, as a pre-condition for the firm's success when becoming more involved in international markets. As noted above, Bartlett and Ghoshal (1989) contains three important insights. First, that changes in strategy and structure are to some extent conditioned by the MNE's administrative heritage. Second, that a stronger focus on socialization to effect coordination and control can go a long way toward moving from a conventional "multinational," "international," and "global" mentality to the transnational solution. Third, that corporate-level management cannot treat the set of business operations under its control through a "United Nations" model of decision making. All operating units within the MNE cannot be treated in the same way.

The importance of administrative heritage is now widely accepted as a critical parameter to which sufficient attention must be devoted when the MNE undertakes a process of strategic and structural change, with the caveat that this administrative heritage may act as an administrative rigidity in host regions. In contrast, Bartlett and Ghoshal's (1989), perhaps somewhat overly optimistic, perspective on the use of socialization mechanisms rather than bureaucratic and market-based coordination and control mechanisms inside the MNE has been questioned extensively, see Rugman and Verbeke (2001a). The implementation of socialization mechanisms, as with any other set of coordination and control devices, is not costless. We noted in the previous section that such internal institutionalization logic could also be detrimental to subsidiary effectiveness in locally embedded host-country clusters.

The above criticism has failed, however, to identify what is perhaps the most important limitation of Bartlett and Ghoshal (1989), namely its stylized unbundling of geographic space into two components: national space and global (meaning worldwide) space. The clearest expression of this approach is found in Bartlett and Ghoshal's (1989) conceptual framework for differentiating among subsidiary roles and responsibilities. However, as we noted in the previous section, this approach also appears to suffer from a significant weakness.

It is not clear that CEOs and senior management committees in MNEs consistently think in terms of "global" (meaning worldwide) versus "national" components of strategy and structure. In fact, when contemplating international expansion plans, rationalization investments, and plant closures etc., senior management often adopts a regional, rather than a "global" or merely "national" focus. For example, *Bayer* reorganized its European activities into regional groups to improve its competitiveness in Europe, and the company is also split along regional lines, with EMEA, the Americas, and Asia-Pacific regions. Similarly, *Sony* Music recently realigned its affiliates in Poland, the Czech Republic, Slovakia, and Hungary into a sub-regional division called Sony Music Central Europe. Sony also took special measures to strengthen its "regional strategies for East Asia, the Americas, and Europe," Sony Annual Report (2003: 17).

Imagine a group of senior MNE executives looking at a map of the world and trying to formulate strategy. In many cases, these executives will try to identify "regions," in the sense of geographic areas, that share sufficient similarities to warrant a coherent, market-based pattern of firm-level decisions and actions. Such "regions" could be sub-national or they may span several countries simultaneously. There is a similarity here with Porter's (1990) analysis of the competitive advantage of nations. There too, the problem appeared that other geographical units of analysis than the nation may be critical to explain why particular firms and industries, originating from a particular country, are competitive. At the sub-national level, localized knowledge clusters may be very narrow in geographic scope; at the other end of the spectrum, a double diamond or multiple diamond framework (spanning two or more countries) is sometimes needed to understand why a particular firm or industry originating from a particular country is internationally competitive, Rugman and Verbeke (1993a).

In this book, we argue, building upon Ohmae (1985), and Rugman and Verbeke (2004), that for the largest 500 companies, the triad constitutes a legitimate starting point for regional analysis. The importance of a regional component in strategy and structure can be usefully illustrated through figure 10.3. (This is basically similar to figure 3.5, but is now

Figure 10.3.
Geographic
components of MNE
market strategy and
structure

components of structure

		global	regional	national
	global	1	4	7
components of strategy	regional	2	5	8
	national	3	6	9

developed further). Figure 10.3 presents a framework that distinguishes among the global, regional, and national components of market strategy and structure for large MNEs.

The vertical axis in this case refers to observed behavior of strategy in the market place; it reflects the existence of market strategies that can range from global product standardization to regional and national adaptation.

In contrast, the horizontal axis reflects organizational structure, supporting some components of strategic decision making to be concentrated globally, and others dispersed across regions or countries. More specifically, the horizontal axis measures whether the MNE has a structure that supports centralized strategic decision making (e.g. choice of product/market niches, choice of strategic management tools to outperform rivals), or whether it supports a dispersion of at least a substantial portion of these decisions across nations and regions.

Figure 10.3 is an extension of Rugman and Verbeke's (1993b) framework on "global" strategies. They have argued that MNEs can be usefully classified according to two elements. First, the deployment of non-location bound versus location-bound FSAs needs to be investigated. This deployment is evaluated here on the vertical axis by looking at the efforts to engage in a market strategy of global product standardization, versus national and regional adaptation. Second, it is critical to assess the number of locations where important strategic decisions are taken. Here, we focus on the organizational structure on the horizontal axis of figure 10.3, as supporting decision making at various geographic levels. The difference with Rugman and Verbeke's (1993b) resource-based perspective on the integration/national responsiveness model, is that figure 10.3 explicitly introduces a regional dimension to the analysis, building upon the empirical evidence presented in the previous section. More specifically, on the horizontal axis this regional dimension implies the presence of organizational structure components that support strategic decisions at the regional, rather than merely the global and national levels. The vertical axis implies effectively deploying downstream FSAs at the geographic level of a region. These are region-bound company strengths; they can contribute to survival, profitability, and growth beyond the geographic scope of a single nation, but they are still location bound, in the sense that they cannot be deployed globally, Morrison, Ricks, and Roth (1991), Morrison and Roth (1991).

In this context, Yip's (2002, p. 7) view that a global company (the use of the term global is unrelated to the Bartlett and Ghoshal MNE archetype) "has the capability to go anywhere, deploy any assets, and access any resources, and it maximizes profits on a global basis," may be a useful normative message, but one that applies to very few, if any, MNEs in practice. Indeed, the empirical evidence shows that most MNEs rely largely on sets of location-bound and region-bound FSAs as the basis for their competitiveness.

Figure 10.3 helps identify some of the more important mistakes made by proponents of globalization and a global strategy for MNEs. We can illustrate this with a few well-known examples from the automobile industry, Belis-Bergouignan, et al. (2000). Here, we should emphasize that all nine cells may be relevant to a single MNE at one point in time, as different strategic business units may need tailored approaches.

The proponents of globalization view as a reflection of a global strategy not only cell 1, but also cells 2, 3, 4, and 7 (where other strategy-structure combinations other than global product standardization and centralization are required). In cell 1, globalization efforts indeed take place. When *Ford*, the US based automobile producer started manufacturing in Europe in 1911, this was a cell 1 approach, sometimes called the "expatriation of the Model T," with European plants simply assembling standardized component kits sent by the US parent and basically selling a single, US product.

In cells 2 and 3, the focus is still on the decisions and actions taken at the corporate center, typically by the CEO, the top management committee, and the MNE's board of directors. However, even if the organizational structure supports many corporate strategy decisions to be taken centrally (left column of figure 10.3), cells 2 and 3 reflect, respectively at the margin, the existence of substantial regional and national responsiveness regarding product/service offerings. A move to cell 2 occurred at *Ford* in 1932 and 1934, when the Y and C models, specifically designed for the European market, were launched. The Second World War physically divided Ford's operations between the German and allied sides, further reinforcing the tendency away from global products. After the Second World War, Ford kept its hierarchical approach, but German based and UK based operations were permitted to tailor their market strategies to local needs, placing Ford closer to cell 3. In other words, MNEs with centralized decision-making that tailor their market strategy to regional and national circumstances do not pursue a simple global strategy as suggested by cell 1. Considerable resources must be allocated to allow for the required level of sub-global responsiveness in terms of the products delivered to the market. In 1967, Ford Europe was created, and this implied, again at the margin, a move from cell 3 to cell 5, this time leading to Pan-European rationalization of operations, and less dependence on the UK. This was associated with increased intra-firm regional trade, expansion in Southern Europe etc. A similar move, closer to cell 5 occurred in North America, with the signing of the Auto Pact between Canada and the United States.

During the last few decades, Ford has, again at the margin, been characterized by a shift toward cell 4, with attempts to develop a "world car strategy," but with decision making for compact vehicles with Ford of Europe, for large vehicles with Ford of America, and for small vehicles, with the Ford-controlled Japanese automobile producer *Mazda*. This implies that, even with a (partly) standardized, global product offering (top row of figure 10.3), not all the important market strategy decisions are taken centrally. Bounded rationality constraints are likely to force corporate management to delegate important decisions to components of the organizational structure at the regional and national levels, thereby positioning the firm closer to cells 4 and 7.

Too much focus on a "multinational" approach in cell 9 has now become unrealistic in many industries, although this was characteristic of the early international expansion of some European MNEs, such as the automobile manufacturer *Fiat*, see Bartlett (1986). It may lead to overlapping efforts and duplication in innovation, inconsistent national strategies, opportunistic behavior by subsidiary managers, and more generally a waste of resources and lack of clear strategic direction, Bartlett, Ghoshal, and Birkinshaw (2003). The great strength of an MNE is that it can overcome market imperfections characterizing national markets and develop systemic, network-related rather than asset-based FSAs, see Dunning and Rugman (1985). Even for MNEs with a polycentric administrative heritage, cells 6 and 8 are likely much more relevant than cell 9.

In cell 6, attempts are made to achieve decision-making synergies across markets, by developing pan-European, pan-American, or pan-Asian strategies in particular functional areas, Rugman and Verbeke (1991).

In cell 8, subsidiary managers pursue economies of scale and scope themselves, through standardizing at the regional level their product/ service offering across those national markets that have strong similarities in demand. In that case, subsidiary initiative is critical, Birkinshaw (2000), Rugman and Verbeke (2001a). For example, a number of recent *Honda* car models, produced and sold in the United States, were specifically designed and marketed for North America, with substantial local R&D and market research, placing these activities in cell 8. More generally, Honda now functions with five regional operations:

(1) North America; (2) Europe, the Middle and Near East and Africa; (3) Asia and Oceania; (4) Japan; (5) China (newly established in April 2003), Honda Annual Report (2003: 33). All regions have substantial autonomy in non-core research, manufacturing and sales, whereby products are tailored to the requirements of each market, a clear example of the relevance of cell 5 in figure 10.3 for many Honda activities. For example, at Honda it was the Japanese R&D unit that developed the global platform for the 1998 Accord series, but market-related decision making on the exact size of the car was delegated to regional centers. The North American region, based on regional market research, decided to build a somewhat larger model than in Europe and Japan, placing this strategy-structure combination in cell 5 of figure 10.3.

Bartlett and Ghoshal's work is good at distinguishing between cells 1 and 9, but it has not addressed most of the other cells. For example, the basic matrix of integration (cell 1) and national responsiveness (cell 9) popularized by Bartlett and Ghoshal (1989) distinguished between a pure global cell 1 strategy and the "act local" national responsiveness strategy of cell 9. In addition, the key contribution of their "transnational solution" framework was the prescription that MNEs should usefully combine strategies in cells 1 and 9. They should attempt to develop for each separate business, for each function within that business, and for each task within that function, the capability to implement either a national or a global approach.

As discussed in chapter 3, the Bartlett and Ghoshal (1989) framework thus can usefully explain cell 3 (a structure supporting centralized decision making combined with local market adaptation), i.e. the global think-local act approach, a strategy typical of many Japanese companies such as Toyota. This constitutes an approach likely adopted by the "global" and "international" firms evolving toward the transnational solution. The framework also permits the analysis of less common cases in cell 7, whereby rather powerful national subsidiaries are responsible for delivering global products, but choose themselves which products have the most potential in their national markets and largely take responsibility for the delivery. This is a typical approach found in formerly "multinational" archetypes evolving toward the transnational.

Yet, Bartlett and Ghoshal's framework cannot handle cell 5, triad-based strategy-structure combinations very well, nor the intermediate cases of cells 2, 4, 6, and 8, i.e. all cases in which the regional level is important. The present book suggests that, at the margin, regional elements are becoming increasingly important in many MNEs, both in terms of organizational structure and market approach. Even the operations of the original nine firms (Kao, Procter & Gamble, Unilever, General Electric, Matsushita, Philips, Ericsson, ITT, and NEC), used by Bartlett and Ghoshal as the empirical basis for the development of the transnational solution, have a significant regional component in their strategy and structure, as discussed below.

REVISITING THE TRANSNATIONAL
SOLUTION CASES

In fact, Bartlett and Ghoshal, in their preface to the paperback edition of their 1998 book, recognize the increased complexity of the international business environment, including the broadening of the regionalization of trading blocks. They also refer to "a social, political and economic revolution . . . opening up whole regions of the world for the first time and . . . creating political blocks and economic alliances that were radically changing the context for companies' operations," Bartlett and Ghoshal (1998, p. X).

The following analysis attempts to identify regional components of strategy and structure in the nine companies examined by Bartlett and Ghoshal (1989). In all cases, a sampling of publicly available information permits to conclude that a regional component is present. This indicates the relevance "at the margin" of cell 5 in figure 10.3. It should be noted that the consumer electronics businesses of GE and ITT were sold to Thomson and Alcatel respectively. In this context, we tried to identify regional elements at Thomson and Alcatel. The nine cases, taken together, suggest that future work on the transnational solution should, at least, recognize the possible significance of regional elements in MNE strategy and structure.

Kao

Kao is still a largely Asian, home-region oriented MNE. Its reported sales by geographic segment are as follows: Asia and Oceania 86%, of which 75% is in Japan. In both North America and Europe together, it has only 14% of sales (Kao, Annual Report 2002: 35).

Kao has changed its organizational structure from a management by country approach to a management by region approach: "a shift from management by country to management by region, such as ASEAN is aimed at strengthening Kao's management structure and speeding the pace of development," Kao, Annual Report (2000: 8). As an example of a more regional market approach, Kao Consumer Products (Southeast Asia) Co. Ltd. has been newly established as the ASEAN regional headquarters, to manage the entire ASEAN region by optimizing the manufacturing base, product development and marketing activities. It will work closely with consumers in the ASEAN region, and monitor the trends of the AFTA (ASEAN Free Trade Area), Kao, News Release, (September 4, 2000). As another example of a more regional component in the strategy–structure interface, Kao established regional headquarters in Barcelona, Spain in September 1999, for its European chemical products operations. Kao Chemicals Europe's mandate will be to "unify the company's various businesses in Europe, while also raising business efficiency and contributing to speedier decision-making," Kao Business Results (1999: 14). As one example of regional product adaptation by regional headquarters: "we took initiatives to promote improved Feather shampoo and conditioner with a new package design through the regional headquarters company in Thailand, which was established to unify regional operations," Kao Business Results (2002: 13).

Procter & Gamble

Procter & Gamble (P&G) is not a truly global company in terms of sales distribution because it derives the majority of its sales from its home region and it has a weak penetration in Asian markets. The reported geographic dispersion of sales is as follows: North America (55%), Europe/Middle East/Africa (27%), Asia-Pacific (10%), and corporate and other (8%), Braintrust Research Group (2003).

Before 1995, P&G managed its businesses under two geographic regions: US and international. Then it moved to four regions: America, Latin America, Asia, and Europe/Middle East/Africa, which reported to the chief operating officer, P&G Annual Report (2002). At present, P&G has adopted a more complex "four pillars" structure, which includes Global Business Units (GBUs); Market Development Organizations (MDOs), with seven MDO regions: North America, Asia/India/Australia, Great China, North East Asia, Central-Eastern Europe/Middle East/Africa, Western Europe, and Latin America; Global Business Services (GBS), with three GBS centers: GBS America located in Costa Rica, GBS Asia located in Manila, and GBS Europe, Middle East and Africa located in Newcastle; and Corporate Functions (CF). The functioning of this structure, and the role of the regional operations, can be described through the following example of the Pantene product:

> The MDOs ensure Pantene excels in their region. In the US, this could mean focusing on Club Stores, which might entail partnering with the GBU to develop large size packaging the outlet demands to maximize value for their shoppers. Conversely, the focus in Latin America might be to develop the smallest possible package, like a sachet, as consumers in that region want to minimize their out-of-pocket costs. Same overall brand equity, but very different executions by region. The GBS Center in Costa Rica would be providing support for both the US and Latin America MDO in this example (and for any other brand business team from these regions). Some of the services would include accounting, employee benefits, and payroll, order management and product logistics, and systems operations.   (website of P&G)

Unilever

Unilever is close to achieving a balanced distribution of sales across the triad, with the following reported distribution: Europe (38.7%), North America (26.6%), Asia and Pacific (15.4%), and 19.3% in other regions, Braintrust Research Group (2003). According to Unilever's Annual Report (2002), the company's operations are structured as two business groups:

Home and Personal Care and Unilever Bestfoods. Home and Personal Care is divided into several regions, including: Asia, Europe (with its regional headquarters in Waterloo, Belgium), North America, and Latin America. Unilever Bestfoods has four regional operations, which manage the ice cream and frozen food product lines: Bestfoods Asia (with its regional headquarters in Singapore), North America, Europe (with its regional headquarter in Rotterdam), and Africa. At the level of market strategy, Unilever has adopted a variety of local and regional brands.

Matsushita

The electronics giant Matsushita Electric, in spite of remaining largely an Asian based company, now has less than 50% of reported sales in its home country but 67.3% in Asia. Its sales distribution is as follows: Asia and Pacific (64.9%), of which 45% is derived from Japan, North and South America (12.4%), Europe (6.9%), others (15.8%), Braintrust Research Group (2003). Matsushita operates with four regional headquarters: China, Europe, Asia/Oceania, and Americas. As an example of the responsibilities given to its regional headquarters, Matsushita describes the purpose of its regional planning center in Asia as "[to] take charge of regional planning and strategy designing" (Matsushita website). To further integrate regional service functions, Asia Matsushita Electric even established a company called Asia Matsushita Technical Service in 1999, responsible for the supply of parts, digital product support, and customer support; Panasonic Semiconductor of South Asia was also established in 1999 to integrate semiconductor sales functions in South Asia, Matsushita Electric (1999). Moreover, other activities, such as environmental management, are also organized separately for the four regions. Matsushita has also introduced the regional dimension in its brand strategy, with the Panasonic brand defined as the global brand, National as the region/product-specific brand in the Japanese market, the Quasar brand in North America, etc.

Matsushita has also voiced its intent to move further away from its administrative heritage, as it will "encourage greater autonomy in its locally-established headquarters overseas, thus enabling more prompt decision making in respective regions", Matsushita, Annual Report (2001: 6). It recently reorganized its companies into fourteen new business domains, which are supposed to act as customer-oriented and autonomous organizations, responsible for "all aspects of business in their respective domains, from R&D and manufacturing, to sales", Matsushita Electric Annual Report (2003: 8).

Philips

The Dutch electronics firm, Philips, has a truly global distribution of sales: Europe (43%), USA/Canada (28.7%), Asia-Pacific (21.5%) and another 6.8% in Latin America and Africa, Braintrust Research Group (2003). Philips operates with four regional headquarters, located in Hong Kong (Asia), New York (North America), Sao Paulo (Latin America), and Amsterdam (Europe, Middle East, and Africa or EMEA region). The regional headquarters for Asia were originally located in Singapore, and the role of that regional office consisted of overseeing services such as strategic management, legal services, treasury and taxation, Philips Annual Report (2002).

Philips has also focused on emerging regions, as its Chairman and CEO Gerard Kleisterlee said in 2001 in the Philippines, "our attention on the Asia-Pacific region is an extremely sound geographic strategy, and we continue to explore all opportunities in the region," Business World Philippines (November 30, 2001).

The traditional "multinational" Philips, Bartlett and Ghoshal (1989) is also changing, under the global strategic program called "transforming into One Philips" (TOP program), which started in 2002. For example, a series of service centers for the Asia-Pacific region has been established to integrate the separate companies in terms of organization, branding and corporate culture, such as the Asia-Pacific financial services center in Thailand and the information technology center in China, Bangkok Post, (September 3, 2003).

NEC

NEC's sales are geographically concentrated in Japan. Its reported sales by market area are: Japan (79.6%), North America (7%), others (13.4%), NEC, Annual Report (2002). NEC has regional headquarters in the United States and Singapore. NEC set up the Singapore headquarters to manage the Asia-Pacific region (outside Japan). More specifically, it established the NEC Business Coordination Centre (Singapore) (NEC BCCS) in 1990, as operational regional headquarters (OHQ) to seamlessly integrate its businesses in the Asia-Pacific. Moreover, NEC also operates its Global Identity Solutions Group (NECSIN-GIS) out of Singapore. It is well established with the region's governments and financial services industries for its market-proven, world-class solutions and its commitment to quality and innovation. NECSIN-GIS is responsible for launching and managing enterprise solutions for the Asia-Pacific market, including design, development, implementation and maintenance (see the NEC website)

Ericsson

Ericsson has strongly diversified sales across the world, but is not solely focused on the triad. Its reported sales by market area are: Europe, Middle East, and Africa (46%), Asia Pacific (25.9%), North America (13.2%), and others (14.9%). However, the top 10 markets (by country) in sales are the United States, China, Mexico, Italy, UK, Brazil, Japan, Spain, Sweden, and Turkey. Activities in developing countries include: China 12%, Mexico 6%, Brazil 5%, and Turkey 3%, Ericsson Annual Report (2001). The firm's corporate headquarters are located in Stockholm, and it has in the past operated with four additional regional headquarters, located in London, Dallas, Miami and Hong Kong, Ericsson, Annual Report (2000: 47). A new market organization with distinct customer units for large global companies was announced in 2001, Ericsson News Release (August 17, 2001). The market area organization was restructured and now includes only three distinct areas: Americas, Asia-Pacific, and Europe, Middle East, and Africa. The presence of regional components in strategy and structure is at least partly driven by the existence of regional standards in the telecommunications industry (see Ericsson's website "Understanding Telecommunications").

Thomson (purchased relevant General Electric operations)

Thomson acquired the consumer electronics business and RCA from General Electric (GE) in 1986, created Thomson Consumer Electronics in 1988, and changed its name to Thomson multimedia in 1995 after the integration with Thomson Broadcast Systems. Thomson has a well-diversified geographic distribution of sales: Europe (27%, including 9% in France), Asia (33%), Americas (40%, including 18% in the United States), Thomson, Annual Report (2001). The firm has a few regional headquarters, most notably the one in Indianapolis for the Americas, and the one in Boulogne (near Paris) for Europe. Thomson deploys regional brands such as RCA in the United States, and Thomson in Europe.

Alcatel (purchased relevant ITT operations)

ITT sold its entire worldwide telecommunications products business to Alcatel in 1989. However, in 1992 Alcatel sold what had formerly been ITT's customer premises equipment business in the United States to a group of private investors. Therefore, the information below on Thomson may capture, only in part, ITT's original consumer electronics business described in Bartlett and Ghoshal (1989). Alcatel is still a home-region based MNE, with the following reported sales by market area: Europe (62.9%), United States (19.8%), Asia-Pacific (7.4%), and rest of world (9.9%), Alcatel, Annual Report (2002: 6). In the mid-nineties, Alcatel decided to adopt a largely regional structure, replacing the powerful national subsidiaries, which until then had dominated the firm, based upon the presence of powerful national telecoms, which chose primarily domestic suppliers. Telecom liberalization was creating an entirely new environment conducive to regional strategy and structure. The organization of the firm into regional divisions varies in the different SBUs. Alcatel now has five SBUs (Alcatel Website): service provider, enterprise networks, consumer products, home space, and additional businesses. The service provider SBU operates on the basis of four regions: North America, Asia Pacific, EMAI (Europe, Middle East, Africa, and India), and Latin/Central America. The enterprise networks SBU is largely European based or at best closely based in only two triads regions. The home space SBU is primarily a European based company. The consumer products – SBU has three divisions: mobile phones, residential phones (part of ATLINKS, a joint venture between Alcatel and Thomson), and DSL modems (sold to Thomson Multimedia). The business of mobile phones is largely European based.

CONCLUSIONS

In this chapter, we explored the implications of introducing a regional dimension in MNE strategy and structure. Such a regional dimension is warranted, given the observed geographic concentration of sales in most MNEs.

The regional issues discussed in this book cast doubts on the validity of the transnational solution model as the panacea for global corporate success. The main weakness of the transnational solution model is its internal complexity. The regional aspects identified here further compound this complexity, and this despite the financial markets' demands for transparency and simplicity in strategy and structure. Regional components in strategy and structure may go a long way towards improving large MNEs' management of distinct geographic zones, especially in the triad regions of NAFTA, the EU, and Asia. However, the main implication of our analysis for smaller MNEs may well be the introduction of more selectivity in the geographic scope of their international expansion, especially as far as downstream, or customer-end activities are concerned. Rather than engaging in a path of rapid "global roll out" of their products and services, these firms should select a narrow geographic market focus, as well as a narrow product focus. This will help to develop the FSAs capable of providing maximum value added to customers.

If MNEs face a higher liability of foreignness in downstream activities as compared to upstream activities, this has significant managerial implications from a dynamic perspective. Learning (in the sense of lowering the liability of foreignness) occurs at a different pace in different activities of the value chain. Foreign market penetration success ultimately is constrained by the activity area with the lowest rate of learning. Managers should thus try to identify the most constraining activities in the critical time paths to achieve international market growth. To put it simply, managers need to recognize that parts of the firm (especially at the downstream end) may operate regionally, whereas other parts (at the upstream end) may function globally.

11 Regional multinationals and government policy

Contents

The interaction between multinational enterprises (MNEs) and the governments of nation states has been studied for over thirty years, going back to the classic analysis of Vernon (1971). The interaction between MNEs and home and host governments has been further developed by Stopford and Strange (1991) in a model of triangular economic diplomacy. The entire development of a scholarly field known as international political economy (IPE) takes as its focus the interactions between MNEs and states. What can be added to this literature given the new evidence that MNEs operate predominately on a regional basis rather than on a global basis, as many earlier IPE studies have assumed? In brief, a focus on regionalization is now required to analyze states and firms.

The issues to be explored in this chapter are the following:

(1) Given the new evidence on the economic interdependence within each region of the triad, is this being facilitated by regional or multilateral trade agreements? The EU is much more of an integrated common market than the looser free trade agreements of NAFTA, the FTAA, and the Asian Agreement of November 2002. Do international agreements really matter when 56% of all Asian trade was already intra-regional in 2001, before a formal trade agreement was announced?

(2) With the trend towards increasing regionalism, is the WTO doomed? The United States is now negotiating many bi-lateral trade agreements, and it is not as focused on the WTO. The EU and United States still disagree over agricultural subsidies; China still has difficulty in

respecting intellectual property; the dispute settlement system at the WTO is being challenged not only by governments, but also by NGOs, especially environmentalists, Rugman, Kirton, and Soloway (1999), and Kobrin (1998). Brazil, India, China, and other mid-range economies, on behalf of the "poorer" countries, largely destroyed the current WTO round at Cancun in October 2003. The agenda of the civil society has targeted the WTO but largely neglected regional trade agreements, except for Mexico's role in NAFTA. Can the small staff of 300 people at the WTO deliver on multilateralism when they are vastly outnumbered by the EU bureaucracy and a growing NAFTA-based set of environmental and labor/human rights institutions?

(3) How do MNEs and states actually interact today on a regional and multilateral basis? Are MNEs beginning to develop "regional" strategies instead of "global" ones? Do states understand this new emphasis?

REGIONAL, NOT GLOBAL, BUSINESS AND TRADE AGREEMENTS

This chapter investigates the current interaction between states and firms within the institutional context of international trade and investment agreements. The basic logic of the chapter is that, today, multinational enterprises (MNEs) largely operate within their home-triad markets, or, at best, are bi-regional (competing only across two of the triads of the EU, NAFTA, and Asia). Few MNEs are "global," and thus few MNEs are really interested in multinational trade and investment agreements. Instead, today, most of the largest 500 MNEs are interested in the deepening of regional agreements in Europe, the Americas, and Asia.

From the viewpoint of the state, we observe a greater emphasis by trade experts and trade negotiators to facilitate regional agreements than to complete the Doha Round of the World Trade Organization (WTO). Recently the following examples of events leading to regional integration occurred:

(a) The EU agreed to a list of ten accession countries in Central and Eastern Europe, to join the EU in mid 2004. In Brussels, a vast bureaucracy of many thousands labors to deepen the economic, social, cultural, political, and financial integration of the EU. Over 2003, a new constitution for the EU was developed.

(b) In November 2002, in Quito, Ecuador, trade ministers for thirty-four countries agreed to continue to negotiate the terms and conditions for a Free Trade Agreement of the Americas (FTAA), first accepted by them, in principle, at the Quebec City Summit of April 2001. These meetings continued in Miami in November 2003 although no agreement occurred in Trinidad in October 2003. The FTAA is due to start in early 2005, and the implementing committee is co-chaired by the United States and Brazil. The FTAA builds on the twin principles of tariff reduction and national treatment from foreign direct investment established in NAFTA, Rugman (1994).

(c) On November 4, 2002, the ten members of ASEAN economies agreed to a new trade and investment agreement with China. This may well be expanded to include Japan and South Korea. Throughout 2003, a set of bilateral trade agreements were negotiated by Asian countries.

One of the arguments in Rugman (2000) was the prediction that economic multilateralism, especially in the form of the WTO, would be challenged by the logic of regional integration. Obviously, in the last three years this prediction has been confirmed. Between Seattle in 1999 and Cancun in 2003, the WTO has failed to develop a consensus for further trade liberalization, and the future success of the WTO is now in doubt. In contrast, over this period, the EU has moved towards greater political and social integration, and it has even developed a draft constitution. Ten new members are to enter in 2004. In Asia, many bilateral and other intra-regional trade agreements have been signed and implemented. The FTAA meeting, in Miami in November 2003, kept the Americas moving towards implementation of the full FTAA in 2005.

The evidence from economic diplomacy shows that regional agreements are still being developed whereas multilateralism has slowed down. It is important that managers be realistic about these developments and focus strategic decision more at regional than global levels. We are now seeing a greater congruence between the economic reality of regionalization and the political nature of regional rather than global agreements.

In Spring 2003, the war in Iraq illustrated the military power of the US hegemon, operating in a world where most European countries (except for the UK) were not supportive of the war, and Asian countries (with the primary exceptions of Japan and Australia) were also critical of the US military power. The result of the war will likely be to reinforce regional economic policies, at the expense of multilateral institutions, (especially the United Nations and the WTO). The United States already exports 37% of its goods and services to its NAFTA partners, and its trade with Canada alone exceeds US exports to all fifteen member states of the EU. In terms of energy, the United States already obtains the majority of its oil and gas from the Americas, and this regional self-sufficiency is likely to increase as security concerns remain. This issue is also discussed in a section below in more detail.

Figure 11.1.
Intra-regional trade in
the triad, 1980–2000

	intra-regional exports (%)		
YEAR	EU	NAFTA	ASIA
2000	62.1	55.7	55.7
1997	60.6	49.1	53.1
1980	52.1	33.6	35.3

Source: IMF, Direction of Trade Statistics Yearbook, 1983–2001 and OECD, International Direct Investment Statistics Yearbook, 2001.

REGIONAL ECONOMIC DETERMINISM IN THE TRIAD

The importance of economic-based regionalization in the triad, and the lack of globalization, is now reflected in political alignments. Following the definitive change to US political attitudes towards national security after the September 11, 2001, terrorist attacks, a new world political system is emerging. This is based on the triad reality of regionalization.

The United States already has a significant degree of economic security on a regional basis. This was affirmed by the NAFTA agreement of 1994, Rugman (1994). Now Canada and Mexico supply energy and other natural resources to the United States in exchange for the enhanced business access to the world's single largest and richest market. The NAFTA does not provide the depth of economic integration of the EU, and it has none of its political and currency integration. Yet it ties together these three economies in a gigantic and highly successful free trade area to the mutual economic benefit of all three partners.

So successful is NAFTA in terms of increased intra-regional trade that it is in the process of being expanded to the FTAA in 2005. This will bring all thirty-four countries of the Americas into an extension of NAFTA. The US economy will serve as the regional regime for growth and renewed prosperity for the states of Latin America and the Caribbean, just as it has done for Mexico (and Canada) under NAFTA.

The economic data on NAFTA show ever increasing interdependence in trade and FDI. Figure 11.1 shows that intra-regional trade has increased from 49% to 55.7% between 1997 and 2000. Today the United States has 22.6% of its exports going to Canada and 14.1% to Mexico, for a total of 36.7%. It has only 21.3% to all fifteen member states of the EU. The United States is now a regional player in terms of trade. Similar data exist for FDI. In addition, at firm level, the 169 US firms in the list of the world's largest 500 firms have an average of 77.3% of all their sales within NAFTA. Of course, Canada and Mexico are more than pulling their weight on intra-regional trade. Canada has 87% of its exports to the United States; Mexico has 88.7%.

Figure 11.1 also demonstrates that Europe and Asia are becoming increasingly regionalized. Intra-regional trade in the EU increased from 60.6% to 62% over the 1997–2001 period. In Asia, even without a formal trade agreement across the region, the intra-regional trade increased from 53.1% to 55.7%. Intra-regional FDI increases from 36% in 1986 to 46% in 1999 in the EU. In Asia intra-regional FDI increased from 20.5% in 1986 to 26.2% in 1999.

Regionalism is now the dominant economic force. As a direct corollary to this trend, there is even less trade between the triad blocks. Elsewhere I have shown that the blocks are closing and becoming more inward looking and less global over time, Rugman (2000). Indeed, there has been increasing regionalization over the last twenty to thirty years, not increasing globalization, as shown by trade and FDI data, Rugman (2000). This economic reality is now being reflected in politics.

Analysis of the decision of the UN Security Council in February 2003, not to endorse a second resolution to authorize US led military action in Iraq shows that the trans-Atlantic political relationships now reflect the broken economic one. Only the UK actually has any significant economic interest in North America. This is now through FDI (not trade) since the UK now has a majority of its trade with its EU partners. As shown in Rugman and Kudina (2002), the UK now has about 40% of its outward stock of FDI in North America. This is matched by a similar inward stock. In contrast, Germany and France have most of their FDI within the EU, not across the Atlantic.

Today the economic lenses of France and Germany are inward looking. Only the UK still needs a political alliance with the United States to match its economic interest. The political support of Spain and Italy for the United States in Iraq reflects more on internal EU politics than on any long-term economic affiliation of these states with the United States. Basically the EU now represents, as a block, an economic alternative to North America. The European-based MNEs have 80% of their sales within Europe. European business does not really need America, just as America does not need Europe, as there is relatively little inter-block trade.

All of this economic analysis also works for Asia. This region is becoming more interdependent, and it has almost identical intra-regional growth in trade and FDI to match its major triad partners of North America and Europe. Again, most of the sales of Asian-based MNEs are within the Asian region, see figure 11.1. This trend is increasing.

The world political picture is also one of expanding regionalism. As noted earlier, the EU expanded by ten new members in 2004, and it may admit ten more a few years later. The NAFTA will extend from three nations to thirty-four in the FTAA by 2005. In Asia, China, Japan, and South Korea will develop stronger ties with the ASEAN countries. These are all signals that regional integration is being fostered by new sets of rules to further facilitate intra-regional trade and FDI. The basic strategy of any business outside the triad is that it needs to become affiliated to a triad region to grow and succeed. Firms inside a triad region will continue to grow intra-regionally.

The Iraq war of 2003 simply reflects the economic reality of the triad. The United States, as a hegemon, does not need support from the leading countries in Europe or Asia. It does not even need it from its NAFTA partners, both of whom made the mistake of not supporting the United States in its political hour of need. This was not smart policy when they are both totally dependent on the United States for economic success. This serious political mistake is unlikely to be repeated by the new Canadian Prime Minister, Paul Martin, or tolerated again by business interests in Mexico.

What is the role of France, Germany, Italy, the UK, Russia, and Japan after the Iraq war? Except for the UK, all have demonstrated their military irrelevancy in fighting the international war on terrorism. In early 2004 Canada has sought to re-align itself with US policy leadership in North America, agreeing to common border security and customs measures. The UK–US relationship is strong, and it provides the UK with independent leverage across the EU and all of Europe. France has largely destroyed its ability to influence current US policy. It now ranks below Russia as a political US ally, and Germany ranks below Italy and Spain. The United States is unlikely to look to the G8 for any military or political alliance in the near future. It does not need the G8 as much as the G8 needs the United States.

In the future, due to this regional business integration, the United States and US MNEs will be better placed to achieve their goals of economic and national security by a regional focus on NAFTA and the FTAA. It is apparent that most European nations and European MNEs still fail to understand the long-run political implications of September 11, 2001. Now the United States places national security first. This will lead, in time, to deeper North American regional economic and political integration. The Iraq war was not for oil, or even for energy security, but to reduce future terrorist threats such as another September 11th. The United States is still at war with terrorism, and it will continue to attack governments that help to foster terrorism when this threatens US national security interests. The United States has relatively less interest in multilateralism than in regionalism, given this overarching domestic security objective. The G8 members need to understand the new US concern over its own regional security and work with it to enhance US security.

Ultimately, the United States does not need to use multilateral agencies such as the United Nations or even the WTO. The huge US economy, now complemented by NAFTA and with the likely prospect of an FTAA, already provides the United States with a great deal of regional economic security, including energy security. But it still needs national security. Future policies will lead to tighter border inspections, more difficult landing and visiting requirements for immigrants, and a growing fortress North America. The internal market of NAFTA may then deepen, driven by MNEs and business interests, partly along the lines of the old EC, with a common immigration policy and border inspections across NAFTA. Canada has already signaled its support for such integrated border measures, and it will thereby become further integrated with the United States. The rest of the G8 will become outsiders; regional interests will dominate multilateral ones.

SECURITY AND REGIONAL US ENERGY SUPPLY

The importance of NAFTA, and a potential FTAA, is highly relevant to the United States in terms of energy security. Despite the widespread popular feeling that the US-led military action in Iraq in March 2003, was due to Iraq's oil; there is no economic logic to support this belief.

The United States has 57.2% of all its oil produced within NAFTA. It produces 41% of its own consumption internally and imports another 16.3% from its two NAFTA partners. Another 9.2% comes from Venezuela and Colombia, so over two-thirds of all US oil consumption is from the Americas. The United States does not need oil from Iraq. Indeed, it only consumes 13.9% of all of its oil from all the states in the Persian Gulf, i.e. Bahrain, Iraq, Kuwait, Qatar, Saudi Arabia, and the UAE. Even though this area has large oil reserves there are similarly large oil reserves in Canada (in the Athabaska tar sands but at a higher cost of development), so this position of oil security is not likely to be threatened for many years. While the Persian Gulf states, through control of OPEC, can influence the world price of oil, the United States can move to ensure safe supplies of oil on a long-range basis through regional sourcing.

In strictly economic terms Iraq and the rest of the Middle East is of minimal importance to the United States. Although the United States has free trade agreements with Israel and Jordan, total trade to these areas is under 1% of its trade. In contrast, the United States has 37% of its trade with its NAFTA partners. In short, Iraq does not matter to North America. It may matter to Europe and Asia, but that is a different issue.

In terms of consumption of oil the United States produces 40.9% of its total needs. Another 9.1% comes from Canada and 7.2% from Mexico as can be seen in table 11.1. Thus, the NAFTA region supplies 57.2% of all the oil required by the

Table 11.1. US consumption of petroleum, by country of origin, 2001: thousand barrels per day

	2001	% of total
United States	8,031	40.9
Canada	1,786	9.1
Mexico	1,423	7.2
North America	11,240	57.2
Venezuela	1,538	7.8
Colombia	280	1.4
Persian Gulf	2,731	13.9
Others	3,861	19.6
Total	19,650	100.0

Table 11.2. US petroleum imports: thousand barrels per day		
	2001	% of total
Canada	1,786	15.4
Mexico	1,423	12.2
North America	3,209	27.6
Venezuela	1,538	13.2
Colombia	280	2.4
Persian Gulf	2,731	23.5
Others	3,861	33.2
Total	11,619	100.0

Sources: 1981–2000 – EIA, Petroleum Supply Annual, annual reports. 2001 – EIA, Petroleum Supply Monthly (February 2002).
Persian Gulf = Bahrain, Iran, Iraq, Kuwait, Qatar, Saudi Arabia, and United Arab Emirates.

United States. A further 7.8% comes from Venezuela and 1.4% from Colombia, so as much as 66.4% of all the oil consumed in the United States is from the Americas. The Persian Gulf as a whole only supplies 13.9% of all US oil. These data are reported in table 11.1.

In terms of imports of oil in 2001 by the United States (remembering that it produces 41% of its consumption itself) the Persian Gulf supplies 23.5% of all US imports. Yet this is lower than the NAFTA partners of the United States, as Canada supplies 15.4% and Mexico 12.2% of all US oil imports (a total of 27.6% from these two neighbors). In addition, Venezuela supplies 13.2% and Colombia 2.4%, so a total of 43.2% of all US oil imports are from the Americas. These data are reported in table 11.2.

Looking at US oil import data for 2002 confirms this picture of regional dependence. Between 2001 and 2002, oil imports from Canada increased from 15.4% to 17.1% and those from Mexico from 12.2% to 13.4%, i.e. NAFTA imports increased from 27.6% to 30.5%. Another 14.4% comes from Venezuela and Colombia (down from 15.6% in 2001). By 2002, US oil imports from all of the Persian Gulf had fallen to 22.0% (from 23.5% in 2001).

IMPLICATIONS OF REGIONALIZATION FOR BUSINESS–GOVERNMENT RELATIONS

The implications of MNE activity for societal welfare and public policy have been the subject of a particularly large and varied literature in economics and political science, Rugman and Verbeke (1998a). Regional trade and investment agreements have also been studied extensively, especially in the context of North American and European integration processes, as discussed earlier in this chapter. Much of the relevant literature has focused on two issues. First, the gains from regional free trade – the issue of trade creation versus trade diversion, whereby insiders and outsiders may be affected differently by a regional integration program. Second, the relative merits of regionalization versus multilateralism, such as through the General Agreement on Tariffs and Trade (GATT) and the World Trade Organization (WTO).

Rugman and Verbeke (2004) show that regionalism is an efficient substitute for ill-functioning multilateral institutions in terms of economic outcomes. Regional integration (with only a limited number of participants that are geographically close) is working better than the multilateral integration process requiring concession of all the 144 countries in the WTO. Regional clusters now drive regional integration. It reflects bottom-up efforts by a multitude of economic actors, who wish to expand their geographical business horizon, guided by immediate opportunities that are geographically close and associated with low transaction costs, as well as a high potential for agglomeration economies. This has been confirmed in NAFTA for autos and chemicals, Rugman, Kirton and Soloway (1999). In the long run, such agglomeration, in the sense of improved "regional diamond conditions" may improve the MNEs' capabilities to penetrate other triad markets, Rugman and Verbeke (2004).

Future research now needs to pay attention to the MNE as the appropriate unit of analysis in regional integration. Each firm's regional integration preferences and role will depend upon its FSA configuration, much in line with its preferences regarding trade and investment protection at the national level. These preferences may even vary from business to business in a single firm, Rugman and Verbeke (2004). As implied by earlier sections of this chapter, the main question for the MNE is to assess how regional integration may reduce the need for location-specific adaptation investments in the various national markets, when expanding the geographic scope of activities.

Rather than merely analyzing macro-economic or sectoral data, there is a rich avenue of work to be pursued on firm-level adaptation processes to regional integration, with a focus on the region-specific adaptation investments needed to link the MNE's existing FSAs (non-location-bound and location-bound ones) with the regional/location advantages, and on the nature of these investments (internal development versus external acquisition), Rugman and Verbeke (2004). An analysis of such new knowledge development in MNEs may be critical to understand fully the societal effects of increased regionalization.

The impacts of regional trading agreements have often been interpreted in terms of changes in entry barriers facing insiders and outsiders, at the macro, industry, and strategic-group levels. From a resource-based perspective, however, there is a real need to understand how regional integration processes affect the creation or elimination of isolating mechanisms, and thereby economic performance, at the level of individual MNEs and subunits within MNEs.

Regional integration also has implications for knowledge exchange, as it is likely to increase the geographic reach of MNE networks in terms of backward and forward linkages, and even the MNEs' broader flagship networks, Rugman and D'Cruz (2000). To the extent that such linkages and networks are associated with knowledge diffusion spill-overs, these should also be taken into account in any analysis of the regional integration welfare effects.

Finally, regional integration can have an impact on the MNE's internal distribution of resources and FSAs; more specifically, firm-level investments in regional adaptation often imply the relocation of specific production facilities to the most efficient subunits, in order to capture regional scale economies and a re-assessment of subsidiary charters. This implies to some extent a zero sum game with "winning" and "losing" subsidiaries.

Interestingly, it has also been observed that regional integration may energize subsidiaries to start new initiatives and to develop new capabilities, Rugman and Verbeke (2001b). This really implies a non-zero sum game, again with macro-level welfare improvements as an outcome. Will the deepening of a regional trading block, even if it has positive net welfare effects inside the region and at the world level, strengthen the affected insider MNEs in other legs of the triad? Or will it, on the contrary, act as an incentive to focus these MNEs' resource allocation processes and market expansion plans even more on intra-regional growth opportunities? The empirical data presented in this chapter appear to indicate that regional integration during the past decade has had little effect on the abilities of MNEs to increase their globalization capabilities.

CONCLUSIONS

The evidence is that the world economy is now a triad one; the economic regions of North America, the EU, and Asia dominate international business. Both aggregate data, and disaggregated data, on the sales of the world's largest multinational enterprise show the regional pattern of economic activity. What does this mean for business–government relations?

The lack of globalization means a lack of multilateralism for governments and a lack of global strategy for firms. As economic power is regional, so is political power. The United States can achieve all of its post-September 11th national security desires within NAFTA. The United States does not need Europe or Asia, for support in the Iraq war. This is just another example of the end of multilateralism. The United States calls the military tune. Other nations either need to dance to it or further deepen their own intra-regional economic relations. Canada and Mexico, in general, experience the strong economic benefits of NAFTA and have learned to live with US political power, with the Iraq war bring a notable exception. Indeed, the Canadians in 2003 seemed to be operating on the old-fashioned model of multilateralism rather than the new reality of regionalism. As Canada was the first major country to negotiate its joining a triad power (in the 1987 Canadian–US Free Trade Agreement) it is likely in the future to return to being a regional player as with Mexico.

Transaction cost economics reasoning largely explains this phenomenon of regionalization. Market-seeking expansion in host regions is often associated with high, location-specific adaptation investments to link the MNE's existing knowledge base with host-region location advantages. The firm's FSAs and CSAs do not simply meld together without managerial intervention. As the required investments to meld FSAs and CSAs become larger, driven by the cultural, administrative, geographic, and economic distance between home country/region and host regions, the attractiveness of foreign markets declines. Then regional, rather than global, strategies are needed to reflect the differential need for "linking" investments in each region. Only in a few sectors, such as consumer electronics, can a balanced, global distribution of sales be achieved.

It is likely that the upstream end of the value chain can be globalized more easily than the customer end, where sales data have been the focus of this chapter. Upstream location-specific investments are not one-sided (in the sense of lacking reciprocal commitments from the other economic actors involved, which is a critical problem at the customer end). Upstream globalization obviously need not be expressed in a balanced geographic distribution of R&D, manufacturing, etc., but rather in the MNE's ability to choose and access locations around the globe where the firm's upstream FSAs can easily be melded with foreign CSAs and location advantages, without the need for major, location-specific adaptation investments. Yet, the available data on production also suggest the importance of home-region based production clusters and networks, as in the automobile sector. This indicates that the hazards of cultural, administrative, geographic, and economic distance between the home country/region and host regions are often also present at the upstream side.

For firms, this dominance of intra-regional activity means that their managers need to pay much more attention to regional trade agreements like NAFTA, regional political integration agreements like the EU, and a potential regional agreement in Asia. These managers already know how to achieve their FSAs on a regional basis and that outsourcing of the supply chain to Asia (as with Nike and Wal-Mart) is to take advantage of locational CSAs (in cheap labor), rather than to reconfigure their basic business model. Overall, business-government relations need to move toward a regional level of analysis, building upon the old-fashioned national sovereignty framework of states and markets. There is no evidence that globalization, global strategy, or multilateralism is of much relevance to either policy makers or managers.

12

Regional multinationals: the new research agenda

One of the puzzles of international business research is that the key actor, the multinational enterprise (MNE), appears to have a very unevenly distributed geographic dispersion of sales. The MNE is usually a regionalized rather than a globalized business. Three definitions matter:

(i) multinational enterprise: a firm with operations across national borders;
(ii) global business: a firm with major operations (at least 20% of its total sales) in each of the three regions of the "broad triad" of the European Union (EU), North America, and Asia-Pacific, but without one dominating region;
(iii) regional business: a firm with the majority of its sales inside one of the triad regions, usually the home region.

The following empirical observations have also been made:

(i) the world's 500 largest MNEs account for over 90% of the world's stock of foreign direct investment (FDI) and over half of world trade, usually in the form of intra-firm sales (Rugman, 2000);
(ii) of these 500 MNEs, only nine are "global";
(iii) the vast majority of the 500 MNEs (320 of the 380 for which data are available) are home-region based and derive an average of 80% of their sales intra-regionally.

These stylized facts suggest a new research agenda for the international business field, as requested by Buckley (2002). In this chapter, we explore some aspects of this. The observed regionalization can be given a simple transaction cost economics (TCE) explanation. Host regions require substantial "linking" or "melding" investments (a form of asset specificity), in order to integrate the MNE's existing firm-specific advantages (FSAs) and exogenous country-specific advantages (CSAs), whereas such investments, driven by cultural, administrative, geographic, and economic distance, are much lower in the home region. This perspective on international business leads to a new "big question" for the field: why are we still teaching global business when much of it is actually regional?

REGIONALIZATION AND NEW THEORY

As discussed earlier in this book, especially in chapter 4, further research should be undertaken to test for the regional dimension of international strategy. Specifically, key analytical devices used in international business research will need to be modified. For example, the economic integration/ national responsiveness matrix popularized by Bartlett and Ghoshal (1989) needs to be complemented with a regional dimension, as discussed below.

One of the clearest examples of regionalization is the automobile industry. This industry is characterized by triad-based clusters with regionally-situated MNEs. The data on foreign sales of the world's largest automobile MNEs show that sales, as well as assembly and production are regional, Rugman (2000). GM has 81% of its sales in North America; Ford has 61%; BMW and VW have the majority of their sales in Europe. DaimlerChrysler, Nissan Motors, Honda, and Toyota are bi-regional. None of these firms is global.

In terms of the value chain, a number of MNEs source offshore. Nike has 99% of its production outside of the United States; almost all of this is in Southeast Asia. This type of globalization, at the upstream end of the value chain, is easier to achieve than at the customer end, because the linking investments required to meld the MNE's key FSAs (brand names and logistics skills) with location advantages in production do not, in this case at least, require high location-specific adaptation investments to tap into the foreign-location advantages.

The service sectors are even more local and regional than is manufacturing. In retail, only one of the largest forty-nine retail firms is global (LVMH), and only two are bi-regional, Rugman and Girod (2003). In banking, all the companies have the vast majority of their assets in the home region.

Despite Levitt's (1983) prediction of standardization through globalization, and of global brands, there is no discernible trend towards either standardization or global branding. Indeed, banks remain stubbornly local or regional. Only a few MNEs, with Coca-Cola leading the way, are global. Even McDonalds is bi-regional not global. In marketing, research shows that location-driven adaptation costs are incurred, in order to be successful. There is little evidence of an increased commonality in demand for products and services. Even successful MNEs, with internationally recognized brands, need to allocate substantial resources to craft linkages between their FSAs and foreign-location advantages, in order to outperform local rivals.

Health care is not a global business, as it is delivered locally and is subject to local regulations. Even within the EU, there are separate national systems for health-care delivery and for pharmaceuticals. Within NAFTA, there are three distinct health-care systems, so health care is not even regional, let alone global. Patents are registered at the national level; the most active is the US patent office where all active MNEs attempt to register.

REGIONAL OR GLOBAL THEORY

There is a potential dynamic in the matrix of figures 3.2 and 10.1, the new "regional" matrix of this book. Firms in cell 2 may move to cell 4 by expanding the reach of their FSAs from regional to global. They could achieve this, for example, by integration strategies of seeking low cost or common brand names. However, movement from cell 2 to cell 1 is rare, as firms will not be able to develop global scope from a regional reach of FSAs. Regional FSAs act as a constraint on the development of global scope. Only if a firm goes from cell 2 to cell 4, is it possible to then, perhaps, move to cell 3.

In other words, global strategy is achieved by development of FSAs, in particular by transforming them from a regional to a global reach. With a global reach in FSAs, the firm is then well positioned to develop a global scope, defined here as a significant presence in all three regions of the triad (at least 20% of sales in each triad region). Globalization is attained through changing FSAs, rather than by expanding scope.

It is tempting to label the dynamics of moving from cell 2 to cell 4 to cell 3 as a "globalization" strategy; at the beginning firms are regional; at the end they are global. However, as we observe only nine firms are in cell 4, it is apparent that this is not really a typical picture of firm strategy. Rather, the vast majority of large 500 firms reside in cell 2. This suggests that there are long-term barriers to the development of a global reach in FSAs. It further suggests that most FSAs are being fully utilized on a regional, not a global, dimension. For most firms, scale economies must be fully realized regionally. Brand names must be fully exploited regionally. There are few, if any, additional advantages to "going global" for 320 of the 380 firms which provide data on intra-regional sales. This is a rather shocking, empirically-based, refutation of the need for global strategy. Instead, for most large firms, it's regional that works.

In this book it was not possible to provide a complete test of performance of regional or global firms. The main contribution of this book is to provide objective firm-level data on intra-regional sales for the 500 firms which dominate international business. Future work can examine the performance of the global firms versus the regional firms. But with so few pure globals (only nine) and only a further three dozen bi-regionals and "near miss" globals, as against 320 home-regional firms, it is highly unlikely that statistically meaningful tests of performance can be achieved. Indeed, we know from other studies of the 500 large firms, Gestrin, Knight, and Rugman (2000) that while financial performance is positively related to the degree of multinationality, it is highly unlikely to be dependent upon the extent of regionalization versus globalization, as defined here. However, this issue awaits further research.

Finally, another issue deserves a word or two. The data here focus on percentages of intra-regional sales. Yet some firms can have a large market share in a region with still a low percentage share of their own sales in that region. An example is Toyota. It has a low percentage of sales in Europe, but a significant market share, especially in certain categories of vehicles. So does Ford. In contrast, while Honda has an even higher percentage of sales in North America than does Toyota, Honda's market share is lower than Toyota's in North America, as Honda is a much smaller firm than is Toyota.

All this means is that the data presented here on intra-regional sales have to be properly interpreted, keeping in mind the size of the firm and its market share, especially its market shares by business unit. As the latter data are not disclosed by firms, they need to be assembled across these 500 firms in a careful manner. Again, this is work that needs to be undertaken in the future.

Overall, the new data on intra-regional sales presented here, and analyzed across fifty to sixty firms in some detail, offer a challenge for scholars of international business to renew their efforts at the empirical level. For too long international business research has been dominated by the "special case" – the few global, transnational, metanational, or whatever name is given to firms with a presence in all three regions of the triad. This work has been overemphasized. It is work that is not based on basic empirical observation. In contrast, as shown here, when research proceeds from a strong empirical base, new theories are needed to explain the predominance of home region activity. This is the general case; global firms are the exception. International business is too important to be left to case writers, consultants, and ad hoc theorists. Across the 500 largest firms in the world global strategy strikes out.

This book suggests a new research agenda. The embeddedness of FSAs at regional level requires serious new thinking, case studies, data analysis, surveys of managers within MNEs, etc. The tools of analytical research should yield new scholarship and insight far beyond the basic work attempted here. This book provides an empirically drawn rationale and potential research agenda for regional strategy. No longer can globalization be confused with multinationality. Most MNEs are not global, but regional. International business is not just foreign sales; it matters where those sales occur – if in the home region (as for most large firms) then forget global and focus on regional issues. The regional geographic scope of most MNEs is matched by a regional reach of their FSAs. Large firms have a regional alignment, not a global one.

IMPLICATIONS FOR MNE THEORY

Conventional international business theory suggests that international sales arise because firms possess firm-specific advantages (FSAs), i.e. proprietary knowledge, which can be exploited profitably across national borders, whether through exports, foreign direct investment, market contracts, or hybrid modes. Further, and especially in the context of market-seeking investment, internalization advantages, in the sense of comparatively higher efficiency of hierarchy vis-à-vis other entry modes, are critical to the explanation of foreign direct investment and the establishment of foreign subsidiaries. Finally, location advantages or country-specific advantages (CSAs), are important in explaining the precise geographic scope of international expansion, Dunning (1993), Rugman (1981, 1996). Given the above, the regional concentration of sales of the world's 500 largest MNEs is puzzling. Why would most American, European, and Asian MNEs in a single industry have a concentration of their sales in their home region, if they (a) possess proprietary knowledge that is internationally transferable/exploitable, (b) can benefit from similar internalization advantages associated with FDI, building upon this proprietary knowledge, and (c) most importantly, face similar location advantages critical to successful market-seeking investment?

One, albeit unsatisfactory, explanation is provided by internationalization theory, Johansson and Vahlne (1977, 1990). This theory argues that MNEs expand first in geographically proximate markets and engage in modest resource commitments. As experiential learning is built up, firms venture into more distant markets and engage in more complex and more far-reaching resource commitments. The problem with internationalization theory is that it lacks serious conceptual grounding and generalizability, especially in regards as to what exactly constitutes geographic proximity or experiential learning, and the mechanisms through which these concepts influence FDI decisions and geographic sales dispersion.

A more useful explanation of regional MNE activity, fully in line with the modern TCE theory of the firm, is that the scope of geographic expansion is determined by the MNE's ability to link its FSAs with location advantages abroad. International success does not simply follow from proprietary knowledge in, e.g. R&D or marketing, but from the MNE's ability to adapt successfully the deployment of its existing FSAs to the specific circumstances of foreign markets, i.e. by better aligning FSAs and CSAs. We have argued elsewhere, Rugman and Verbeke (1992, 2001a, 2003c, and 2004) that such adaptation can take several forms, especially (a) investments in the development of location-bound FSAs in foreign markets (leading to benefits of national responsiveness) to complement non-location-bound FSAs, and (b) investments in the development of new, non-location-bound FSAs in foreign subsidiaries.

It could be argued that there is nothing new in this analysis; MNEs are faced with the liability of foreignness, i.e. additional costs of doing business abroad, and such costs are simply higher in host-region markets than in home-region markets. However, our proposition is that, at the market side, these costs could be viewed as the result of implicit contracts with foreign locations, whereby the intended outcome is stronger embeddedness of the firm's extended knowledge base in these foreign locations, and therefore higher sales. In other words, asset specificity (in the form of additional, location-specific linking investments) is incurred, implying that such transactions, even if successful, come at a cost, as compared to the conventional deployment of FSAs in locations where no such linking investments need to be made to increase sales.

This problem is compounded by the fact that the MNE's commitment of resources to link its existing pool of FSAs with foreign-location advantages (such as the presence of a large market), through crafting location-bound FSAs or even new, non-location-bound FSAs in foreign markets, in no way guarantees success. The resource commitments made to attract potential foreign customers and to increase sales are fully one-sided. This is in contrast with, e.g. resource-seeking or strategic asset-seeking FDI, whereby foreign locations may again require location-specific linking investments from the MNE, but whereby all relevant parties, such as foreign suppliers, workers, and acquired companies themselves, engage in reciprocal commitments to make these investments worthwhile.

The above analysis suggests that the puzzle of regional concentration of sales has transaction cost-related origins: in the case of market-driven geographic expansion, what is conventionally viewed as the MNE's proprietary knowledge (its FSAs), is not just deployed in geographic space in those locations where exogenously determined CSAs (in this case an attractive market) are the greatest in an objective sense. Each foreign location requires location-specific linking investments to meld existing FSAs with CSAs, and it is, *ceteris paribus*, the extent of these adaptation costs, taking into account the redeployability of the resulting additional knowledge in the relevant locations, that explains why most MNEs expand first in their home region, and may face great difficulty expanding to other regions.

More specifically, many so-called non-location-bound FSAs can only be exploited profitably within the home region, without the need for substantial, location-specific adaptation investments. In addition, location-bound FSAs developed in the home country or in other countries in the home region can be "tuned up" to be fully deployable in the entire region, with low-linking investments required, if the countries involved are subject to a low cultural, administrative, geographic, and economic distance among themselves, in the spirit of Ghemawat (2001). Hence, these FSAs can easily be made "region bound," to the extent that linking investments with high cultural specificity, administrative specificity, geography-related specificity, and economy-related specificity can be avoided. This process is further enhanced if governments in this region pursue policies that promote internal coherence via administrative and political harmonization (as in the EU) or even merely via economic integration (as in NAFTA and Asia), thereby reducing the MNE's needs to engage in idiosyncratic, location-specific adaptation investments to meld existing FSAs and foreign-location advantages. In contrast, host regions may require large adaptation investments driven by home/host region differences in the cultural, administrative, geographic, and economic sphere in order to meld the MNE's existing knowledge base and the host-region location advantages. This requirement for high, region-specific "linking" investments acts as an entry deterrent for many MNEs.

A related point is that inter-block business is likely to be restricted relative to intra-regional sales by government-imposed barriers to entry. For example, the EU and the United States are likely to fight trade wars and be responsive to domestic business lobbies seeking shelter in the form of subsidies and/or protection. Cultural, administrative, geography-related, and economy-related differences among members of a single triad region may remain, but these will mostly be less significant than across triad regions, Rugman (2000). The end result is the persistence of MNEs that will continue to earn 80% or more of their income in their home-triad region. There will only be a limited number of purely "global" MNEs in the top 500.

In contrast, as mentioned above, transactions that do not relate to sales (or the customer end of the value chain) but to more upstream activities, are not one-sided (meaning the MNE engages in location-specific adaptation investments without any customer guarantees to purchase the MNEs' products). Upstream value-chain activities entail transactions whereby all relevant economic actors may make credible commitments to craft a highly efficient manufacturing or logistics chain apparatus (including workers, outside component suppliers, logistics providers, etc.).

IMPLICATIONS OF REGIONALIZATION FOR BUSINESS STRATEGY

In this chapter, globalization is defined in terms of geographic dispersion of sales across regions, with regional effects being potentially very different in upstream and customer-end activities, given the differential ease to develop linkages between the firm's FSA base and the relevant location advantages at the upstream versus customer end. For example, some firms, such as Nike and Wal-Mart, have sourcing structures that may be much more geographically dispersed than their sales. Global sourcing of primary and intermediate inputs, as well as dispersed production, may greatly contribute to a firm's success in its home region. However, ultimately it is market penetration (if achieved in a profitable way) that provides the best, in fact the only, indicator of global corporate success. What are the immediate managerial implications of the observed geographic concentration of sales in most MNEs, beyond the broader research issues discussed above? The following five managerial implications are critical.

First, the regional issues discussed in this chapter, whether viewed as opportunities or threats, cast additional doubts on the validity of the transnational solution model as the panacea for global corporate success. The main weakness of the transnational solution model is its internal complexity, as discussed in Rugman and Verbeke (2001a, 2003c). The regional aspects identified here further compound this complexity, and this despite the financial markets' demands for transparency and simplicity in strategy and structure. The empirical evidence suggests that MNEs, especially smaller ones, should try to capitalize on opportunities in their home region as far as customer-end activities are concerned, rather than engaging in a path of rapid "global roll out" of their products and services. A narrow geographic market focus may thus be required as much as a narrow product focus, so as to guarantee the presence of FSAs capable of providing maximum value added to customers, without the need for additional, one-sided, location-specific investments.

Second, from a strategic management perspective, a key problem associated with attempts to implement the transnational solution is the implicit assumption that every activity in the firm requires a careful analysis of its need for location-bound versus non-location-bound company strengths, and resulting managerial decisions to develop and deploy such strengths. The managerial reality, however, is that not all individual activities conducted in the MNE require FSAs instrumental to outperforming rivals, or requiring location-specific adaptation investments abroad. It is therefore important to identify those activities for which FSAs are critical to success, and that may require location-specific adaptation investments abroad. In addition, various combinations of location-bound and non-location-bound strengths may lead to equivalent performance outcomes. Hence, it is necessary to first identify those activities for which access to specific FSA bundles, and location-specific adaptation investments are critical to the MNE's ultimate economic performance (in terms of market penetration and profitability). In addition, as noted above, it is likely that many of the identified upstream and customer-end activities will require a different composition of FSA bundles, and location-specific adaptation investments, but even if this requisite variety imposed by the external environment can be correctly assessed, this does not guarantee market success. Market success requires three more conditions to be fulfilled: first, the appropriate bundling of critical activities with similar FSA requirements in properly functioning organizational units; second, the effective coordination among these units; third, the differentiation of these units across geographic regions, as a reflection of the MNE's idiosyncratic market position in each region, and the differential need for location-specific adaptation investments in each region.

Third, even in allegedly global functions, such as finance (due to the result of liberalized financial capital markets), there are elements of regionalization that need to be examined. Here are three:

(1) The world financial system is now largely dominated in terms of financial intermediation by the three major currencies: the US dollar, the euro, and the yen. The pound sterling is increasingly affiliated with the euro, reflecting British exports of 64% with the rest of the EU and 50% of its inward FDI stock in 1999 from there, Rugman and Kudina (2002).

(2) The leading stock markets appear to largely serve local companies. For example 91% of the new issues on the US NASDAQ are by US companies; in the German Neuer Market 83% of new issues were German, and most of the remaining ones were by other EU companies.

(3) The foreign exchange traders in New York and Tokyo exhibited strong isomorphic behavior guided by home-country patterns of legitimate behavior, according to Zaheer (1995). Even in a perfect market with instantaneous transmission of information, American foreign exchange traders behaved differently from Japanese traders. Hence, even for tasks and functional areas for which the non-location-bound nature of successful patterns of decisions and actions is widely accepted in the firm, it may be necessary to revisit the old assumption of international transferability. Specifically, the location-specific adaptation investments needed to meld FSAs and CSAs in particular foreign markets may be influenced to an important extent by the MNE's country of origin, Zaheer and Mosakowski (1997). In other words, a home-region competence may lead to a host-region competence trap.

Fourth, the largest service companies appear even less global than manufacturing companies. In retail, only one of the largest forty-nine retail firms is global (LVMH), and only five are bi-regional, Rugman and Girod (2003). In banking, all but one (Santander Central Hispano Group) of the forty companies have the vast majority of their sales in the home region. Insurance is even more local. Even knowledge intensive service industries are largely local. For example, professional service firms – such as law firms, consultants, accountants – are usually embedded in local clusters, with partners being largely immobile and their loose networks being, at best, regionally based.

This situation was anticipated by Campbell and Verbeke (1994), who assessed the validity of the transnational solution for service MNEs. They concluded that the potential for scope economies resulting from the transfer of non-location-bound FSAs is usually lower in service firms, because of the impossibility in many cases of separating the upstream and customer-end segments of the value chain (inseparability of production and delivery). In this context, this implies that regional-market responsiveness at the customer end is only possible if innovation at the upstream end is also decentralized. In other words, decentralization of decision-making power to the regional level may require that large sets of decisions be delegated to that level, and this is usually associated with high, location-specific adaptation investments. Such investments thus imply, paradoxically, a reduction rather than an increase of the MNE's globalization approach at the upstream end, namely if upstream practices appropriate in a host region differ from the home region (e.g. in case of the required use of local resources and network participants).

Fifth, if MNEs face a higher liability of foreignness in customer-end activities as compared to upstream activities, this has two managerial implications from a dynamic perspective. First, learning in the sense of lowering the liability of foreignness, through location-specific adaptation investments in market knowledge, occurs at a different pace in particular activities of the value chain. Foreign market penetration success ultimately is constrained by the activity area with the lowest rate of learning (or the highest required level of location-specific adaptation investments). Managers should thus try to identify the most constraining activities in the critical time paths to achieve international market growth. Second, whereas upstream activities can often be appropriately upgraded, in the sense of successfully linking the MNE's initial set of FSAs with foreign CSAs, as a result of (inexpensive) observational learning and selective imitation, this does not appear so simple at the customer end. Hence, Ohmae (1985) may be correct when he suggests that the deep market penetration of host-triad regions should be performed by collaborative instruments (consortia, joint ventures etc.). These lead to rapid local embeddedness and access to social network ties. However, collaborating with foreign partners and permitting foreign affiliates to develop local network ties, though avoiding the need for high, location-specific adaptation investments, brings its own set of managerial problems. First is the danger of FSA dissipation through intentional appropriation by the foreign partner, but also in a broader sense through knowledge diffusion as a result of proximity induced imitation, Hamel et al. (1989). Second is the danger of reduced coherence within the MNE, if affiliates become locally embedded in host-region networks at the expense of the MNE's overall institutionalization logic, Campbell and Verbeke (2001). The challenges above reflect critical trade-offs to be made, much in line with the decision-making challenges on product diversification in large firms Ollinger (1994).

IMPLICATIONS OF REGIONALIZATION FOR SOCIETY

The implications of MNE activity for societal welfare and public policy have been the subject of a particularly large and varied literature in economics and political science, Rugman and Verbeke (1998a). The topic of the integration impacts resulting from regional trade and investment agreements has been studied extensively, especially in the context of North American and European integration processes, see Pomfret (2001) for an extensive review. Much of the relevant literature has focused on two issues. First, building upon the seminal work of Viner (1950), the problem of trade creation versus trade diversion, whereby insiders and outsiders may be affected differently by a regional integration program. Second, the relative merits of regionalization vis-à-vis efforts toward multilateralism, such as through the General Agreement on Tariffs and Trade (GATT) and the World Trade Organization (WTO).

Here, four contradictory perspectives have been formulated, Poon (1997). First, an emphasis on the economic inferiority of regional vis-à-vis multilateral integration outcomes, Bhagwati (2002). Second, the view that regionalism is an efficient substitute for ill-functioning multilateral institutions in terms of economic outcomes, Rugman and Verbeke (2003a). Third, a focus on the comparative ease of conducting a regional integration process (with only a limited number of participants that are geographically close) vis-à-vis a multilateral integration process that could involve all the 144 countries in the WTO. Fourth, a focus on the organic nature of economic integration in regional clusters, Krugman (1993), Frankel et al. (1995). Here, regional integration is not driven primarily by the strategic intent of government agencies and powerful economic actors to increase or consolidate economic exchange within a region through new institutions in a top-down fashion. Rather, it reflects bottom-up efforts by a multitude of economic actors, who wish to expand their geographical business horizon, guided by immediate opportunities that are geographically close and associated with low transaction costs, as well as a high potential for agglomeration economies. In the long run, such agglomeration, in the sense of improved 'regional diamond conditions' may improve the MNEs' capabilities to penetrate other triad markets, Rugman and Verbeke (2003b).

None of these four perspectives has paid much attention to the MNE as the appropriate unit of analysis, with some exceptions that include Rugman and Verbeke (1990a, 1990b, 1991), Rugman, Verbeke, and Luxmore (1990), Rugman (1994). This is a fruitful avenue for future IB research, for five reasons.

First, the role of individual MNEs in the institutional processes of regional integration could be investigated in more depth, without starting from the ideological assumption that all MNEs pursue a narrow and homogenous business agenda. Each firm's regional integration preferences and role will depend upon its FSA configuration, much in line with its preferences regarding trade and investment protection at the national level, Milner (1988), Salorio (1993). These preferences may even vary from business to business in a single firm, Rugman, Verbeke, and Luxmore (1990). As implied by earlier sections of this chapter, the main question for the MNE is to assess how regional integration may reduce the need for location-specific adaptation investments in the various national markets, when expanding the geographic scope of activities.

Second, rather than merely analyzing macro-economic or sectoral data, there is a rich avenue of work to be pursued on firm level adaptation processes to regional integration, with a focus on the region-specific adaptation investments needed to link the MNE's existing FSAs (non-location-bound and location-bound ones) with the regional/location advantages, and on the nature of these investments (internal development versus external acquisition), Rugman and Verbeke (1991). An analysis of such new knowledge development in MNEs may be critical for understanding fully the societal effects of increased regionalization.

Third, the impacts of regional trading agreements have often been interpreted in terms of changes in entry barriers facing insiders and outsiders, at the macro, industry, and strategic-group levels. From a resource-based perspective, however, there is a real need to understand how regional integration processes affect the creation or elimination of isolating mechanisms, and thereby economic performance, at the level of individual MNEs and subunits within MNEs.

Fourth, regional integration also has implications for knowledge exchange, as it is likely to increase the geographic reach of MNE networks in terms of backward and forward linkages, and even the MNEs broader flagship networks, Rugman and D'Cruz (2000). To the extent that such linkages and networks are associated with knowledge diffusion spillovers, these should also be taken into account in any analysis of the regional integration welfare effects.

Finally, regional integration can have an impact on the MNE's internal distribution of resources and FSAs; more specifically, firm-level investments in regional adaptation often imply the relocation of specific production facilities to the most efficient subunits, in order to capture regional scale economies and a re-assessment of subsidiary charters. This implies to some extent a zero sum game with "winning" and "losing" subsidiaries.

Interestingly, it has also been observed that regional integration may energize subsidiaries to start new initiatives and to develop new capabilities, which really implies a non-zero sum game, Birkinshaw (2000), again with macro-level welfare improvements as an outcome. Will the deepening of a regional trading block, even if it has positive net welfare effects inside the region and at the world level, strengthen the affected insider MNEs in other legs of the triad? Or will it, on the contrary, act as an incentive to focus these MNEs' resource allocation processes and market expansion plans even more on intra-regional growth opportunities? The empirical data presented in this chapter appear to indicate that regional integration during the past decade has had little effect on the abilities of MNEs to increase their globalization capabilities.

THE REGIONAL DATA ARE ROBUST

As a final word on the challenge to our thinking provided by the lack of evidence on globalization let us revisit the key data presented in this book. As developed and explained in detail in chapter 2, this book is the first to report data on intra-regional sales of the 500 largest firms in the world. The data bank was constructed over the 2002–03 period based on basic listings in the *Fortune* 500 of August 2002, which reports the published data from the annual reports of the 500 firms for the year 2001. In table 2.11 these 2001 data were updated for sixty firms for 2002, the latest year available at the time of writing. These are the 60 firms discussed in some detail in this book, especially in the brief case studies reported in chapters 5 through 9, and in the analysis of chapters 3 and 10. As reported in chapter 2, the addition of 2002 data only caused reclassification of two firms: Nokia ceased being global; and GlaxoSmithKline became a host-region bi-regional.

As a final check on the reliability of the 2001 data, let us consider the main group of 320 home-regional firms identified in this study. In table 12.1 we report the intra-regional sales of each tenth firm in this list, based on the 2001 sales used in chapter 2 and the Appendix to this book.

In table 12.2 we report the 2002 sales data for this set of thirty-two home-region based firms. All the firms remain in the home-region classification. The average intra-regional sales for the thirty-two firms actually increases slightly from 82.4% to 84.6%.

Table 12.3 shows that the average intra-regional sales of the sample of thirty-two firms with 2001 data is 82.4%. The intra-regional sales increase, to 84.6%, for 2002 data. Far from a trend towards globalization; these home-region firms are becoming even more regional. Of the thirty-two

Table 12.1. Geographic revenue for the world's 32 largest home-region oriented MNEs, 2001

500 rank	company	revenues in bn US $	F/T sales	% intra regional	North America % of total	Europe % of total	Asia-Pacific % of total
1	Wal-Mart Stores (q)	219.8	16.3	94.1	94.1	4.8	0.4
22	Siemens	77.4	78	52	30.0 [l]	52.0	13.0
32	Hitachi	63.9	31	80	11.0	7.0	80.0
49	Fiat	51.9	65.6	73.3	13.0	73.3	na
62	Merck	47.7	16.4	83.6	83.6 [z]	na	na
78	Dynegy	42.2	23.7	90.7	90.7	na	na
92	Pemex (q)	39.4	34.4	91.7	91.7	3.7	na
104	Kmart	36.2	–	100	100.0	–	–
122	Conoco	32.8	42.4	57.6	57.6 [z]	na	na
134	United Parcel Service	30.6	13.7	86.3	86.3 [z]	na	na
155	Saint-Gobain	27.2	67.9	63.9	22.3	63.9	na
169	Enel	25.8	1.5	98.6	0.2	98.6	na
182	Lockheed Martin	24.8	17	83	83.0 [z]	na	na
195	Honeywell Intl.	23.7	26.3	73.7	73.7 [z]	18.0	na
209	American Express	22.6	24.7	75.3	75.3	11.0	6.5
222	Royal and Sun Alliance	21.5	55.1	64.8	27.1 [l]	64.8 [m]	na
247	Best Buy	19.6	–	100	100.0	–	–
267	Volvo	18.3	na	51.6	30.2	51.6	6.0
283	Washington Mutual	17.7	na	100	100.0	na	na
304	US Bancorp	16.4	na	100	100.0	–	–
319	AmerisourceBergen	15.8	–	100	100.0	–	–
336	Valero Energy	15	na	100	100.0	–	–
351	May Dept. Stores	14.2	–	100	100.0	–	–
366	Bank of Nova Scotia (q)	13.7	35.9	71.2	71.2 [a]	na	na
380	Accenture (q)	13.3	na	54.8	54.8 [l]	38.3 [m]	6.9
397	Anheuser-Busch	12.9	5.3	94.7	94.7 [z]	na	na
410	WellPoint Health Netwks.	12.4	–	100	100.0	–	–
428	British Airways	11.9	50.8	64.8	18.6 [l]	64.8	na
441	Eli Lilly	11.5	36.2	63.8	63.8 [a]	16.9	na
453	Old Mutual (q)	11.1	6.6	93.4	na	na	na
465	Sun Life Financial Services	10.9	76.9	83.5	83.5 [a]	12.4	2.8
483	Manulife Financial (q)	10.5	70.3	71.1	71.1 [a]	na	20.1

Notes: [q] Wal-Mart: Estimated using number of stores. Pemex: Estimated using 1999 date (latest available); North America refers to Mexico and the US; Bank of Nova Scotia: Revenues are estimated using income figures as reported in the Annual Report; Accenture: Includes information on India in its EMEA geographic segment; Old Mutual: Fortune Magazine reports Old Mutual as a British company because it is headquartered there. However, the company is South African. Revenues are estimated using "total new premium income" as reported in the Annual Report under "segmented analysis"; Manulife Financial: The data are estimated using sales by division (US, Canada and Asia) as reported in the Annual Report. [z] United States only; [l] includes Latin America; [a] Canada and the United States; [m] Europe, Middle East, and Africa.

firms in the sample, six have 100% of their sales in the home region. Twelve of the thirty-two experienced an increase in intra-regional sales between 2001 and 2002, whereas eleven experienced a decrease. However, the large increases in intra-regional sales of ConocoPhillips at 26.4%; Saint-Gobain, at 10.4%; Dynergy at 8.8%; and Volvo at 8% offset the much smaller decreases in intra-regional sales, with only Bank of Nova Scotia

Table 12.2. Geographic revenue for the world's 32 largest home-region oriented MNEs, 2002

2001 rank	2002 rank	company	revenues in bn US$	F/T sales	% intra regional	North America % of total	Europe % of total	Asia % of total
1	1	Wal-Mart Stores (q)	246.5	16.7	94.5	94.5	4.6	0.5
22	21	Siemens	77.2	77.0	57.0	25.0[l]	57.0	12.0
32	26	Hitachi	67.2	32.0	80.0	11.0	7.0	80.0
49	46	Fiat	52.6	64.0	74.0	13.0	74.0	na
62	50	Merck	51.8	16.0	84.0	84.0	na	na
78	na	Dynegy	5.6	13.5	99.5	99.5[a]	0.5	na
92	95	Pemex	38.0	34.3	86.0	86.0	2.1	na
104	121	Kmart	30.8	–	100.0	100.0[z]	–	–
122	36	Conoco Phillips	56.7	17.8	84.0	84.0[a]	na	na
134	120	United Parcel Service	31.3	16.0	84.0	84.0[z]	na	na
155	133	Saint-Gobain	28.6	68.8	74.3	22.4	74.3	na
169	138	Enel	28.3	5.1	98.3	1.7	98.3	na
182	153	Lockheed Martin	26.8	14.0	86.0	86.0[z]	na	na
195	197	Honeywell Intl.	22.3	30.3	69.7	69.7[z]	18.8	na
209	176	America Express	23.8	21.3	78.7	78.7[z]	7.9	6.9
222	233	Royal and Sun Alliance	19.7	58.3	63.1	26.5[l]	63.1[m]	10.4
247	188	Best Buy	22.7	7.2	100.0	100.0	na	na
267	243	Volvo	19.2	na	59.6	24.1	59.6	9.0
283	246	Washington Mutual	19.0	–	100.0	100.0[z]	–	–
304	320	US Bancorp	15.4	–	100.0	100.0	–	–
319	67	AmericansourceBergen	45.2	–	100.0	100.0	–	–
336	150	Valero Energy	27.0	–	100.0	100.0[l]	–	–
351	376	May Dept. Stores	13.5	–	100.0	100.0	–	–
366	432	Bank of Nova Scotia	11.6	43.7	65.4	65.4	na	na
380	436	Accenture	11.6	na	50.4	50.4[l]	42.9[m]	6.7
397	369	Anheuser-Busch	13.6	6.9	93.1	93.1[z]	na	na
410	272	WellPoint Health Netwks.	17.3	–	100.0	100.0	–	–
428	429	British Airways	11.9	52.7	63.8	19.3[l]	63.8	7.4
441	456	Eli Lilly	11.1	41.0	59.0	59.0	19.5	na
453	366	Old Mutual (q)	13.7	na	na	na	na	na
465	323	Sun Life Financial Services	15.3	72.0	80.0	80.0[a]	8.0	3.0
483	479	Manulife Financial (q)	10.5	67.2	73.9	73.9	na	21.4

Notes: [q] Wal-Mart: Estimated using number of stores. Pemex: Estimated using 1999 date (latest available); North America refers to Mexico and the US; Bank of Nova Scotia: Revenues are estimated using income figures as reported in the Annual Report; Accenture: Includes information on India in its EMEA geographic segment; Old Mutual: Fortune Magazine reports Old Mutual as a British company because it is headquartered there. However, the company is South African. Data for 2002 is not available; Manulife Financial: The data are estimated using sales by division (US, Canada and Asia) as reported in the Annual Report. [z] United States only; [l] includes Latin America; [a] Canada and the United States; [m] Europe, Middle East and Africa.

at 5.8%, Pemex at 5.7%; Eli Lilly at 4.8%; and Honeywell at 4%; showing significant increases in intra-regional sales.

It can be concluded that the 2001 sales data provide reliable classifications of firms and that using data for a later year provides no changes. Indeed, table 12.3 shows that firms became more intra-regional over the

Table 12.3. Intra-regional revenues for the world's 32 largest home-region oriented MNEs, 2001–2002

2001 rank	2002 rank	company	region	intra-regional sales (%) 2001	2002	change
1	1	Wal-Mart Stores	North America	94.1	94.5	0.4
22	21	Siemens	Europe	52.0	57.0	5.0
32	26	Hitachi	Asia-Pacific	80.0	80.0	–
49	46	Fiat	Europe	73.3	74.0	0.7
62	50	Merck	North America	83.6	84.0	0.3
78	na	Dynegy	North America	90.7	99.5	8.8
92	95	Pemex	North America	91.7	86.0	(5.7)
104	121	Kmart	North America	100.0	100.0	–
122	36	ConocoPhillips	North America	57.6	84.0	26.4
134	120	United Parcel Service	North America	86.3	84.0	(2.3)
155	133	Saint-Gobain	Europe	63.9	74.3	10.4
169	138	Enel	Europe	98.6	98.3	(0.3)
182	153	Lockheed Martin	North America	83.0	86.0	3.0
195	197	Honeywell Intl.	North America	73.7	69.7	(4.0)
209	176	America Express	North America	75.3	78.7	3.4
222	233	Royal and Sun Alliance	Europe	64.8	63.1	(1.7)
247	188	Best Buy	North America	100.0	100.0	–
267	243	Volvo	Europe	51.6	59.6	8.0
283	246	Washington Mutual	North America	100.0	100.0	–
304	320	US Bancorp	North America	100.0	100.0	–
319	67	Americansource Bergen	North America	100.0	100.0	–
336	150	Valero Energy	North America	100.0	100.0	–
351	376	May Dept. Stores	North America	100.0	100.0	–
366	432	Bank of Nova Scotia	North America	71.2	65.4	(5.8)
380	436	Accenture	North America	54.8	50.4	(4.4)
397	369	Anheuser-Busch	North America	94.7	93.1	(1.6)
410	272	WellPoint Health Netwks.	North America	100.0	100.0	–
428	429	British Airways	Europe	64.8	63.8	(1.0)
441	456	Eli Lilly	North America	63.8	59.0	(4.8)
453	366	Old Mutual	Europe	93.4	na	na
465	323	Sun Life Financial Services	North America	83.5	80.0	(3.5)
483	479	Manulife Financial	North America	71.1	73.9	2.8
Average intra-regional sales*				82.4	84.6	2.2

Notes: * refers to weighted average intra-regional sales according to revenues and does not include Old Mutual, for which 2002 data are not available.

2002 period than in 2001. Similarly, sales data for earlier periods are highly unlikely to provide much new information or cause us to reclassify more than a handful of the 380 firms of the top 500 for which a classification was possible.

Yet some colleagues still seem to question these data. There must be a trend towards globalization over time they say. Well no – actually the aggregate data of chapter 11 strongly suggests the opposite; over the last twenty-five years there is a trend towards increased intra-regional trade and investment. Naturally, these aggregate data trends are likely to be mirrored in the firm-level data. At the very least the data for 2001 sales present an up-to-date snapshot of the lack of globalization and the dominance of regional firm-level economic activity. It is now up to other scholars to advance on this research and to extend the debate on global versus regional strategy.

CONCLUSIONS

The evidence is that most of the world's largest firms are stay-at-home multinationals. The great majority of MNEs (320 out of 380 with available data) have, on average, 80% of all their sales in their home region of the triad. The world of international business is a regional one, not a global one. Only a handful of MNEs (a total of nine) actually operate successfully as key players in each region of the triad. For 320 of 365 cases of MNEs for which data are available and classifiable, the data indicate they operate on a home-triad basis. This is very strong evidence of regional/triad activity. There are twenty-five bi-regional MNEs and another eleven host-country based ones. There are so few "global" MNEs as to render the concept of "globalization" meaningless. This research suggests that scholars of international business need to pay less attention to models of "global" strategy – as this is a special case. The "big question" for research in international business is: why do MNEs succeed as regional organizations without becoming global?

Transaction cost economics reasoning largely explains this phenomenon: market-seeking expansion in host regions is often associated with high, location-specific adaptation investments to link the MNE's existing knowledge base with host-region location advantages. FSAs and CSAs do not simply meld together without managerial intervention. As the required investments to meld FSAs and CSAs become larger, driven by the cultural, administrative, geographic, and economic distance between home country/region and host regions, the attractiveness of foreign markets declines, and regional, rather than global, strategies are needed to reflect the differential need for "linking" investments in each region. Only in a few sectors, such as consumer electronics, can a balanced, global distribution of sales be achieved.

It is likely that the upstream end of the value chain can be globalized more easily than the customer end, which has been the focus of this chapter, because upstream location-specific investments are not one-sided (in the sense of lacking reciprocal commitments from the other economic actors involved, which is a critical problem at the customer end). Upstream globalization obviously need not be expressed in a balanced geographic distribution of R&D, manufacturing, etc., but rather in the MNE's ability to choose and access locations around the globe where the firm's upstream FSAs can easily be melded with foreign location advantages, without the need for major, location-specific adaptation investments. Yet the available data on production also suggest the importance of home-region based production clusters and networks, as in the automobile sector, thus indicating that the hazards of cultural, administrative, geographic, and economic distance between the home country/region and host regions are often also present at the upstream side.

Appendix
The 500 companies with triad
percent sales, alphabetical, 2001

company	region	revenues in bn US$	F/T sales	% intra regional	NA % of total	EUR % of total	AP % of total	C
1 3M (q)	North America	16.1	53.1	46.9	46.9^z	24.6	18.9	B
2 ABB	Europe	23.7	na	53.9	25.1	53.9	11.3	D
3 Abbey National	Europe	17.8	4.0	99.5	0.5	99.5	–	D
4 Abbott Laboratories	North America	16.3	37.1	65.8	65.8^a	na	4.6^j	D
5 ABN Amro Holding	Europe	39.7	na	na	na	na	na	N
6 Accenture (q)	North America	13.3	na	54.8	54.8^l	38.3^m	6.9	D
7 Adecco	Europe	16.1	na	60.0	28.0	60.0	9.0	D
8 AdvancePCS	North America	13.1	–	100.0	100.0^z	–	–	D
9 Aegon	Europe	28.6	na	na	na	na	na	N
10 AEON	Asia-Pacific	23.6	na	na	na	na	na	N
11 Aetna	North America	25.2	–	100.0	100.0^z	–	–	D
12 Agricultural Bank of China	Asia	10.7	na	na	na	na	na	N
13 Air France Group (q)	Europe	11.1	49.8	50.2	na	50.2	na	D
14 Akzo Nobel	Europe	12.6	na	na	na	na	na	N
15 Albertson's	North America	37.9	–	100.0	100.0	–	–	D
16 Alcan	North America	12.6	95.4	41.1	41.1^a	39.6	13.9	B
17 Alcatel	Europe	22.7	69.5	62.9	19.8^z	62.9	7.4	D
18 Alcoa	North America	22.9	34.0	73.0	73.0^l	20.0	7.0	D
19 Allegheny Energy	North America	10.4	–	100.0	100.0^z	–	–	D
20 Alliance Unichem	Europe	10.5	na	100.0	–	100.0	–	D
21 Allianz	Europe	85.9	69.4	78.0	17.6^l	78.0	4.4^f	D
22 Allstate	North America	28.9	na	100.0	100.0^a	na	na	D
23 Almanij	Europe	18.1	21.0	97.9	1.9	97.9	–	D
24 Alstom	Europe	20.7	88.0	45.1	28.0	45.1	16.1	B
25 Amerada Hess	North America	13.4	26.8	73.2	73.2^z	23.7	na	D
26 American Electric Power	North America	61.3	12.3	87.7	87.7^z	11.8^u	na	D
27 American Express	North America	22.6	24.7	75.3	75.3	11.0	6.5	D
28 American International Group	North America	62.4	na	59.0	59.0^a	na	na	D

Continued

company	region	revenues in bn US$	F/T sales	% intra regional	NA % of total	EUR % of total	AP % of total	C
29 AmerisourceBergen	North America	15.8	–	100.0	100.0^z	–	–	D
30 AMR	North America	19.0	28.0	72.0	72.0^z	14.4	2.6	D
31 Anglo American	Europe	14.8	86.7	46.1	18.9	46.1	17.8	I
32 Anheuser-Busch (q)	North America	12.9	5.3	94.7	94.7^z	na	na	D
33 Anthem	North America	10.4	–	100.0	100.0	–	–	D
34 AOL Time Warner	North America	38.2	14.6	86.4	86.4	na	na	D
35 Aquila	North America	40.4	18.4	91.0	91.0^a	na	na	D
36 Arbed (q)	Europe	11.2	na	na	na	na	na	N
37 Arcelor	Europe	13.0	na	75.0	12.0	75.0	na	D
38 Archer Daniels Midland	North America	20.1	34.6	65.4	65.4^z	na	na	D
39 Arrow Electronics	North America	10.1	na	62.0	62.0	29.4	8.6	D
40 Asahi Glass	Asia	10.1	40.7	74.5	12.1^l	13.4	74.5	D
41 Asahi Mutual Life Insurance	Asia-Pacific	33.1	na	na	na	na	na	N
42 Assicurazioni Generali (q)	Europe	51.4	67.2	91.4	1.7^a	91.4	na	D
43 AstraZeneca	Europe	16.5	na	32.0	52.8^z	32.0	5.2^j	S
44 AT&T	North America	59.1	na	na	na	na	na	N
45 AutoNation	North America	20.0	–	100.0	100.0	–	–	D
46 Aventis (q)	Europe	20.5	87.2	32.1	38.8^a	32.1	6.4^j	B
47 Aviva	Europe	52.3	na	na	na	na	na	N
48 Avnet	North America	12.8	na	68.3	68.3^z	27.4^m	4.3	D
49 AXA (q)	Europe	65.6	77.3	51.2	24.1^z	51.2	19.9	D
50 BAE Systems	Europe	13.0	82.7	38.1	32.3^a	38.1	2.7	B
51 Banco Bilbao Vizcaya Argentaria	Europe	23.8	na	na	na	na	na	N
52 Banco Bradesco	Other	15.0	na	na	na	na	na	N
53 Banco Do Brasil	Other	11.7	na	na	na	na	na	N
54 Bank of America Corp.	North America	52.6	na	92.9	92.9^a	3.5^m	2.7	D
55 Bank Of China	Asia-Pacific	17.9	na	na	na	na	na	N
56 Bank of Montreal (q)	North America	11.2	46.5	70.7	70.7^a	na	na	D
57 Bank of Nova Scotia (q)	North America	13.7	35.9	71.2	71.2^a	na	na	D
58 Bank One Corp.	North America	24.5	na	100.0	100.0	na	na	D
59 Bankgesellschaft Berlin (q)	Europe	10.6	22.2	77.8	na	77.8	na	D
60 Barclays	Europe	27.6	na	88.0	6.0^z	88.0	na	D
61 BASF	Europe	29.1	77.8	55.3	23.6	55.3	14.4^f	D
62 Bayer	Europe	27.1	na	40.3	32.7	40.3	16.1	B
63 Bayerische Landesbank	Europe	15.8	na	82.1	12.9^z	82.1	5.2	D
64 BCE	North America	14.9	14.7	90.5	90.5^a	na	na	D
65 BellSouth	North America	24.1	11.3	88.7	88.7^z	na	na	D
66 Berkshire Hathaway	North America	37.7	na	na	na	na	na	N
67 Bertelsmann	Europe	17.9	69.4	62.1	32.2^z	62.1	na	D
68 Best Buy	North America	19.6	–	100.0	100.0	–	–	D
69 BHP Billiton	Asia-Pacific	17.8	67.9	66.1	12.6	13.0	66.1	D
70 BMW	Europe	34.4	73.4	57.3	31.7^l	57.3	na	D

(cont.)

Continued

company	region	revenues in bn US$	F/T sales	% intra regional	NA % of total	EUR % of total	AP % of total	C
71 BNP Paribas	Europe	55.0	na	na	na	na	na	N
72 Boeing	North America	58.2	33.3	66.7	66.7^z	14.5	16.3	D
73 Bombardier	North America	13.9	92.2	60.7	60.7^a	30.9	4.5	D
74 Bouygues	Europe	18.3	53.0	62.0	2.0^l	62.0	13.0	D
75 BP	Europe	174.2	80.4	36.3	48.1^z	36.3	na	B
76 Bridgestone	Asia-Pacific	17.6	61.2	38.8	43.0^l	10.1	38.8^j	B
77 Bristol-Myers Squibb	North America	21.7	32.3	67.7	67.7^z	18.6^m	7.0	D
78 British Airways	Europe	11.9	50.8	64.8	18.6^l	64.8	na	D
79 British American Tobacco (q)	Europe	18.1	na	31.3	na	31.3	9.9	I
80 BT (q)	Europe	30.0	26.6	87.0	8.3^l	87.0	4.7	D
81 Canadian Imperial Bank of Commerce (q)	North America	13.9	39.8	79.7	79.7^a	na	na	D
82 Canon	Asia-Pacific	23.9	71.5	28.5	33.8^l	20.8	28.5^j	G
83 Cardinal Health	North America	47.9	2.1	97.9	37.9^z	na	na	D
84 Carrefour	Europe	62.2	50.8	81.3	na	81.3	6.6	D
85 Carso Global Telecom	North America	11.9	na	na	na	na	na	N
86 Caterpillar (q)	North America	20.5	na	53.9	53.9	26.9^m	10.6	D
87 Cathay Life	Asia	11.6	–	100.0	–	–	100.0	D
88 Central Japan Railway	Asia	10.9	na	na	na	na	na	N
89 Centrica	Europe	18.2	11.0	93.8	6.2	93.8	na	D
90 Chevrontexaco	North America	99.7	56.5	43.5	43.5^z	na	na	I
91 China Construction Bank	Asia-Pacific	13.1	na	na	na	na	na	N
92 China Mobile Communications	Asia-Pacific	17.4	na	na	na	na	na	N
93 China National Petroleum	Asia-Pacific	41.5	na	na	na	na	na	N
94 China Telecom-munications	Asia-Pacific	22.3	na	na	na	na	na	N
95 Chinese Petroleum	Asia	10.8	na	na	na	na	na	N
96 Chubu Electric Power	Asia-Pacific	17.8	na	na	na	na	na	N
97 Cigna	North America	19.1	4.9	95.1	95.1^z	na	na	D
98 Cinergy	North America	12.9	1.4	98.6	98.6^z	na	na	D
99 Circuit City Stores	North America	12.8	–	100.0	100.0^z	–	–	D
100 Cisco Systems	North America	22.3	na	59.7	59.7^l	24.8^m	15.5	D
101 Citigroup	North America	112.0	na	na	na	na	na	N
102 CMS Energy	North America	13.0	5.2	94.8	94.8^z	na	na	D
103 CNP Assurances	Europe	20.1	na	na	na	na	na	N
104 Coca-Cola	North America	20.1	na	38.4	38.4	22.4^m	24.9	G
105 Coca-Cola Enterprises	North America	15.7	na	76.8	76.8	23.2	na	D
106 COFCO	Asia-Pacific	13.0	na	na	na	na	na	N
107 Coles Myer	Asia	12.6	0.5	100.0	na	na	100.0	D
108 Commerzbank	Europe	23.8	na	85.5	8.5	85.5	3.0	D
109 Compaq Computer (q)	North America	33.6	62.0	38.0	38.0^z	36.0^m	na	I

Continued

company	region	revenues in bn US$	F/T sales	% intra regional	NA % of total	EUR % of total	AP % of total	C
110 Compass Group	Europe	12.6	67.0	67.6	32.4	67.6	–	D
111 Computer Sciences	North America	11.4	36.0	64.0	64.0^z	25.0	na	D
112 ConAgra	North America	27.2	14.7	85.3	85.3	na	na	D
113 Conoco	North America	32.8	42.4	57.6	57.6^z	na	na	D
114 Consignia	Europe	12.0	na	na	na	na	na	N
115 Corus Group	Europe	11.1	69.9	82.7	11.5	82.7	5.8	D
116 Cosmo Oil	Asia	10.6	<10	>90	na	na	>90^j	D
117 Costco Wholesale (q)	North America	34.8	24.3	95.5	95.5	2.4^u	2.1	D
118 Crédit Agricole	Europe	35.7	na	na	na	na	na	N
119 Crédit Lyonnais (q)	Europe	18.8	28.0	82.0	8.0	82.0	7.0	D
120 Crédit Suisse	Europe	64.2	73.3	60.9	34.9^j	60.9	4.1^f	D
121 CVS	North America	22.2	–	100.0	100.0	–	–	D
122 Dai Nippon Printing	Asia	10.5	10.5	89.5	na	na	89.5^j	D
123 Daido Life Insurance	Asia	10.5	na	na	na	na	na	N
124 Daiei	Asia-Pacific	20.1	1.0	99.5	0.5	–	99.5	D
125 Dai-Ichi Mutual Life Insurance	Asia-Pacific	43.1	na	na	na	na	na	N
126 DaimlerChrysler	Europe	136.9	na	29.9	60.1	29.9	na	S
127 Daiwa Bank Holdings	Asia	10.9	<10	>90	na	na	>90^j	D
128 Dana	North America	10.5	na	74.8	74.8	17.4	3.2	D
129 Danske Bank Group (q)	Europe	10.9	27.5	94.3	5.1	94.3	0.6	D
130 Deere	North America	13.3	na	76.0	76.0^a	na	na	D
131 Delhaize 'Le Lion'	Europe	19.6	84.0	22.0	75.9	22.0	1.0	S
132 Dell Computer	North America	31.2	na	71.7	71.7^l	20.1	8.2	D
133 Delphi	North America	26.1	na	77.7	77.7	18.4	na	D
134 Delta Air Lines	North America	13.9	na	81.3	81.3	na	na	D
135 Denso	Asia-Pacific	19.2	32.4	73.1	20.0^l	6.8	73.1	D
136 Dentsu	Asia-Pacific	14.3	5.0	95.0	na	na	95.0	D
137 Deutsche Bahn	Europe	14.1	na	na	na	na	na	N
138 Deutsche Bank	Europe	66.8	69.0	63.1	29.3	63.1	6.5	D
139 Deutsche Post	Europe	31.3	32.9	91.6	5.0^l	91.6	2.7	D
140 Deutsche Telekom (q)	Europe	43.2	27.3	93.1	6.3	93.1	na	D
141 Dexia Group	Europe	19.0	na	na	na	na	na	N
142 Diageo	Europe	18.6	na	31.8	49.9	31.8	7.7	B
143 Dior (Christian) (q)	Europe	11.3	83.4	36.0	26.0^z	36.0	32.0	G
144 Dominion Resources	North America	10.6	19.6	100.0	100.0	na	na	D
145 Dow Chemical	North America	27.8	57.9	42.1	42.1^z	32.0	na	I
146 Duke Energy	North America	59.5	13.1	96.5	96.5	na	na	D
147 DuPont de Nemours (E.I.)	North America	25.4	51.2	55.1	55.1	26.0^m	14.8	D
148 Dynegy	North America	42.2	23.7	90.7	90.7	na	na	D
149 DZ Bank (q)	Europe	26.0	na	85.6	na	85.6	na	D
150 EON	Europe	66.5	43.4	80.1	9.4^z	80.1	na	D

(cont.)

Continued

company	region	revenues in bn US$	F/T sales	% intra regional	NA % of total	EUR % of total	AP % of total	C
151 EADS	Europe	27.6	na	44.9	33.7	44.9	10.2	B
152 East Japan Railway	Asia-Pacific	20.3	0	100.0	–	–	100.0^j	D
153 Eastman Kodak	North America	13.2	na	48.5	48.5^z	24.7^m	17.2	B
154 Edison	Europe	14.1	na	na	na	na	na	N
155 Edison International	North America	12.2	8.3	91.7	91.7^z	na	na	D
156 El Paso	North America	57.5	2.8	97.2	97.2^z	na	na	D
157 Électricité De France	Europe	36.5	34.2	93.9	na	93.9	na	D
158 Electrolux	Europe	13.1	na	47.0	39.0	47.0	9.0	B
159 Electronic Data Systems	North America	21.5	42.6	57.4	57.4^z	15.6^u	na	D
160 Eli Lilly	North America	11.5	36.2	63.8	63.8^z	16.9	na	D
161 Emerson Electric	North America	15.5	40.0	60.0	60.0^z	19.9	9.1	D
162 Endesa	Europe	13.9	na	na	na	na	na	N
163 Enel	Europe	25.8	1.5	98.6	0.2	98.6	na	D
164 ENI	Europe	44.6	44.3	80.4	12.1^l	80.4	3.1	D
165 Enron	North America	138.7	na	na	na	na	na	N
166 Exelon	North America	15.1	na	100.0	100.0	–	–	D
167 Exxon Mobile	North America	191.6	69.6	37.5	37.5^a	8.9^u	10.4^j	I
168 Fannie Mae	North America	50.8	–	100.0	100.0^z	–	–	D
169 Farmland Industries	North America	11.8	na	na	na	na	na	N
170 Federated Dept. Stores	North America	16.9	na	na	na	na	na	N
171 FedEx	North America	19.6	24.3	75.7	75.7	na	na	D
172 Fiat	Europe	51.9	65.6	73.3	13.0	73.3	na	D
173 FleetBoston	North America	19.2	na	na	na	na	na	N
174 Fleming	North America	15.6	–	100.0	100.0	na	na	D
175 Flextronics International	Asia-Pacific	13.1	na	22.4	46.3^z	30.9	22.4	G
176 Foncière Euris	Europe	20.5	na	na	na	na	na	N
177 Ford Motor	North America	162.4	33.3	66.7	66.7^z	21.9	na	D
178 Fortis (q)	Europe	40.5	na	64.3	21.4^z	64.3	na	D
179 France Télécom (q)	Europe	38.5	35.8	64.2	na	64.2	na	D
180 Franz Haniel	Europe	18.2	78.7	95.0	na	95.0	na	D
181 Freddie Mac	North America	35.5	na	na	na	na	na	N
182 Fuji Heavy Industries	Asia	10.9	34.0	66.0	33.7	na	66.0^j	D
183 Fuji Photo Film	Asia-Pacific	19.2	51.6	48.4	na	na	48.4^j	I
184 Fujitsu	Asia-Pacific	40.0	28.2	71.8	11.4^l	12.2	71.8^j	D
185 Gap	North America	13.8	13.1	86.9	86.9^z	na	na	D
186 Gaz de France (q)	Europe	12.9	15.0	85.0	na	85.0	na	D
187 Gazprom	Europe	20.1	na	na	na	na	na	N
188 General Dynamics	North America	12.2	10.7	90.4	90.4	4.6	1.3	D
189 General Electric	North America	125.9	40.9	59.1	59.1^z	19.0	9.1	D
190 General Motors	North America	177.3	25.5	81.1	81.1	14.6	na	D
191 George Weston	North America	15.9	10.5	100.0	100.0^a	–	–	D
192 Georgia-Pacific	North America	25.3	13.2	86.8	86.8^z	na	na	D
193 GlaxoSmithKline	Europe	29.5	50.8	49.2	49.2^z	28.6	na	B

Continued

company	region	revenues in bn US$	F/T sales	% intra regional	NA % of total	EUR % of total	AP % of total	C
194 Goldman Sachs Group	North America	31.1	35.6	65.9	65.9^l	25.0	9.1	D
195 Goodyear Tire & Rubber (q)	North America	14.1	45.9	54.1	54.1^z	na	na	D
196 Great Atl. & Pacific Tea	North America	11.0	na	100.0	100.0	–	–	D
197 Groupama	Europe	12.3	na	na	na	na	na	N
198 Groupe Auchan	Europe	23.4	na	na	na	na	na	N
199 Groupe Caisse d'Épargne	Europe	16.7	na	na	na	na	na	N
200 Groupe Danone	Europe	13.0	74.3	60.3	na	60.3	na	D
201 Groupe Pinault-Printemps	Europe	24.9	54.7	69.1	21.2	69.1	5.6	D
202 Halliburton	North America	13.4	62.4	37.6	37.6^z	13.8^u	na	I
203 Hartford Fin. Services	North America	15.1	na	na	na	na	na	N
204 HBOS	Europe	27.8	7.9	92.1	na	92.1^u	na	D
205 HCA	North America	18.0	–	100.0	100.0^z	na	na	D
206 Henkel	Europe	11.7	77.2	72.1	14.8	72.1	8.0	D
207 Hewlett Packard (q)	North America	45.2	58.4	41.6	18.8^z	na	na	I
208 Hitachi	Asia-Pacific	63.9	31.0	80.0	11.0	7.0	80.0	D
209 Home Depot	North America	53.6	6.2	100.0	100.0	–	–	D
210 Honda Motor	Asia-Pacific	58.9	73.1	26.9	53.9	8.1	26.9^j	S
211 Honeywell Intl.	North America	23.7	26.3	73.7	73.7^z	18.0	na	D
212 Household International	North America	13.9	9.2	92.5	92.5^a	na	na	D
213 HSBC Holdings	Europe	46.4	na	na	na	na	na	N
214 Humana	North America	10.2	–	100.0	100.0	–	–	D
215 Hypovereinsbank	Europe	39.4	na	na	na	na	na	N
216 Hyundai	Asia-Pacific	21.7	46.2	56.3	24.2	10.5	56.3	D
217 Hyundai Motor	Asia-Pacific	30.9	20.9	81.6	18.1	0.3	81.6	D
218 Idemitsu Kosan	Asia-Pacific	15.7	na	na	na	na	na	N
219 Indian Oil	Asia-Pacific	20.9	na	na	na	na	na	N
220 Industrial & Commercial Bank of China	Asia-Pacific	19.8	na	na	na	na	na	N
221 ING Group	Europe	83.0	77.3	35.1	51.4	35.1	3.4	S
222 Ingram Micro	North America	25.2	46.4	53.6	53.6^z	28.4	na	D
223 Intel	North America	26.5	64.6	35.4	35.4^z	24.5	40.2	G
224 International Paper	North America	26.4	22.0	78.0	78.0^z	10.0	7.0	D
225 IntesaBci	Europe	19.9	31.6	80.4	na	80.4	na	D
226 Intl. Business Machines	North America	85.9	64.8	43.5	43.5^l	28.0^m	20.0	G
227 Isuzu Motors	Asia	12.8	30.8	69.2	39.6	na	69.2^j	D
228 Itausa	Other	10.2	na	na	na	na	na	N
229 Itochu	Asia-Pacific	91.2	19.1	91.2	5.5	1.7	91.2	D
230 Ito-Yokado	Asia-Pacific	26.8	40.0	66.6	30.2	na	66.6	D
231 J. Sainsbury	Europe	24.6	na	83.3	16.7	83.3	–	D
232 J. C. Penney (q)	North America	32.6	na	100.0	100.0^l	na	na	D
233 Japan Airlines	Asia-Pacific	12.9	<10	>90	na	na	>90	D
234 Japan Energy	Asia-Pacific	13.2	na	na	na	na	na	N

(cont.)

Continued

company	region	revenues in bn US$	F/T sales	% intra regional	NA % of total	EUR % of total	AP % of total	C
235 Japan Postal Service	Asia-Pacific	20.3	na	na	na	na	na	N
236 Japan Telecom	Asia-Pacific	13.6	<10	>90	na	na	>90	D
237 Japan Tobacco	Asia-Pacific	16.3	9.5	90.5	na	5.8	90.5^j	D
238 Johnson & Johnson	North America	33.0	32.7	67.3	67.3^z	20.9	na	D
239 Johnson Controls	North America	18.4	na	62.9	62.9	25.6	na	D
240 JP Morgan Chase & Co	North America	50.4	na	67.7	67.7^z	23.2^m	6.7	D
241 Kajima	Asia-Pacific	16.5	9.9	92.2	6.9	1.0	92.2	D
242 Kansai Electric Power	Asia-Pacific	21.2	na	na	na	na	na	N
243 KarstadtQuelle	Europe	14.4	11.0	100.0	–	100.0	–	D
244 KDDI	Asia-Pacific	22.7	<10	>90	na	na	>90^j	D
245 Kimberly-Clark	North America	14.5	na	55.0	55.0	15.0	na	D
246 Kingfisher (q)	Europe	16.1	40.2	98.3	0.8	98.3	0.6	D
247 Kmart	North America	36.2	–	100.0	100.0	–	–	D
248 Korea Electric Power	Asia-Pacific	15.7	na	na	na	na	na	N
249 Kreditanstalt für Wiederaufbau	Europe	10.5	na	na	na	na	na	N
250 Kroger	North America	50.1	–	100.0	100.0	–	–	D
251 KT	Asia	12.3	na	na	na	na	na	N
252 Kyushu Electric Power	Asia	11.7	–	100.0	–	–	100.0	D
253 L. M. Ericsson	Europe	22.4	97.0	31.0	13.2	46.0	25.9	B
254 La Poste	Europe	15.2	na	na	na	na	na	N
255 Lafarge	Europe	12.3	na	40.0	32.0	40.0	8.0	B
256 Lagardère Groupe	Europe	11.9	65.8	71.1	20.4^a	71.1	8.5	D
257 Landesbank Baden-Wurttemberg	Europe	16.9	na	94.8	2.7	94.8	2.5	D
258 Lear	North America	13.6	51.4	58.2	58.2	31.6	na	D
259 Legal & General	Europe	13.5	na	na	na	na	na	N
260 Lehman Brothers Hldgs.	North America	22.4	37.0	63.0	63.0^z	29.0	na	D
261 LG Electronics	Asia-Pacific	23.1	na	na	na	na	na	N
262 LG International	Asia-Pacific	19.5	na	na	na	na	na	N
263 Liberty Mutual Group	North America	14.3	na	na	na	na	na	N
264 Lloyds TSB Group	Europe	22.8	na	81.2	na	81.2^u	na	D
265 Lockheed Martin	North America	24.8	17.0	83.0	83.0^z	na	na	D
266 Loews	North America	18.8	–	100.0	100.0^z	na	na	D
267 L'Oréal	Europe	12.3	na	48.5	32.4	48.5	na	B
268 Lowe's	North America	22.1	–	100.0	100.0	–	–	D
269 Lucent Technologies	North America	25.1	35.3	64.7	64.7^z	na	na	D
270 Lufthansa Group	Europe	14.9	na	61.7	19.5	61.7	11.6	D
271 Lukoil	Europe	12.1	na	na	na	na	na	N
272 LVMH	Europe	11.0	83.4	36.0	26.0^z	36.0	32.0	G
273 Magna International	North America	11.0	67.2	67.7	67.7	31.4	na	D
274 Man Group	Europe	14.6	72.6	68.7	15.6	68.7	12.7	D
275 Manpower	North America	10.5	80.9	19.1	19.1^z	68.6	na	S
276 Manulife Financial (q)	North America	10.5	70.3	71.1	71.1^a	na	20.1	D

Continued

company	region	revenues in bn US$	F/T sales	% intra regional	NA % of total	EUR % of total	AP % of total	C
277 Marathon Oil	North America	35.0	3.6	96.4	97.6^a	na	na	D
278 Marks & Spencer	Europe	11.6	14.9	85.1	na	85.1^u	na	D
279 Marriott International	North America	10.2	na	na	na	na	na	N
280 Marubeni (q)	Asia-Pacific	71.8	28.2	74.5	11.6^z	na	74.5	D
281 Mass. Mutual Life Ins.	North America	19.3	na	na	na	na	na	N
282 Matsushita Electric Industrial	Asia-Pacific	55.0	35.1	64.9	12.4^l	6.9	64.9	D
283 May Dept. Stores	North America	14.2	–	100.0	100.0	–	–	D
284 Mazda Motor	Asia-Pacific	16.8	34.3	65.7	24.4	7.0	65.7^j	D
285 MBNA	North America	10.1	na	na	na	na	na	N
286 McDonald's (q)	North America	14.9	63.7	40.4	40.4^a	31.9	14.8	B
287 McKesson (q)	North America	50.0	6.6	93.4	93.4^z	na	na	D
288 Meiji Life Insurance	Asia-Pacific	25.3	na	na	na	na	na	N
289 Merck	North America	47.7	16.4	83.6	83.6^z	na	na	D
290 Merrill Lynch (q)	North America	38.8	31.0	73.0	73.0	16.6^m	8.7	D
291 MetLife	North America	31.9	na	na	na	na	na	N
292 Metro	Europe	44.3	42.7	97.3	–	97.3	2.3	D
293 Michelin	Europe	14.6	na	47.0	40.0	47.0	na	B
294 Microsoft	North America	25.3	na	na	na	na	na	N
295 Migros	Europe	12.0	na	na	na	na	na	N
296 Mirant	North America	31.5	16.0	95.2	95.2^a	1.8^u	na	D
297 Mitsubishi	Asia-Pacific	105.8	13.2	86.8	5.4^z	1.7^u	86.8^j	D
298 Mitsubishi Chemical	Asia-Pacific	14.2	13.1	86.9	na	na	86.9^j	D
299 Mitsubishi Electric	Asia-Pacific	29.2	26.3	83.1	8.9	6.0	83.1	D
300 Mitsubishi Heavy Industries	Asia-Pacific	22.9	7.9	93.2	4.7	1.9	93.2^j	D
301 Mitsubishi Motors	Asia-Pacific	25.6	40.9	62.8	22.1	12.1	62.8	D
302 Mitsubishi Tokyo Financial Group	Asia-Pacific	26.1	na	64.4	23.6	7.0	64.4	D
303 Mitsui	Asia-Pacific	101.2	34.0	78.9	7.4	11.1	78.9	D
304 Mitsui Mutual Life Insurance	Asia-Pacific	21.7	na	na	na	na	na	N
305 Mitsui Sumitomo Insurance	Asia-Pacific	15.2	2.0	98.0	na	na	98.0^j	D
306 Mizuho Holdings	Asia-Pacific	41.5	30.3	74.4	19.7	5.8	74.4	D
307 Morgan Stanley (q)	North America	43.7	25.0	75.0	75.0^z	17.9	6.3	D
308 Motorola	North America	30.0	56.0	44.0	44.0^z	14.0	26.0	B
309 Munich Re Group (q)	Europe	41.9	54.7	72.3	19.3	72.3	4.1	D
310 National Australia Bank	Asia-Pacific	16.5	na	na	na	na	na	N
311 Nationwide	North America	15.1	na	na	na	na	na	N
312 NEC	Asia-Pacific	40.8	20.4	79.6	7.0	na	79.6^j	D
313 Nestlé	Europe	50.2	na	31.6	31.4	31.6	na	I
314 New York Life Insurance	North America	25.7	na	na	na	na	na	N
315 News Corp.	Asia-Pacific	13.8	na	9.0	75.0^z	16.0^u	9.0	S

(cont.)

Continued

company	region	revenues in bn US$	F/T sales	% intra regional	NA % of total	EUR % of total	AP % of total	C
316 Nichimen	Asia-Pacific	16.4	15.0	91.5	0.6^l	2.3^m	91.5	D
317 Nippon Express	Asia-Pacific	13.7	14.9	85.1	na	na	85.1^j	D
318 Nippon Life Insurance	Asia-Pacific	63.8	na	na	na	na	na	N
319 Nippon Mitsubishi Oil	Asia-Pacific	23.5	19.2	87.9	1.9	10.2	87.9	D
320 Nippon Steel	Asia-Pacific	20.6	17.8	82.2	na	na	82.2^j	D
321 Nippon Telegraph & Telephone	Asia-Pacific	93.4	na	na	na	na	na	N
322 Nissan Motor	Asia-Pacific	49.6	50.3	49.7	34.6	11.0	49.7^j	B
323 Nissho Iwai	Asia-Pacific	43.7	21.4	88.9	7.5	3.0	88.9	D
324 NKK	Asia-Pacific	13.2	30.5	69.5	na	na	69.5^j	D
325 Nokia	Europe	27.9	98.5	49.0	25.0^l	49.0	26.0	G
326 Norddeutsche Landesb. (q)	Europe	10.6	18.9	94.8	2.9	94.8	2.3	D
327 Nordea (q)	Europe	12.2	na	100.0	na	100.0	na	D
328 Norinchukin Bank	Asia-Pacific	12.9	na	90.6	2.2	7.2	90.6	D
329 Norsk Hydro	Europe	17.0	91.8	77.0	11.8^a	77.0	4.2	D
330 Nortel Networks	North America	18.5	94.6	54.4	54.4^a	na	na	D
331 Northrop Grumman	North America	13.6	9.6	90.4	90.4^z	na	na	D
332 Northwestern Mutual	North America	16.2	na	na	na	na	na	N
333 Novartis	Europe	19.0	na	32.0	43.0^z	32.0	na	I
334 Obayashi	Asia	11.2	<10	>90	na	na	>90	D
335 Occidental Petroleum	North America	14.1	13.2	87.7	87.7^a	na	na	D
336 Office Depot	North America	11.2	15.3	84.7	84.7^z	na	na	D
337 Old Mutual (q)	Europe/Other	11.1	5.1	93.4	na	na	na	D
338 Olivetti	Europe	28.7	na	na	na	na	na	N
339 Onex	North America	15.4	77.0	65.0	65.0^a	22.0	na	D
340 Oracle	North America	10.9	48.6	53.9	53.9	na	7.0	D
341 Otto Versand	Europe	13.6	na	na	na$^\#$	na	na	N
342 PacifiCare Health Sys.	North America	11.8	–	100.0	100.0^z	–	–	D
343 PDVSA	Other	46.3	na	na	na	na	na	N
344 Pemex (q)	North America	39.4	34.4	91.7	91.7	3.7	na	D
345 PepsiCo	North America	26.9	32.4	67.6	67.6^z	na	na	D
346 Petrobrás (q)	Other	24.5	12.0	88.0	na	na	na	D
347 Petronas	Asia-Pacific	17.7	na	na	na	na	na	N
348 Peugeot	Europe	46.3	na	na	na	na	na	N
349 Pfizer	North America	32.3	38.2	61.8	61.8^z	na	6.5^j	D
350 PG&E Corp.	North America	23.0	na	100.0	100.0	–	–	D
351 Pharmacia	North America	19.3	43.5	56.5	56.5^z	na	6.7^j	D
352 Philip Morris	North America	72.9	42.1	57.9	57.9^z	25.8	na	D
353 Phillips Petroleum	North America	24.2	9.1	90.9	90.9^z	na	na	D
354 POSCO	Asia	10.2	na	na	na	na	na	N
355 Power Corp. of Canada	North America	11.9	32.4	100.0	100.0^a	–	–	D
356 Procter & Gamble	North America	39.2	48.2	55.0	55.0	27.0^m	10.0	D
357 Prudential	Europe	35.8	na	na	na	na	na	N

Continued

company	region	revenues in bn US$	F/T sales	% intra regional	NA % of total	EUR % of total	AP % of total	C
358 Prudential Financial	North America	27.2	17.0	83.0	83.0[z]	na	13.3[j]	D
359 Publix Super Markets	North America	15.3	–	100.0	100.0	–	–	D
360 Qwest Communications	North America	19.7	na	na	na	na	na	N
361 Rabobank	Europe	21.1	na	na	na	na	na	N
362 RAG	Europe	13.7	29.2	83.8	na	83.8	na	D
363 Raytheon	North America	16.9	16.4	83.6	83.6[z]	na	na	D
364 Reliant Energy	North America	46.2	8.6	91.4	91.4[z]	na	na	D
365 Renault	Europe	32.6	60.8	89.1	na	89.1	na	D
366 Repsol YPF	Europe	39.1	na	na	na	na	na	N
367 Ricoh	Asia-Pacific	13.4	39.5	60.5	16.4[l]	16.1	60.5[j]	D
368 Rite Aid	North America	15.2	–	100.0	100.0	–	–	D
369 Robert Bosch	Europe	30.5	na	na	na	na	na	N
370 Roche Group	Europe	17.3	98.2	36.8	38.6	36.8	11.7	B
371 Royal & Sun Alliance	Europe	21.5	55.1	64.8	27.1[l]	64.8	na	D
372 Royal Ahold	Europe	59.6	85.0	32.8	59.2	32.8	0.6	S
373 Royal Bank of Canada (q)	North America	16.5	28.3	71.7	71.7[c]	na	na	D
374 Royal Bank of Scotland	Europe	33.8	19.0	81.0	12.0[z]	81.0[u]	na	D
375 Royal Dutch/Shell Group	Europe	135.2	na	46.1	15.6[z]	46.1	na	I
376 Royal KPN (q)	Europe	11.1	22.0	78.0	na	78.0	na	D
377 Royal Philips Electronics	Europe	29.0	na	43.0	28.7[a]	43.0	21.5	G
378 RWE	Europe	50.7	37.9	75.0	19.5[l]	75.0	5.1	D
379 Safeway	Europe	12.3	–	100.0	na	100.0	na	D
380 Safeway (q)	North America	34.3	12.0	100.0	100.0	–	–	D
381 Saint-Gobain	Europe	27.2	67.9	63.9	22.3	63.9	na	D
382 Samsung	Asia-Pacific	33.2	na	na	na	na	na	N
383 Samsung Electronics	Asia-Pacific	36.0	na	na	na	na	na	N
384 Samsung Life Insurance	Asia-Pacific	17.5	na	na	na	na	na	N
385 Santander Central Hispano Group	Europe	30.4	66.1	44.3	55.7[l]	44.3	na	S
386 Sanyo Electric	Asia-Pacific	16.9	49.0	72.7	17.0	8.7	72.7	D
387 Sara Lee	North America	17.7	42.9	57.1	57.1[z]	na	na	D
388 SBC Communications (q)	North America	45.9	0.4	99.6	99.6[z]	na	na	D
389 Schlumberger	North America	14.0	na	na	na	na	na	N
390 Sears Roebuck	North America	41.1	12.6	100.0	100.0	–	–	D
391 Sekisui House	Asia	10.6	<10	>90	na	na	>90[l]	D
392 Sharp	Asia-Pacific	14.4	32.5	80.0	18.7[l]	9.5	80.0	D
393 Shimizu	Asia	12.7	5.5	94.5	na	na	94.5[j]	D
394 Showa Shell Sekiyu	Asia	10.4	12.8	90.8	na	na	90.8	D
395 Siemens	Europe	77.4	78.0	52.0	30.0[l]	52.0	13.0	D
396 Sinochem	Asia-Pacific	16.2	na	na	na	na	na	N
397 Sinopec	Asia-Pacific	40.4	na	na	na	na	na	N
398 SK	Asia-Pacific	33.0	na	na	na	na	na	N
399 SK Global	Asia-Pacific	17.2	na	na	na	na	na	N

(cont.)

Continued

company	region	revenues in bn US$	F/T sales	% intra regional	NA % of total	EUR % of total	AP % of total	C
400 Skanska (q)	Europe	15.9	83.0	40.0	41.0	40.0	na	B
401 SNCF	Europe	18.0	na	na	na	na	na	N
402 Société Générale	Europe	23.9	na	77.3	15.6	77.3	3.6	D
403 Sodexho Alliance	Europe	10.6	na	42.0	50.0	42.0	na	S
404 Solectron	North America	18.7	50.8	49.2	49.2^z	18.2	na	I
405 Sony	Asia-Pacific	60.6	67.2	32.8	29.8^z	20.2	32.8^j	G
406 Southern	North America	10.2	na	na	na	na	na	N
407 Sprint	North America	26.1	na	na	na	na	na	N
408 Standard Life Assurance	Europe	18.4	na	na	na	na	na	N
409 Staples	North America	10.7	na	93.3	93.3	6.7	na	D
410 State Farm Insurance Cos.	North America	46.7	–	100.0	100.0	–	–	D
411 State Power	Asia-Pacific	48.4	na	na	na	na	na	N
412 Statoil	Europe	26.3	24.6	86.8	10.0^z	86.8	na	D
413 Stora Enso	Europe	12.1	94.3	69.2	19.5	69.2	7.1	D
414 Suez	Europe	37.9	50.0	74.0	11.0	74.0	5.0	D
415 Sumitomo	Asia-Pacific	77.1	12.7	87.3	4.8^z	na	87.3^j	D
416 Sumitomo Electric Industries	Asia	11.9	24.8	82.8	13.5^l	na	82.8^j	D
417 Sumitomo Life Insurance	Asia-Pacific	32.5	na	na	na	na	na	N
418 Sumitomo Metal Industries	Asia	10.8	6.8	95.1	na	na	95.1	D
419 Sumitomo Mitsui Banking	Asia-Pacific	30.2	22.4	83.4	11.1^l	5.6	83.4	D
420 Sun Life Financial Services	North America	10.9	76.9	83.5	83.5^a	12.4	2.8	D
421 Sun Microsystems	North America	18.3	52.6	47.4	47.4^z	30.2^m	17.2	B
422 Sunoco	North America	12.4	–	100.0	100.0	–	–	D
423 Suntory	Asia	10.4	na	na	na	na	na	N
424 Supervalu	North America	20.9	–	100.0	100.0^z	–	–	D
425 Suzuki Motor	Asia-Pacific	13.3	31.6	68.4	13.3	14.9	68.4^j	D
426 Swiss Life Ins. & Pension	Europe	13.5	na	na	na	na	na	N
427 Swiss Reinsurance	Europe	20.2	na	na	na	na	na	N
428 Sysco (q)	North America	21.8	na	100.0	100.0	–	–	D
429 Taisei	Asia-Pacific	13.4	<10	>90	na	na	>90	D
430 Taiyo Mutual Life Insurance	Asia	12.8	na	na	na	na	na	N
431 Takenaka	Asia	10.1	na	na	na	na	na	N
432 Target	North America	39.9	–	100.0	100.0	–	–	D
433 Tech Data (q)	North America	17.2	44.9	55.1	55.1^z	38.2	na	D
434 Telefónica (q)	Europe	27.8	43.1	56.9	–	56.9	–	D
435 Telstra (q)	Asia	12.4	na	92.6	na	na	92.6	D
436 Tenet Healthcare	North America	12.1	–	100.0	100.0	–	–	D
437 Tesco	Europe	33.9	15.4	93.6	–	93.6	6.4	D
438 Textron	North America	12.3	34.4	70.7	70.7^a	na	4.2	D

Continued

company	region	revenues in bn US$	F/T sales	% intra regional	NA % of total	EUR % of total	AP % of total	C
439 Thyssen Krupp	Europe	33.8	63.8	61.1	21.9^z	61.1	na	D
440 TIAA-CREF	North America	24.2	na	na	na	na	na	N
441 TJX	North America	10.7	na	na	na	na	na	N
442 Tohoku Electric Power	Asia-Pacific	13.6	–	100.0	–	–	100.0	D
443 Tokio Marine & Fire Insurance	Asia-Pacific	16.2	na	na	na	na	na	N
444 Tokyo Electric Power	Asia-Pacific	41.8	<10	>90	na	na	>90^j	D
445 Tomen	Asia-Pacific	19.1	na	na	na	na	na	N
446 Toppan Printing	Asia	10.4	<10	>90	na	na	>90^j	D
447 Toronto-Dominion Bank	North America	13.6	28.5	86.6	86.6^a	na	na	D
448 Toshiba	Asia-Pacific	43.1	37.0	75.3	13.9	8.7	75.3	D
449 Total Fina Elf	Europe	94.3	na	55.6	8.4	55.6	na	D
450 Toyota Motor	Asia-Pacific	120.8	50.8	49.2	36.6	7.7	49.2^j	B
451 Toyota Tsusho	Asia-Pacific	18.0	na	na	na	na	na	N
452 Toys 'R' Us	North America	11.0	18.5	81.5	81.5^z	na	na	D
453 TransCanada Pipelines (q)	North America	11.7	37.6	74.7	74.7^a	na	na	D
454 TRW	North America	16.4	40.7	59.3	59.3^z	na	na	D
455 TUI	Europe	21.3	na	na	na	na	na	N
456 TXU	North America	27.9	49.0	51.0	51.0	46.0	3.0	D
457 Tyco International	North America	36.4	na	65.4	65.4	21.2	12.4	D
458 Tyson Foods	North America	10.8	na	na	na	na	na	N
459 US Bancorp	North America	16.4	na	100.0	100.0	–	–	D
460 US Postal Service (q)	North America	65.8	3.0	97.0	97.0^z	na	na	D
461 UAL	North America	16.1	na	66.1	66.1	na	na	D
462 UBS (q)	Europe	48.5	62.0	58.0	37.0^l	58.0	5.0	D
463 UFJ Holdings (q)	Asia-Pacific	25.3	29.4	78.5	15.5	6.1	78.5	D
464 UniCredito Italiano	Europe	15.8	na	na	na	na	na	N
465 Unilever	Europe	46.1	na	38.7	26.6	38.7	15.4	B
466 Union Pacific	North America	12.0	na	na	na	na	na	N
467 United Parcel Service	North America	30.6	13.7	86.3	86.3^z	na	na	D
468 United Technologies	North America	27.9	53.0	47.0	47.0^z	17.0	12.0	I
469 UnitedHealth Group	North America	23.5	na	na	na	na	na	N
470 Valero Energy	North America	15.0	na	100.0	100.0	–	–	D
471 Verizon Communications	North America	67.2	3.8	96.2	96.2^z	na	na	D
472 Viacom	North America	23.2	16.0	84.0	83.9^z	na	na	D
473 Vinci	Europe	16.3	38.0	89.0	5.0	89.0	na	D
474 Visteon	North America	17.8	29.0	71.0	71.0^z	15.6	na	D
475 Vivendi Universal	Europe	51.4	na	68.0	22.0^z	68.0	na	D
476 Vodafone	Europe	32.7	36.2	93.1	0.1^z	93.1	4.8	D
477 Volkswagen	Europe	79.3	72.3	68.2	20.1	68.2	5.3	D
478 Volvo	Europe	18.3	na	51.6	30.2	51.6	6.0	D
479 Wachovia Corp.	North America	22.4	na	100.0	100.0	–	–	D

(cont.)

Continued

company	region	revenues in bn US$	F/T sales	% intra regional	NA % of total	EUR % of total	AP % of total	C
480 Walgreen	North America	24.6	–	100.0	100.0^z	na	na	D
481 Wal-Mart Stores (q)	North America	219.8	16.3	94.1	94.1	4.8	0.4	D
482 Walt Disney	North America	25.3	na	83.0	83.0^a	10.3	4.9	D
483 Washington Mutual	North America	17.7	na	100.0	100.0	na	na	D
484 Waste Management	North America	11.3	4.3	99.9	99.9	0.1	–	D
485 WellPoint Health Netwks.	North America	12.4	–	100.0	100.0^z	–	–	D
486 Wells Fargo	North America	26.9	na	na	na	na	na	N
487 Westdeutsche Landesbank	Europe	23.1	na	80.0	12.8	80.0	5.1	D
488 Weyerhaeuser	North America	14.5	18.9	86.4	86.4^a	2.9	4.8^j	D
489 Whirlpool	North America	10.3	na	62.7	62.7	19.6	3.6	D
490 Williams	North America	11.1	12.9	87.1	87.1^z	na	na	D
491 Winn-Dixie Stores	North America	12.9	–	100.0	100.0	–	–	D
492 Wolseley (q)	Europe	10.4	79.1	28.7	66.3	28.7	na	S
493 Woolworths	Asia	11.5	–	100.0	–	–	100.0	D
494 WorldCom	North America	35.2	10.7	89.3	89.3^z	na	na	D
495 Wyeth	North America	14.1	36.1	63.9	63.9^z	na	na	D
496 Xcel Energy	North America	15.0	na	na	na	na	na	N
497 Xerox	North America	16.5	41.0	59.0	59.0^z	29.6	na	D
498 Yasuda Fire & Marine Insurance (q)	Asia	11.3	–	100.0	–	–	100.0	D
499 Yasuda Mutual Life Insurance	Asia-Pacific	16.6	na	na	na	na	na	N
500 Zurich Financial Services	Europe	38.7	na	51.0	38.3	51.0	na	D

Notes: ^{a} includes only US and Canada; ^{c} refers to Canada only; ^{u} refers only to the United Kingdom; ^{l} refers to Americas; ^{m} refers to EMEA: Europe, Middle East and Africa; ^{z} refers only to the United States; ^{j} Japan; ^{f} includes Africa. C = Classification: G = Global; D = Home-Region Oriented; S = Host-Region Oriented; B = Biregional; N = Not Available; I = Insufficient Information.

Company notes

(In alphabetical order)

3M Data for Europe include the Middle East.

Accenture Includes information on India in its EMEA geographic segment.

Air France Group Data on Europe include only domestic (France) sales.

Anheuser-Busch Estimated using information on domestic vs. international revenues from beer sales.

Arbed Acquired by Usinor, now Arcelor.

Assicurazioni Generali Used premium income (45.6 billion) to estimate geographic distribution of revenues.

Aventis Estimated using sales for core business (which totaled 17,674 in 2001).

AXA Europe represents France, the UK, Germany, and Belgium. An additional category "other countries" might include other European nations.

Bank of Montreal Estimated using net incomeas reported in the Annual Report.

Bank of Nova Scotia Revenues are estimated using income figures as reported in the Annual Report.

Bankgesellschaft Berlin Estimated using income data as reported in the Annual Report. Data for Europe only includes Germany.

British American Tobacco The Annual Report does not report data on North America or the Americas, instead it reports data on Americas-Pacific.

BT data are for 2002.

Canadian Imperial Bank of Commerce Revenues are estimated using total revenues as reported in the Annual Report.

Caterpillar Estimated using sales of machine and engines as reported in the annual report.

Compaq Computer merged with HP in 2002.

Costco Wholesale Estimated using data on number of stores.

Crédit Lyonnais Estimated using net banking income percentages.

Danske Bank Group Estimated using gross income figures as reported in the Annual Report. Geographic segmentation is based on the location where the individual transactions are recorded.

Deutsche Telekom Estimated using geographic information for net revenues.

Dior (Christian) Acquired by LVMH.

Dominion Resources Includes revenues (net of royalties and interest expenses).

DZ Bank European data are only for Germany.

Fortis Europe is Belgium, The Netherlands and Luxembourg. Numbers are estimates using total revenues, net of interest expense.

France Telecom Number for Europe includes only France.

Gaz de France European data only include France.

Goodyear Tire & Rubber Based on the location of the selling subsidiary (i.e. exports are not included).

Hewlett Packard   No individual country outside the United States accounts for more than 10% of HP's revenue.

JC Penney   The firm has operations in the United States, Mexico, Puerto Rico and Brazil.

Kingfisher   Figures are estimated using number of stores.

Manulife Financial   The data are estimated using sales by division (US, Canada and Asia) as reported in the Annual Report.

Marubeni   Asia includes only Japan and Singapore.

McDonald's   Data for Asia include the Middle East and Africa.

McKesson   International revenues (non-US) comprise operations of a wholly-owned subsidiary in Canada, an equity investment in a distributor in Mexico and an IT business in the UK and Europe.

Merrill Lynch   Estimated using net revenues from Annual Report.

Morgan Stanley   Estimated using geographic information for net revenues.

Munich Re Group   Calculated using geographic information on premiums (totaling 36.1 billion). This represents 84% of revenues.

Norddeutsche Landesb.   Data are calculated using income figures as reported in the Annual Report.

Nordea   Based on Note 48 of Annual Report.

Old Mutual   Fortune Magazine reports Old Mutual as a British company because it is headquartered there. However, the company is South African. Revenues are estimated using "total new premium income" as reported in the Annual Report under "segmented analysis".

Pemex   Estimated using 1999 date (latest available). North America refers to Mexico and the US.

Petrobras   Only 12% of its revenues originate outside of Brazil. Its intra-regional number might be underestimated as it doesn't include revenues from other Latin American countries, the US and Canada.

Royal Bank of Canada   Revenues are estimated using gross revenues as reported in the Annual Report.

Royal KPN   Data on Europe only include domestic (Netherlands) sales.

Safeway   Data are estimates.

SBC Communications   Foreign investments are accounted for under the equity method of accounting, and therefore are not included in operating revenues. However, an appendix in the Annual Report shows that 87% of foreign investments are located in the US.

Skanska   Europe refers to: Sweden, Great Britain, Norway, Finland and Denmark. If we add Czech Rep. and Poland, Europe would account for 49%.

Sysco   Annual Report does not include international operations because these are considered insignificant.

Tech Data   European figure includes the Middle East.

Telefonica   Estimated using EBITDA; Europe refers to Spain, all other EBITDA is located in Latin America.

Telstra   Data for Asia are only for Australia.

Transcanada Pipelines   Data do not include Canadian sales for export, which might be intra-regional.

UBS   Calculated using data on operating income from the Annual Report.

UFJ   Estimated using ordinary income figures from the Annual Report.

US Postal Service   US data reflect an Annual Report statement that says less than 3% of total revenues originate outside the United States.

Wal-Mart   Estimated using number of stores.

Wolseley   Data for Europe only include turnover in the UK and France.

Yasuda Fire & Marine Insurance   Now part of Sompo, the Annual Report describes overseas sales as immaterial and does not report them.

Case references

Adidas www.adidas.com

Adidas-Salomon. 2002. *Annual Report*
Adidas-Salomon. 2002. *Social and Environmental Report*

Alcatel www.alcatel.com

Alcatel. 2001. *Annual Report*
Alcatel. 2002. *Annual Report*

AOL Time Warner www.aoltimewarner.com

AOL Time Warner. 2003. *Annual Report*
AOL Time Warner. 2003. *European Factbook*
Burt, T. and Larsen, P. T. 2003. "Time Warner may drop AOL name." *Financial Times*, August 12

Asahi Glass www.agc.co.jp

AstraZeneca www.astrazeneca.com

AstraZeneca. 2002. *Annual Report*
CBS. 2003. "Drug linked to 124 deaths in Japan." *CBSNews.com*, January 10, 2003
Philadelphia Business Journal. 2003. "FTC investigates AstraZeneca marketing." March 10
USA Today. 2003. "Misleading drug ads slip under regulators radar." *USA Today.com* January 5

Aventis www.aventis.com

Aventis. 2002. *Annual Report*
Economist. 2002. "Rhine or shine." *Economist*, March 7
O'Reilly, B. 2001. "Reaping a Biotech Blunder." *Fortune*, February 8

Bank of America www.bankofamerica.com

Bank of America. 2002. *Annual Report*
Economist. 2001. "Deal-making Done." *Economist*, January 25

Bayer www.bayer.com

Bayer. 2002. *Annual Report*
BBC. 2001. "Bayer beats Canada in Anthrax row." *BBC News*, October 23

BBC. 2003. "Bayer wins second Baycol case." *BBC News*, April 4
Economist. 2002, "Making up for lost time." *Economist*, August 25

British Petroleum www.bp.com

British Petroleum. 2002. *Annual Report*
Bahree, B. and Whalen, J. 2003. "BP Aims to Cut Price of Stake in TNK Venture by $1 Billion." *Wall Street Journal*, June 26
British Petroleum. 2002. *Annual Accounts*
Guyon, J. 1999. "When John Browne Talks, Big Oil Listens." *Fortune*, July 5
Guyon, J. 2000. "A Big-Oil Man Gets Religion." *Fortune*, March 6
Johnston, T. 2003. "BP sidesteps extortion of Indonesia's army." *The Times*, May 3
McNulty, S. 2002. "Inquiry may threaten BP operations." *Financial Times*, August 24
Murphy, C. 2002. "Is BP Beyond Petroleum? Hardly." *Fortune*, September 30

Canon www.canon.com

Canon. 2002. *Annual Report*
Canon. 2002. *Canon Fact Book*
Canon. 2002. *The Canon Story*
William J. H. 2002. "Canon Takes Aim at Xerox." *Fortune*, September 19

Carrefour www.carrefour.com

Carrefour. 2001. *Annual Report*
Economist. 1999. "French fusion." *Economist*, September 2
Economist. 2001. "A hypermarket." *Economist*, April 5

Cemex www.cemex.com

Economist. 2000. "The Cemex way." *Economist*, June 14

Citigroup www.citigroup.com

Citigroup. 2002. *Annual Report*
The People's Daily. 2000. "Citigroup Allowed to Build Mansion in Shanghai." 2000. *The People's Daily*, December 4
Shari, M., Bremner, B., Timmons, H., and Gaylord, B. 2001. "Citibank Conquers Asia." *Business Week* (int'l edition), February 26

Cisco Systems www.cisco.com

Cisco Systems. 2003. *Annual Report*
Carter, L. 2001. "Cisco's Virtual Close." *Harvard Business Review*, April, pp. 22–23
Cisco System. 2003. *Value Line Report*, April

Coca-Cola www.cocacola.com

Coca-Cola. 2002. *Annual Report*
Economist. 2002. "Regime change." *The Economist*, October 31
Janardhan, N. 2003. "Politics on the rocks with a twist of religion." *Asia Times*, January 24
Murphy, V. 2003. "Mecca Cola challenges US rival." *BBC News*, January 8

Crédit Suisse www.credit-suisse.com

Credit Suisse Group. 2002. *Annual Report*
BBC. 2002. "CSFB in Enron Probe." *BBC News*, March 1
BBC. 2002. "UK Slaps Record Fine on Swiss Bank." *BBC News*, December 19
BBC. 2003. "Jobs Go At Credit Suisse." *BBC News*, February, 25

DaimlerChrysler www.daimlerchrysler.com

DaimlerChrysler. 2002. *Annual Report*
BBC. 2001. "Daimler's Chrysler Mistakes." *BBC News*, February 26
DaimlerChrysler. 2002. *Key Figures*

Deutsche Bank www.db.com

Deutsche Bank. 2002. *Annual Report*
BBC. 2003. "'We're Staying Deutsche' Says Deutsche Bank." *BBC News*, February 24
Economist. 2000. "Deutsche's Big Gamble." *Economist*, May 9
Economist. 2002. "Deutsche's American Dream." *Economist*, January 31
Economist. 2002. "The Great Swiss Hope." *Economist*, May 16
Fairlamb, D. 2002. "Germany's Banking Titans Are in Trouble." *Business Week*, May 13
Miller, K. and Ewing, J. 1999. "Fixing Deutsche Bank." *Business Week*, July 19

DuPont www.dupont.com

DuPont. 2002. *Annual Report*
Economist. 1999. "DuPont's punt." *Economist*, September 20
Economist. 1999. "Stretch-pockets." *Economist*, September 30
Economist. 2002. "Trading hot air." *Economist*. October 17

Eastman Kodak www.Kodak.com

Eastman Kodak. 2002. *Annual Report*
Economist. 2000. "Develop or die." *Economist*, September 28
Wilke, J. and Bandler, J. 2001. "Kodak tangles with Microsoft over Win XP." *The Wall Street Journal Online*, July 1

Eli Lilly www.lilly.com

Eli Lilly. 2002. *Annual Report*
Economist. 2002. "Bloom and blight." *Economist*, October 24
Economist. 2001. "Marketing madness." *Economist*, July 19
McLean, B. 2001. "A Bitter Pill." *Fortune*, July 24

Ericsson www.ericsson.com

Ericsson. 2000. *Annual Report*
Ericsson. 2001. *Annual Report*

Flextronics www.flextronics.com

Flextronics. 2002. *Annual Report*
BBC. 2001. "Xerox sells half its plants for $220 million." *BBC News*, October 2
Economist. 2000. "Have factory, will travel." *Economist*, February 10
Economist. 2001. "Let the bad times roll." *Economist*, April 5
Economist. 2001. "Gadget wars." *Economist*, May 8
Sprague, J. 2002. "Invasion of the Factory Snatchers." *Fortune*, August 15

Foot Locker www.footlocker.com

Foot Locker. 2002. *Annual Report*

Ford www.ford.com

Ford. 2002. *Annual Report*

General Electric (GE) www.ge.com

BBC. 2001. "EU rejects latest GE offers." *BBC News*, June 29
BBC. 2001. "EU blocks GE/Honeywell deal." *BBC News*, July 3
BBC. 2001. "US Senators lash out at EU over GE deal." *BBC News*, June 15
General Electric. 2002. *10K SEC Filing*

General Motors (GM) www.gm.com

General Motors. 2002. *Annual Report*
General Motors. 2003. *Annual Report*
Economist. 2002. "A Duo of Dunces." *Economist*, March 7

GlaxoSmithKline www.gsk.com

GlaxoSmithKline. 2002. *Annual Report*
Economist. 2002. "Searching for a new formula." *Economist*, May 21
Economist. 2000. "Glaxo's expanding galaxy." *Economist*, November 23
Walt. V. 2001. "AIDS Drug War Heats Up." *Fortune*, June 20

Haier www.haier.com

Qingdao Haier. 2002. *Annual Report*

Honda www.honda.com

Honda. 2002. *Annual Report*
Boorstin, J. 2002. "Going Cheap: Japan's Hottest Carmakers." *Fortune*, May 15
CNN. 2002. "Honda, Toyota Missing From White House 'hybrid car' Event." *CNN.com*, February 25
Taylor, A. III. 2002. "Honda Goes Its Own Way." *Fortune*, July 8

IBM www.ibm.com

IBM. 2002. Annual Report
IBM. 2003. Annual Report

JP Morgan www.jpmorgan.com

BBC. 2003. "JP Morgan Sets Up Research Team in India." *BBC News*
BBC. 2002. "Enron-tainted Bank Reassures Investors." *BBC News*, July 24

Kao www.kao.co.jp

Kao. 2000. *Annual Report*
Kao. 2002. *Annual Report*
Kao. 2003. *Annual Report*
Kao. 1999. *Business Results*
Kao. 2000. *Business Results*

Lafarge www.lafargecorp.com

Lafarge. 2002. *Annual Report*
Economist. 1999. "Bagged Cement." *Economist*, July 17
Economist. 2000. "The Cemex way." *Economist*, June 4

Legend www.legendgrp.com

Spaeth, A. 2000. "China's Legend In The Making." *Time.com*, May 8

L'Oreal www.loreal.com

L'Oreal. 2002. *Annual Report*
L'Oreal. 2001. *Annual Report*
BBC. 2001. "Euro MPs fight 'cruel' cosmetics." *BBC News*, April
BBC. 2002. "Changing the face of China." *BBC News*, November 5
BBC. 2002. "Inside China's 'Me' generation." *BBC News*, November 6
Economist. 2003. "The colour of money." *Economist*, March 6

LVMH www.lvmh.com

LVMH. 2001. *Annual Report*
Business Week. 2001. "The Sweet Smell of Success." *Business Week*, July 16
Matlack, C. 2000. "Identity Crisis at LVMH?" *Business Week*, December 11
Merril Lynch. 2001. "European Luxury Goods." *Merrill Lynch Equities*, May 2001

Marubeni www.marubeni.com

Marubeni. 2002. *Annual Report*

Matsushita http://panasonic.co.jp/maco/en

Matsushita. 2001. *Annual Report*

McDonald's www.mcdonalds.com

McDonald's. 2002. *Annual Report*
Economist. 2002. "Delicious irony." *Economist*, April 25
Hindu Business Line. 2002. "Animal flavouring – McDonald's Indian arm says it's
    clear." *Hindu Business Line*, March 9

Merck www.merck.com

Merck. 2002. *Annual Report*
Economist. 2002. "The acceptable face of capitalism?" *The Economist*, December 12
Warner, M. 2001. "Can Merck Stand Alone?" *Fortune*, July 9

Motorola www.motorola.com

Motorola. 2002. *Annual Report*
BBC. 2001. "Motorola boosts China investment." *BBC News*, November 7
BBC. 2001. "Customers hang up on Motorola." *BBC News*, April 11
Lukas, P. 2003. "The Great American Company – Motorola: Radio Days." *Fortune*,
    April 18
Schoenbeger, K. 1996. "Motorola bets big on China." *Fortune*, May 27

NEC www.nec.com

NEC. 2002. *Annual Report*
BBC. 2001. "NEC weighs anti-dumping complaint." *BBC News*, October 24
BBC. 2001. "NEC confirms job cuts." *BBC News*, July 27
BBC. 2002. "NEC to switch plant to China." *BBC News*, February 27

Nestlé www.nestle.com

Nestlé. 2002. *Annual Report*
Economist. 2002. "A dedicated enemy of fashion." *Economist*, August 29
Foulkes, I. 2003. "Nestlé and Ethiopia settle dispute." *BBC News*, January 24
Valdmanis, T. 2002. "Nestlé offers $11.5B for Hershey." *USA Today*, August 26

News Corp. www.newscorp.com

News Corp. 2002. *Annual Report*
Economist. 1999. "Rupert laid bare." *The Economist*, March 18
Gunther, M. 2003. "Murdoch's Prime Time." *Fortune*, February 3
Hopkins. N. 2001. "News Corp buys into China telecom group." *CNN.com*, February 20
O'Reilly, B. 2001. "Reaping a biotech blunder." *Fortune*, February 8

Nike www.nikebiz.com

Nike. 2002. *Annual Report*
Nike. 2001. *Annual Report*

Pfizer www.pfizer.com

Pfizer. 2002. *Annual Report*
Clifford, L. 2001. "Pharmacia: Tyrannosaurus Rx." *Fortune*, February 18
Pfizer. 2003. "Pfizer and Pharmacia Combine Operations, Creating World's Largest Research-Based Pharmaceutical Company." *News Release*, April 16
Simons, J. 2003. "King of the Pill." *Fortune*, March 30
USA Today. 2003. "Misleading Drug Ads Slip Under Regulators' Radar." *USA Today*, January 5

Philips www.philipsusa.com

Philips. 2002. *Annual Report*

Procter & Gamble (P&G) www.pg.com

Procter & Gamble. 2002. *Annual Report*

Puma www.puma.com

Puma. 2002. *Annual Report*
Puma. 2002. *Environmental and Social Report*

Royal Ahold www.ahold.com

Royal Ahold. 2001. *Annual Report*
BBC. 2003. "Worries mount for Ahold." *BBC News*, February 26
Economist. 2003. "Europe's Enron," *Economist*, February 27
Masters, B. A. 2003. "Ahold ousts CEO of US Foodservice." *Washington Post*, May 14

Royal Dutch/Shell Group www.shell.com

Royal Dutch Petroleum Company. 2002. *Annual Report and Accounts*
Royal Dutch Petroleum Company. 2002. *Financial and Operational Information 1998–2002 Royal Dutch/Shell Group of Companies*

Siemens www.siemens.com

Siemens. 2002. *Annual Report*

Starbucks www.starbucks.com

Starbucks. 2002. *Annual Report*
Economist. 2002. "Mug Shot." *Economist*, September 19
Financial Times. 2001. "Survey of the World's Most Respected Companies." *Financial Times*, December 21, p. VII, Supplement
Starbucks. 2002. *Annual Report*
Stein, N. 2002. "Crisis in a Coffee Cup." *Fortune*, December 4
Williams, J. 2002. "Starbucks Takes on its Critics." *BBC News*, February 27

Thomson www.thomson.com

Thomson. 2001. *Annual Report*

TotalFinaElf www.total.com

TotalFinaElf. 2002. *Annual Report*
BBC. 2001. "French Elite Hit by Sleaze claims." *BBC News*, June 18
BBC. 2003. "French Court Clears Ex-minister." *BBC News*, January 29
BBC. 1999. "Elf counterbid for Totalfina." *BBC News*, July 19
CNN. 2003. "TotalFinaElf sues Iraqi contracts." *CNN.com*, April 22
Economist. 2003. "Elfs and Dwarfs." *Economist,* November 13
Tomlinson, R. 2001. "Building an Empire Drop by Drop." *Fortune*, October 10

Toyota www.toyota.com

Toyota. 2002. *Annual Report*
BBC. 2001. "Toyota commits $8bn to target minorities." *BBC News*, August 10
BBC. 2002. "Toyota targets European expansion." *BBC News*, March 6
Boorstin, J. 2002. "Going Cheap: Japan's Hottest Carmakers." *Fortune*, May 15
Economist. 2002. "Twenty years down the road." *Economist*, September 12

Unilever www.unilever.com/home/

Unilever. 2002. *Annual Report*

Volkswagen www.vw.com

Volkswagen. 2002. *Annual Report*
Tierney, C. C. and Muller, J. 2001. "Another Trip Down Memory Lane." *Business Week*, July 23
Tierney, C., Zammert, A., Muller, J. and Kerwin, K. 2001. "Volkswagen." *Business Week*, July 23

Wal-Mart www.walmart.com

Wal-Mart. 2002. *Annual Report*

Other non-academic references

FDA, Europe Standardizing Drug Approval Process. 2003. *FDA News*, May 30

Academic references

Agarwal, J, Malhotra, N., and Wu, T. 2002. "Does NAFTA Influence Mexico's Product Image? A Theoretical Framework and an Empirical Investigation in Two Countries," *Management International Review* 42(4): 441–71.

Barkema, H., Bell, J., and Pennings, J. 1996. "Foreign Entry, Cultural Barriers and Learning," *Strategic Management Journal* 17(2): 151–66.

Bartlett, C. 1986. "Building and Managing the Transnational: The New Organizational Challenges" in Porter, M. E. (ed.) *Competition in Global Industries*, Boston, MA: Harvard Business School Press, pp. 367–406.

Bartlett, C. and Ghoshal, S. 1989. *Managing Across Borders: The Transnational Solution,* Cambridge, MA: Harvard Business School Press.

  1998. *Managing Across Borders: The Transnational Solution (Second Edition)*, Boston, MA: Harvard Business School Press.

  2000. *Text, Cases and Readings in Cross-Border Management*, New York: Irwin/McGraw-Hill.

  2002. "The Transnational and Beyond: Reflections and Perspectives at the Millennium" in M. A. Hitt and J. C. Cheng (eds.) *Managing Transnational Firms: Resources, Market Entry and Strategic Alliances*, Oxford: Elsevier, pp. 3–36.

Bartlett, C., Ghoshal S., and Birkinshaw, J. 2003. *Transnational Management: Text and Cases*, Boston, MA: McGraw Hill.

Belis-Bergouignan, M. C., Bordenave, G., and Lung, Y. 2000. "Global Strategies in the Automobile Industry," *Regional Studies* 34(1): 41–54.

Bhagwati, J. 2002. *Free Trade Today*, Princeton, NJ: Princeton University Press.

Birkinshaw, J. 2000. *Entrepreneurship in the Global Firm*, London: Sage.

Braintrust Research Group 2003. *The Regional Nature of Global Multinational Activity*, Toronto: Braintrust Research Group.

Buckley, P. 2002. "Is the International Business Research Agenda Running Out of Steam?" *Journal of International Business Studies* 33(2): 365–73.

Buckley, P. and Casson, M. 1976. *The Future of the Multinational Enterprise*, London: Macmillan.

  1981. "The Optimal Timing of a Foreign Direct Investment," *Economic Journal*, 91(361): 75–87.

Buckley, P., Dunning, J., and Pearce, R. 1977. "The Influence of Firm Size, Sector, Nationality, and Degree of Multinationality in the Growth and Profitability of the World's Largest Firms," *Weltwirtschaftliches Archiv* CXIV, pp. 243–57.

  1984. "An Analysis of the Growth and Profitability of the World's Largest Firms 1972 to 1977," *Kyklos* 37(1): 3–27.

Campbell, A. and Verbeke, A. 1994. "The Globalization of Service Multinationals," *Long Range Planning* 27(2): 95–102.

  2001. "The Multinational Management of Multiple External Network", in Van den Bulcke, D. and Verbeke, A. (eds.) *Globalisation and the Small Open Economy*, Cheltenham: Elgar, pp. 193–209.

Cartwright, W. R. 1993. "Multiple Linked Diamonds and the International Competitiveness of Export-Dependent Industries: The New Zealand Experience," *Management International Review* 33(2): 55–70.

Cohen, W. and Levinthal, D. 1990. "Absorptive Capacity: A New Perspective on Learning and Innovation," *Administrative Science Quarterly* 35: 128–52.

D'Cruz, J. 1986. "Strategic Management of Subsidiaries" in H. Etemad and L. S. Dulude (eds.) *Managing the Multinational Subsidiary*, London: Croom Helm, pp. 75–80.

Daniels, J. 1987. "Bridging National and Global Marketing Strategies Through Regional Operations," *International Marketing Review* 4(3): 29–44.

Dunning, J. H. 1981. *International Production and the Multinational Enterprise*, London: George Allen and Unwin.

1993. *The Globalization of Business*, London: Routledge.

1996. "The Geographic Sources of Competitiveness of Firms: Some Results of a New Survey," *Transnational Corporations* 5(3): 1–30.

2001. *Global Capitalism at Bay?* London: Routledge.

Dunning, J. and Mucchielli, J. 2002. *Multinational Firms: The Global-Local Dilemma*, London: Routledge.

Dunning, J. and Norman, G. 1987. "The Location Choice of Offices of International Companies," *Environmental Planning A* 19: 613–31.

Dunning, J. and Rugman, A. M. 1985. "The Influence of Hymer's Dissertation on the Theory of Foreign Direct Investment," *American Economic Review*, Papers and Proceedings 75 (2): 228–32.

Egelhoff, W. 1982. "Strategy and Structure in Multinational Corporations: An Information-processing Approach," *Administrative Science Quarterly*, 27: 435–58.

Enright, M. 2000. "The Globalization of Competition and the Localization of Competitive Advantage: Policies Towards Regional Clustering" in N. Hood and S. Young (eds.) *Globalization of Economic Activity and Economic Development*, Macmillan, Basingstoke, UK, pp. 303–31.

European Commission, 2002. *Report on United States Barriers to Trade and Investment, 2000*, Brussels: European Commission, July.

Fina, E. and Rugman, A. 1996. "A Test of Internalization Theory and Internationalization Theory: The Upjohn Company," *Management International Review* 36 (3): 199–213.

Frankel, J., Stein, E., and Wei, S. J. 1995. "Trading Blocs and the Americas: The Natural, the Unnatural and the Super-natural," *Journal of Development Economics* 47: 61–95.

Freeland, R. F. 1996. "The Myth of the M-Form? Governance, Consent, and Organizational Change," *American Journal of Sociology* 102: 2 (September): 483–526.

Geringer, J. M., Beamish, P., and daCosta, R. C. 1989. "Diversification Strategy and Internationalization: Implications for MNE Performance," *Strategic Management Journal* 10(2): 109–19.

Gestrin, M. 2000. "The Globalization of Retail: On Your Marks . . ." *European Retail Digest*, 26: 6–8.

Gestrin, M., Knight, R., and Rugman, A. 2000. *The Templeton Global Performance Index 2000*, Templeton College, University of Oxford.

Ghemawat, P. 2001. "Distance Still Matters: The Hard Reality of Global Expansion," *Harvard Business Review* 79 (8) (September): 137–47.

2003. "Semiglobalization and International Business Strategy," *Journal of International Business Studies* 34(2): 138–52.

Govindarajan, V. and Gupta, A. 2001. *The Quest for Global Dominance*, San Francisco: Josey-Bass/Wiley.

Grosse, R. 1981. "Regional Offices of MNCs," *Management International Review* 21(1): 48–55.

Hamel, G., Doz, Y., and Prahalad, C. 1989. "Collaborate With Your Competitors and Win," *Harvard Business Review* 67 (1): 133–9.

Heenan, D. A. 1979. "The Regional Headquarters Division: A Comparative Analysis," *Academy of Management Journal* 22 (2): 410–15.

Henderson, Fritz, 2003. "Capitalizing on Global Growth," presentation at 2003 Tokyo Analyst Conference, October 20.

Hitt, M. A., Hoskisson, R. E., and Kim, H. 1997. "International Diversification: Effects on Innovation and Firm Performance in Product-diversified Firms," *Academy of Management Journal* 40: 767–98.

Hymer, S. 1976. *The International Operations of National Firms,* Cambridge: MIT Press.

Jeannet, J. 2000. *Managing with a Global Mindset,* London: Financial Times / Prentice Hall, Pearson.

Johansson, J. and Vahlne, J. E. 1977. "The Internationalization Process of the Firm: A Model of Knowledge Development and Increasing Foreign Market Commitments," *Journal of International Business Studies* 8 (1): 23–32.

　1990. "The Mechanism of Internationalization," *International Marketing Review* 7(4): 1–24.

Kobrin, Stephen 1998. "The MAI and the Clash of Globalization," *Foreign Policy* (112): 97–109.

Kogut, B. 1983. "Foreign Direct Investment as a Sequential Process" in C. P. Kindleberger and D. B. Audretsch (eds.) *The Multinational Corporation in the 1980s.* Cambridge, Mass.: MIT Press, pp. 38–56.

Kogut, B. and Kulatilaka, N. 1994. "Operating Flexibility, Global Manufacturing, and the Option Value of a Multinational Network," *Management Science* 40 (1): 123–39.

Kogut, B. and Zander, U. 1993. "Knowledge of the Firm and the Evolutionary Theory of the Multinational Enterprise," *Journal of International Business Studies* 24 (4): 625–45.

Koza, M. P. and Lewin, A. Y. 1998. "The Co-Evolution of Strategic Alliances," *Organization Science* 9 (3): 255–64.

Krugman, P. 1993. "Regionalism Versus Multilateralism: Analytical Note" in J. de Melo and A. Panagarily (eds.) *New Dimensions in Regional Integration,* New York: Cambridge University Press, pp. 58–79.

Lasserre, P. 1996. "Regional Headquarters: The Spearhead for Asia Pacific Markets," *Long Range Planning* 29: 30–37.

Levitt, T. 1983. "The Globalization of Markets," *Harvard Business Review,* (May–June): 92–102.

Milner, H. V. 1988. *Resisting Protectionism: Global Industries and the Policies of International Trade,* Princeton, NJ: Princeton University Press.

Moon, C., Rugman, A., and Verbeke, A. 1998. "A Generalized Double Diamond Approach to the Global Competitiveness of Korea and Singapore," *International Business Review* 7(2): 135–50.

Morck, R. and Yeung, B. 1991. "Why Investors Value Multinationality," *Journal of Business,* 64(2): 165–87.

Morris, R. W. 2000. "Motor Vehicles 2000," *Survey of Current Business,* (February 2001).

Morrison, A. and Roth, K. 1991. The Regional Solution: An Alternative to Globalization, *Transnational Corporations* 1(2): 37–55.

Morrison, A., Ricks, D., and Roth, K. 1991. "Globalization Versus Regionalization: Which Way for the Multinational?" *Organizational Dynamics,* 19(3): 17–29.

Nelson, R. and Winter, S. 1982. *An Evolutionary Theory of Economic Change,* Cambridge, Mass: Belknapp Press.

Ohmae, K. 1985. *Triad Power: The Coming Shape of Global Competition,* New York: The Free Press.

Ollinger, M. 1994. "The Limits of Growth of the Multidivisional Firm: A Case Study of the US Oil Industry from 1930–90," *Strategic Management Journal* 15(7): 503–520.

Perlmutter, H. 1969. "The Tortuous Evolution of the Multinational Enterprise", *The Columbia Journal of World Business* 4(1): 9–18.

Pomfret, R. 2001. *The Economics of Regional Trading Arrangements*, University of Oxford: Oxford University Press.

Poon, J. 1997. "The Cosmopolitanization of Trade Regions: Global Trends and Implications," *Economic Geography* 73: 390–404.

Porter, M. 1986. (ed.) *Competition in Global Industries*, Boston, MA: Harvard Business School Press.

1990. *The Competitive Advantage of Nations*, New York: Free Press-Macmillan.

Ronan, S. and Shenkar, O. 1985. "Clustering Countries on Attitudinal Dimensions: A Review and Syntheses," *Academy of Management Review* 10: 435–54.

Rugman, A. 1976. "Risk Reduction by International Diversification," *Journal of International Business Studies* 7(2): 85–90.

1981. *Inside the Multinationals: The Economics of Internal Markets*, New York: Columbia University Press.

1990. *Multinationals and Canada US Free Trade*, Columbia, SC: University of South Carolina Press.

(ed.) 1994. *Foreign Investment and NAFTA*, Columbia, SC: University of South Carolina Press.

1996. *The Theory of Multinational Enterprises*, Cheltenham: Elgar.

2000. *The End of Globalization*, London: Random House and New York: Amacom-McGraw Hill.

2003. "Regional Strategy and the Demise of Globalization," *Journal of International Management* 9 (4): 409–17.

Rugman, A. and Brain, C. 2003."Multinationals are Regional, not Global," *Multinational Business Review* 11 (1) Spring 2003: 3–12.

Rugman, A. and D'Cruz, J. R. 1993. "Developing International Competitiveness: The Five Partners Model," *Business Quarterly* 58(2): 60–70.

2000. *Multinationals as Flagship Firms: Regional Business Networks*, Oxford: Oxford University Press.

Rugman, A. and Girod, S. 2003. "Retail Multinationals and Globalization: The Evidence is Regional," *European Management Review* 21 (1): 24–37.

Rugman, A. and Hodgetts, R. 2003. "The End of Global Strategy," *European Management Journal* 19(4): 333–43.

Rugman, A., Kirton, J., and Soloway, J. 1999. *Environmental Regulations and Corporate Strategy*, Oxford: Oxford University Press.

Rugman, A. and Kudina, A. 2002. "Britain, Europe and North America" in M. Fratianni et al. (eds.), *Governing Global Finance*, Aldershot, UK: Ashgate, pp. 185–95.

Rugman, A., Van den Broeck, J. and Verbeke, A. 1995 (eds.) *Research in Global Strategic Management (5) Beyond the Diamond*. Greenwich, Conn: JAI Press.

Rugman, A. and Verbeke, A. 1990a. *Global Corporate Strategy and Trade Policy*, London and New York: Routledge.

1990b. "Strategic Planning, Adjustment and Trade Liberalisation" in A. Rugman, *Multinationals and Canada-United States Free Canada*, Columbia, SC: University of South Carolina Press, pp. 146–78.

1991. "Environmental Change and Global Competitive Strategy in Europe" in A. Rugman and A. Verbeke (eds.), *Research in Global Strategic Management, (2): Global Competition and the European Community*, Conn.: JAI Press, pp. 3–28.

1992. "A Note on the Transnational Solution and the Transaction Cost Theory of Multinational Strategic Management," *Journal of International Business Studies* 23(4): 761–71.

1993a. "Foreign Subsidiaries and Multinational Strategic Management: An Extension of Porter's Single Diamond Framework," *Management International Review* 33(2): 71–84.

1993b (eds.) *Global Competition: Beyond the Three Generics. Research* in *Global Strategic Management* (4), Greenwich, Connecticut/London, England: JAI Press Inc.

1998a. "Multinational Enterprises and Public Policy," *Journal of International Business Studies* 29(1): 115–36.

1998b. "Corporate Strategies and Environmental Regulations: An Organizing Framework," *Strategic Management Journal* 19(3): 363–75.

2000. "Six Cases of Corporate Strategic Response to Environmental Regulation," *European Management Journal* 18(4): 377–85.

2001a. "Subsidiary-Specific Advantages in Multinational Enterprises," *Strategic Management Journal* 22(8): 237–50.

2001b. "Location, Competitiveness and the Multinational Enterprise," in A. Rugman and T. Brewer, (eds.), *The Oxford Handbook of International Business*, Oxford: Oxford University Press, pp. 150–80.

2002. "Edith Penrose's Contribution to the Resource-based View of Strategic Management," *Strategic Management Journal* 23 (8): 769–80.

2003a. "The World Trade Organization, Multinational Enterprises, and the Civil Society" in John Kirton (ed.) *Sustaining Global Growth and Development*, Aldershot, UK: Ashgate, 81–97.

2003b. "Multinational Enterprises and Clusters: An Organizing Framework, *Management International Review* 43: Special Issue 3: 151–69.

2003c. "Extending the Theory of the Multinational Enterprise: Internalization and Strategic Management Perspectives," *Journal of International Business Studies* 34(2): 125–37.

2003d. "Regional Multinationals and Triad Strategy" in A. Rugman (ed.) *Leadership in International Business Education and Research*. Oxford: Elsevier, pp. 253–68.

2004. "A Perspective on Regional and Global Strategies of Multinational Enterprises," *Journal of International Business Studies* 35 (1): 3–18.

Rugman, A., Verbeke, A. and Luxmore, S. 1990. "Corporate Strategy and the Free Trade Agreement: Adjustment by Canadian Multinational Enterprises," *Canadian Journal of Regional Science* 13 (2/3): 307–30.

Ruigrok, W. and Wagner, H. 2003. "Internationalization and Performance: An Organizational Learning Perspective," *Management International Review* 43(1): 63–83.

Salorio, E. 1993. "Strategic Use of Import Protection: Seeking Shelter for Competitive Advantage" in A. Rugman and A. Verbeke (eds.), *Beyond the Three Generics*, Greenwich, Conn.: JAI Press, pp. 101–24.

Schlie, E. and Yip, G. 2000. "Regional Follows Global: Strategy Mixes in the World Automotive Industry," *European Management Journal* 18: 343–56.

Stopford, J. and Strange, S. 1991. *Rival States, Rival Firms*, Cambridge: Cambridge University Press.

Stopford, J. M. and Wells, L. T. 1972. *Managing the Multinational Enterprise: Organization of the Firm and Ownership of the Subsidiaries*, New York: Basic Books.

Tallman, S. B. and Yip, G. S. 2001. "Strategy and the Multinational Enterprise" in A. Rugman and T. Brewer (eds.) *The Oxford Handbook of International Business*, Oxford: Oxford University Press, pp. 317–48.

United Nations 2001. *World Investment Report 2001*, New York and Geneva: United Nations Conference on Trade and Development.

2002. *World Investment Report 2002*, New York and Geneva: United Nations Conference on Trade and Development.

Van Den Bulcke, D. and Verbeke, A. 2001. *Globalization and the Small Open Economy*, Cheltenham and Northampton: Elgar.

Vermeulen, F. and Barkema, H. 2002. "Pace, Rhythm, and Scope: Process Dependence in Building a Profitable Multinational Corporation," *Strategic Management Journal* 23: 637–53.

Vernon, R. 1966. "International Investment and International Trade in the Product Cycle," *Quarterly Journal of Economics* 80: 190–207.

1971. *Sovereignty at Bay*, New York: Basic Books.

Viner, J. 1950. *The Customs Union Issue,* New York: Carnegie Endowment for International Peace.

Wan, W. P. and Hoskisson, R. E. 2003. "Home Country Environments, Corporate Diversification Strategies and Firm Performance," *Academy of Management Journal* 46(1): 27–45.

Westney, E. and Zaheer S. 2001. "The Multinational Enterprise as an Organization" in Rugman A. M. and Verbeke, A. (eds.) *The Oxford Handbook of International Business*, Oxford: Oxford University Press, 2001, pp. 349–79.

Williamson, O. E. 1975. *Markets and Hierarchies: Analysis and Antitrust Implications*, New York: Free Press.

Wolf, J. and Egelhoff, W. G. 2002. "A Reexamination and Extension of International Strategy-Structure Theory," *Strategic Management Journal* 23: 181–89.

Yeung, H., Wai-chung, P., Martin, J. and Martin, P. 2001. "Towards a Regional Strategy: The Role of Regional Headquarters of Foreign Firms in Singapore," *Urban Studies* 38(1): 157–83.

Yip, G. 2002. *Total Global Strategy II*, Upper Saddle River, NJ: Prentice Hall.

Zaheer, S. 1995. "Overcoming the Liability of Foreignness," *Academy of Management Journal* 38(2): 341–63.

Zaheer, S. and Mosakowski, E. 1997. "The Dynamics of the Liability of Foreignness: A Global Study of Survival in Financial Services," *Strategic Management Journal* 18(6): 439–64.

Author index

General index